Tort Liability and Autonomous Systems Accidents

Tort Liability and Autonomous Systems Accidents

Common and Civil Law Perspectives

Edited by

Phillip Morgan

Reader in Law, York Law School, University of York, UK

Edward Elgar
PUBLISHING

Cheltenham, UK • Northampton, MA, USA

Published by
Edward Elgar Publishing Limited
The Lypiatts
15 Lansdown Road
Cheltenham
Glos GL50 2JA
UK

Edward Elgar Publishing, Inc.
William Pratt House
9 Dewey Court
Northampton
Massachusetts 01060
USA

A catalogue record for this book
is available from the British Library

Library of Congress Control Number: 2023942566

This book is available electronically in the **Elgar**online
Law subject collection
http://dx.doi.org/10.4337/9781802203844

ISBN 978 1 80220 383 7 (cased)
ISBN 978 1 80220 384 4 (eBook)

Printed and bound by CPI Group (UK) Ltd, Croydon, CR0 4YY

Contents

Contributors

Ryan Abbott, Professor of Law and Health Sciences, University of Surrey School of Law (United Kingdom), Adjunct Assistant Professor of Medicine, David Geffen School of Medicine at University of California, Los Angeles (United States of America) and Partner, Brown, Neri, Smith, & Khan, LLP, Los Angeles, CA (United States of America).

Henrique Sousa Antunes, Associate Professor, Faculty of Law (Lisbon School), Universidade Católica Portuguesa (Portugal).

Simon Baughen, Professor of Shipping Law, The Institute of International Shipping and Trade Law, Swansea University (United Kingdom).

Ayşegül Buğra Şar, Assistant Professor of Maritime and Insurance Law, Koç University Law School (Turkey).

Özgün Çelebi, Assistant Professor of Civil Law, Koç University Law School (Turkey).

Jan De Bruyne, Research Expert, KU Leuven Centre for IT & IP law – imec (CiTiP) (Belgium); Assistant Professor of eLaw, Leiden University (The Netherlands).

Orian Dheu, Doctoral Researcher in Law, KU Leuven Centre for IT & IP Law – imec (CiTiP) (Belgium).

Maria Glynou, LLM candidate and Research Assistant at the London School of Economics and Political Science (United Kingdom).

Mitja Kovac, Professor of Civil and Commercial Law, University of Ljubljana School of Economics and Business (Slovenia).

Attila Menyhárd, Professor of Civil Law and the Head of the Department of Civil Law, Eötvös Loránd University, Budapest (Hungary).

Phillip Morgan, Reader in Law (Associate Professor), York Law School, University of York (United Kingdom).

Kyriaki Noussia, Associate Professor in Commercial Law, School of Law, University of Reading (United Kingdom).

Erica Palmerini, Associate Professor of Private Law, Scuola Superiore Sant'Anna, Pisa (Italy).

1. Tort Liability and Autonomous Systems Accidents – Challenges and Future Developments

Phillip Morgan[1]

I.   BACKGROUND

The introduction of autonomous systems driven by artificial intelligence ('AI')[2] technologies, particularly machine learning, has been widely described

[1]   Reader in Law, University of York. This book is part of a project that has received funding from the European Research Council ('ERC') under the European Union's Horizon 2020 research and innovation programme (Grant agreement No. 824990) (Robotics for Infrastructure Inspection and Maintenance ('RIMA')). The editor would also like to thank Jochem Koers for formatting and editorial assistance.

[2]   For a definition see Communication from the Commission to the European Parliament, the European Council, the Council, the European Economic and Social Committee and the Committee of the Regions on Artificial Intelligence for Europe (COM (2018) 237 final): '[a]rtificial intelligence (AI) refers to systems that display intelligent behaviour by analysing their environment and taking actions – with some degree of autonomy – to achieve specific goals. AI-based systems can be purely software-based, acting in the virtual world (e.g. voice assistants, image analysis software, search engines, speech and face recognition systems) or AI can be embedded in hardware devices (e.g. advanced robots, autonomous cars, drones or Internet of Things applications).' cf High-Level Expert Group on Artificial Intelligence, *A definition of AI: Main capabilities and scientific disciplines* (European Commission, 2018): '[a]rtificial intelligence (AI) refers to systems designed by humans that, given a complex goal, act in the physical or digital world by perceiving their environment, interpreting the collected structured or unstructured data, reasoning on the knowledge derived from this data and deciding the best action(s) to take (according to pre-defined parameters) to achieve the given goal. AI systems can also be designed to learn to adapt their behaviour by analysing how the environment is affected by their previous actions...' As noted by Christoph Bartneck, Christoph Lütge, Alan Wagner and Sean Welsh, *An Introduction to Ethics in Robotics and AI* (Springer, 2021) 8, 'the definition of AI itself is volatile and has changed over time'. Ryan Calo, 'Artificial Intelligence Policy: a Primer and Roadmap' (2017) 51 UCDL Rev 399, also notes that there is a lack of consensus over a definition of AI.

as a key element within the Fourth Industrial Revolution.[3] Autonomous systems are systems which 'make decisions independently of human control'.[4] There is a spectrum of such systems. At the one end there are highly autonomous systems which make decisions and implement the subsequent actions. At the other end are systems which make decisions which are advisory, and the human in charge is responsible for the implementation of the recommendation.[5] The full potential of autonomous systems is still to be realised, but it is clear that such systems are here to stay, and that they will play an increasing role in our lives. There is significant potential for such systems to increase productivity and improve safety in a wide range of sectors, including oil and gas, nuclear, water supply, transportation, civil engineering, medical, agricultural, extraction, manufacturing and infrastructure industries, amongst many others. Sadly, even if autonomous systems prove safer than humans, such systems will cause accidents, and the law needs an adequate way to respond to these accidents and to compensate those wrongfully injured. In most jurisdictions accident law primarily invokes tort/delict, although there are of course some non-fault accident compensation schemes, and some social security schemes. Even if criminal law and regulatory law also interface with accidents, the heavy lifting of accident compensation is carried out by tort, and its interplay with liability insurance.

Autonomous systems present tort law with unique challenges to overcome, which are discussed in more detail throughout this book, and below. The adequacy of accident compensation systems designed around the human wrongdoer, or a human whose conduct can be attributed to a wrongdoer who is a legal person, are brought into question when the 'wrongdoer' is an autonomous system. This problem is widely recognised, and rapid solutions need to be found, since such technology is increasingly deployed in real-world settings. Liability proposals have been advanced by the European Parliament,[6] by the European Commission[7] and also by some individual jurisdictions, some of which have also rapidly legislated for autonomous vehicles, such as the United Kingdom.[8] The purpose of this book is to examine the difficulties

---

[3]   For example, Klaus Schwab, *The Fourth Industrial Revolution* (WEF, 2016).

[4]   Simon Burton, Ibrahim Habli, Tom Lawton, John McDermid, Phillip Morgan and Zoe Porter, 'Mind the Gaps: Assuring the Safety of Autonomous Systems from an Engineering, Ethical, and Legal Perspective' (2020) 279 Artificial Intelligence 103201.

[5]   ibid.

[6]   European Parliament resolution of 20 October 2020 with recommendations to the Commission on a civil liability regime for artificial intelligence (2020/2014(INL)).

[7]   European Commission, Proposal for a Directive of the European Parliament and of the Council on adapting non-contractual civil liability rules to artificial intelligence (AI Liability Directive) (COM(2022) 496 final).

[8]   Automated and Electric Vehicles Act 2018.

that autonomous systems create for existing accident compensation systems founded on tort, and to propose solutions. A number of key themes emerge from the chapters in this book, including: 1) the type of liability regime best suited to autonomous systems; 2) the role of product liability; 3) the question of legal personality for autonomous systems,[9] and its interface with liability; 4) the role of liability insurance, and the regulatory function of insurance; and 5) whether specialised liability regimes are required for particular autonomous systems contexts and sectors.

Autonomous systems also represent a problem for how tort lawyers think. Tort lawyers typically operate in a forensic manner, analysing incidents/ accidents after the fact, and assigning responsibility for damage ex-post. In the autonomous systems context, we are being asked to think prospectively and assume an ex-ante mindset more typically found amongst regulators. Tort lawyers will thus need to consider what the problems and potential accidents *may* be across a broad range of autonomous systems technologies, and actors, and how tort law *might* interface with these, regulate and compensate. In order for actors to be able to deploy such technologies in real-world settings it is likely that both deployers and insurers will need to be able to predict their liability exposure in advance.[10] Knowing the liability rules is thus not something we can simply defer until after the first wave of autonomous systems accidents.

This book seeks to be a dedicated academic treatment on accident compensation for the operation of autonomous systems. The authors in this book propose a variety of solutions, and also take into account the regulatory consequences, and the potential regulatory role of tort, considering its interface with the objectives of autonomous systems regulation (see in particular Chapters 3 and 6).[11] Within their chapters the authors draw on a wide variety of jurisdictions, both from common and civil law traditions. Views on the potential tort solutions to autonomous systems will inevitably differ, as the chapters of this book show. However, this is not necessarily a problem, since diversity of ideas will provide a pool of possibilities for jurisdictions designing solutions. Further, in considering these proposed solutions, the editor suggests that it is possible that one size may not necessarily fit all, either technologically or in

---

[9]   Which the majority of the authors in this book do not consider to be a viable option. For a wider discussion see: Simon Chesterman, 'Artificial Intelligence and the Limits of Legal Personality' (2020) 69 ICLQ 819 and Robert van den Hoven van Genderen, 'Legal Personhood in the Age of Artificially Intelligence Robots' in Woodrow Barfield and Ugo Pagallo (eds.), *Research Handbook on the Law of Artificial Intelligence* (Edward Elgar Publishing, 2018).

[10]   See text to (n 39).

[11]   In Chapter 6 Menyhárd draws on law and economics methods to assess this balance.

relation to the solution's wider fit with the existing accident compensation schemes within particular jurisdictions.

Concerning the fit with technology, autonomous systems represent a diverse field, with many potential applications. Perhaps more specific solutions may be suitable for particular uses of such technologies? This is not unusual in tort. For instance, compensation for motor vehicle accidents is dealt with differently in some jurisdictions when compared to other accidents.[12] It is possible that a technology-by-technology application might be how the law progresses. This book consequently includes a number of chapters focused on particular key industries which will deploy autonomous technologies, such as the maritime industry (Chapter 9), medical profession (Chapter 7) and the oil and gas extraction industry (Chapter 10). However, with such an approach technology impartiality will need to be considered (see below).

With regard to the wider fit with existing liability schemes, De Bruyne and Dheu note in Chapter 2 that there is a 'dilemma' regarding international tort initiatives and harmonisation measures. In particular there is the need to take into consideration that national law is still the most important source of law regarding tort liability for autonomous systems, and also the need to preserve the coherence of national systems of tort liability. In considering potential liability regimes, too often there is an assumption that an autonomous systems liability regime designed for one legal system will operate equally well within different legal systems. This is a concern that might also be levied in relation to the European Commission's proposed AI Liability Directive,[13] which aims to supplement existing national liability regimes. Further, supranational liability harmonisation regimes, which surgically alter existing national causes of action and draw on national law definitions, may not necessarily lead to uniform outcomes, or may be less likely to achieve this than more complete regimes such as that found in the European Product Liability Directive.[14] The diversity of approaches within this book (even if some are, or have been, rejected by leading national and supranational bodies) is therefore of value to future legislators in tailoring a solution for their jurisdiction which best fits with their existing national legal system.

---

[12]   For instance, via specific schemes. Even in jurisdictions which purport to use the same fault-based torts for motor vehicle accidents as for other accidents, the manner in which the standard of care is approached may significantly vary in the motor accident context (see below).

[13]   See above (n 7).

[14]   Council Directive 85/374/EEC of 25 July 1985 on the approximation of the laws, regulations and administrative provisions of the Member States concerning liability for defective products.

In considering the problems which autonomous systems cause for tort, a number of the authors give specific focus to European Union ('EU') regimes and proposals (for an overview see Chapters 2, 3, 5 and 6), and the European tort tradition. This is not simply a product of the jurisdictional training of many of the authors, but also stems from the fact that the EU has been a thought leader in considering regulatory and liability aspects of autonomous technologies, and in designing specific tort adjustments to deal with these technological advances. These European developments are also relevant to other jurisdictions which are considering how to deal with liability issues concerning such technology. Other jurisdictions are watching the first movers, and thus analysing a variety of proposals and regimes (even those not subsequently taken forward, such as the European Parliament's proposed model of liability, which Antunes discusses in detail in Chapter 5) has real value for other jurisdictions which are considering acting. Further, the nature and scale of the EU's market means that its regulatory reach is significant, and it will impact on product design, even for products used in other parts of the world.[15] Likewise analysis of the currently applied European liability regimes has long-term value, even if the EU subsequently amends instruments such as the Product Liability Directive in the light of recent proposals. This is since the United Kingdom, through the Consumer Protection Act 1987, will continue to apply the current product liability regime, and it too may need to consider amendments.

It is unlikely that liability issues for autonomous systems will be static. We can only design solutions for the problems we foresee. Subsequent developments and experience might also tell us that particular solutions are not optimal. This was also shown to be the experience with the developments in tort prompted by previous industrial revolutions.[16] It is thus likely that the lived experience of tort law and autonomous systems will mean that other possibilities, including previously rejected proposals for autonomous systems, may need to be revisited.

---

[15] The EU's attempts to regulate technology in this sphere are also likely to have wide-reaching effects in other jurisdictions, see for example Dan Svantesson, 'The European Union Artificial Intelligence Act: Potential Implications for Australia' (2022) 47 Alternative Law Journal 4.

[16] Ken Oliphant, 'Tort Law, Risk, and Technological Innovation in England' (2014) 59 McGill Law Journal 819; John Bell and David Ibbetson, *European Legal Development: The Case of Tort* (CUP 2012); Donald Gifford, 'Technological Triggers to Tort Revolutions: Steam Locomotives, Autonomous Vehicles, and Accident Compensation' (2018) 11 J Tort L 71; Bryan McMahon, 'The Reactions of Tortious Liability to Industrial Revolution: A Comparison: I' (1968) 3 Irish Jurist 18; Wolfgang Ernst (ed.), *The Development of Traffic Liability* (CUP 2010); Gert Brüggemeier, 'The Civilian Law of Delict: A Comparative and Historical Analysis' (2020) 7 European Journal of Comparative Law and Governance 339.

II.   AUTONOMOUS SYSTEMS ACCIDENTS

Autonomous systems accidents are not simply science fiction, and as with any other accident the law will need to be able to deal with them. Few readers will be unfamiliar with the Tempe incident, which has become a cause célèbre within the autonomous systems safety community and has been widely reported by the international media.[17] An Uber automated test vehicle in Tempe, Arizona, which was operated by an automated driving system ('ADS'), struck and fatally injured a pedestrian whilst she pushed her bicycle. Whilst the ADS detected the pedestrian, it did not classify her as a pedestrian, instead repeatedly misclassifying her in different categories,[18] nor did the ADS predict her actual path of movement. The design of the system did not include any consideration of 'jaywalking' pedestrians, and due to the system not considering the tracking history of reclassified objects it could not correctly predict her path.[19] Immediately before the collision the system determined that a collision was imminent, however the response specifications of the ADS were exceeded, and the human safety driver failed to intervene in time.[20]

Although, perhaps the most high profile Uber vehicle collision, it was not the first.[21] Other high profile incidents have been reported in the international media involving other systems, including fatal accidents involving Tesla's Level 2 'autopilot' systems where the vehicles collided with crossing trucks;[22]

---

[17] For example, Sam Levin and Julia Carrie Wong, 'Self-driving Uber kills Arizona woman in first fatal crash involving pedestrian' (*The Guardian*, 19 March 2018) www .theguardian.com/technology/2018/mar/19/uber-self-driving-car-kills-woman-arizona -tempe accessed 26 January 2023; BBC, 'Uber in fatal crash had safety flaws say US investigators' (*BBC*, 6 November 2019) www.bbc.co.uk/news/business-50312340 accessed 26 January 2023; David Shepardson, 'In review of fatal Arizona crash, US agency says Uber software had flaws' (*Reuters*, 5 November 2019) www.reuters.com/ article/us-uber-crash-idUSKBN1XF2HA accessed 26 January 2023.

[18] National Transportation Safety Board, *Collision Between Vehicle Controlled by Developmental Automated Driving System and Pedestrian, Tempe, Arizona, March 18, 2018* (Highway Accident Report NTSB/HAR-19/03, 2019) 15–16.

[19] ibid 16–17.

[20] ibid. Subsequently, questions have been raised into the corporate culture, training, the conduct of the human in the loop and the engineering decisions made, including the decision to turn off the car's collision avoidance system.

[21] It must be noted that in 33 of these cases the ADS-driven vehicle was struck by another vehicle: Reuters Staff, 'Uber test vehicles involved in 37 crashes before fatal self-driving incident' (*Reuters*, 5 November 2018) www.reuters.com/article/uber-crash -idUSL2N27L1D2 accessed 26 January 2023.

[22] National Transportation Safety Board, *Collision Between a Car Operating With Automated Vehicle Control Systems and a Tractor-Semitrailer Truck Near Williston, Florida, May 7, 2016* (Highway Accident Report NTSB/HAR-17/02, 2017); National

an Amazon-owned Zoosk vehicle operating in fully autonomous mode rear-ending a tractor-trailer;[23] an Amazon warehouse robot puncturing a can of bear spray resulting in 24 warehouse workers being admitted to hospital, one requiring intensive care;[24] a security robot running over a one-year-old child;[25] and a chess robot that grabbed and broke the finger of its seven-year-old opponent,[26] amongst others.

There are also widely catalogued examples of AI failures.[27] Although many of these failures did not lead to accidents, they are illustrative that autonomous systems do not always carry out their expected function or operate in a safe manner. The source of potentially dangerous autonomous system failures varies, but includes engineering mistakes, environmental impacts and malevolent actors.[28] Analysing known failures Yampolskiy predicts 'that both the frequency and seriousness of such events will steadily increase as AIs become

---

Transportation Safety Board, *Collision Between Car Operating with Partial Driving Automation and Truck-Tractor Semitrailer Delray Beach, Florida, March 1, 2019* (Highway Accident Brief NTSB/HAB-20/01).

[23]   Mick Akers, 'Vehicle in self-driving test crashes just off Las Vegas Strip' (*Las Vegas Review-Journal*, 15 November 2022) www.reviewjournal.com/local/traffic/vehicle-in-self-driving-test-crashes-just-off-las-vegas-strip-2677041/ accessed 26 January 2023.

[24]   Jasper Jolly, 'Amazon robot sets off bear repellent, putting 24 workers in hospital' (*The Guardian*, 6 December 2018) www.theguardian.com/technology/2018/dec/06/24-us-amazon-workers-hospitalised-after-robot-sets-off-bear-repellent; Catherine Olsson, '(2018-12-05) Incident Number 2' in Sean McGregor (ed.), 'Artificial Intelligence Incident Database. Responsible AI Collaborative' incidentdatabase.ai/cite/2 accessed 21 November 2022.

[25]   Melia Robinson, 'A real-life robocop patrolling Silicon Valley allegedly ran over a child in a mall' (*Insider*, 12 July 2016) www.insider.com/robotic-mall-cop-injury-at-stanford-mall-2016-7 accessed 26 January 2023; Steven Hoffer, '300-pound security robot runs over toddler at California shopping center' (*Huffington Post*, 13 July 2016) www.huffingtonpost.co.uk/entry/security-robot-toddler_n_57863670e4b03f c3ee4e8f3a accessed 26 January 2023.

[26]   Jon Henley, 'Chess robot grabs and breaks finger of seven-year-old opponent' (*The Guardian*, 24 July 2022) www.theguardian.com/sport/2022/jul/24/chess-robot-grabs-and-breaks-finger-of-seven-year-old-opponent-moscow accessed 26 January 2023.

[27]   See the AI Incident Database: https://incidentdatabase.ai/ accessed 26 January 2023; Sean McGregor, 'Preventing Repeated Real World AI Failures by Cataloging Incidents: The AI Incident Database' (2021) 35(17) Proceedings of the AAAI Conference on Artificial Intelligence 15458–15463; also Roman Yampolskiy, 'Predicting Future AI Failures from Historic Examples' (2019) 21 Foresight 138, 140–3; Peter Scott and Roman Yampolskiy, 'Classification Schemas for Artificial Intelligence Failures' (2019) 2 Delphi 186.

[28]   Yampolskiy, 'Predicting Future AI Failures from Historic Examples' (n 27) 138–39.

more capable'.[29] He further considers that 'we can arrive at a simple generalization: an AI designed to do X will eventually fail to do X.'[30]

In June 2021 the United States National Highway Traffic Safety Administration ('NHTSA') issued an order[31] which required manufacturers and operators to report crashes occurring on public roads in the US involving ADSs, which were defined as Level 3–5 systems,[32] and also those involving Level 2 Advanced Driver Assistance Systems ('ADAS'), where the systems were engaged during the crash or within 30 seconds of the commencement of the crash, and the crash resulted in an airbag deployment, towaway, fatality, person transported to hospital for medical treatment or the involvement of a vulnerable road user.[33] From 29 June 2021 to 15 May 2022 NHTSA received 392 reports of crashes involving Level 2 systems, five involving serious injuries, and six fatal injuries. Three crashes involved a pedestrian, and one a cyclist.[34] In the same period, incident reports were received for 130 crashes involving ADS vehicles; one crash involved serious injuries, three crashes involved moderate injuries and 12 minor injuries. Some crashes involved vulnerable road users, including seven involving cyclists and two involving electric scooters.[35] It must be noted that the number of reports is not the same as the total number of crashes, and is thus not a reliable metric. The reports also do not deal with the cause of the incident but are nevertheless still illustrative of the fact that autonomous systems will be involved in accidents.

Organisational sociology, in the shape of normal accident theory, would also suggest that some autonomous systems accidents are inevitable, since many such systems are tightly coupled (typically illustrated by systems which are highly automated, with little opportunity for human intervention),[36] complex (that is have many interlocking parts) and high risk, thus leaving

---

[29]   ibid 138.
[30]   ibid 142.
[31]   United States Department of Transportation NHTSA, Standing General Order 2021-01.
[32]   This adopts the definitions used in SAE International, 'J3016 Taxonomy and Definitions for Terms Related to Driving Automation Systems for On-Road Motor Vehicles' (*SAE International*, 2021) www.sae.org/standards/content/j3016_202104/ accessed 26 January 2023.
[33]   Request No 1 C.
[34]   NHTSA, *Summary Report: Standing General Order on Crash Reporting for Level 2 Advanced Driver Assistance Systems* (NHTSA 2022).
[35]   NHTSA, *Summary Report: Standing General Order on Crash Reporting for Automated Driving Systems* (NHTSA 2022).
[36]   Andrew Hopkins, 'The Limits of Normal Accident Theory' (1999) 32 Safety Science 93, 95.

very little room for error.[37] Indeed, safety specialists regularly make the link between normal accidents and autonomous systems;[38] further, it has been advanced that such systems are more susceptible to normal accidents than the previous 'textbook' examples.[39] Potential industrial users of such technologies also appear to be highly aware of the potential for accidents, indeed resultant liability concerns are a major barrier to the adoption of such technologies.[40]

Reinforcing the fact that such accidents *will* occur is the knowledge that there have been numerous accidents involving robotic technologies, particularly in factory contexts.[41] Most of these accidents were in closed contexts and did not involve autonomous, machine learning systems, operating in real-world environments. Thus, physical barriers and worker training have been used to reduce such accidents.[42] The ability to control access to the environment means that personal protective equipment ('PPE') may also be used to mitigate the severity of accidents. However, such techniques will be less effective with the new industrial revolution which deploys autonomous systems in open contexts. New hazards will also emerge which existing techniques are poor at recognising or mitigating.[43] This is particularly the case given that in open contexts systems are more likely to interact with a wide range of actors (including malevolent ones) and other (and potentially unpredictable) systems, than if their use was confined to carefully controlled and restricted areas such as factories, where their human interaction can be limited to highly trained

---

[37]   Charles Perrow, *Normal Accidents. Living with High Risk Technologies* (2nd ed., Princeton University Press, 1999) 141. Considering the full body of Perrow's work this is not a solely technological determinist argument, and also includes organisational failures: Jean-Christophe Le Coze, '1984–2014. Normal Accidents. Was Charles Perrow Right for the Wrong Reasons?' (2015) 23 J Contingencies & Crisis Man 275.

[38]   For example, Matthijs Maas, 'Regulating for 'Normal AI Accidents': Operational Lessons for the Responsible Governance of Artificial Intelligence Deployment' (2018) Proceedings of the 2018 AAAI/ACM Conference on AI, Ethics, and Society December 2018, 223; Robert Williams and Roman Yampolskiy 'Understanding and Avoiding AI Failures: A Practical Guide' (2021) 6 Philosophies 53.

[39]   Maas (n 38) 226.

[40]   Liability concerns for potential damage were cited as the most recurrent major external barrier to using such technologies by potential European users of AI technologies (European Commission, Directorate-General for Communications Networks, Content and Technology, 'European enterprise survey on the use of technologies based on artificial intelligence: final report') (*Publications Office*, 2020) https://data.europa .eu/doi/10.2759/759368 accessed 26 January 2023.

[41]   Balbir S Dhillon, *Robot Reliability and Safety* (Springer, 1991) Chapter 4.

[42]   The National Institute for Occupational Safety and Health, *Preventing the Injury of Workers by Robots* (DHHS 85–103, 1984).

[43]   John Sammarco, 'Operationalizing Normal Accident Theory for Safety-related Computer Systems' (2005) 43 Safety Science 697.

personnel. Accidents involving autonomous systems are likely to become more common as they become more widely used.

However, that many readers will be able to easily recall examples of autonomous systems accidents which feature prominently in the media, suggests that these are currently rare and noteworthy incidents, particularly when compared to the frequency of accidents involving the technologies such systems are replacing. For instance, car accidents, including fatal accidents, are sadly a frequent occurrence; the World Health Organization has estimated that approximately 1.3 million people are killed a year by road traffic accidents,[44] yet these accidents rarely feature prominently in the media. We should thus be careful not to fall foul of the availability heuristic,[45] whereby the probability of noteworthy events, or events of the type that have been brought to public attention, is overestimated, since people rate risks more seriously where they can recall an incident or examples.[46] Further, we should also be careful not to allow the existing examples of autonomous systems accidents to limit our intellectual horizons as to the types of autonomous systems accidents, which for instance might be cascading failures within the context of networked and opaque systems.[47] The point of this section is not to demonstrate that autonomous systems are unsafe or accident prone, far from it, indeed it is possible that in some contexts in the future they may be significantly safer. However, its purpose is to demonstrate that the law *will* need to be able to deal with autonomous systems accidents, and such accidents may occur in unexpected ways.

III.   AUTONOMOUS SYSTEMS ACCIDENTS AND TORT

The Tempe incident attracted the attention of regulators, the criminal justice system and tort lawyers.[48] The tort case brought on behalf of the victim's family and estate against Uber was confidentially settled by Uber for an undis-

---

[44]   The World Health Organization, 'Road traffic injuries' (*WHO*, 2021) www.who .int/news-room/fact-sheets/detail/road-traffic-injuries#:~:text=Approximately%201.3 %20million%20people%20die,result%20of%20road%20traffic%20crashes   accessed 26 January 2023.

[45]   Amos Tversky and Daniel Kahneman, 'Availability: A Heuristic for Judging Frequency and Probability' (1973) 5 Cognitive Psychology 207.

[46]   Edward Cartwright, *Behavioral Economics* (2nd ed., Routledge, 2014) 232.

[47]   Maas (n 38) 224.

[48]   John McDermid, Zoe Porter and Phillip Morgan 'Autonomous driving, accidents and fatalities…where does responsibility lie?' (*AAIP*, 2019) www.york.ac.uk/assuring -autonomy/news/blog/autonomous-driving-responsibility/ accessed 26 January 2023.

closed sum.[49] This book is concerned with tort. Whilst there has been much work on autonomous system regulation, one notable example being the EU's proposed Artificial Intelligence Act ('AI Act'),[50] such ex-ante regulation will not eliminate the need to consider the consequences of what should happen when an accident occurs, and where the losses should lie.[51] Further, not all jurisdictions will be drawn to the EU's comprehensive regulatory strategy for AI, some wishing to remain more competitive by retaining light touch ex-ante regulation. In such jurisdictions tort and insurers may play a greater regulatory role. The potential role of insurer regulation is examined in Chapter 7 where Çelebi and Buğra-Şar advance that liability insurers will play a role in encouraging explainable systems since this will both reduce defence costs and increase the predictability of litigation.

Although autonomous systems may result in a range of harms, from personal injury to psychological harm, privacy harms, and reputational and economic losses, this work focuses on accident compensation. It does so as it is one of the most pressing issues to examine, and since the right to life and bodily integrity is high in the hierarchy of values. In doing so, it raises the issue of who should pay for the injuries, or bear their burden, and to what extent, in exchange for society benefiting from technological advancement.

As noted above, accident compensation in most jurisdictions is typically dealt with through the interface between tort (either fault-based or strict liability) and liability insurance, the two having a symbiotic relationship.[52] In focusing on accidents this work recognises that this is often a distinct field within tort law,[53] this is even the case in legal systems where at first glance it appears to be addressed through the same causes of action as other harms. For instance, in an English common law context this is demonstrated by the fault-based requirement of the tort of negligence being watered down to

---

[49] 'Uber settles with family of woman killed by self-driving car' (*The Guardian*, 29 March 2018) www.theguardian.com/technology/2018/mar/29/uber-settles-with-family -of-woman-killed-by-self-driving-car accessed 26 January 2023.

[50] Proposal for a Regulation of the European Parliament and of the Council laying down harmonised rules on artificial intelligence (Artificial Intelligence Act) and amending certain Union legislative acts (COM/2021/206 final).

[51] The European Commission also recently noted in its proposals for an AI Liability Directive that regulation does not entirely eliminate risks, '[s]afety and liability are two sides of the same coin: they apply at different moments and reinforce each other'. AI Liability Directive Proposal (n 7), Explanatory Memorandum, 2.

[52] Rob Merkin and Jenny Steele, *Insurance and the Law of Obligations* (Oxford University Press, 2013); Kenneth S Abraham, *The Liability Century Insurance and Tort Law from the Progressive Era to 9/11* (Harvard University Press, 2008).

[53] See generally Peter Cane and James Goudkamp, *Atiyah's Accidents, Compensation and the Law* (9th ed., Cambridge University Press, 2018).

essentially a strict liability system in a motor vehicle accident context,[54] or by the fact that limitation periods for personal injury torts are distinct and capable of being extended beyond the periods for other losses.[55] Accidents are also often provided with more obvious differential treatment in some jurisdictions, as illustrated by the existence of no-fault schemes such as the New Zealand Accident Compensation Scheme,[56] workers' compensation schemes[57] and strict liability automobile accident schemes in a number of European juris-dictions.[58] Nevertheless, it is recognised that there is highly likely to be some spill over from how tort law deals with autonomous systems accidents into other areas of tort. Some of the core doctrinal challenges within tort caused by the use of autonomous systems, such as problems with causation and proof of fault (see below), will apply to a wide range of scenarios and torts. Indeed, one experience of previous industrial revolutions is the spill over to other areas from changes to tort law brought in to deal with new technologies.[59]

Inevitably this focus on accidents means that many of the examples dis-cussed in this book primarily concern embodied technologies, such as autono-mous vehicles and ships, as these are more likely (at least in the near term) to cause injuries – although it also considers unembodied systems (see Chapter 7 on medical uses), which include systems with a human in or on the loop, including those which are advisory systems. However, given the cognitive limitations of the human in/on the loop, combined with potentially high speeds of human response being required, anchoring bias and perhaps the lack of situational awareness when compared with a human using a traditional system, such systems can also raise similar legal problems in an accident context.

The current tort liability regimes which govern the situations in which the persons associated with autonomous systems are civilly liable for accidents are

---

[54]   *Nettleship v Weston* [1971] 2 QB 691 (CA) 699–701 (Lord Denning MR); *Henderson v Henry E Jenkins & Sons* [1970] AC 282 (HL); *Daly v Liverpool Corporation* [1939] 2 All ER 142 (AS) 144; *Government Insurance Office of New South Wales v Ergul* [1993] NSWCA 108 [35]–[40] (Clarke JA): 'since the advent of compulsory insurance, and consequential notions of risk sharing, the courts have, in substance, elevated the "reasonably prudent driver" to the role of the perfection-ist.' See generally James Goudkamp, 'The Spurious Relationship Between Moral Blameworthiness and Liability for Negligence' (2004) 28 MULR 343.

[55]   Limitation Act 1980, s 33.

[56]   NZ Accident Compensation Act 2001.

[57]   For example, Joseph LaDou, 'The European influence on workers' compensa-tion reform in the United States' (2011) 10 Environ Health 103.

[58]   Konrad Zweigert and Hein Kötz, *An Introduction to Comparative Law* (Tony Weir tr, 3rd ed., Oxford University Press, 1998) 660.

[59]   Reinhard Zimmermann, *The Law of Obligations: Roman Foundations of the Civilian Tradition* (Clarendon Press, 1996) 1132.

a mix of fault based, strict liability or product liability based, depending on the particular circumstances. Fault-based standards may in some circumstances import otherwise non-binding industry standards and guidelines into the law.[60]

Autonomous systems produce a considerable challenge for accident compensation systems based on tort. Increasingly sophisticated autonomous systems raise significant problems on how to appropriately assign responsibility. This raises questions as to how we should approach autonomous systems accidents, which this book addresses. As further developed later in this book, autonomous systems cause problems for legal notions such as fault, causation[61] and remoteness of damage.[62] Given connectivity, data sharing,[63] opaqueness, the multiple parties involved with their development and use,[64] and post deployment learning,[65] identifying tortfeasors or where the costs should lie is highly complex.[66] The burden of proof on claimants may be difficult and expensive to meet. This problem may be particularly acute in lower value cases. Jurisdictional complexities also arise. Unembodied systems may operate

---

[60] Stephan Kirste, 'Concept and Validity of Law' in Pauline Westerman, Jaap Hage, Stephan Kirste et al. (eds.) *Legal Validity and Soft Law* (Springer, 2018) 50.

[61] Jos Lehmann, Joost Breuker and Bob Brouwer, 'Causation in AI and Law' (2004) AIL 279, 280–86; Chris Holder, Vikram Khurana, Faye Harrison et al., 'Robotics and Law: Key Legal and Regulatory Implications of the Robotics Age (Part I of II)' (2016) 32 CLSR 383, 386; Yavar Bathaee, 'The Artificial Intelligence Black Box and the Failure of Intent and Causation' (2018) 31 Harv JL & T 889; Curtis Karnow, 'Liability for Distributed Artificial Intelligences' (1996) 11 Berkeley Tech LJ 147.

[62] Woodrow Barfield, 'Towards a Law of Artificial Intelligence' in Barfield and Pagallo (n 9) 4; Jason Miller and Ian Kerr, 'Delegation, Relinquishment, and Responsibility: The Prospect of Expert Robots' in Ryan Calo, A Michael Froomkin and Ian Kerr (eds.), *Robot Law* (Edward Elgar Publishing, 2016) 107; Curtis Karnow, 'The Application of Traditional Tort Theory to Embodied Machine Intelligence' in Calo, Froomkin, and Kerr (n 62) 60; Expert Group on Liability and New Technologies, *New Technologies Formation, Liability for Artificial Intelligence and Other Emerging Digital Technologies* (European Union, 2019) 54. As Pagallo notes '[e]ven the best-intentioned and best-informed designer cannot foresee all the possible outcomes of robotic behaviour'. Ugo Pagallo, *The Laws of Robots, Crimes, Contracts, and Torts* (Springer, 2013) 138, see also 47. Note also Bathaee (n 61) 923–25.

[63] F Patrick Hubbard, 'Allocating the Risk of Physical Injury from "Sophisticated Robots": Efficiency, Fairness, and Innovation' in Calo, Froomkin, and Kerr (n 62) 31.

[64] Natalia Porto and Daniel Preiskel, 'United Kingdom Chapter' in Alain Bensoussan and Jérémy Bensoussan (eds.) *Comparative Handbook: Robotic Technologies Law* (Larcier, 2016) 346–47; Miriam Buiten, 'Towards Intelligent Regulation of Artificial Intelligence' (2019) 10 EJRR 41.

[65] Matt Hervey and Matthew Lavy, *The Law of Artificial Intelligence* (Sweet and Maxwell, 2021) [5–023].

[66] Chris Reed, 'How Should We Regulate Artificial Intelligence?' (2018) 376 Philos Trans A 20170360; Expert Group on Liability and New Technologies (n 62) 21; Pagallo (n 62) x.

across multiple jurisdictions and have the potential to cause harm in multiple locations. Even where the systems are embodied, they will not be static and will potentially move between jurisdictions, and operate in both national and international waters and airspace.

The problems that such systems cause to tort is widely recognised, both by scholars and policymakers.[67] However, a balance needs to be struck. Such technology appears essential for a jurisdiction to be economically competitive in the future, but at what price to the important rights protected by tort, in particular the rights to life and bodily integrity, which accident compensation systems are primarily designed to protect? Tort law may also have a regulatory function, and play a role in accident reduction, but we also need to ensure that it does not prohibit technology where it will be highly beneficial to society.

Different balances are struck by the authors within this book – for instance, both Palmerini (Chapter 3) and Abbott (Chapter 4) suggest that strict liability for autonomous systems will stand in the way of innovation. Indeed, Abbott argues that a negligence standard should be implemented as a way of encouraging the development of such systems. On the other hand, Menyhárd (Chapter 6) argues that since autonomous systems endanger key protected interests, such as life, health and bodily integrity, this points towards strict liability being appropriate. This introduction is not the place to resolve this particular debate, although it should be noted that non-autonomous technologies and human acts may *also* endanger these important interests, and that currently many such claims where these interests are violated are governed by fault-based liability. However, it should be noted that strict liability is often engaged in certain limited circumstances, such as in the case of ultra-hazardous activities and product liability claims.

As Kovac (Chapter 8) notes, it is possible that this balance may need to vary from sector to sector. This is a theme further developed by Baughen when considering autonomous shipping in Chapter 9. Some industries are subject to highly specific regulation and also liability regimes, and any regime concerning autonomous systems regulation and liability may need to accommodate this. Although Baughen considers this issue from the context of the maritime

---

[67]   See for example: F Patrick Hubbard, 'Sophisticated Robots: Balancing Liability, Regulation, and Innovation' (2014) 66 Fla LR 1803; Samir Chopra and Laurence White, *A Legal Theory for Autonomous Artificial Agents* (Michigan University Press, 2011); Pagallo (n 62); Ryan Abbott, *The Reasonable Robot* (CUP 2020); Jonathan Morgan, 'Torts and Technology' in Roger Brownsword, Eloise Scotford and Karen Yeung (eds.), *The Oxford Handbook of Law, Regulation and Technology* (Oxford University Press, 2017) 522; European Parliament resolution of 20 October 2020 (n 6); Law Commission, *Automated Vehicles A Joint Preliminary Consultation Paper* (Law Com CP No 240, 2018).

sector, this issue is of broader concern. Overlaps between regimes will need to be mapped out within a variety of sectors, and their interrelation studied. Care should be taken so as to ensure that any general regulatory and liability regimes for autonomous systems, such as the generalised regimes proposed by the European Commission, take account of the regimes applicable to specific sectors, and do not clash with them. That one size might not fit all is further reinforced by the fact that certain sectors might generate different types of risk, for instance that of significant levels of environmental damage, an issue noted by Noussia and Glynou when considering the oil and gas sector in Chapter 10.

It is important to note that not *all* autonomous systems accidents will necessarily cause legal difficulties for victims. In the Tempe incident, the role of the safety driver, and her alleged failure to duly monitor the driving (whilst she was allegedly watching videos), meant that negligence could be easily pleaded, and a claim brought against her employer via vicarious liability. However, there may be many situations where there is no human in the loop, or where the human in the loop is not at fault. Further, we need to be careful not to use any human in the loop as a liability sink,[68] particularly where it is not cognitively possible for them to have prevented the accident.

IV.   TECH-IMPARTIALITY AND AVOIDING THE SUBSIDY PROBLEM

Various proposals to deal with autonomous systems are proposed by the authors in this book. How is a reader or policymaker to decide which liability proposal is best suited for a particular jurisdiction and/or a particular technology? The editor advances that the best prism is a concept called technology impartiality ('tech-impartiality'), and that policymakers should attempt to implement the most tech-impartial solution.[69]

The risk of tort liability factors into the decision-making of actors, including as to how they carry out work, the level of care they exercise and the precautions they implement.[70] Properly deployed tort law deters harmful conduct

---

[68]   Tom Lawton, Phillip Morgan, Zoe Porter et al., 'The Problem With Clinicians Becoming a "Liability Sink" for AI?' (forthcoming).

[69]   This section on tech-impartiality draws on Phillip Morgan, 'Tort Law and AI – Vicarious Liability' in Ernest Lim and Phillip Morgan (eds.), *The Cambridge Handbook of Private Law and Artificial Intelligence* (Cambridge University Press, forthcoming) Chapter 6.

[70]   Richard Posner and Francesco Parisi (eds.), *Economic Foundations of Private Law* (Edward Elgar Publishing, 2002) 5; Richard Posner, *Tort Law: Cases and Economic Analysis* (Little Brown and Company, 1982) 1–9; Steven Shavell, *Economic Analysis of Accident Law* (Harvard University Press, 1987) 5; Don Dewees, David Duff and Michael Trebilcock, *Exploring the Domain of Accident Law* (Oxford University

and encourages the use of safer methods.[71] Deterrence is present even in the presence of insurance since insurers reduce moral hazards through a range of sophisticated devices[72] and also provide a governance function.[73]

Within tort law there is a calculus between safety and technological innovation.[74] Tech-impartiality requires that tort should neither encourage nor discourage the use of new technologies, where the risk of legally recognised harms that such technologies pose to third parties are the same when compared to older technologies and methods of work. Tort should only play a role in encouraging or discouraging the use of new technologies where the systems are more, or less safe, than the alternatives. This aspect prevents a perversion of tort's deterrence role. Measuring this in fine grain can be difficult, and where data is lacking this needs to be assessed with a broad brush, examining if particular causes of action are absent for, or materially differ between technologies, or if additional hurdles within claims exist between technologies. This aspect of tech-impartiality is thus intimately connected with the wider tort liability system applicable in a jurisdiction.

Victims also have legally recognised rights which are protected by and vindicated through the law of tort,[75] including rights of bodily security and freedom, reputational rights and rights in property.[76] Such rights may be rendered nugatory from a tort law perspective by the elimination of causes of action or remedies. The second aspect of tech-impartiality insists that an actor cannot strip a victim of their rights through the use of new technology in place of existing systems of work. If the same harm is inflicted on a person, a similar remedy, or remedies of equal value, should be provided in tort whether or not that harm is inflicted by a person or a new technology. For instance, a pedes-

---

Press, 1996); Gary Schwartz, 'Reality in the Economic Analysis of Tort Law: Does Tort Law Really Deter?' (1994–1995) 42 UCLA LR 377; Cane and Goudkamp (n 53) 405–33.

[71]   Posner and Parisi (n 70) 5; Posner (n 70) 1–9; Shavell (n 70) 5.

[72]   See Malcolm Clarke, *Policies and Perceptions of Insurance* (Clarendon Press, 1997) 216–26; Merkin and Steele (n 52) 322; R Ian McEwin, 'No-Fault and Road Accidents: Some Australasian Evidence' (1989) 9 IRLE 13, 18; Tom Baker and Peter Siegelman, 'The Law & Economics of Liability Insurance' in Jennifer Arlen (ed.), *Research Handbook on the Economics of Torts* (Edward Elgar Publishing, 2013) Chapter 7.

[73]   Richard Ericson, Aaron Doyle and Dean Barry, *Insurance as Governance* (University of Toronto Press 2003); Tom Baker and Rick Swedloff, 'Regulation by Liability Insurance: From Auto to Lawyers' Professional Liability' (2013) 60 UCLA LR 1412; Gary Schwartz, 'The Ethics and Economics of Tort Liability Insurance' (1990) 75 Cornell LR 312, 356.

[74]   Hubbard, 'Allocating' (n 63) 26.

[75]   Robert Stevens, *Torts and Rights* (Oxford University Press 2007) 2–3.

[76]   *Allen v Flood* [1898] AC 1 (HL) 29 (Cave J).

trian injured by a collision with a vehicle driven in a manner which falls below the standard of that of the reasonable driver has their right to bodily integrity violated whether or not the vehicle is autonomous or driven by a human driver. It is of course open to societies to subsidise the adoption of new technologies, for instance through taxes and grants, but it is not the role of tort to do so.[77]

It is thus likely that the tech-impartial autonomous system liability solution may vary somewhat from jurisdiction to jurisdiction, or within families of jurisdictions. This is another warning to jurisdictions observing the current thought leaders and who may be considering legal transplants.

V. WHY SHOULD TORT LAWYERS BE INTERESTED IN AUTONOMOUS SYSTEMS?

Tort lawyers should pay close attention to the law's response to autonomous systems accidents. This is since the systems have the potential to widely impact on tort law doctrines, with effects outside the context of autonomous systems accidents. Previous major socio-technical changes have had major impacts on tort systems[78] and it is difficult to underestimate the changes to tort law that resulted. In the context of US law Gifford refers to each wave of technological change, as 'ruptur[ing] the fabric of the pre-existing liability system'.[79] This statement appears also to reflect the experience of all Western industrial jurisdictions.[80] Legal systems needed to reassess their existing liability rules to account for such technical developments. No tort lawyer can ignore the significant tort law developments driven by the steam engine, motor car, factories, mass production, modern communications or industrial diseases.[81]

The problems generated by new technologies in an accident context have in previous industrial revolutions been addressed by a general trend of easing the legal position of the claimant. This was achieved via a number of mechanisms, in particular the partial replacement of fault-based liability, primarily

---

[77] cf Abbott in Chapter 4. This is not to say that jurisdictions have not dabbled with such an approach. Horwitz controversially advances that during the Industrial Revolution in the US, courts replaced systems of strict liability with systems of fault-based liability as a subsidy to industry: Morton J Horwitz, *The Transformation of American Law, 1780–1850* (Harvard University Press, 1977). This subsidy thesis is not reflected in the English common law experience: Jonathan Morgan, 'Technological Change and the Development of Liability for Fault in England and Wales' in Miquel Martín-Casals (ed.), *The Development of Liability in Relation to Technological Change* (Cambridge University Press, 2010) 40–41, 48.

[78] Zimmermann (n 59) 1130; Brüggemeier (n 16) 340.

[79] Gifford (n 16) 126.

[80] Zimmermann (n 59) 1130

[81] Oliphant (n 16) 837; Bell and Ibbetson (n 16) 38.

through the introduction of strict liability mechanisms, either via specific legislative measures[82] or judicial interpretation of existing provisions;[83] by a re-conceptualisation of what fault requires, lowering the fault threshold;[84] by a removal of existing defences;[85] by introducing special no-fault compensation schemes;[86] and finally, through limited interventions concerning particular tort aspects such as causation.[87]

These changes, brought in to deal with new technologies, spilled over to other areas of tort. For instance, Spencer notes that in the English tort of negligence, the fact that (insured) drivers are only liable for fault, has perverted the general law of negligence.[88] Even in the case where the changes were isolated within special statutes, the ideas infiltrated other traditional areas of tort.[89] Indeed in Chapter 4 of this book Abbott tacitly acknowledges this and makes the case that autonomous systems should set the benchmark for other areas of accident law, and that once such systems become safer than humans they

---

[82]   Specific statutory regimes were introduced in a number of European jurisdictions to deal with railway accidents. Similar regimes were also introduced for motor vehicle accidents, and such motor vehicle schemes are now widespread amongst European jurisdictions: Bell and Ibbetson (n 16) 34; McMahon (n 16) 27; Brüggemeier (n 16) 362. Note also modern European product liability: Council Directive 85/374/EEC of 25 July 1985 (n 14); and in the UK, The Consumer Protection Act 1987.

[83]   For instance the French Cour de Cassation radically reinterpreted Article 1384 to judicially construct no-fault liability for harm caused by any object under the control of the defendant; Zweigert and Kötz (n 58) 659–60; Brüggemeier (n 16) 361; and in England the use of the *Rylands v Fletcher* (1866) LR 1 Ex 265; affirmed (1868) LR 3 HL 330, jurisprudence to establish strict liability for traction engine and steam roller accidents: *Mansel v Webb* [1918–19] All ER Rep 794, 796 (Swinfen Eady MR); J R Spencer, 'Motor-Cars and the Rule in Rylands v. Fletcher: A Chapter of Accidents in the History of Law and Motoring' (1983) 42 CLJ 65, 69; Jonathan Morgan, 'Technological Change' (n 77) 48.

[84]   For instance in France, prior to the development of the Article 1384 jurisprudence, in the light of industrial injuries, difficulties of proof and liability insurance, judges reinterpreted Article 1382 to only require objective fault, not subjective fault; McMahon (n 16) 18. In English law in motor vehicle accident cases, in the light of compulsory motor insurance, the standard of care has been progressively shifted to a standard approaching strict liability. Zimmermann (n 59) 1132; *Daly* (n 54); *Nettleship* (n 54); *Henderson* (n 54).

[85]   For instance in English law, what Morgan terms the 'three ugly sister' defences: contributory negligence, volenti non fit injuria and common employment. Jonathan Morgan, 'Technological Change' (n 77) 40, 53.

[86]   See for instance Bismarck's Industrial Accident Insurance Act, and also the UK's Workman's Compensation Act 1897.

[87]   Michael Jones, Anthony Dugdale and Mark Simpson (eds.), *Clerk & Lindsell on Torts* (23rd ed, Sweet and Maxwell, 2020) [2–27], [2–32].

[88]   Spencer (n 83) 65, 79.

[89]   Zimmermann (n 59) 1132.

should set the baseline for a new standard of care. No tort lawyer should thus ignore autonomous systems.

VI.   RECENT EUROPEAN PROPOSALS

The European Commission is increasingly concerned with regulating autonomous technologies, whilst simultaneously promoting their uptake, and the European Commission considers that a single European approach, based on European values, must be implemented regarding the promotion and development of such technologies. That existing tort regimes are inadequate to deal with the future of autonomous technologies is recognised by Commission reports, which are dealt with in detail in Chapters 2, 3, 5 and 6. It is one of the great fears of any book editor that major new proposals are brought forward at the same time as a book is being submitted for print. Here such fears have been realised. Thus, readers will need to forgive this introduction for discussing the proposed regime in significantly more detail than would be found in a typical book introduction. The European Commission has proposed an AI Liability Directive,[90] alongside revisions to the Product Liability Directive.[91] The revisions to the latter are dealt with in Chapter 2, this section therefore focuses on the former.

The European Commission's headline ambitions are to address the 'compensation gap',[92] by ensuring that victims injured by AI systems receive 'equivalent protection' and 'level of redress' to those injured by other means.[93] The European Commission also considers that the proposal will incentivise compliance with safety rules.[94] These ambitions, which may reflect a nascent notion of tech-impartiality, are justified by the European Commission on the basis that this will promote trust in both the judicial system and AI technology.[95] However, the European Commission's press release also speaks of 'putting consumers on an equal footing with manufacturers',[96] an ambition which may not be tech-impartial, and given the litigation resources of large

---

[90]   See above (n 7).

[91]   European Commission, Proposal for a directive of the European Parliament and of the Council on liability for defective products (COM (2022) 495).

[92]   AI Liability Directive, Recital [3], [8].

[93]   ibid, Explanatory Memo, Recital [3]. The European Commission's press release goes further and refers to the 'same standards of protection'. European Commission, Press Release, 'New liability rules on products and AI to protect consumers and foster innovation' (*European Commission*, 28 September 2022) https://ec.europa.eu/commission/presscorner/detail/en/ip_22_5807 accessed 27 January 2023.

[94]   AI Liability Directive, Recital.

[95]   ibid, Recital [3], [5].

[96]   European Commission, Press Release (n 93).

technology firms is unlikely to be met. Further, the proposal's limitations, perhaps motivated by the need not to stifle innovation, ensure that the proposal is unlikely to meet its own stated objectives.

The European Commission has chosen to intervene in a minimal interim manner, subject to a review. The review will consider the appropriateness of a no-fault liability regime and compulsory insurance.[97] The European Commission justifies its restricted intervention by stating that the systems which might endanger the general public and important rights such as rights to life, health and property, 'are not yet widely available on the market'.[98] However, since the review is to take place five years after a two-year transposition period, and given the pace of development, testing and the current commercial availability of such systems, this opinion may prove untimely.

The European Commission acknowledges that system characteristics such as complexity, opacity and autonomous behaviour,[99] and consequent high up-front litigation costs[100] render existing national fault-based liability systems problematic. In particular, they highlight the problem of proving causation.[101] The proposal is for a minimum harmonisation regime grafted on to the existing member state non-contractual fault-based civil liability systems.[102] Member states are also permitted to adopt or retain national rules which are more favourable to claimants.[103]

Two primary mechanisms are contained within the proposal, the rebuttable 'presumption of causality'[104] and a right to the disclosure of evidence relating to high-risk AI systems.[105] These mechanisms also apply to subrogated claims.[106] Notwithstanding the headline description of the causation mechanism, there is a significant burden imposed on the claimant to trigger the presumption, and it is somewhat convoluted and more complex to engage than the common law doctrine of res ipsa loquitur. The proposal does not change the national definitions of fault, standards of care, burdens of proof, standards of proof or notions of remoteness of damage, or approaches to multiple tortfeasors or contributory conduct (amongst others).[107] National definitions of causality are

---

[97]   Article 5(1)–(3).
[98]   AI Liability Directive, Explanatory Memo.
[99]   Recital [3].
[100] AI Liability Directive, Explanatory Memo.
[101] Recital [3].
[102] Article 1(2).
[103] Article 1(4).
[104] AI Liability Directive, Explanatory Memo; Recital [22], [29].
[105] Article 1(1).
[106] Article 2(6)(b).
[107] AI Liability Directive, Explanatory Memo; Recital [10]; see also Article 1(3).

also maintained.[108] There is thus likely to be diversity in outcome in litigation from member state to member state.

The proposal applies only to highly autonomous systems. It does not apply to advisory AI systems, where a human actor acts after receiving information or advice from an AI system.[109] How far this exclusion extends within the category of human in/on the loop systems is not currently clear. It thus potentially excludes classes of case which also cause problems for existing tort systems. The proposal is directly linked to the EU's draft AI Act, and definitions within the proposed liability directive, for instance in relation to 'high-risk AI systems', 'provider' and 'user', are expressly linked to those contained within the AI Act.[110]

A.   Rebuttable Presumption

The presumption contained in Article 4 is narrowly drawn, and the defendant has the right to rebut it.[111] The presumption establishes that for lower risk systems national courts are to presume a causal link between the defendant's fault and the AI system's output or failure to produce an output, where: 1) the claimant proves that the defendant or someone for whom they are responsible was in breach of a duty of care in national or EU law (or that the Article 3(5) presumption is triggered due to the defendant's failure to disclose evidence), and that duty was 'directly intended to protect against the damage that occurred';[112] 2) that it is 'reasonably likely' that the fault influenced the system's output, or lack of output;[113] and 3) the claimant demonstrates that the output or lack of output caused the damage.[114] Importantly, this only establishes an element of causation concerning the link between the defendant's fault and the output (or lack of output) and is not the same as establishing causation for the purposes of the tort, in that the claimant still needs to prove that the system itself caused the damage.[115] Unlike the proposal of the European Parliament, the AI Liability Directive does not establish a rebuttable presumption of fault itself.

The presumption is somewhat narrower for high-risk systems. For high-risk systems the same process is followed, save that proving fault is not sufficient, instead the claimant needs to prove that the defendant failed to comply

---

[108] Recital [10].
[109] Recital [15].
[110] Article 2(1)–(4).
[111] Article 4(7).
[112] Article 4(1)(a).
[113] Article 4(1)(b).
[114] Article 4(1)(c).
[115] AI Liability Directive, Explanatory Memo; Recital [22].

with specific obligations contained within the AI Act, including where the defendant is the provider of the system and the data used to train, test and validate the system did not meet the AI Act's quality criteria; or the system did not meet the transparency, oversight, robustness, accuracy or cybersecurity requirements of the AI Act;[116] and where the defendant is merely the user of the system, that the defendant did not comply with their obligations under the AI Act to use/monitor the system in accordance with the instructions which accompany the system, or suspend its use; or they exposed the system to data controlled by the defendant which was irrelevant to the system's intended purpose.[117] Critically with high-risk systems, for a claimant's claim to succeed the claimant faces an additional hurdle over that of the victim of an incident involving a lower risk system. To establish the tort both claimants will have to prove that the defendant was in breach of the duty of care, but to benefit from the presumption the claimant in a high-risk system incident will *also* need to prove that the defendant was in breach of a relevant AI Act obligation. Making the presumption less accessible to victims harmed by high-risk systems is odd, since such systems are more highly regulated *because* they represent a higher level of risk to victims.[118]

Further, this causation presumption only applies for lower risk AI systems where the court considers that it is 'excessively difficult' for the claimant to prove causation,[119] and for high-risk systems it does not apply 'where the defendant demonstrates that sufficient evidence and expertise is reasonably accessible for the claimant to prove the causal link'.[120] The stated purpose of this exception is to incentivise disclosure obligations.[121] A claimant relying solely on the rebuttable presumption to establish causation is thus likely to be in a weak position, since if a claimant benefits from the presumption by definition in many high-risk cases they will lack access to the expertise necessary to counter the defendant's rebuttal. Moreover, proving a breach of a duty, which is necessary to trigger the presumption, might itself require significant forensic expertise, particularly within a 'many hands' context. It is therefore unlikely that this presumption will place consumers on an equal footing with manufacturers.

---

[116] Article 4(2).

[117] Article 4(3).

[118] Orian Dheu, Jan De Bruyne and Charlotte Ducuing, 'The European Commission's Approach to Extra-Contractual Liability and AI – A First Analysis and Evaluation of the Two Proposals' (2022) CiTiP Working Paper, 20, https://lirias.kuleuven.be/3875635?limo=0 accessed 27 January 2023.

[119] Article 4(5).

[120] Article 4(4).

[121] AI Liability Directive, Explanatory Memo.

Additionally, the presumption does not apply to personal, non-professional uses of AI systems, unless the defendant 'materially interfered' with the conditions of the system's operations, or 'if the defendant was required and able to determine the conditions of operation of the AI system and failed to do so'.[122] This difference may be motivated by a desire not to discourage consumer uptake of such systems, and/or by ideas of enterprise liability. However, from a tech-impartiality perspective this is problematic if it disapplies a presumption intended to provide a similar level of protection to victims of AI harms to victims of other harms. This also excludes many potential uses of autonomous vehicles, and much of the wide range of domestic robotics coming on to the market. It also leads to the problem that the use of some systems will regularly alternate between being covered by the presumption or not, even with the same user using the system to carry out tasks with the same risk profile. For instance, where an autonomous vehicle is used by an individual on the same day to travel to their doctor's surgery for a medical appointment, then commuting to work, then undertaking a journey as part of their employment and then travelling on holiday, in relation to the user, only elements of this day's journey will be covered by the presumption. From the victim's perspective their rights may thus only be discernible after examining which leg of this journey they were injured on. Likewise, the legal and commercial structure used to provide and manage AI services may make a difference to the rights victims may assert against users.

B.   Right of Access to Evidence

The second mechanism which the AI Liability Directive proposes is a 'right of access to evidence'. It applies only to high-risk AI systems.[123] The proposal establishes a disclosure regime, whereby on the claimant's request the court is permitted to order evidential disclosure from a user or provider in relation to a specific high-risk AI system suspected of having caused damage, where the claimant has undertaken all proportionate attempts at gathering the relevant evidence,[124] and where it is proportionate to do so, taking into account the legitimate interests of all parties, including third parties, and specifically protecting trade secrets and confidential information.[125] Where a defendant refuses to provide evidence to a potential claimant, they may also make such a request,

---

[122]   Article 6(3).
[123]   Article 3(1).
[124]   Article 3(2).
[125]   Article 3(4).

but additionally a potential claimant is required to present facts and evidence which are sufficient to support the plausibility of their claim.[126]

The proposal introduces a rebuttable presumption that where a defendant user or provider refuses to comply with such an order to disclose or preserve evidence at its disposal,[127] the court should presume that the defendant has not complied with the relevant duty of care. However, the defendant has a right to rebut this presumption.[128] This disclosure obligation may make little difference if applied in common law systems, or in some mixed jurisdictions. For instance in an English, Irish or Cypriot context,[129] the existing disclosure obligations within the English Civil Procedure Rules,[130] Irish Superior Court Rules[131] and the Cypriot Civil Procedure Rules[132] would cover the disclosure obligation, and the sanctions for a defendant's non-compliance with the court's order to disclose may include inferences similar to the proposal's, but also the striking out all of parts of the defence,[133] which constitutes significantly stronger leverage to force disclosure compared to a mere rebuttable presumption relating to a single element of the claim. However, the proposed level of pre-proceedings disclosure for potential claimants may represent an expansion in court powers for some civil law jurisdictions which do not have discovery regimes comparable to common law jurisdictions.[134]

The rebuttable presumption potentially makes this disclosure obligation weak, particularly when compared to systems which include a sanction of striking out the defence. This is since a defendant may subsequently deploy evidence favourable to it at trial to rebut the presumption, whilst at the same time continuing to withhold potentially damaging evidence, to which the claimant does not have access. Further, this mechanism would not appear to level the playing field between consumers and manufacturers, since the mere provision of evidence, particularly when it consists of large quantities

---

[126]   Article 3(1).

[127]   ibid.

[128]   Article 3(5).

[129]   Nikitas Hatzimihail, 'Cyprus as a Mixed Legal System' (2013) 6 JCLS 37, 38–41; in Cyprus, procedural law is purely common law, whereas private law is primarily common law.

[130]   CPR Part 31.

[131]   SCR Order 31; Commercial Litigation Association of Ireland, *Good Practice Discovery Guide* (2nd ed., CLAI 2015).

[132]   Cyprus CPR Order 28.

[133]   *Byers and others v Samba Financial Group* [2020] EWHC 853 (Ch); SCR Order 31, Rule 21; Cyprus CPR Order 28, Rule 12.

[134]   Gloria de la Rosa, 'Taking Discovery in the European Union' (2013) 9 ESJ 982; cf ELI-UNIDROIT, *Model European Rules of Civil Procedure* (Oxford University Press, 2021) Rules 100–103.

of complex data, does not address the problems that the claimant will have in interpreting it and identifying fault. Common law systems, which already have such disclosure obligations in place, also have significant problems in providing equivalent protection in tort to the victims of AI harms. Further, the limitation of this obligation to high-risk systems does not address the problems encountered in litigation concerning other AI systems.

Whilst the proposal represents some improvements on existing systems of liability, both mechanisms provided in the proposed AI Liability Directive fail to solve many of the core problems of AI liability, which have been identified throughout this book, including problems concerning duty, fault, remoteness and 'many hands'. The proposal is therefore unlikely to bridge the liability gap. Further, its interconnected nature with the proposed AI Act also makes it an inappropriate template for non-EU jurisdictions to follow.

VII.   CONCLUSION

Autonomous systems are here to stay, and they are likely to play an increasingly important role in society, including in safety critical roles. They have the potential to improve both productivity and safety. However, autonomous systems accidents will occur, and the law will need to be able to adequately deal with them. Even in jurisdictions with extensive ex-ante regulation for autonomous systems there will still be a need to consider the consequences of what should happen when an accident occurs, and where the losses should lie. Currently tort law, combined with liability insurance, carries out the heavy lifting within accident compensation. The chapters in this book explore the significant challenges autonomous systems cause for existing tort law. As developed throughout the chapters it is clear that the current law of tort is likely to be found wanting in an autonomous system context, further that tort law will need to be adjusted to accommodate such technologies. This conclusion should not surprise us. A liability system designed around human wrongdoers, or the attribution of the conduct of human wrongdoers to legal persons, is likely to be challenged, if the 'wrongdoer' is a machine. Further, in previous industrial revolutions tort law required significant adjustments to accommodate new technologies, and new types and scales of accidents. As demonstrated by these adjustments over-spilling and leading to major revisions across tort law, all tort lawyers should be keeping an eye on autonomous system developments, and how tort law is being crafted to meet the problems which such systems will cause.

Autonomous systems also represent a challenge for how tort lawyers think, as we are required to adopt an ex-ante mindset more familiar to regulators. However, we cannot simply wait for the first wave of autonomous systems accidents to be litigated before we resolve the problems autonomous systems cause for tort. Predictability as to liability exposure is important to deployers of such technologies and their insurers if such technologies are to be successfully used in a wide range of contexts. The authors in this book propose a broad range of solutions to these challenges, both general and sector specific. Inevitably they differ, but as advanced above there is strength in this diversity of opinion. It provides policymakers with more to draw on. Further, the tech-impartial solution may vary from jurisdiction to jurisdiction, autonomous system to autonomous system, sector to sector, or even over time. Tort liability may also evolve as the technology evolves, and previously rejected proposals might therefore need to be reconsidered. This introduction also discusses the proposed AI Liability Directive, highlighting its key features, mechanisms, advances and some of its problems.

2. Liability for Damage Caused by Artificial Intelligence – Some Food for Thought and Current Proposals

Jan De Bruyne[1] and Orian Dheu[2]

I. INTRODUCTION

Artificial intelligence (AI) and robots are becoming increasingly important in our daily lives.[3] AI systems are already used for a variety of purposes and

---

[1] Research Expert, KU Leuven Centre for IT & IP law – imec (CiTiP); Assistant Professor, eLaw Leiden; Senior Researcher, Knowledge Centre Data & Society. This chapter is partly based on previous research done by Jan De Bruyne, Elias Van Gool and Thomas Gils on tort law for the book Jan De Bruyne and Cedric Vanleenhove, *Artificial Intelligence and the Law* (Intersentia 2021) 520.

[2] Doctoral researcher in law, KU Leuven Centre for IT & IP Law – imec (CiTiP). Part of this research has received funding from the European Union's Horizon 2020 Research and Innovation – Marie Skłodowska-Curie actions program under the Safer Autonomous Systems (SAS) project, grant agreement n° 812.788: https://etn-sas.eu/. This publication reflects only the author's view, exempting the European Union from any liability. This chapter was submitted for review prior to the release of two recent proposals for an 'AI Liability Directive' and a 'revised Product Liability Directive'. However, some of these proposals' most important elements are identified in this chapter.

[3] Ronald Leenes and others, 'Regulatory Challenges of Robotics: Some Guidelines for Addressing Legal and Ethical Issues' (2017) 9(1) Law, Innovation and Technology 2. The scope of this chapter does not allow for an in-depth discussion of the concept of AI. We use the concept as it is defined in Article 3(1) in the Proposed EU Artificial Intelligence Act (European Commission, Proposal for a Regulation of the European Parliament and of the Council laying down harmonised rules on artificial intelligence (Artificial Intelligence Act) and amending certain Union legislative acts, COM(2021) 206 final). It refers to software that is developed with one or more of the techniques and approaches listed in Annex I of the Proposal (e.g. machine learning approaches, logic- and knowledge-based approaches and statistical approaches) and that can, for a given set of human-defined objectives, generate outputs such as content, predictions, recommendations or decisions influencing the environments they interact with.

deployed in many sectors.[4] The rise of AI systems is no surprise considering their many benefits. They are more accurate and efficient because they are faster and can process information 'better' than humans.[5] AI systems and robots can also have advantages for the specific sector in which they are to be used. For instance, traffic is expected to become safer as the result of deploying autonomous vehicles.[6] At the same time, however, several challenges remain as well. Ethical questions include the human-machine relationship, and especially what role humans may still play in an era of AI. AI systems will also raise many safety challenges (e.g. how to provide evidence that such systems are safe enough).[7] Finally, the commercialisation of robots will pose several challenges from a legal and regulatory perspective.[8]

In this chapter, we will focus on the allocation of liability when AI systems and/or robots cause damage. AI systems and robots will raise (extra-)contractual liability issues as they will inevitably cause damage. Reference can be made to recent accidents involving self-driving cars. The autopilot sensors of a Tesla car, for instance, were not able to distinguish a white tractor-trailer crossing the road from the bright sky above, leading to a fatal crash.[9] An Uber self-driving car hit a pedestrian in Arizona who later died in hospital.[10] A surgical robot at a hospital in Philadelphia malfunctioned during a prostate

---

[4]   See in general: OECD, *Artificial Intelligence in Society* (OECD Publishing, 2019) 152.

[5]   Spyros G Tzafestas, *Roboethics: A Navigating Overview* (Springer, 2015) 147.

[6]   Many studies point to similar results. A NTHSA study, for instance, found that around 94% of road accidents in the US were related to human error: S Singh, 'Critical Reasons for Crashes Investigated in the National Motor Vehicle Crash Causation Survey' (*NHTSA Website*, 2018) crashstats.nhtsa.dot.gov/Api/Public/Publication/812506 accessed 27 November 2020.

[7]   See for example: Roman V Yampolskiy, *Artificial Intelligence Safety and Security* (CRC Press, 2018) 474.

[8]   Ronald Leenes and others (n 3) 2. See in general: Martin Ebers and Susana Navas (eds.), *Algorithms and Law* (Cambridge University Press, 2020) 319; Marcelo Corrales, Mark Fenwick and Nikolaus Forgó, *Robotics, AI and the Future of Law* (Springer, 2018) 237; Jacob Turner, *Robot Rules: Regulating Artificial Intelligence* (Springer, 2018) 377; Jan De Bruyne and Cedric Vanleenhove, *Artificial Intelligence and the Law* (Intersentia, 2021) 520; Matt Hervey and Matthew Lavy, *The Law of Artificial Intelligence* (Sweet & Maxwell, 2021) 588.

[9]   The Tesla Team, 'A Tragic Loss' (*Tesla*, 30 June 2016) www.teslamotors.com/blog/tragic-loss accessed 3 March 2022.

[10]   Sam Levin and Julia Carrie, 'Self-driving Uber kills Arizona woman in first fatal crash involving pedestrian' *The Guardian* (London, 19 March 2018) www.theguardian.com/technology/2018/mar/19/uber-self-driving-car-kills-woman-arizona-tempe accessed 3 March 2022.

surgery, thereby severely injuring the patient.[11] These examples illustrate that liability issues in an AI context will become prevalent in the future. Things may get even more complicated as the characteristics of AI systems such as opaqueness, autonomy, connectivity, data dependency or self-learning abilities make it difficult to trace back potentially problematic decisions made with the involvement of such systems.[12] This, in turn, may make it challenging for victims to obtain compensation under existing liability regimes at the national level and at the level of the European Union (EU). There is also some uncertainty regarding the allocation of responsibilities between different economic operators in the supply chain of AI systems. Several parties can be involved, such as the developers of the software/algorithms, the producer of the hardware, owners/keepers of the AI product, suppliers of data, public authorities and the users of the product. Persons who have suffered harm may not have effective access to the evidence that is necessary to build a case in court and may have less effective redress possibilities compared to situations where the damage is caused by 'traditional' products.[13]

In this chapter, we will examine some issues regarding tort and product liability for damage caused by AI systems from an EU perspective. We will first provide a short overview of the regulatory evolutions and mention recent proposals on tort liability at the supranational level (Part II). Once this background has been provided, we will focus on how AI systems challenge the existing liability frameworks. We will take product liability as a case study and see how such a recent proposal tries to address some of these challenges (Part III). We will then provide some ideas that can be relied upon for future discussions, thereby also focusing on procedural elements such as the burden of proof (Part IV). The main findings are briefly summarised in a conclusion (Part V).

---

[11]   *Mracek v Bryn Mawr Hospital*, 363 Fed. Appx. 925 (3d Cir. 2010) as reported in Trevor N White and Seth D Baum, 'Liability for Present and Future Robotics Technology' in Patrick Lin and others (eds.), *Robot Ethics 2.0: From Autonomous Cars to Artificial Intelligence* (Oxford University Press, 2017) 66–79.

[12]   Expert Group on Liability and New Technologies, New Technologies Formation, 'Liability for Artificial Intelligence and Other Emerging Digital Technologies' (Report for the European Commission 2019) 32–4.

[13]   European Commission, 'White Paper on Artificial Intelligence – A European approach to excellence and trust' (Communication) COM(2020) 65 final, 13; Gerhard Wagner, 'Robot Liability' (Colloquium on EU Law and Digital Economy, Liability for Robotics and the Internet of Things, Münster, March 2018) 1; Jan De Bruyne, Elias Van Gool and Thomas Gils, 'Tort Law and Damage Caused by AI Systems' in Jan De Bruyne and Cedric Vanleenhove (eds.), *Artificial Intelligence and the Law* (Intersentia 2021) 359–403.

II.   THE EUROPEAN UNION FRAMEWORK ON LIABILITY AND AI: SETTING THE SCENE

The EU considers AI as a strategic set of technologies that Europe must foster and enable,[14] although adequate regulation must ensure its safety and guarantee the respect of fundamental rights. The EU has long been aware of the potential liability bottlenecks that may hamper innovation and stifle trust in the development and deployment of AI applications. Striking a balance between facilitating the victim's claim and fostering innovation, however, is not straightforward. One of the first reports on this issue was published by the European Parliament (EP) in 2017.[15] It considered, among other things, creating electronic personhood for sophisticated robots. It also called upon the European Commission (EC) to consider a legislative instrument that would deal with the liability for damage caused by autonomous systems and robots. The feasibility of a strict liability or a risk management approach had to be evaluated as well. The risk management approach focuses on the person who is able, under certain circumstances, to minimise risks and deal with negative impacts. Strict liability requires only the proof 'that damage has occurred and the establishment of a causal link between the harmful functioning of the robot and the damage suffered by the injured party'.[16]

In March 2018, the EC set up an expert group on liability and new tech- nologies, which was divided into two formations. The first subgroup is the 'Product Liability Directive Formation' (PLDF). It was tasked with assess- ing the Product Liability Directive (PLD). The second subgroup, the 'New Technologies Formation' (NTF), explored the main liability challenges raised by these new technologies. The latter subgroup published a report on the 'Liability for Artificial Intelligence and Other Emerging Digital Technologies' in November 2019.[17] The report adopts a macro level analysis of the liability challenges raised by AI and digital technologies. The report, therefore, refrains from diving into details of specific sectoral liability regimes, which are plenty,

---

[14]   See: European Commission, 'Communication on Artificial Intelligence for Europe' (Communication) COM(2018) 237 final; European Commission, 'Coordinated Plan on Artificial Intelligence' (Communication) COM/2018/795 final (2018).

[15]   European Parliament, 'Report with recommendations to the Commission on Civil Law Rules on Robotics' (2017) 2015/2103(INL). Note that several reports have also been published upon request by European institutions (e.g. Andrea Bertolini, *Artificial Intelligence and Civil Liability* (Report for the European Parliament JURI committee 2020)).

[16]   ibid. para 54.

[17]   Expert Group on Liability and New Technologies, New Technologies Formation (n 12).

especially in the transportation field.[18] After a quick overview of the various liability regimes, the report describes the specific challenges posed to current tort law by AI technologies. It concludes that liability regimes 'in force in Member States ensure at least basic protection of victims whose damage is caused by the operation of such new technologies'.[19] However, their effective implementation may be problematic due to these technologies' intrinsic characteristics, such as their complexity, self-learning abilities, opacity and limited predictability.[20] The report then stresses the idea that current liability mechanisms may not offer an adequate, efficient and fair allocation of liabilities when such technologies cause damage. The report offers several recommendations, some of which will be addressed later in this chapter. The operators of emerging digital technologies which are, for example, operated in a 'non-private environment' and which could cause 'significant harm' should bear strict liability, as they carry the risks of operating such systems. A distinction is made between two types of operators. Front-end operators primarily decide and benefit from the use of the technology (e.g. a user of an autonomous vehicle). Back-end operators are those actors who continuously define the features of the relevant technology and provide essential and ongoing back-end support (e.g. the parties that provide continuous software updates as well as back-end services).[21]

In February 2020, the EC published its White Paper on AI. It sets out options to consider when regulating AI systems and their applications. The White Paper has two main building blocks, namely an 'ecosystem of trust' and an 'ecosystem of excellence'. Creating an ecosystem of trust will give citizens the confidence to take up AI applications, and companies and public organisations the legal certainty to innovate by using AI. The White Paper adheres to a risk-based approach, meaning that any regulatory intervention should be targeted and proportionate. That is why the EC does not want to regulate all AI systems but only high-risk systems. Such systems will have to comply with several additional requirements. AI systems that are not considered high risk should only be covered by more general legislation, for example on

---

[18]   See for instance the (national) specific regimes for third party damages on the surface by aircraft or road traffic liability laws.

[19]   Expert Group on Liability and New Technologies, New Technologies Formation (n 12) 3.

[20]   Also see *infra* part III.A.

[21]   Expert Group on Liability and New Technologies, New Technologies Formation (n 12) 39–41. Also see: Orian Dheu, 'EU report on AI, new technologies and liability: key take-aways and limitations' (*CiTiP Blog*, 9 January 2020) www.law.kuleuven .be/citip/blog/eu-report-on-ai-new-technologies-and-liability-key-take-aways-and -limitations accessed 27 September 2021.

data protection, consumer protection and product safety/liability. These rules may, however, need some targeted modifications to effectively address the risks created by AI systems.[22] The issue of liability and AI is not extensively addressed in the White Paper. Nevertheless, it acknowledges that the legal framework could be improved to address the uncertainty regarding the allocation of responsibilities between different actors. The features of AI systems may challenge aspects of liability frameworks and could reduce their effectiveness. For instance, AI technologies' characteristics would make it harder for victims to 'trace the damage back to a person', which can be required for fault-based liability schemes.[23] The White Paper also stresses that persons who have been injured or suffered damage as the result of an AI system should benefit from an equal level of protection as those having suffered harm caused by other technologies. The current PLD may need to be amended, while a targeted harmonisation of national liability rules is suggested as well.[24]

This White Paper was accompanied by a report on safety and liability, which signalled the importance that the EC gave to addressing the issue of liability. After a brief assessment of the legal framework, it focuses on several points that need further attention, such as clarifying the scope of the PLD *inter alia* by considering revising the notion of putting a product into circulation. The reversal or alleviation of the burden of proof for damage caused by the operation of AI systems also needs to be examined, for instance through an 'appropriate EU initiative'. For the operation of AI applications with a specific risk profile (e.g. those with a high risk), the Commission is seeking views 'on whether and to what extent strict liability [...] may be needed in order to achieve effective compensation of possible victims. The Commission is also gathering views on coupling strict liability with a possible obligation to conclude available insurance.'[25] Finally, the report raises the question of whether or not to adapt the burden of proof regarding fault and causation for other AI systems (e.g. those with a low risk).[26]

In October 2020, the EP adopted a Resolution with recommendations to the EC on a civil liability regime for AI. It contained a proposal for a horizontal

---

[22]   European Commission, 'White Paper on Artificial Intelligence – A European approach to excellence and trust' (n 13) 9–22.

[23]   Ibid. 15.

[24]   Ibid. 14–15. We will see below that this is the path that has been chosen by the European Commission in its two recent proposals.

[25]   Ibid. 16.

[26]   European Commission, 'Report on the safety and liability implications of Artificial Intelligence, the Internet of Things and Robotics' (Report) COM(2020) 64 final (2020), 12–16. Also see: Jan De Bruyne and Orian Dheu, 'An EU perspective on liability and Artificial Intelligence' (*RAILS Blog*, 14 March 2020) blog.ai-laws.org/an -eu-perspective-on-liability-and-artificial-intelligence/ accessed 20 October 2020.

regulation of liability for the operation of AI systems. According to this proposal, the operator of a high-risk AI system should be strictly liable for any harm or damage that was caused by a physical or virtual activity, device or process driven by that AI system.[27] Operators of high-risk systems would not be able to exonerate themselves from liability by arguing that they acted with 'due diligence or that the harm or damage was caused by an autonomous activity, device or process driven by their AI system'.[28] Operators would not be held liable if the harm or damage was caused by force majeure.[29] The operator of an AI system that does not constitute a high-risk AI system should be subject to 'fault-based liability for any harm or damage that was caused by a physical or virtual activity, device or process driven by the AI system'.[30] This provision, however, contains a reversal of the burden of proof. The operator would not be liable if he/she can prove that the harm or damage was caused without his/her fault, relying on either of the following grounds: '(a) the AI system was activated without his/her knowledge while all reasonable and necessary measures to avoid such activation outside of the operator's control were taken, or (b) due diligence was observed by performing all the following actions: selecting a suitable AI system for the right task and skills, putting the AI system duly into operation, monitoring the activities and maintaining the operational reliability by regularly installing all available updates'.[31]

In April 2021, the EC issued its draft AI Act (AIA).[32] It adheres to a risk-based approach as well. Whereas certain AI systems are prohibited, several additional requirements apply for the placing of high-risk AI systems on the market. These, for instance, relate to the establishment of a risk management system, the need to ensure human oversight and the requirement of record-keeping. The draft AIA also imposes obligations upon several parties, such as providers and users of high-risk AI systems.[33] Providers of high-risk AI systems have to ensure that their systems are compliant with the applicable requirements in the draft AIA. They should also have a quality management system in place, comply with the applicable registration requirements and draw up the technical documentation of the AI system. Providers need to keep

---

[27]   European Parliament, 'European Parliament resolution of 20 October 2020 with recommendations to the Commission on a civil liability regime for artificial intelligence' (Report) 2020/2014(INL), Art 4 (1).

[28]   ibid. Art 4 (3).

[29]   ibid. Art 4 (3).

[30]   ibid. Art 8 (1).

[31]   ibid. Art 8 (2).

[32]   European Commission, 'Proposal for a Regulation of the European Parliament and of the Council laying down harmonised rules on artificial intelligence (Artificial Intelligence Act) and amending certain Union legislative acts', COM(2021) 206 final.

[33]   ibid. Arts 16–29.

the logs automatically generated by their high-risk AI systems when under their control. They need to ensure that the high-risk AI system undergoes the relevant conformity assessment procedure prior to its placing on the market or putting into service. Users of high-risk AI systems in turn have to use such systems in accordance with the instructions of use accompanying them.[34] Those obligations will be important when it comes to establishing the potential liability of such parties, for instance when determining that an operator or user committed a fault (i.e. violation of a specific legal norm or negligence). Member States must also lay down effective, proportionate and dissuasive penalties, including administrative fines, when AI systems that are put on the market do not respect the requirements of the Regulation.[35]

Finally, most recently, in September 2022, the EC published two proposals for Directives to adapt liability rules to the digital age – one 'adapting non contractual civil liability rules to artificial intelligence' ('AI Liability Directive')[36] and another revising the Product Liability Directive ('revised Product Liability Directive').[37] The AI Liability Directive lays down rules on the disclosure of evidence on high-risk AI that allow a claimant to substantiate a non-contractual civil liability claim as well as rules regarding the burden of proof for damages caused by AI systems.[38] The revised Product Liability Directive also provides substantive changes to the current product liability regime. These two proposals will not be thoroughly assessed here, as the following chapter was written prior to their release, though some of their main provisions will be identified and explained. However, many elements in these proposals echo observations made in this chapter. [39]

---

[34]   ibid. Art 29 (1).

[35]   ibid. Arts 71–72.

[36]   Proposal for a Directive of the European Parliament and of the Council on adapting non contractual civil liability rules to artificial intelligence, European Commission, COM(2022) 496 final, 2022 (hereafter referred to 'AI Liability Directive').

[37]   Proposal for a Directive of the European Parliament and of the Council on liability for defective products, European Commission, COM(2022) 495 final, 2022 (hereafter referred to 'revised Product Liability Directive').

[38]   Article 1 of the AI Liability Directive.

[39]   For an overview and critical analysis of these two Directives, one may refer to the following paper: Orian Dheu, Jan De Bruyne and Charlotte Ducuing, 'The European Commission's Approach to Extra-Contractual Liability and AI – A First Analysis and Evaluation of the Two Proposals', SSRN, 2022, 43 p. (https://papers.ssrn.com/sol3/papers.cfm?abstract_id=4239792).

III.   THE CHALLENGES CAUSED BY AI SYSTEMS AND WAYS THEY ARE ADDRESSED

Although AI technologies are expected to increase levels of safety and reliability, it has already been mentioned that their applications may still cause damage to life, health, physical integrity and property. Liability issues will thus eventually arise. Much legal uncertainty exists when it comes to prospectively assessing the liability risks at play. With complex and dynamic technologies and a multi-stakeholder ecosystem, identifying and allocating liability may not be straightforward. That is why after mapping some of AI's disruptive characteristics (Part A), we will briefly explore how current liability regimes may be challenged by this set of technologies and how a new European proposal aims to tackle these challenges (Part B). We will take the product liability regime as a case study.

A.   Artificial Intelligence as (an Evolving) Challenge to Existing Civil Liability Mechanisms

AI systems represent a protean and multifaceted reality that is hard to reduce to a few elements.[40] However, building on the many European reports and studies, common features can be observed that challenge the application of traditional extra-contractual liability regimes. AI systems are characterised by their autonomy, dynamicity and opacity as well as their complexity and high data reliance. Such characteristics will undoubtedly have an impact on the applicability and implementation of current (national) liability frameworks across the EU.

First and foremost, one of AI systems' distinctive features resides in their autonomy. The concept of autonomy is by itself difficult to define due to the heterogeneous nature of these technologies and their applications. Different taxonomies related to the apprehension of autonomy exist. However, if we base the definition of autonomy on the notion of human control,[41] AI systems, specifically those using probabilistic or statistical methods, will enable systems

---

[40]   See also Chapter 1.

[41]   The notion of control is usually a crucial element in ascribing responsibility to agents. See for instance: Mark Fischer, *Responsibility and Control: A Theory of Moral Responsibility* (Cambridge University Press, 1998). Some authors contend that with AI technologies, the control criteria will no longer be attributable to a human agent and could therefore lead to a responsibility gap. See for instance: Andreas Matthias, 'The Responsibility Gap: Ascribing Responsibility for the Actions of Learning Automata' (2004) 6(3) Ethics and Information Technology 175; Zoe Porter and others, 'The Moral Responsibility Gap and the Increasing Autonomy of Systems' in B Gallina and others

to take decisions with few if any human inputs based on the data they receive and process. With autonomous systems, the human operator partially or totally disengages him/herself from providing direct instructions to the machine or software, therefore parting from traditional automation paradigms. This autonomy will raise questions when the systems cause harm to persons or damage property. Determining and attributing liability for AI systems' decisions can be extremely complex in certain circumstances. Moreover, AI systems may embed machine learning algorithms allowing them to learn from data and adapt their decision-making process accordingly. Such dynamicity, resulting from their self-learning capacities, may prove challenging when implementing some of the existing liability mechanisms.[42]

Second, AI systems are also often characterised by opacity and a lack of transparency.[43] The intrinsic opacity of some AI technologies makes it difficult to understand why (and how) the system took a specific decision.[44] Indeed, technologies that embed machine learning usually work as 'black boxes', meaning that it is extremely difficult to apprehend why (and how) their decisional process led to a specific output. This may be problematic when a victim tries to trace the source of the damage or, more importantly, when attributing liability. Yet, understanding the cause of the damage is a crucial element in implementing some liability regimes.[45]

Thirdly, the complexity of AI technologies and their associated applications will make the tracing of the damage back to a liable party extremely difficult, if not impossible. Indeed, in the case of autonomous systems embedding AI technologies, numerous cyber-physical components and actors interact with each other, therefore blurring even further the identification and the attribution of liability (cf. the 'many hands' issue). Furthermore, these technologies are highly data reliant. Data is the essential fuel and enabler on which AI algorithms feed themselves in order to train and take decisions. However, this means that any flaw or issue with the quality of the data may lead the system to take incorrect decisions or erroneously self-learn, which could ultimately

---

(eds.), *Computer Safety, Reliability, and Security. SAFECOMP 2018. Lecture Notes in Computer Science, vol 11094* (Springer 2018) 487–93.

[42]   Expert Group on Liability and New Technologies, New Technologies Formation (n 12) 33. See also: Benedikt Buchner, 'Artificial Intelligence as a Challenge for the Law: The Example of "Doctor Algorithm"' [2022] Int. Cybersecur. Law Rev 2.

[43]   Expert Group on Liability and New Technologies, New Technologies Formation (n 12) 33.

[44]   On the lack of predictability and the responsibility gap see: Matthias (n 41) 175–83 (he seems to suggest that neither the operator nor the manufacturer should be held responsible since they no longer have control over the system).

[45]   Expert Group on Liability and New Technologies, New Technologies Formation (n 12) 33.

lead to damage. This also means that most AI systems are highly prone to cybersecurity threats. And with some safety-critical AI applications, this could mean liability exposure.[46]

B.   The Challenges under the PLD as a Case Study

This quick overview of AI systems' disruptive features hints at the many legal hurdles that may arise from their development and deployment, especially in the field of civil liability. An important example in this regard is product liability, which has already attracted much academic attention.[47] Article 1 of the current Product Liability Directive ('PLD') states that the producer will be held liable for damage caused by a defect in his/her product. We will examine whether the current applicable framework is adapted to the AI reality by focusing on three elements, namely whether software can be qualified as a 'product' (Part 1), when a product can be considered 'defective' (Part 2) and the moment when the product incorporating AI is 'put into circulation' (Part 3).[48] Although the focus will be on the PLD, the situation in Belgium will be considered as well. We include that jurisdiction considering our expertise as well as the fact that several elements under the PLD still touch upon national law. We will also mention the recent proposal on a revised Product Liability Directive. Though not limited to AI-related products, it provides some answers to the questions raised in this chapter.

---

[46]   Expert Group on Liability and New Technologies, New Technologies Formation (n 12) 33–4. See on the cybersecurity of autonomous vehicles: C Warren Axelrod, 'Cybersecurity challenges of systems-of-systems for fully-autonomous road vehicles' (13th International Conference and Expo on Emerging Technologies for a Smarter World (CEWIT), Stony Brook, NY, 2017) 1–6.

[47]   See the many contributions on product liability in: Sebastian Lohsse and others, 'Liability for Artificial Intelligence' in Sebastien Lohsse, Reiner Schulze and Dirk Staudenmayer (eds.), *Liability for Artificial Intelligence and the Internet of Things* (Nomos 2019) 352; Kevin Funkhouser, 'Paving the Road Ahead: Autonomous Vehicles, Products Liability, and the Need for a New Approach' (2013) 1 Utah Law Review 437. More recently: Bertolini, (n 15) 47–62.

[48]   See for a more extensive analysis in the context of autonomous vehicles: Jan De Bruyne and Jochen Tanghe, 'Liability for Damage Caused by Autonomous Vehicles: A Belgian Perspective' (2017) 8(3) Journal of European Tort Law 324. See for more information: De Bruyne, Van Gool and Gils (n 13) 359–403; Andrea Bertolini and Massimo Riccaboni, 'Grounding the Case for a European Approach to the Regulation of Automated Driving: the Technology-selection Effect of Liability Rules' (2021) 51 European Journal of Law and Economics 243.

1.   Is software a product?

A producer will be liable for damage caused by a defect in the product. Technology and industry, however, have evolved drastically over the last decades. The division between products and services is no longer as clear-cut as it was. Producing products and providing services are increasingly intertwined.[49] Moreover, software and AI systems merit specific attention in respect of product liability. Software is essential to the functioning of many products and affects their safety. It is integrated into products, but it can also be supplied separately to enable the use of the product as intended. Consequently, an important question is whether stand-alone software can be qualified as a product within the meaning of the PLD.[50]

Article 2 of the PLD defines a product as all movables, with the exception of primary agricultural products and game, even though incorporated into another movable or into an immovable. There are several reasons why software cannot be seen as a product. For instance, software might be qualified as a service and not as a product.[51] However, some scholars argue that software is not a service but the object of a service. It would, therefore, be covered by the PLD.[52] The fact that software is not qualified as a service does not necessarily mean that it is a product. As the PLD mentions 'movables', some argue that it cannot relate to tangible goods only.[53] Others, by contrast, conclude that it does.[54] It would otherwise make no sense to explicitly include electricity in the scope of the

---

[49] See: Bert Keirsbilck, E Terryn and Elias Van Gool, 'Consumentenbescherming bij *servitisation* en product-dienst-systemen (PDS)' [2019] TPR 817. See on the notion of blurred product versus service dichotomy in the context of autonomous systems: Orian Dheu, Charlotte Ducuing and Peggy Valcke, 'The Emperor's New Clothes: A Roadmap for Conceptualizing the "New Vehicle"' (2020) 75 Revue Transidit.

[50] Report on the safety and liability implications of Artificial Intelligence, the Internet of Things and Robotics (n 26) 14; De Bruyne, Van Gool and Gils (n 13) 359–403.

[51] See the references in: De Bruyne and Tanghe (n 48) 355, footnote 121. This is also acknowledged by Bertolini (n 15) 57 ('One of the major obstacles for a case to be successfully actioned under the PLD, is that the device whose defect caused a damage may not be considered a "product", but rather a «service», and thus falls outside the scope of application of the directive').

[52] See for example: Michel Flamée, '"Malfunction 54" of het produktkarakter van software', in *Liber Amicorum E. Krings* (Story-Scientia 1991) 124, no 124; Thiery Vansweevelt, 'De Wet van 25 februari 1991 inzake produktenaansprakelijkheid' [1992] TBBR 96, 105, no 17.

[53] Joost Verlinden, 'Veiligheid van producten en diensten en productaansprakelijkheid' in N Betsch and others (eds.), *Huur van diensten – Aanneming van werk: vormingsprogramma 2005-2006* (Larcier 2007) 62–3.

[54] See: Thierry Vansweevelt and Britt Weyts, *Handboek Buitencontractueel Aansprakelijkheidsrecht* (Intersentia 2009) 503.

Directive.[55] The Belgian Product Liability Act confirms this line of reasoning and stipulates that the regime only concerns tangible goods.[56] This requirement is problematic for software products. Software is a collection of data and instructions that is imperceptible to the human eye. A software system is thus often regarded as intangible. Accordingly, it might not fall within the scope of the PLD as it is not a physical product.[57]

However, not everyone agrees with this conclusion. Some authors claim that software should be regarded as a product because it is captured on a tangible medium or device (e.g. USB or hard drive). The EC has expressed this point of view in the past.[58] According to other scholars, software itself qualifies as a tangible good.[59] Even though codes used in software systems might be imperceptible to humans, they are part of our tangible world according to the standards of physics. Software differs from abstract ideas such as political or philosophical opinions.[60] Following a teleological interpretation, the PLD can also apply to software even if it is qualified as an intangible good. After all, the inclusion of electricity shows that the drafters aimed at a wide material scope. It is not surprising that legislators did not think of software in the early 1980s as personal computers only became commercially widespread during the second half of the 1980s. The inclusion of software in the PLD would reflect the current economic reality in which software is a commercial product just as any other product that may entail risks for users and third parties.[61] In

---

[55]   Art 2 Council Directive 85/374/EEC of 25 July 1985 on the approximation of the laws, regulations and administrative provisions of the Member States concerning liability for defective products [1985] OJ L 210/29 ('Product Liability Directive').

[56]   Art 2 Act of 25 February 1991 concerning liability for defective products (BS 22 March 1991) ('Belgian Product Liability Act').

[57]   On 'algorithms that are not embedded in a physical product', see: Eric Tjong Tjin Tai, 'Liability for (Semi)Autonomous Systems: Robots and Algorithms' (2018) Tilburg Law School Legal Studies Research Paper Series No. 09/2018 16 papers.ssrn.com/sol3/papers.cfm?abstract_id=3161962 accessed 25 September 2021; Dimitri Verhoeven, *Productaansprakelijkheid en productveiligheid* (Intersentia 2018) 55–6.

[58]   See in this regard: Written Question no. 706/88 (5 July 1988) and Answer by Lord Cockfield on behalf of the Commission (15 November 1988), *OJ* 114/42, 8 May 1989.

[59]   See for example: Jean-Paul Triaille, 'The EEC Directive (25 July 1985) on product liability and its application to databases and information' [1993] Computer Law and Practice 217.

[60]   De Bruyne and Tanghe (n 48) 356–7.

[61]   ibid. 357. Also see: Bernhard Koch, 'Product Liability 2.0 – Mere Update or New Version?' in Sebastian Lohsse and others (eds.), *Liability for Artificial Intelligence and the Internet of Things* (Nomos 2019) 106; Gerhard Wagner, 'Robot Liability' in Sebastian Lohsse and others (eds.), *Liability for Artificial Intelligence and the Internet of Things* (Nomos 2019) 42.

this regard, Wendehorst eventually concludes that the 'current product definition leads to serious uncertainties with regard to the liability for software. Although there are good reasons why software should be considered a product under the current PLD and convincing attempts in legal literature have been made to bridge the existing inconsistencies, the many diverging views – not only between Member States but also within jurisdictions – on how to treat software under the PLD, render a revision by the European legislator necessary.'[62] Regardless of the qualification of software, the victim of an accident involving an AI system may have a claim against the producer of a product incorporating software, such as an autonomous vehicle or a household robot.[63] Software steering the operations of a tangible product could be considered as a part or component of that product.[64] This means that an autonomous vehicle or material robot used for surgery is a product in the sense of the PLD, and can be defective if the software system it uses is not functioning properly.

The Commission's recent proposal for a revised Product Liability Directive puts an end to such discussions by providing a clear answer to these questions: software and digital manufacturing files are considered products and are therefore included within its scope.[65] This means that an injured person may claim compensation for damages relating to defective software, and therefore possibly defective software embedding artificial intelligence.

2.   When is an AI system defective?

Liability under the current PLD requires a defect in the product. A product is defective if it does not provide the safety that a person is entitled to expect, taking all circumstances into account (cf. 'consumer expectations test').[66] This does not refer to the expectations of a particular person but to the expectations of the general public[67] or the target audience.[68] The criterion of legitimate expectations is normative as well. The question is not what expectations the

---

[62]   Christiane Wendehorst, 'Safety and Liability Related Aspects of Software' (Report for the European Commission, 2021) 66.

[63]   ibid. 65.

[64]   European Commission, 'Report on the safety and liability implications of Artificial Intelligence, the Internet of Things and Robotics' (n 26) 14.

[65]   Art 4 (1) revised Product Liability Directive.

[66]   Art 6 (1) Product Liability Directive.

[67]   Recital 6 Product Liability Directive. Bocken argues that it concerns the consumer as part of a group (Hubert Bocken, 'Buitencontractuele aansprakelijkheid voor gebrekkige producten' in *Bijzondere overeenkomsten – PUC W. Delva nr. 34* (Kluwer 2008) 367.

[68]   Belgian Court of cassation, 26 September 2003, Arr.Cass., 2003, 1765, RW, 2004–05, 22, annotation by Britt Weyts; Court of Appeal Antwerp 13 April 2005, RW, 2008–09, 803; Court of Appeal Antwerp 28 October 2009, TBBR, 2011, 381.

general public or the audience actually have but what expectations they are entitled to have, in other words, which expectations are legitimate.[69]

The assessment of the legitimate expectations is done in concrete terms.[70] Several elements can be used to determine the legitimate expectations regarding the use of AI systems. These include the presentation of the product, the normal or reasonably foreseeable use of it and the moment in time when the product was put into circulation.[71] This enumeration of circumstances, however, is not exhaustive, as other factors may play a role as well.[72] The presentation of a product is especially important for manufacturers of autonomous vehicles or medical robots. That is because they often tend to market their products explicitly as safer than existing alternatives, which increases the risk of liability.[73] The criterion of legitimate expectations remains rather vague and it gives judges a wide margin of appreciation.[74] As a consequence, it is difficult to predict how this criterion will be applied in the context of AI systems. The safety expectations will be very high for AI systems used in high-risk contexts, such as health care or mobility.[75] At the same time, however, the concrete application of this test remains difficult for AI systems because of their novelty, the complexity of comparing these systems with human or technological alternatives and the characteristics of autonomy and opacity.[76] The 'interconnectivity of products and systems also makes it hard to identify the defectiveness'.[77] In addition, sophisticated AI systems 'with self-learning capabilities raise the question of whether unpredictable deviations in the decision-making process can be treated as defects. Even if they constitute a defect, the state-of-the-art defence may apply.'[78] The 'complexity

---

[69]   Vansweevelt and Weyts (n 54) 510.

[70]   Hubert Bocken and Ingrid Boone with cooperation by M Kruithof, *Inleiding tot het schadevergoedingsrecht* (Die Keure 2014) 196.

[71]   Art 5 (1) Belgian Product Liability Act.

[72]   Bocken and Boone (n 70) 148, footnote 18.

[73]   Koen Swinnen, 'De inpassing van digitale producten in het Belgisch privaatrecht' [2018] TPR 1087.

[74]   Bocken (n 67) 368.

[75]   See for example: Case C-503/13 *Boston Scientific* [2015] ECLI:EU:C:2015:148, consideration 39; Thomas Malengreau, 'Automatisation de la conduite: quelles responsabilités en droit belge? (Première partie)' (2019) (5) RGAR 15578–15607, no 27

[76]   On the assessment of an algorithm's defectiveness, see: Jean-Sébastien Borghetti, 'How can Artificial Intelligence be Defective?' in Sebastian Lohsse (eds.), *Liability for Artificial Intelligence and the Internet of Things* (Nomos 2019) 66-67; De Bruyne and Tanghe (n 48) 358–62.

[77]   Expert Group on Liability and New Technologies, New Technologies Formation (n 12) 28.

[78]   Under this defence, the producer will not be held liable if he/she proves that the state of scientific and technical knowledge at the time when he/she put the product into

and the opacity of emerging digital technologies, such as AI systems, further complicate the chance for the victim to discover and prove the defect and/or causation.'[79] In addition, 'there is some uncertainty on how and to what extent the PLD would apply in the case of certain types of defects, for example those resulting from weaknesses in the cybersecurity of the product'.[80]

The revised Product Liability Directive does give answers to some of these questions.[81] While it still refers to the general public's safety expectations,[82] it includes an expanded and adapted list of circumstances under which the product may be assessed for its defectiveness. These include the 'the effect on the product of any ability to continue to learn after deployment'and 'the effect on the product of other products that can reasonably be expected to be used together with the product'.[83] However, another circumstance listed in the proposal may be problematic. Namely, the circumstance that takes into account 'the specific expectations of the end users for whom the product is intended'.[84] As observed by Dheu, De Bruyne and Ducuing, it remains unclear how such a provision would interplay with the general expectations test as this circumstance seems to refer to the subjective expectations of the end user.[85]

3.   Putting the product into circulation and AI?

Under the current PLD, the victim only needs to prove that the product was defective at the moment of the accident. There are, however, some possibilities for the producer to escape liability.[86] For instance, the manufacturer of the product can escape liability when he/she establishes that it is probable that the defect causing the damage did not exist at the time when the product was put into circulation or that this defect came into being afterwards.[87] According to Article 6 of the Belgian Product Liability Act, 'putting into circulation' means the first act embodying the producer's intention to bestow upon the product

---

circulation was not such as to enable the existence of the defect to be discovered (Art 7 (e) Product Liability Directive).

[79]   Expert Group on Liability and New Technologies, New Technologies Formation (n 12) 28.

[80]   European Commission, 'White Paper on Artificial Intelligence – A European approach to excellence and trust' (n 13) 13.

[81]   Dheu, De Bruyne and Ducuing (n 39) 29.

[82]   Art 6.1 revised Product Liability Directive.

[83]   Art 6.1 (c) and (d) revised Product Liability Directive.

[84]   Art 6.1 (h) revised Product Liability Directive.

[85]   Dheu, De Bruyne and Ducuing (n 39) 36.

[86]   Art 7 Product Liability Directive.

[87]   Art 7 (b) Product Liability Directive. Also see: Belgian Court of Cassation, 4 May 2007 RW 2007, 1286–7 with annotation by Daily Wuyts. Also, see: Wendehorst (n 60) 68–9.

the usage that he/she intends for it through the transfer of the product to a third party or the use of it for the benefit of that person. According to the European Court of Justice, a product must be considered as having been put into circulation when 'it leaves the production process operated by the producer, and enters a marketing process in the form in which it is offered to the public to be used or consumed'.[88] Despite this broad interpretation, the notion of 'putting into circulation' can be challenging for products incorporating software or AI systems that may change and evolve over time.[89] AI's self-learning and autonomous nature, as well as the associated frequent safety and security updates of such systems, display a 'continuous production process', even without external interaction.[90]

Some scholars conclude that if software is seen as a product, any update thereof could be considered an act by which the producer brings a new product into circulation. Consequently, the software producer would not be able to escape liability all too easily by referring to the provision in Article 7(b) of the PLD.[91] It becomes more difficult with self-learning systems, as they continually improve themselves. For defects that are created this way, a moment of putting the product into circulation cannot be indicated, as the manufacturer did not perform an act to that end. It is also unrealistic to qualify a software system as defective merely because it is able to adjust itself.[92] Against this background, completely disallowing this defence may be considered in the context of AI systems. This makes it possible for victims to file a claim against the manufacturer of the software even when the defect is created through the continuous self-development of software.[93] Other scholars, however, are more nuanced and conclude that the potential defect in an AI system should find its origins in the production process. This may eventually lead to the producer's liability.[94]

---

[88] Case C-127/04 *Declan O' Byrne v Sanofi Pasteur MSD Ltd & Sanofi Pasteur SA* [2006] ERC I-1313, para 27.

[89] European Commission, 'Report on the safety and liability implications of Artificial Intelligence, the Internet of Things and Robotics' (n 26) 15.

[90] Elias Van Gool, Jan De Bruyne and Michiel Fierens, 'De regulering van artificiële intelligentie (deel 2) – Een analyse van buitencontractuele aansprakelijkheid' (2021) 26 Rechtskundig Weekblad 1014–15.

[91] De Bruyne and Tanghe (n 48) 370.

[92] See, however, more nuanced: Jean-Benoit Hubin, 'La responsabilité du fait des robots – Le droit de la responsabilité à l'ère de la révolution numérique' in Hervé Jacquemin and others (eds.), *Responsabilités et numérique* (Anthemis 2018) 272.

[93] De Bruyne and Tanghe (n 48) 370. One will however have to consider that the statute of limitation (periods) may be revised as well.

[94] See for example: Hubin (n 92) 272; Thomas Malengreau, 'Automatisation de la conduite: quelles responsabilités en droit belge? (Deuxième partie)' [2019] (6) RGAR

The possibility of the producer escaping liability by relying on this defence is also a reoccurring topic in many EU studies. The Expert Report on liability and AI issued by the New Technologies Formation is important in this regard. It states that 'when the defect came into being as a result of the producer's interference with the product already put into circulation (by way of a software update for example) or the producer's failure to interfere, it should be regarded as a defect in the product for which' he/she can be held liable.[95] It further adds that 'the point in time at which a product is placed on the market should not set a strict limit on the producer's liability for defects where, after that point in time, the producer or a third party acting on behalf of the producer remains in charge of providing updates or digital services'.[96] The producer should, therefore, remain liable where the defect has its origin '(a) in a defective digital component or digital ancillary part, or in other digital content or services provided for the product, with the producer's assent after the product has been put into circulation; or (b) in the absence of an update of digital content, or of the provision of a digital service which would have been required to maintain the expected level of safety within the time period for which the producer is obliged to provide such updates'.[97] The producer should thus be strictly liable for defects in emerging digital technologies even if these defects 'appear after the product was put into circulation, as long as the producer was still in control of updates to, or upgrades on, the technology'.[98]

The revised Product Liability Directive clarifies some of these issues.[99] Indeed, by derogation to the 'latter defect defence' provision, it states that the economic operators (which is the term that refers more broadly to i.e. manufacturers, component manufacturers, importers, fulfilment service providers, etc.) may not benefit from this exemption when the defectiveness of the product is due to '(a) a related service; (b) software including software updates or upgrades; (c) or lack of software updates or upgrades necessary to maintain safety' *provided* that they are under the manufacturer's control.[100] Such control is defined as the manufacturer of a product 'authorises (a) the integration, inter-connection or supply by a third party of a component including software updates or upgrades, (b) the modification of the product'.[101] Moreover, the

---

15582–611, no 42.

[95] Expert Group on Liability and New Technologies, New Technologies Formation (n 12) 43.

[96] ibid.

[97] ibid.

[98] ibid. 42–4.

[99] For a preliminary analysis, see: Dheu, De Bruyne and Ducuing (n 39) 33.

[100] Art 10.1 (c) and 10.2 revised Product Liability Directive.

[101] Art 4 (5) revised Product Liability Directive.

moment of putting into circulation is no longer strictly limited to the moment where the manufacturer placed the product on to the market, but extends to the moment where the product was put into service or where the manufacturer 'retains control over the product after that moment, the moment in time where the product left the control of the manufacturer'.[102] This therefore extends and addresses the issues of software updates or upgrades which could still be considered under the revised Product Liability Directive's regime. However, one question remains: whether such provisions would nonetheless be suited (or not) for machine learning software that can continue to evolve after being released on the market. In this situation, such software would not necessarily be under the control of the manufacturer, meaning that the product would not be defective as such.[103]

The development risk defence may also be relevant in an AI context. This defence implies that the manufacturer will not be liable when proving that the state of scientific and technical knowledge at the time when he/she put the product into circulation was not such as to enable the existence of the defect to be discovered.[104] This defence may become more important considering that producers of sophisticated AI systems will probably frequently invoke it to refute liability.[105] The question, however, is how this defence should be applied with regard to AI systems. Due to the autonomous nature of AI systems, their behaviour cannot be completely foreseeable. Nevertheless, the fact that damage will occur is foreseeable.[106] Judges interpret this defence in a very restrictive way. This defence is not specifically directed at the practices and safety standards in use in the industrial sector in which the producer is operating but, unreservedly, at the state of scientific and technical knowledge, including the most advanced level of such knowledge at the time when the product was put into circulation. This defence does not contemplate the state of knowledge of which the producer actually or subjectively was or could have been apprised. Instead, it relates to the objective state of scientific and technical knowledge of which the producer is presumed to have been informed.[107]

---

[102] Art 6.1 (e) revised Product Liability Directive.

[103] See: Dheu, De Bruyne and Ducuing (n 39) 34–5.

[104] Art 7 (e) Product Liability Directive.

[105] Expert Group on Liability and New Technologies, New Technologies Formation (n 12) 28–9; Hervé Jacquemin and Jean-Benoit Hubin, 'Aspects contractuels et de responsabilité civile en matière d'intelligence artificielle' in Hervé Jacquemin and Alexandre de Streel (eds.), *Intelligence Artificielle et le droit* (Larcier 2017) 137.

[106] See: De Bruyne, Van Gool and Gils (n 13) 387.

[107] See: Case C-300/95, *Commission v United Kingdom* [1997] ECR I-2649, paras 26–9; Duncan Fairgrieve and others, 'Product Liability Directive' in Piotr Machnikowski (ed.), *European Product Liability: An Analysis of the State of the Art in the Era of New Technologies* (Intersentia 2017) 78.

The relevant scientific and technical knowledge must have been accessible at the time when the product was put into circulation.[108] Therefore, it seems possible to maintain this defence for AI systems.[109] Its assessment should, however, not be limited to the 'traditional' moment of putting the product into circulation but should be continuously assessed over time in the light of a producer's update and monitoring obligations.[110] The expert report eventually concludes that the development risk defence should not be available in cases 'where it was predictable that unforeseen developments might occur'.[111] Despite these identified issues, the revised Product Liability Directive retains the development risk defence and extends it to products that were under the manufacturer's control (such as software).[112] Moreover, contrary to the current version of the Directive, it does not leave the possibility to Member States to derogate from this provision.

4.   The difficult burden of proof, access to information and proposed solutions

In the current PLD, the burden of proof falls on the injured party. Moreover, it is up to the victim to gather evidence that demonstrates the product's defectiveness as well as the causal link between the defective product and the damage. However, in the context of AI-related products, these two requirements will be difficult, if not mostly impossible, for the injured party to establish.

First and foremost, the burden of proof for victims will especially remain difficult when the potential defect relates to the AI software itself, such as a programming error in the source code. In those circumstances, the discussion will more likely relate to potential 'design defects/flaws' in AI systems for which 'the reasonable design alternative' is the most commonly used criterion.[113] Comparing an AI system with a human or human-controlled technological alternative, however, is challenging. Over time, AI systems by their

---

[108] *Commission of the European Communities v United Kingdom of Great Britain and Northern Ireland* (n 107) considerations 26–9.

[109] Also see: Malengreau (n 75) 15582–611, no 43.

[110] Expert Group on Liability and New Technologies, New Technologies Formation (n 12) 42–3; Piotr Machnikowski, 'Conclusions' in Piotr Machnikowski (ed.), *European Product Liability. An Analysis of the State of the Art in the Era of New Technologies* (Intersentia 2016) 704.

[111] Expert Group on Liability and New Technologies, New Technologies Formation (n 12) 43.

[112] Art 10.1 (e) revised Product Liability Directive.

[113] Borghetti (n 76) 66–8; Mark A Geistfeld, 'A Roadmap for Autonomous Vehicles: State Tort Liability, Automobile Insurance, and Federal Safety Regulation' (2017) 105 California Law Review 1634–6.

very nature may also become safer than existing alternatives.[114] Therefore, it seems appropriate to make the comparison with a functionally comparable reference AI system placed in the same circumstances. Not only should the basic algorithm be considered, but also the technical context in which the AI system operates, such as the underlying algorithms and used datasets.[115] Several additional (legal) challenges arise as well. An advanced AI system works with probability calculation and tries to achieve a sufficiently safe behaviour through self-learning training.[116] Therefore, it cannot be assumed that an AI system that causes damage in a specific case in which another system does not do so would by itself be a more dangerous system than the latter one.[117] As such, the overall safety performance of an AI system should be compared statistically with that of a reference AI system, whereby this performance may be lowered by a certain percentage without resulting in a qualification as a defective product. Indeed, the situation should be avoided that any AI system that is not the safest on the market is automatically considered to be defective.[118] Nevertheless, the question remains how to identify a reference AI system, how to collect information on the performance of both AI systems and how to determine the percentage of deviation allowed.[119]

Secondly, while both parties may have similar knowledge regarding the events and underlying causes in 'traditional' cases of fault liability, this is no longer true when the damage is a result of AI systems that have been developed, controlled or used by the defendant (cf. information asymmetry). AI technology can be especially complex and inaccessible (cf. black box).[120] Moreover, the injured party will likely be a natural person, while the defendant will mostly be a legal person with considerable knowledge on the specific AI system or on AI technology in general.[121] Only when the defendant is not the

---

[114] Borghetti (n 76) 68–9; Also see: De Bruyne and Tanghe (n 48) 360 with further references.

[115] See: Anton Vedder and Laurens Naudts, 'Accountability for the Use of Algorithms in a Big Data Environment' (2017) 31(2) International Review of Law, Computers & Technology 209.

[116] Geistfeld (n 113) 1645–6. See also: Herbert Zech, 'Liability for Autonomous Systems: Tackling Specific Risks of Modern IT' in Sebastian Lohsse and others (eds.), *Liability for Artificial Intelligence and the Internet of Things* (Nomos 2019) 188–92.

[117] Borghetti (n 76) 70.

[118] ibid. 70–71.

[119] Van Gool, De Bruyne and Fierens (n 90) 1010–14; Wendehorst (n 62) 67–8.

[120] See specifically regarding the 'discreet, diffuse, discrete and opaque' nature of the development of AI systems: Matthew U Scherer, 'Regulating Artificial Intelligence Systems: Risks, Challenges, Competencies, and Strategies' (2016) 29(2) Harvard Journal of Law & Technology 369–73.

[121] Regarding asymmetry in access to evidence, see: Wannes Vandenbussche, *Bewijs en onrechtmatige daad* (Intersentia 2017) 221–5.

developer but a non-professional user, for example the user of an individual autonomous car or housekeeping robot, less informational asymmetry may exist between the parties. Nevertheless, even these non-professional defendants still enjoy easier access to the AI system's data, its features, developers and service providers. Likewise, a victim faces a high burden of proof under the current PLD. The injured person must prove the damage, the defect in a product and the causal relationship between the defect and damage under the PLD. Especially the proof of a design defect in an AI system is by no means straightforward.[122] The expert report also states that proving that some hardware defect caused damage to a person is difficult. It is more difficult to establish that the underlying cause was a flawed algorithm. It is even more complicated if the algorithm 'suspected of causing harm has been developed or modified by the AI system itself', using machine learning and/or deep learning techniques, while being fuelled by external data that it has collected since the start of its operation.[123] Algorithms often no longer come as easily readable code but as a 'black box' that has evolved through self-learning and that can be tested as to its effects, but cannot be fully understood (and explained). It is, therefore, becoming increasingly complex for victims to identify such technologies as even a possible source of harm, let alone why and how they have caused it.[124] Considering that the proof of causation can thus be quite challenging and sometimes even impossible, mechanisms have been developed by national judges to overcome this hurdle (e.g. the theory of *res ipsa loquitur*, lowering the standard of proof or the loss of a chance doctrine).[125]

Thirdly, an AI developer or the producer of products incorporating AI can be the actor facing the least problems gathering the necessary evidence, both in terms of the timing to provide it as well as regarding the workload that it would thereby incur.[126] More generally, a reversal of the burden of proof may be desirable as there can be an information (and resource) asymmetry between the parties.[127] It has already been mentioned that AI developers or producers

---

[122] See *supra* part III.B.2.

[123] Expert Group on Liability and New Technologies, New Technologies Formation (n 12) 20.

[124] ibid. 32–4.

[125] ibid. 50–51.

[126] Wannes Vandenbussche, *Bewijs en onrechtmatige daad* (Intersentia 2017) 714–15.

[127] Michael G Faure, *Tort Law and Economics* (Edward Elgar Publishing, 2009) 30; Jurgen Basedow, *Private Enforcement of EC Competition Law* (Kluwer Law International, 2007) 298; Ivo Giesen, *Bewijs en aansprakelijkheid: een rechtsvergelijkend onderzoek naar de bewijslast, de bewijsvoeringslast, het bewijsrisico en de bewijsrisico-omkering in het aansprakelijkheidsrecht* (Boom Juridische Uitgevers, 2001) 537; Bernhard A Koch, *Damage Caused by Genetically Modified Organisms:*

and companies marketing AI will in most cases possess more relevant information about the actual AI systems. Such parties may be required by law or following 'best practices' to keep the necessary documents and track records that they obtained during the development process (cf. the relevant provisions in the draft AIA). Victims of damage caused by AI systems may sometimes be considered as weak or 'unsophisticated persons'[128] who trust AI developers or producers.

One could also burden the party whose 'bad' behaviour should be deterred. This idea relates to the social objectives of legislation. Burdening the developer of AI systems to prove compliance with its obligations during the process can make litigation a worse outcome for this defendant due to the time and efforts put into the legal procedure. This might give that party a greater incentive to avoid litigation, which it can do by taking adequate precautions during the development of an AI system.[129] A more important and relevant but somehow more contested reason justifying a reversal of the burden of proof relates to a party's possibility to gather evidence. The 'burden of proof could be placed on the party with better access to relevant information'.[130] This deals with the ability of a party to gather the necessary evidence. One has to examine for which actor collecting the evidence would be the less burdensome.[131] This can, for instance, be the developer of an AI system or the producer of a product incorporating AI. Some scholars, however, argue that this element should in principle not be a reason to shift the burden of proof. The party with better access to relevant information is not necessarily best placed to provide evidence when bearing the burden of proof. The party with better access to proof

---

Comparative Survey of Redress Options for Harm to Persons, Property or the Environment (Walter de Gruyter, 2010) 847; Jan De Bruyne, *Third-Party Certifiers* (Kluwer Law International, 2019) 343.

[128] See in context of credit ratings: *Bathurst Regional Council v Local Government Financial Services Pty Ltd (No 5)* (2012) FCA 120, [2767]–[2778]; *ABN AMRO Bank NV v Bathurst Regional Council* (2014) FCAFC 65, [580], [599], [890]–[891], [1211], [1263]–[1269].

[129] Chris W Sanchirico, 'A Primary Activity Approach to Proof Burdens' (2008) 37(1) The Journal of Legal Studies, 276; De Bruyne, *Third-Party Certifiers* (n 127) 339.

[130] See for an overview: Sanchirico (n 129) 275, footnote 3; Eric A Posner, 'Fault in Contract Law' (2009) 107(8) Michigan Law Review 1444.

[131] Benoit Allemeersch, Ilse Samoy and Wannes Vandenbussche, 'Overzicht van rechtspraak. Het burgerlijk bewijsrecht 2000–2013, [De burgerlijke bewijslast] Concrete toepassing van de basisregel' (2015) 43(2) Tijdschrift voor Privaatrecht 726; Jean Laenens and others, *Handboek Gerechtelijk Recht* (Intersentia, 2016) 563; De Bruyne, *Third-Party Certifiers* (n 127) 342.

might also be the one trying to manipulate the evidence.[132] Yet, a producer's or developer's access to information and the ability to provide evidence should be an element that needs to be taken into account when determining the burden of proof.[133] Victims do not always have access to the required (confidential) information to prove that a producer or developer of AI systems did not comply with its obligations during the process.[134] The proof of a developer's or producer's act potentially leading to liability can, therefore, become quite challenging.[135] In those circumstances, a reversal of the burden of proof could be useful.[136]

The Commission seems to have heard such concerns and suggestions since its proposed revision of the PLD provides new circumstances to assess the product's defectiveness, and most importantly, it creates legal presumptions of defectiveness and causality under certain conditions. Indeed, it establishes new circumstances under which the product, and therefore the machine learning software, may be assessed as defective. One of such circumstances includes the 'effect on the product of any ability to continue to learn after deployment'.[137]

---

[132] See for example: Jef De Mot, 'De verdeling van de bewijslast economisch bekeken' in Jef De Mot (ed.), *Liber amicorum Boudewijn Bouckaert. Vrank en vrij* (Die Keure, 2012) 18; Benoit Samyn, 'De bewijslast. Rechtsleer getoetst aan tien jaar cassatierechtspraak' [2010] (1) Tijdschrift voor Procesrecht en Bewijsrecht- Revue de Droit Judiciaire et de la Preuve 17.

[133] Several other scholars in Belgium also argue that a party's ability to gather evidence and access to the evidence can be taken into account when allocating the burden of proof. See for example: Stefan Rutten, 'Beginselen van behoorlijke bewijsvoering in het burgerlijk proces: enkele aandachtspunten' in A De Boeck and others (eds), *Het vermogensrechtelijk bewijsrecht vandaag en morgen* (Die Keure, 2009) 22; Matthias E Storme, 'Goede trouw in geding en bewijs – De Goede trouw in het geding? De invloed van de goede trouw in het privaat proces- en bewijsrecht' [1990] (2) Tijdschrift voor Privaatrecht 509, no 112; Wannes Vandenbussche, *Bewijs en onrechtmatige daad* (Intersentia 2017) 707–8.

[134] See in the context of credit rating agencies: *Abu Dhabi Commercial Bank v Morgan Stanley & Co. Inc.*, 651. F. Supp. 2d 155, 180–1 (S.D.N.Y. 2009); *California Public Employees' Retirement System v Moody's Corp.*, no. A134912, 28–30 (Cal. Ct. App. 2014).

[135] De Mot (n 132) 24.

[136] ibid. 24; Mohammed Hemraj, *Credit Rating Agencies: Self-regulation, Statutory Regulation and Case Law Regulation in the United States and European Union* (Springer 2015) 175; De Bruyne, *Third-Party Certifiers* (n 127) 342–3. See also Belgian cases where the link between the reversal of the burden of proof and a party's ability/capacity to gather evidence has been acknowledged: Commercial Court Brussels, December 3, 1996 (1999) Revue Générale des Assurances et des Responsabilités no. 13.059; Court of Appeal Antwerp, June 15, 2015, (2016) Le Droit des Affaires-Het Ondernemingsrecht 31.

[137] Art 6.1 (c) revised Product Liability Directive.

It therefore seems that such ability of machine learning software that could have an impact on the product after its deployment could be used as a way to assess the product's defectiveness. However, as noted by Dheu, De Bruyne and Ducuing, one may wonder whether such a provision would make the AI product more prone to being qualified as defective.[138] This could impact the willingness of machine learning enabled software manufacturers to market such products. Most importantly, the revised Product Liability Directive provides the injured party with a presumption of defectiveness if certain conditions are met. Under these alternative conditions, the claimant must either prove that the defendant failed to comply with the Directive's disclosure requirements with regard to 'relevant evidence', or must prove that 'the product does not comply with mandatory safety requirements laid down in Union law that are intended to protect against a risk of the damage that occurred' or must prove that the damage 'was caused by an obvious malfunction of the product during normal use or under ordinary circumstances'.[139] The Commission also suggests a presumption of causal link between the product's defectiveness and the product when 'it is established that the product is defective and the damage caused is of a kind typically consistent with the defect in question'.[140] Finally, a more general legal presumption of the product's defectiveness and/or causal link between its defectiveness and the damage is provided in the revised Product Liability Directive. However, to apply this provision, the claimant must prove that the 'product contributed to the damage' and that 'it is likely that the product was defective or that its defectiveness is a likely cause of the damage, or both'.[141] Many interrogations subsist, such as the interpretation of concepts like 'reasonably foreseeable', 'reasonably', 'substantial', 'relevant', 'proportionate' and 'necessary'.[142] To counterbalance such a legal presumption, the revised Product Liability Directive provides the defendant with the right to 'contest the existence of excessive difficulties or the likelihood' previously referred to in the proposal[143] as well as a more general rebuttal right.[144]

Finally, the question of collecting relevant evidence and information about these systems, which will be extremely challenging for the injured party, is also partially addressed in this proposed Directive. In that perspective, the revised Product Liability Directive has proposed imposing upon manufacturers (and, more generally, so-called 'economic operators') an obligation

---

[138] Dheu, De Bruyne and Ducuing (n 39) 36.
[139] Art 9.2 revised Product Liability Directive.
[140] Art 9.3 revised Product Liability Directive.
[141] Art 9.4 revised Product Liability Directive.
[142] Dheu, De Bruyne and Ducuing (n 39) 36.
[143] Art 9.4 paragraph 2 revised Product Liability Directive.
[144] Art 9.5 revised Product Liability Directive.

to disclose relevant evidence to the injured person when such a person has 'presented facts and evidence sufficient to support the plausibility of claim'.[145] However, the same Directive limits such disclosure to what is 'necessary and proportionate to support a claim'.[146] Again the understanding of certain terms/ concepts will be open to the interpretation of Member States' courts.[147] This could potentially lead to legal variations between jurisdictions, therefore possibly resulting in the victim's differentiated treatment.

IV.   GENERAL CONSIDERATIONS ON LIABILITY FOR AI

Several challenges and potential answers have already been raised and provided in the previous part. In this last section, we briefly discuss the AI 'tort law dilemma' (Part A), the challenges of AI to the tort law foundations (Part B) and the importance of considering procedural law, such as the burden of proof which seems to be echoed in the newly published EC proposal on a liability regime for AI and more specifically the revised Product Liability Directive (Part C).

A.   The AI 'Tort Law Dilemma'

It has already been mentioned that much is happening at EU level regarding liability for damage caused by AI. Some even urge the EU legislator to consider the introduction of a new Directive on AI liability. This plea seems to have been heard since the Commission recently adopted two proposals on an AI Liability Directive and a revised Product Liability Directive. The problem, however, is that the European liability landscape is a rather heterogeneous one, since civil liability usually falls under Member States' scope of competence. Except for the current PLD and now the newly proposed AI Liability Directive, as well as some other specific regimes, contractual and extra-contractual (tort) liability laws are usually national. This is what we refer to as the AI tort law dilemma – while initiatives are especially taken at the EU level, national law remains the most important source when it comes to tort liability and AI systems. This can also be seen within the newly proposed AI Liability Directive as well as the revised Product Liability Directive where many provisions still refer to national law or will rely on the national courts for the interpretation of certain provisions.

---

[145]   Art 8.1 revised Product Liability Directive.
[146]   Art 8.2 revised Product Liability Directive.
[147]   Dheu, De Bruyne and Ducuing (n 39) 36–7.

The current PLD acknowledges the importance of national law. Pursuant to Article 13, for instance, the current PLD shall not affect any rights which an injured person may have according to the rules of the law of contractual or non-contractual liability or a special liability system. Moreover, each Member State may, by way of derogation from Article 7(e), maintain or provide in legislation that the producer shall be liable even if he/she proves that the state of scientific and technical knowledge at the time when he/she put the product into circulation was not such as to enable the existence of a defect to be discovered. This defence is relevant in an AI context,[148] potentially leading to diverging rules across the EU.[149]

The revised Product Liability Directive and the proposed AI Liability Directive both rely on national laws for important elements of a claim. Indeed, while the latter establishes a legal presumption of causal link between the damage and the fault of the defendant, it relies on national law to determine the scope and definition of 'fault' and 'causal link'.[150] Moreover, the Directive provides that Member States 'may adopt or maintain national rules that are more favourable for claimants to substantiate a non-contractual civil law claim for damages caused by an AI system'.[151] As noted by some authors, this approach can 'preserve the coherence of the national tort liability systems'.[152] The revised Product Liability Directive will also rely on the national court's interpretation of certain key concepts/provisions based on their legal tradition and case law solutions. Such terms submitted to interpretation include 'plausibility of claim', 'relevant evidence', 'obvious malfunction', 'ordinary circumstances' and 'likely cause of the damage'.[153]

These examples show that national judges ultimately have to explain and interpret these concepts. Though European legislation could improve legal certainty, the dependency on the national court's interpretation raises the question to what extent an EU horizontal approach or a specific regime for liability caused by AI systems would be effective and feasible after all.[154] The aim of harmonisation and unification could partially be undermined.[155]

---

[148] See *supra* part III.B.3.

[149] Art 13 Product Liability Directive.

[150] Art 4.1 AI Liability Directive.

[151] Art 1.4 AI Liability Directive.

[152] Dheu, De Bruyne and Ducuing (n 39) 16–17. See also: Miriam Buiten *et al.*, 'EU Liability rules for the age of artificial intelligence', Centre on Regulation in Europe, 9 April 2021, p. 59.

[153] Dheu, De Bruyne and Ducuing (n 39) 36–7. Art 8.1, Art 9.2 (a), Art 9.2 (c), Art 9.4 (b) revised Product Liability Directive.

[154] Dheu, De Bruyne and Ducuing (n 39) 41–2. See also: Bertolini (n 15) 87–8.

[155] This not only is the case for AI systems but also for third-party certifiers. The European Union, for instance, introduced a liability regime for credit rating agencies

Currently, many national regimes already exist that could be relied upon in an AI context. Think of the general liability for wrongful acts (e.g. negligence), liability of the custodian for defective things or liability for the owner of an animal (though implementation difficulties could also arise). One may also distinguish between general liability frameworks such as fault which can apply horizontally irrespectively of the domain, and sector-specific regimes that apply in determined contexts (e.g. transportation). Such regimes may eventually extend to autonomous vehicles. For instance, instead of a horizontal liability regime, it has been suggested that the EU could take a more tailored approach through the adoption of liability regulations for specific classes of AI applications.[156] Bertolini also suggests that the PLD should constitute a general rule that covers both traditional and new technologies. However, 'for the latter category it should play a residual role' and specific legislation should apply to 'specific classes of applications' at the European level.[157] This does not seem to be the exact direction the EC is leaning towards.

B.   The Foundations of Tort Law and AI Systems[158]

There are several (academic) views on the role of tort law.[159] Some scholars look at tort law as a way of achieving corrective justice.[160] Corrective justice embodies the idea that tort liability rectifies the injuries inflicted by one person to another one.[161] Tort law can also be seen as a matter of distributive justice. It then deals with the fair apportionment of the burdens and benefits of risky activities or resources between members of the society or a community.[162] In addition to corrective or distributive justice, law and economics scholars

---

(Regulation (EU) No 462/2013 of the European Parliament and of the Council of 21 May 2013 amending Regulation (EC) No 1060/2009 on credit rating agencies). Art 35(a) contains several concepts that require a national interpretation as well (e.g. 'reasonable' reliance on ratings, 'gross negligence'), which affects the effectiveness of the harmonised regime (see extensively: De Bruyne, *Third-Party Certifiers* (n 127)).

[156]   See for instance: Bertolini (n 15) 61, 99.

[157]   Bertolini (n 15) 61.

[158]   See for an extensive discussion upon which this part is based: De Bruyne, *Third-Party Certifiers* (n 127).

[159]   Gary T Schwartz, 'Mixed Theories of Tort Law: Affirming Both Deterrence and Corrective Justice' (1997) 75(7) Texas Law Review 1801.

[160]   Jules L Coleman, 'Moral Theories of Torts: Their Scope and Limits: Part I' (1982) 2(1) Law and Philosophy 371; Ernest J Weinrib, 'Toward a Moral Theory of Negligence Law' (1983) 2 Law and Philosophy 37.

[161]   Ernest J Weinrib, 'Corrective Justice in a Nutshell' (2002) 52(4) University of Toronto Law Journal 349.

[162]   Gregory C Keating, 'Distributive and Corrective Justice in the Tort Law of Accidents' (2000) 74(1) Southern California Law Review 200.

understand tort law as an instrument aimed largely at the goal of deterrence.[163] According to law and economics scholars, the purpose of damage payments in tort law is not to compensate injured parties but to provide incentives for potential injurers to take efficient cost-justified precautions to avoid causing the accident.[164] An individual or entity makes the decision about whether or how to engage in a given activity by weighing the costs and benefits of the particular activity. The risk of liability and actual imposition of damage awards may lead parties to take into account externalities when they decide whether and how to act.[165] The fact that someone can be held liable ex post can provide the necessary incentives ex ante to act in such a way as to prevent liability.[166] The purpose of tort law is to promote overall social welfare by efficiently deterring and reducing accidents in the future.[167] As such, tort liability aims to deter unreasonable risks.[168] Law and economics scholars thus argue that injurers might adopt cost-justified safety measures if the system holds them liable for the injury costs they generate.[169] The risk of having to bear financial burdens due to liability could serve as an incentive for potential tortfeasors to avoid injury-causing activities or at least to provide them with greater regard

---

[163] Guido Calabresi, *The Costs of Accidents: A Legal and Economic Analysis* (Yale University Press, 1970); Richard A Posner, 'A Theory of Negligence' (1972) 1 Journal of Legal Studies 29.

[164] Paul H Rubin, 'Law and Economics' in David R Henderson (ed.), *The Concise Encyclopaedia of Economics* (Liberty Fund 2008), www.econlib.org/library/Enc/LawandEconomics.html accessed 25 September 2021; Michael G Faure and others, 'Naar een Kostenoptimalisatie van de letselschaderegeling: een verkenning' (2011) 4 Aansprakelijkheid, Verzekering & Schade 3–4.

[165] John CP Goldberg, 'Twentieth-Century Tort Theory' (2003) 91 Georgetown Law Journal 545.

[166] Michael G Faure and Ton Hartlief, *Nieuwe risico's en vragen van aansprakelijkheid en verzekering* (Kluwer, 2002) 19; Ivo Giesen, 'Regulating Regulators through Liability – The Case for Applying Normal Tort Rules to Supervisors' (2006) 2(1) Utrecht Law Review 14–15; Andrew F Popper, 'In Defense of Deterrence' (2012) 75(1) Albany Law Review 181.

[167] Goldberg (n 165) 544; Calabresi (n 163) 24, 26; Michael G Faure, 'Calabresi and Behavioural Tort Law and Economics' (2008) 1(4) Erasmus Law Review 93.

[168] David Rosenberg, 'The Judicial Posner on Negligence Versus Strict Liability: Indiana Harbor Belt Railroad Co. v Am. Cyanamid Co' (2007) 120 Harvard Law Review 1212 (citing *Ind. Harbor Belt R.R. Co. v Am. Cyanamid Co.*, 662 F. Supp. 635, 1181–1182 (N.D. Ill. 1987)); Alan D Miller and Ronen Perry, 'The Reasonable Person' (2012) 82 NYU Law Review 328.

[169] Steven D Smith, 'The Critics and the Crisis: A Reassessment of Current Conceptions of Tort Law' (1987) 72 Cornell Law Review 772 with further references in footnote 28.

for safety.[170] If tort law is working correctly, the threat of civil liability will cause actors to take all and only those precautions that cost less than the harm that is expected to result if those precautions are not taken.[171]

When looking at the previously discussed policy documents adopted at the EU level, one actually notes that many of them rely on the deterring function of tort law when regulating AI. The White Paper on AI, for instance, adopts a risk-based approach when regulating AI to ensure innovation.[172] The accompanying Report on Liability and Safety departs from the same assumptions when concluding that civil liability rules play a double role in the society.[173] It states that on 'the one hand, they ensure that victims of a damage caused by others get compensation. On the other hand, they provide economic incentives for the liable party to avoid causing such damage. Liability rules usually have to strike a balance between protecting citizens from harm while enabling businesses to innovate'.[174] In the 2017 Resolution, the EP urges the EC to determine whether a strict liability or a risk management approach should be applied. The risk management approach does not focus on the person who acted negligently as individually liable but on the person who is able, under certain circumstances, to minimise the risks and deal with negative impacts.[175] Bertolini proposes a risk management approach when dealing with the identified liability challenges in the JURI report. Liability should be attributed to the party best placed to '(i) identify a risk, (ii) control and minimize it through its choices, and (iii) manage it – ideally pooling and redistributing it among all other parties – eventually through insurance and/or no-fault compensation funds'.[176]

---

[170] Craig Brown, 'Deterrence in Tort and No-Fault: The New Zealand Experience' (1985) 73 California Law Review 976–977; Thomas C Galligan, 'Deterrence: The Legitimate Function of the Public Tort' (2001) 58(3) Washington and Lee Law Review 1020; William M Landes and Richard A Posner, *The Economic Structure of Tort Law* (Harvard University Press, 1987) 10; Jennifer H Arlen, 'Compensation Systems and Efficient Deterrence' (1993) 52(4) Maryland Law Review 1133.

[171] Goldberg (n 165) 545.

[172] European Commission, 'White Paper on Artificial Intelligence – A European approach to excellence and trust' (n 13).

[173] European Commission, 'Report on the safety and liability implications of Artificial Intelligence, the Internet of Things and Robotics' (n 26) 12.

[174] ibid. 12.

[175] European Parliament, 'Report with recommendations to the Commission on Civil Law Rules on Robotics' (n 14) paras 49–59.

[176] Bertolini (n 15) 99–100.

The problem, however, is that the assumptions upon which the traditional law and economics literature is based have been challenged in academia.[177] Behavioural law and economics scholars, for instance, question the underlying rational choice assumptions and endeavour to render economic analysis more realistic by using psychological insights.[178] Several (empirical) studies even show that tort law does not always have the expected deterring influence on someone's behaviour.[179] Although it has been argued elsewhere that the deterring effect of tort law can still be relied upon as a valid and convincing starting point,[180] one should take these concerns into account when drafting a regulatory liability regime, especially when considering that the other foundations of tort law can be challenged as well in an AI context. It will be shown below that it can be difficult for victims to obtain proper compensation when damage is caused by AI systems. This in turn may potentially undermine the corrective foundation (i.e. ensuring that victims of damage caused by others get compensation) as well as the distributive foundation (i.e. ensuring a fair apportionment of the burdens and benefits of using AI) of tort law.

Nonetheless, the revised Product Liability Directive relies on safety concepts which could have a prophylactic impact on the manufacturer's conduct. First and foremost, the defectiveness of a product is defined with regard to the safety which the public at large is entitled to expect.[181] Moreover, other different provisions rely on the notion of safety in order to help determine the manufacturer's liability. For instance, when referring to the burden of proving the product's defectiveness, which is presumed under circumstances, one condition relates to the claimant establishing that the product did not 'comply

---

[177] See for instance: Pieter Gillaerts, 'Extracontractual Liability Law as a Policy Instrument: Public Law in Disguise or in Chains?' (2020) 11 Journal of European Tort Law 16. This author stresses the possible 'instrumentalization' of tort law to non-compensatory goals such as prevention.

[178] See for instance: Klaus Mathis, *European Perspectives on Behavioural Law and Economics* (Springer 2015); Christine Jolls, CR Sunstein and Richard Thaler, 'A Behavioral Approach to Law and Economics' (1998) 50(5) Stanford Law Review 1476; Joshua D Wright and Douglas H Ginsburg, 'Behavioral Law and Economics: Its Origins, Fatal Flaws, and Implications for Liberty' (2015) 106(3) Northwestern University Law Review 1033.

[179] See for example: Daniel W. Shuman, 'Psychology of Deterrence in Tort Law' (1993) 42(1) University of Kansas Law Review 165; Richard N Pearson, 'Liability for Negligently Inflicted Psychic Harm: A Response to Professor Bell' (1984) 36(3) University of Florida Law Review 417; Jonathan W Cardi, Randall D Penfield and Albert H Yoon, 'Does Tort Law Deter Individuals? A Behavioral Science Study' (2012) 9(3) Journal of Empirical Legal Studies 567. See for further references: Goldberg (n 165) 513–84.

[180] See the extensive analysis in De Bruyne, *Third-Party Certifiers* (n 127) 270–76.

[181] Art 6.1 revised Product Liability Directive.

with mandatory safety requirements laid down in Union law or national law intended to protect against the risk of the damage that has occurred'.[182] Furthermore, the exemption of liability from the 'later defect' defence does not apply when the product's defectiveness is due, *inter alia*, to the 'lack of software updates or upgrades necessary to maintain safety'.[183] These provisions therefore push the economic operators (manufacturer included) to adopt safe conducts/behaviours with regard to their products and to comply with safety requirements set by the law.

C.   Liability for Damage Caused by AI Goes Hand in Hand with Procedural Law

A 'general, worldwide accepted rule'[184] in the law of evidence is that each party must prove its claims and contentions (*actori incumbit probatio*).[185] Reference can be made to fault-based liability pursuant to Articles 1382–3 of the Old Belgian Civil Code (OBCC). Claimants must establish a party's wrongful act, the incurred loss and a causal link between both elements. This seems to be echoed in the AI Liability Directive as well as the revised Product Liability Directive. In accordance with traditional Belgian civil evidence law, it is in principle up to the injured party as claimant to prove that each condition of liability for fault is fulfilled.[186] Notwithstanding the possibility to refute evidence submitted by the claimant, the defendant only bears the burden of proof when he/she invokes a ground of exemption from liability.[187] The required standard of proof is 'a reasonable level of certainty'.[188] The individual injured party needs to deliver this proof for each liability condition. The only possible

---

[182]   Art. 9.2 (b) revised Product Liability Directive.

[183]   Art 10.2 (c) revised Product Liability Directive.

[184]   Ivo Giesen, 'The Burden of Proof and other Procedural Devices in Tort Law' in Helmut Koziol, Barbara C Steininger and C Alunaru (eds.), *European Tort Law 2008* (Springer, 2009) 50.

[185]   Mojtaba Kazazi, *Burden of Proof and Related Issues: A Study on Evidence Before International Tribunals* (Martinus Nijhoff Publishers 1996) 378.

[186]   Art 8.4(1) New Belgian Civil Code (Act of 13 April 2019, *BS* 14 May 2019, p. 46353); Art 870 Belgian Judicial Code.

[187]   Art 8.4(2) New Belgian Civil Code; Art 870 Belgian Judicial Code. The exemption is either a ground of justification or an external cause (see: Wannes Vandenbussche, *Bewijs en onrechtmatige daad* (Intersentia 2017) 150–151).

[188]   Art 8.5 New Belgian Civil Code.

external support consists of investigatory measures, which a judge may order (e.g. a judicial expertise)[189] and the principle that all parties are required to cooperate in the administration of evidence,[190] which seems difficult to enforce within the opaque, highly complex and multi-actor context of AI technology.[191]

In sum, it will often not be straightforward for injured parties to establish a defendant's wrongful act, the defect of an AI system or the fact of how the damage was caused. Against this background, the European Group on Liability and New Technologies proposed to reverse the burden of proof for fault in a number of cases, namely '(a) when the claimant generally encounters disproportionate difficulties and costs to prove a fault; (b) when the defendant has violated a safety rule which was meant to avoid the damage; or (c) when "logging" information has not been recorded or provided in violation of an obligation to do so'.[192] In its 2020 report, the Commission explicitly considers the possibility of reversing the burden of proof for liability conditions such as fault.[193] There are indeed several reasons – based on factors of logic and policy – why a reversal of the burden of proof can be appropriate when damage is caused by AI systems, implying for example that the producer has to show that an AI system was not defective or that an AI developer did not act negligently during the development process.[194]

When dealing with liability and AI, one has to take procedural aspects into account as well. National law will play an important role in this regard, and an EU initiative may be useful as well. This is even more so as there are already several examples of EU law that provide a reversal of the burden of proof. Article 5 of Regulation 261/2004 on passenger rights stipulates that the burden of proof concerning the questions as to whether and when the passenger has been informed of the cancellation of their flight rests with the operating air

---

[189] Arts 962–91bis Belgian Judicial Code.

[190] Art 8.4 (3) New Belgian Civil Code. Also see: Belgian Court of Cassation, 14 November 2013, *Arr.Cass.* 2013, 2401; Cass. 4 June 2015, C.14.0479.F; Belgian Court of Cassation, 7 June 2019, C.18.0523.N.

[191] De Bruyne, Van Gool and Gils (n 13) 364.

[192] ibid. 47–9 and 52–5. See also on 'logging obligations' as an instrument for ex post verification of potential liability in cases involving AI systems: Ujjayini Bose, 'The Black Box Solution to Autonomous Liability' (2015) 92(5) Washington University Law Review 1342.

[193] European Commission, 'Report on the safety and liability implications of Artificial Intelligence, the Internet of Things and Robotics' (n 26) 14, 16.

[194] Ian H Dennis, *The Law of Evidence* (Sweet & Maxwell, 1999) 388. See for an overview of reasons to shift the legal burden of proof: Ivo Giesen, *Bewijs en aansprake-lijkheid: een rechtsvergelijkend onderzoek naar de bewijslast, de bewijsvoeringslast, het bewijsrisico en de bewijsrisico-omkering in het aansprakelijkheidsrecht* (Boom Juridische Uitgevers 2001) 409–22, 537–8.

carrier.[195] More importantly, the Digital Content Directive also stipulates that the burden of proof with regard to whether the digital content or digital service was supplied in accordance with Article 5 is on the trader.[196] Interestingly, the final section of Article 8.4 of the New Belgian Civil Code now allows a judge to reverse the burden of proof 'in light of exceptional circumstances' when the application of the 'normal rules' would be 'manifestly unreasonable'.[197] The judge can allow a reversal of the burden of proof as a matter of last resort after all useful investigatory measures have been ordered and the obligation of all parties to cooperate in the administration of evidence has already been enforced.[198] The proof of an objective fault in cases of damage created by AI systems seems an appropriate scenario for applying this valuable but far-reaching technique. However, it can be wondered whether strictly limiting it to a measure of last resort may turn out to be too inefficient in this particular context where the informational asymmetry between parties can be extreme from the onset. Efforts by the claimant to provide sufficient proof will often be futile and a judicial expertise will be time- and resource-consuming. It may also still lead to a debatable conclusion. In cases of liability for AI systems, it may consequently be more attractive to provide a more immediate possibility to reverse the burden of proof.[199] Once again, several questions can be asked. Should the reversal of the burden of proof, for instance, apply to all elements of

---

[195]   European Parliament & Council Regulation (EC) 261/2004 of 11 February 2004 establishing common rules on compensation and assistance to passengers in the event of denied boarding and of cancellation or long delay of flights and repealing Regulation (EEC) No 295/91 [2004] OJ L 46.

[196]   European Parliament & Council Directive (EU) 2019/770 of 20 May 2019 on certain aspects concerning contracts for the supply of digital content and digital services [2019] OJ L 136, Art 12.

[197]   In this regard, the Memorandum of explanation states that 'The judge will furthermore be able to consider an important imbalance in the aptitude for delivering evidence, if obtaining, recording or reporting the required evidence would be excessively onerous or expensive for one of the parties. The existence of an economic imbalance between the parties, for example an individual against a large company, should not automatically result in a reversal of the burden of proof. Nevertheless, the judge can take such imbalance into consideration, if the burden of proof incumbent on the individual would require extremely onerous and/or expensive performances from him' (Memorandum of explanation accompanying the Proposed Act to insert Book 8 'Evidence' in the New Civil Code, Parl.St. Kamer 2018–19, no. 3349/001, p. 15, own translation).

[198]   The legislative proposal emphasises that this measure can only be applied as an '*ultimum remedium*' (Memorandum of explanation accompanying the Proposed Act to insert Book 8 'Evidence' in the New Civil Code, *Parl.St.* Kamer 2018–19, no. 3349/001, pp. 14–15).

[199]   De Bruyne, Van Gool and Gils (n 13) 359–403.

a liability claim? Should we not reverse but instead lower the burden of proof? How? For which elements – fault and/or causation?

The Commission has heard such concerns since its revised Product Liability Directive provides the injured party with a presumption of defectiveness if certain (alternative) conditions are met (see *supra* part III.B.3). The Commission also suggests a presumption of a causal link between the product's defectiveness and the product when 'it is established that the product is defective and the damage caused is of a kind typically consistent with the defect in question'.[200] Finally, a more general legal presumption of the product's defectiveness and/ or causal link between its defectiveness and the damage is provided in the revised Product Liability Directive. However, to apply this provision, the claimant must prove that the 'product contributed to the damage' and that 'it is likely that the product was defective or that its defectiveness is a likely cause of the damage, or both'.[201] Many interrogations subsist, such as the interpretation of concepts like 'relevant evidence', 'obvious malfunction', 'ordinary circumstances' and 'likely cause of the damage'.[202] To counter balance such a legal presumption, the revised Product Liability Directive provides the defendant with the right to 'contest the existence of excessive difficulties or the likelihood' previously referred to in the proposal[203] as well as a more general rebuttal right.[204]

V.   CONCLUDING REMARKS

This chapter has shed light on several challenges regarding the liability for damage caused by AI. We first gave an overview of the regulatory initiatives at the EU level dealing with AI and tort liability. The analysis showed that several initiatives have already been taken. We then discussed how AI systems' characteristics may challenge some traditional concepts in tort law and product liability. We also mentioned existing European proposals that (partially) address some of these issues. We discussed three elements that served as a basis for discussions as well as regulatory actions. First, we elaborated upon the AI tort law dilemma with the question how and at which level to regulate the liability for damage caused by AI. Second, we looked at the foundations of tort law and how to apply them for AI systems. Finally, we stressed the importance of procedural law, and especially the need to consider reversing the burden of proof. The current EC proposals seem to echo many of these points and will

---

[200]   Art 9.3 revised Product Liability Directive.
[201]   Art 9.4 revised Product Liability Directive.
[202]   Dheu, De Bruyne and Ducuing (n 39) 26–7.
[203]   Art 9.4 paragraph 2 revised Product Liability Directive.
[204]   Art 9.5 revised Product Liability Directive.

merit further exploration and analysis. It remains to be seen what amendments may be adopted when they pass through the scrutiny of the EP and the Council.

3. AI Systems and the Issue of Liability in the European and National Regulatory Strategies

Erica Palmerini[1]

I. SETTING THE SCENE

The regulation of artificial intelligence ('AI') and robotics is an extremely hot topic. A flurry of initiatives has flourished around this concern at the level of European and national legislative bodies, in academic circuits, research centres, policy institutions and associations grouping together the various stakeholders active in the field. As for the latter, a 2019 article counted 84 projects and proposals,[2] and probably that number has today been exceeded by far. The Organisation for Economic Co-operation and Development has set up an observatory of all the regulatory attempts undertaken at both the public and the private level, which can be browsed by country, type of instrument used and group targeted by specific policies.[3] This tool gives an impressive overview of the ongoing discussion.

The documents addressing the problem of liability for damage caused by AI-powered and cyber-physical systems, thus the most relevant for this chapter, can be found in those produced by the European Commission and the European Parliament, complemented by some national interventions in specific sectors, such as the automotive domain.

The Resolution of the European Parliament on Civil Law Rules on Robotics of 16 February 2017[4] was a first attempt at opening the discussion about the regulation of cyber-physical systems. The document has an extremely wide

---

[1]   Associate Professor of Private Law, Scuola Superiore Sant'Anna, Pisa.
[2]   Brent Mittelstadt, 'Principles alone cannot guarantee ethical AI' (2019) 1 Nature Machine Intelligence 501.
[3]   OECD.AI Policy Observatory oecd.ai/countries-and-initiatives/ accessed 4 November 2021.
[4]   European Parliament resolution of 16 February 2017 with recommendations to the Commission on Civil Law Rules on Robotics (2015/2103 (INL)).

reach, and aims to be almost exhaustive in terms of the issues that regulators should address. Several robotic applications, ranging from autonomous vehicles to drones, from care robots to medical robotic devices – and all their potential legal and ethical implications – are mentioned; the legal problems that may arise from said applications are listed and possible solutions are envisaged. Among these, liability is considered 'a crucial issue'[5] – presented in the Introduction as one of the most urgent matters, it is discussed thoroughly in the following analysis, and hypothetical schemes for dealing with it are advanced, including the controversial proposal of creating electronic persons.[6]

Later on, the attention of the European regulators has shifted from the narrower field of robotics to the wider domain of AI. This change in focus can be traced back to the 2018 Communication of the Commission *Artificial Intelligence for Europe* that uses the same umbrella term for purely software-based AI or AI embedded in a physical system, and it seems to encompass both types of system within a common approach.[7]

In the light of the purpose of establishing a clear ethical and legal framework to foster future developments in the field, the issue of liability is considered key, while other preliminary regulatory actions concerning products' safety and the processes of standardisation are announced. An assessment of the current framework with regard to its adequacy in relation to AI and emerging technologies is envisioned, as well as an evaluation of the defective product liability scheme with an eye to the need for reform. Following on from this, an Expert Group on Liability and New Technologies was set up, working in two formations: a Product Liability Directive formation, providing advice on the applicability of the Directive to novel complex technological products, and a New Technologies formation, assisting the Commission in the possible adaptations of applicable laws at EU and national level relating to new technologies. The latter has released a report containing an in-depth examination of emerging digital technologies against the backdrop of current liability regimes,[8] whose findings need to be closely analysed as they are expected to inform future legislative steps.

---

5   ibid. para 49.
6   ibid. paras 49–59.
7   EU Commission, Communication *Artificial Intelligence for Europe* COM(2018) 237 final. In the same vein, the strategy is further developed by the Commission Communication of 7 December 2018 on a co-ordinated Plan on artificial intelligence (COM(2018) 0795) and the Commission Communication of 8 April 2019 on building trust in human-centric artificial intelligence (COM(2019) 0168).
8   Expert Group on Liability and New Technologies, 'Liability for Artificial Intelligence and Other Emerging Digital Technologies' (Report for the European Commission 2019). For an attentive consideration, see Andrea Bertolini and Francesca Episcopo, 'The Expert Group's Report on Liability for Artificial Intelligence and Other

The strategy started by the 2018 Communication is implemented by several other activities and documents that pinpoint a multi-layered effort towards the definition of a complex regulatory scheme – the White Paper on Artificial Intelligence,[9] released on 19 February 2019, is accompanied by a Report on the safety and liability implications of AI, the Internet of Things, and Robotics.[10] Before its approval, a High-Level Expert Group had been established and charged with the task of elaborating Guidelines on AI that were firstly published in a draft version submitted to an open consultation,[11] and then in a revised version in April 2019.[12]

The European Parliament has also devoted its attention to the regulation of AI and to the problem of liability with two resolutions[13] that were meant to inspire the legislative proposals of the Commission.

The latest step of this regulatory pathway is the proposal for a regulation on AI (Artificial Intelligence Act ('AIA')) that aims at introducing a horizontal, albeit not comprehensive, regulation of AI systems.[14] The text embraces a risk-based approach and focuses especially on ex ante safety measures, but it does not tackle the problem of liability which is left to proximate interventions.

II.   THE TARGET OF REGULATION

Identifying the target of regulation is a critical step, and at the same time a very difficult one. The question is deeply entangled with the problem of defining what AI is, and thus which AI systems would fall into the scope of the said reg-

---

Emerging Digital Technologies: A Critical Assessment' (2021) 12 European Journal of Risk Regulation 644.

[9]   European Commission, 'White Paper on Artificial Intelligence – A European approach to excellence and trust' (Communication) COM(2020) 65 final.

[10]   European Commission, 'Report from the Commission to the European Parliament, the Council and the European Economic and Social Committee on the safety and liability implications of Artificial Intelligence, the Internet of Things, and Robotics' (Report) COM(2020) 64 final.

[11]   European Commission's High-Level Expert Group on Artificial Intelligence, 'Draft Ethics Guidelines for Trustworthy AI' (18 December 2018).

[12]   Independent High-Level Expert Group on Artificial Intelligence, 'Ethics Guidelines for Trustworthy AI' (8 April 2019).

[13]   Respectively, European Parliament Resolution of 20 October 2020 with recommendations to the Commission on a framework of ethical aspects of artificial intelligence, robotics and related technologies (2020/2012(INL)); European Parliament Resolution of 20 October 2020 with recommendations to the Commission on a civil liability regime for artificial intelligence (2020/2014(INL)).

[14]   Proposal for a Regulation of the European Parliament and of the Council laying down harmonised rules on artificial intelligence (Artificial Intelligence Act) and amending certain Union legislative acts COM(2021) 206 final, 21 April 2021.

ulation. The demand for a definition of AI systems is stressed in several analyses: the Resolution of the European Parliament on civil law rules on robotics states the need for 'common Union definitions of cyber-physical systems, autonomous systems, smart autonomous robots and their subcategories'.[15] The White Paper on artificial intelligence affirms that 'a key issue for the future specific regulatory framework on AI intelligence [sic] is to determine the scope of its application ... AI should therefore be clearly defined'. Then it adds that 'the definition of AI will need to be sufficiently flexible to accommodate technical progress while being precise enough to provide the necessary legal certainty'.[16] An updated definition of AI is proposed by the High-Level Group on AI in a document specifically devoted to this task.[17]

The AIA identifies its subject matter by providing a general definition of AI systems in Article 3(1) that is complemented by a list of approaches and techniques to be periodically updated,[18] in order to make it as technology neutral and future-proof as possible.

However, the hypothesis of introducing a special regime that encompasses all possible AI and robotic applications – as previously defined – rarely stems from these propositions. The question is whether all applications are doomed to be regulated with an identical approach (and perhaps within a unique piece of legislation), or different and more nuanced types of intervention (or no intervention at all) for specific types of AI are conceivable.

In fact, an 'exceptionalist' attitude – to some extent embraced by the European Parliament Resolution of 2017 – that regards the technologies to be regulated as completely novel and of an unprecedented nature has disappeared. It cannot be maintained that robotic and AI technologies are endowed with unique features that require building a totally new regulatory environment or creating a separate branch of the law to deal with them. Already, robotic applications fall within the boundaries of diverse law regimes that qualify them

---

[15]   Para 1.

[16]   Para 5C.

[17]   High-Level Expert Group on artificial intelligence set up by the European Commission, 'A definition of AI: main capabilities and disciplines' (8 April 2019).

[18]   Annex 1.

– as products,[19] machinery,[20] medical devices,[21] data collectors[22] – and regulate accordingly. On these premises, regulating robotics cannot mean adopting a single body of laws to address all applications that simply pertain to the same technological domain.[23]

However, these regimes may not be exhaustive of the problems to come and may not be able to properly solve new legal issues that autonomous systems will bring about. Dealing with 'regulatory disconnection'[24] appears then a more suitable attitude that checks the fitness of the current regimes, updates or adapts them to the specific features that robots or AI systems exhibit and assesses whether and for which particular problems an innovative approach is necessary.

Such a methodological stance applies also to the liability problem, soon identified as a key issue in light of the aims of the regulatory endeavour: providing market players with certainty as to the legal duties to comply with and the responsibility associated with their activities, ensuring a proper allocation of the inherent risks, and increasing the trust of end users towards emerging digital technologies.

An analysis of the recent documents enables verification of whether they choose a selective approach or rather aim at a comprehensive solution that tries to establish an overarching framework applicable to all intelligent systems.

While advocacy for setting up very general principles doomed to regulate all forms of AI tools persists,[25] a more focused kind of intervention is taking shape that targets higher risk situations. This line of thinking acknowledges

---

[19]   Directive 2001/95/EC of the European Parliament and of the Council of 3 December 2001 on general product safety [2002] OJ L 11/4.

[20]   Directive 2006/42/EC of the European Parliament and of the Council of 17 May 2006 on Machinery, and amending Directive 95/16/EC [2006] OJ L 157/24.

[21]   Regulation 2017/745 of the European Parliament and of the Council of 5 April 2017 on medical devices, amending Directive 2001/83/EC, Regulation (EC) No 178/2002 and Regulation (EC) No 1223/2009 and repealing Council Directives 90/385/EEC and 93/42/EEC.

[22]   Regulation 2016/679 of the European Parliament and of the Council of 27 April 2016 on the protection of natural persons with regard to the processing of personal data and on the free movement of such data, and repealing Directive 95/46/EC (General Data Protection Regulation).

[23]   Erica Palmerini, 'Regulating Robotics in Europe: A Perplexed View' (*Jusletter IT*, 23 November 2017).

[24]   Roger Brownsword and Morag Goodwin, *Law and the Technologies of the Twenty-First Century* (Cambridge University Press, 2012) 63–8, 372–419.

[25]   The European Parliament Resolution on a civil liability regime for artificial intelligence would approve 'a horizontal and harmonized legal framework based on common principles' (para 2) and insists on hard law and uniform approach, by stating that these 'new common rules should only take the form of a regulation' (para 5).

that different AI systems pose a diverse range of risks, hampering the search for a common solution. New rules should be introduced only for systems that overcome a certain level of dangerousness; other types of AI applications that are barely posing risks or can be considered substantially harmless (for instance, email anti-spam filters or many smartphone apps) should be left untouched. Applications that present risks no different from the ones already dealt with through the extant safety and liability regimes do not demand wide-reaching reforms.

Lastly, such a risk-based approach has been adopted by the recent proposal for an AIA that articulates its rules – as said, mainly preventive and safety measures – precisely on the distinction between AI practices beyond an acceptable level of risk that are prohibited,[26] high-risk systems and practices that are strongly regulated,[27] medium- or low-risk systems,[28] addressed by rules on transparency, and systems with minimal risk that are permitted without restrictions.

III.   HORIZONTAL VERSUS SELECTIVE APPROACH

Also from the perspective of liability, a risk-based approach[29] is considered a plausible strategy – it avoids disproportionate interventions that put excessive burdens on the development of technologies, while ensuring an adequate protection of the interests at stake. However, this very same approach, while being widely shared, entails the difficult passage of identifying the systems that expose users and third parties to high risks, and of defining accurate criteria to that end.[30] In this respect, there are several alternatives that need to be explored: the risk can refer to the likelihood of materialisation in the form of a damage, or to the type of damages that the use of certain applications can cause. For instance, only damages to health, bodily integrity and property could be deemed relevant; or damage to other personality rights or even pure economic losses could be included among the risks that deserve special con-

---

[26]   Art 5.

[27]   Art 6.

[28]   Art 52.

[29]   European Parliament Resolution of 20 October 2020 with recommendations to the Commission on a civil liability regime for artificial intelligence (2020/2014(INL)) para 14; European Commission, 'White Paper on Artificial Intelligence – A European approach to excellence and trust' (Communication) COM(2020) 65 final 18.

[30]   Philipp Hacker, 'AI Regulation in Europe' (7 May 2020) ssrn.com/abstract= 3556532 accessed 5 November 2021, agrees that 'it will be a tremendous challenge to formulate transparent, clearly defined allocation criteria across sectors', notwithstanding that such an approach of assigning certain applications to classes of risk exists in other areas.

sideration. In turn, qualifying the types of damage the system is more likely to cause as indicators of risk leads to the question as to whether only natural persons, or also legal persons, should be compensated.[31]

A broad definition has been attempted that refers both to the severity of possible harms and to the magnitude of the risk, to be assessed taking into account the 'sector' in which the system is deployed, the 'nature of the activities undertaken' and the 'manner' in which it is used.[32]

The White Paper on AI devotes specific attention to the risk of infringement of fundamental rights entailed by the use of algorithms in automated decision-making. Risks can lie in the faulty design of the algorithm, can derive from biased data used for the training or depend on other flaws in the dataset. AI systems deployed by private companies or public administration in the fields of employment, housing, fiscal checks, financial services, surveillance, migration, online commerce and law enforcement increase the possibilities that values and rights to data protection, privacy or dignity are affected and that discriminatory outputs occur. Resting on the analysis that enlarges the spectrum of the risks to take into account, the White Paper suggests an assessment of high-risk applications based on two cumulative criteria: the sectors where they are applied and the tasks they would perform in the said sectors, and thus the potential impact on affected parties deriving from their use. Exceptional situations could be envisaged that should be always considered high-risk, such as the employment sector or remote biometric identification.[33]

The depicted approach raises several problems. It could prove hard to implement in practice, since it requires a clear definition of the qualities of the systems that trigger a higher risk, in combination with the sector or type of activities in which they will be used. Attaining such a level of precision might be challenging; special cases that cannot definitely be attributed to the area covered by the new regime would probably emerge, and this would create overall uncertainty in the application of said norms. In order to reduce these difficulties, the Resolution of the European Parliament resorts to a special list, periodically updated, that details the applications included in the high-risk

---

[31] Sebastian Lohsse, Reiner Schulze and Dirk Staudenmayer, 'Liability for Artificial Intelligence' in Sebastian Lohsse, Reiner Schulze and Dirk Staudenmayer (eds.), *Liability for Artificial Intelligence and the Internet of Things: Münster Colloquia on EU Law and the Digital Economy IV* (Hart Nomos 2019) 20.

[32] European Parliament Resolution of 20 October 2020 with recommendations to the Commission on a civil liability regime for artificial intelligence (2020/2014(INL) para 15.

[33] European Commission, 'White Paper on Artificial Intelligence – A European approach to excellence and trust' (n 9) 17–18.

category.[34] However, the solution seems especially burdensome to apply, also taking into account the pace at which new solutions and devices are developed, and it does not prevent grey situations, difficult to assign to one class or another, from coming up.

The model described has another weakness in that it abstracts from the nature of the diverse applications and the different type of risk they engender. As has been pointed out,[35] AI-powered systems can be classified depending on whether they pertain mainly to a physical dimension, where material damages are the greater concern, or a social dimension that entails risks in terms of discrimination, manipulation and loss of control. Disregarding this difference can obfuscate the fact that several legal tools are already available to counteract the first type of risks (and only require some refinement), while AI-specific risks of the second kind demand a special regulatory response. This need for a tailored reaction derives not so much from the novelty of the risks, but instead from their magnitude, since the empowering effect of AI techniques amplifies their reach, and thus the subsequent potential harms.

In sum, the simple notion of 'high-risk application' as a paradigm to tackle the liability issue has a number of shortcomings: it appears too vague, therefore particularly hard to translate in practice; it may be overreaching and involve applications that are already satisfactorily regulated; to the contrary, it could create gaps of protection when the criteria for being included in the category are not all contextually satisfied.

However, the main weakness is considering the technological features of AI systems and the sectors in which they operate in isolation from the legal landscape. Disentangling the analysis from a comparison with the current applicable regimes basically looks at the new technology as it emerged in a void, and that void had to be filled from scratch. In reality, AI devices are impacted by different bodies of legislation, spanning from safety to liability schemes that would nonetheless apply. And since defining the boundaries of a specially regulated class, with the aim of removing it from the reach of previous rules, is particularly challenging, the potential for overlaps is high, as well as the overall uncertainty that the entire process generates.

---

[34] European Parliament Resolution of 20 October 2020 with recommendations to the Commission on a civil liability regime for artificial intelligence (2020/2014(INL) para 16.

[35] This critique has been formulated by Jens-Peter Schneider and Christiane Wendehorst, 'Response to the public consultation on the White Paper: On Artificial Intelligence – A European Approach to Excellence and Trust COM(2020) 65 final' 5–8, www.europeanlawinstitute.eu/fileadmin/user_upload/p_eli/News_page/2020/ELI _Response_AI_White_Paper.pdf accessed 5 November 2021.

Apart from the methodological issue, the possible contents of the envisaged regulation also raise some doubts – as it has been stressed, a 'one-size-fits-all' approach does not seem to work particularly well.[36] Even for digital products and systems that do not fall already into a domain that is densely regulated, a uniform solution may overestimate the relevance of their intrinsic features and way of functioning, purely autonomous for instance, without considering that the potential for harm varies according to the context of use and the foreseeable impact on the persons involved.

Similar concerns can be directed also to the model chosen in the proposal for a regulation on AI. From its perspective, not directly involved with liability problems, the AIA adopts a complex classification of high-risk systems by distinguishing two main categories: AI products or products equipped with an AI component that are already subject to third-party ex ante conformity assessment according to the EU safety legislation listed in Annex II; and stand-alone AI systems included in Annex III (which is updatable according to the procedure set in Article 7). This second category refers to systems and practices deployed in sensitive areas, such as education, employment, access to social services, predictive policing, etc. They have been identified after screening a large pool of AI use cases, covered in documents and studies of different EU bodies and other organisations, documented in the academic literature, resulting from the pilot application of the HLEG ethics guidelines and the public consultation on the White Paper. The high-risk use cases have been selected by applying the criteria of type, severity and probability of harm.

This model is worth considering; however, it is inevitably tied to the rationale of the proposal, which focuses on safety and does not deal with liability. More precisely, the two categories of high-risk systems are regulated unitarily in the context of the AIA from the point of view of assessing their safety. Each category, however, reflects physical AI systems, on the one hand, causing mainly physical risks, and purely digital AI systems, on the other hand, that can harm other fundamental rights or cause economic losses. In light of the difference between these two types of AI-powered systems in terms of potential uses, the kind of harm they can provoke and regimes already in place to address these damages, the pure transposition of a homogenous set of rules from the area of safety to the field of ex post liability seems quite problematic.

While waiting for the next developments of the legislative trajectory, a feasible pathway could be to analyse the current regulatory landscape and

---

[36] Bernhard A Koch, 'Product Liability 2.0 – Mere Update or New Version?' in Lohsse, Schulze and Staudenmayer (n 31) 113–14.

evaluate its fitness against concrete examples of AI systems.[37] This overview permits highlighting inconsistencies and authentic legal gaps; it also enables identifying, basically by subtraction, the areas or single applications that might need to be tackled head-on with a brand-new approach.

IV.   LIABILITY FOR DEFECTIVE PRODUCTS AT THE CENTRE-STAGE

The regime of liability for defective products – harmonised at the European level by the Product Liability Directive[38] – is poised to have an important role in the allocation of responsibilities for accidents involving intelligent systems. With autonomous devices,[39] the shift in control from the user to the manufacturer puts the latter in the position of being identified as the central figure to whom liability claims should be addressed. In fact, the autonomous mode of operation of the system intuitively enables a wrongful event to be traced back to a defect in the system itself. Therefore, the advent of new technologies seems to render more appropriate than before a conceptual and regulatory framework that places the responsibility for damages caused by complex products on the subject that has launched them on to the market and has a better knowledge of the associated risks.

The central role played by the defective Product Liability Directive has been diffusely acknowledged in different policy circles, as well as the need to maintain and improve such a harmonised regime.[40] Problems created by

---

[37]   Paul Nemitz, 'Constitutional Democracy and Technology in the Age of Artificial Intelligence' [2018] Philosophical Transactions Royal Society A: Mathematical, Physical and Engineering Sciences 376, 10, proposes an analogous approach for the regulation of AI in general: 'Once a challenge of AI is discovered which touches on fundamental rights of individuals or important interests of the state, we have to ask ourselves whether a law already exists which can apply to AI and which addresses the challenge in a sufficient and proportional manner. So before making a new law, the potential scope of application and problem-solving ability of existing law in relation to AI must be determined'.

[38]   Council Directive 85/347/EEC of 25 July 1985 on the approximation of the laws, regulations and administrative provisions of the Member States concerning liability for defective products (Product Liability Directive) [1985] OJ L 210/29.

[39]   Where AI systems are simple decision-assistance tools, thus requiring human-computer interaction, negligence law remains the main legal scheme for assigning responsibility: Andrew D Selbst, 'Negligence and AI's Human Users' (2020) 100 Boston University Law Review 1315.

[40]   Commission Staff Working Document, Evaluation of Council Directive 85/374/ EEC of 25 July 1985 on the approximation of the laws, regulations and administrative provisions of the Member States concerning liability for defective products, Brussels, 7.5.2018, SWD(2018) 157 final, 69–70; Tatjana Evas, 'Civil liability regime

certain frictions between the current text and the ensuing interpretation, on the one hand, and some technological features of advanced products, on the other, seem to demand targeted interventions rather than radical reforms.

A. Immunity for Producers of Autonomous Systems? Not a Good Idea

The appeal to the contrary, that producers should be immunised from liability as a way of fostering innovation, has remained isolated.[41] This solution was intended to support emerging robotic industries by reducing the fears of liability-related costs, thus avoiding a technology chilling effect that would hamper the pace of valuable innovation.

In fact, shielding producers from liability is problematic for different reasons: it assumes – but so far there is no strong evidence (of) – a technology chilling effect, and that effect is regarded as negative. However, as long as new technological devices have not reached a higher level of safety than those currently available, liability rules that prevent from launching on to the market said devices for fear of having to bear the relative costs play precisely the role that is normally assigned to them.

A second policy reason that militates against an immunity for manufacturers relies on the ideas of responsible research and innovation and accountability that are enshrined in the European governance of science making.[42] After all, AI-powered systems are produced intentionally, and equipping them with machine learning capabilities depends on design decisions that make the device more versatile but at the same time augment the risk of unforeseen outcomes. Automating functions and tasks that were previously carried out by

---

for artificial intelligence, European added value assessment' (Study of the European Parliamentary Research Service, September 2020) 7–9; Expert Group on Liability and New Technologies (n 8); European Commission, 'Report from the Commission to the European Parliament, the Council and the European Economic and Social Committee on the safety and liability implications of Artificial Intelligence, the Internet of Things and Robotics' (n 10).

[41] Ryan Calo, 'Open Robotics' (2011) 70 Maryland Law Review 571. With specific regard to autonomous vehicles, Gary E Marchant and Rachel A Lindor, 'The Coming Collision Between Autonomous Vehicles and the Liability System' (2012) 52 Santa Clara Law Review 1321, 1337–8, consider appropriate introduction of legislation protecting against, or limiting, liability of producers in order to foster beneficial innovation. In favour of shifting from strict liability of producers to negligence as a way of fostering automation that improves overall safety, Ryan Abbott, 'The Reasonable Computer: Disrupting the Paradigm of Tort Liability' (2018) 86 George Washington Law Review 1.

[42] René von Schomberg and Jonathan Hankins, *International Handbook on Responsible Innovation. A Global Resource* (Edward Elgar Publishing, 2019).

humans should not serve to shield from liability the very subject who created and made such a device commercially available.[43]

Third, the capacity of control that the producer can exert over the behaviour of the system should not be underestimated.[44] Although the autonomy of the system, coupled with machine learning abilities, certainly diminishes the possibility of anticipating all possible scenarios and installing the appropriate countermeasures within the machine, the design and manufacturing phases still represent the setting where greater efforts can be spent in order to achieve an adequate degree of safety. In addition, in the case of digital products, the capability of controlling the product itself does not end with the sale – thanks to product connectivity, manufacturers/sellers will gradually acquire increasing control over their products, learn more about their post-sale use and potentially discover risks or unveil misuses that they were not previously aware of. As a matter of fact, a number of post-sale obligations such as monitoring and informing customers of newly discovered risks could be fuelled by this flux of information that takes place between the producer/seller and the robotic device. The proximity to the product, to the product user and to the product use could work as a driver of liability:[45] the knowledge gained over the behaviour of the system could be used to improve its performance and enhance its safety, but it may have an impact also on the liability that follows from malfunctioning or inappropriate uses of the product that could have been detected, patched or warned against. The impact on liability could be substantial also because the costs of updating a software or providing a patch are certainly low, compared to the ones that a manufacturer has to sustain for recalling defective products (which explains why a duty to observe and monitor its products exists only in some jurisdictions and is not a widespread issue).[46]

One of the rationales for creating an immunity for producers of advanced products impinges on the capacity to work as a leverage for innovation. However, doubts have been expressed on the appropriateness of using liability

---

[43]   Nemitz (n 37) 6.

[44]   Joanna J Bryson, 'The Artificial Intelligence of the Ethics of Artificial Intelligence: An Introductory Overview for Law and Regulation' in Markus Dubber, Frank Pasquale and Sunit Das (eds.), *The Oxford Handbook of Ethics of Artificial Intelligence* (Oxford University Press, 2020).

[45]   Bryant Walker Smith, 'Proximity-Driven Liability' (2014) 102 Georgetown Law Journal 1777.

[46]   Francesco Paolo Patti, 'Autonomous Vehicles' Liability: Need for Change?' in Alberto De Franceschi and Reiner Schulze (eds.), *Digital Revolution – New Challenges for Law* (Beck Nomos 2019) 209; Gabriele Mazzini, 'A System of Governance for Artificial Intelligence through the Lens of Emerging Intersections between AI and EU Law' in Alberto De Franceschi and Reiner Schulze (eds.), *Digital Revolution – New Challenges for Law* (Beck Nomos, 2019) 262; Hacker (n 30) 15.

rules to foster innovation, with the effect of expanding the launch of potentially dangerous activities.[47] The immunity would basically subsidise the production of sophisticated technological products, raising the question whether an effort in that direction is justified per se or, on the contrary, it should instead be preceded by a choice of the technologies that deserve a more favourable treatment. Provided that any form of immunity would shift the cost of liability on to society, the acceptability of this transfer needs to be assessed against the overall advantages of the decision, taking into account the social gain brought about by different types of innovation at stake.

In addition, not only would the proposal steer liability rules towards an objective that is normally achieved through other means, such as intellectual property rights, but it would also fail to pursue the authentic goals of liability regimes in an effective way – on the one hand, compensating the victims of damages, thus requiring that other mechanisms are put in place with that aim;[48] on the other, preventing the occurrence of future accidents, by giving incentives to those subjects that are in the best position to avoid them.

For all these reasons, the idea formulated with regard to the US environment of introducing an immunity, or even a partial immunity for producers, did not appeal in the European context.[49]

B.   Reforming the PLD

A common understanding is taking shape about the need for tailored interventions in the defective product liability regime in order to make it apt to accommodate more complex technologies than could be envisioned when the Product Liability Directive was approved.

The main criticalities can only be briefly recalled here. First, the scope of the directive is circumscribed by the notion of product, with Article 2 stating

---

[47]   Gerhard Wagner, 'Robot Liability' in Lohsse, Schulze and Staudenmayer (n 31) 30. For a detailed critique of such a rationale for immunising producers see also F Patrick Hubbard, '"Sophisticated Robots": Balancing Liability, Regulation, and Innovation' (2014) 66 Florida Law Review 1803, 1870–71.

[48]   Georg Borges, 'New Liability Concepts: the Potential of Insurance and Compensation Funds' in Lohsse, Schulze and Staudenmayer (n 31) 160 admits that mechanisms such as publicly funded compensation funds, which shield producers from liability while bearing the costs of compensation of the victims, could be used if we agree that the introduction of an autonomous system is a task that engages society as a whole, since it is a key element in the transformation processes needed for the development of a digital society.

[49]   For an earlier critique, see Palmerini (n 23) 18; with a more nuanced view Andrea Bertolini, 'Robots as Products: The Case for a Realistic Analysis of Robotic Applications and Liability Rules' (2013) 5(2) Law, Innovation & Technology 214, 246.

its applicability to 'movables'.[50] Even before the appearance of robotics and AI devices, whether software was included in the concept at stake has been thoroughly discussed. While an AI-based software embedded in a physical appliance would certainly fall within the notion of product, pure digital contents – such as updates downloaded from the internet (for instance, audio or video files, maps for a navigation system) – have a more ambiguous nature. There are already reasons that support a wider interpretation of the notion of product, or at least justify its extension by analogy,[51] which would be entirely consistent with the aim of the Product Liability Directive, as stated in recital 2, of a 'fair apportionment of the risk inherent in modern technological production'.[52] However, according to a number of analyses, it is worth clarifying this point explicitly, by adopting a broader definition that encompasses all forms of digital products including stand-alone software.[53]

The second problem pertains to the concept of defectiveness that the victim is asked to demonstrate. This requirement is problematic because the common understanding of defectiveness refers to the categories of manufacturing defect, design defect and information defect. While manufacturing defects can easily be applied to digital products – for instance a bug included in a single copy of the software code – the area of design defect is less manageable. In particular, the risk-utility test that was developed by the courts requires comparing the product with the performance ensured by an alternative design. The benchmark against which to make this assessment is not straightforward: should it be the algorithm, if it exists, capable of avoiding that particular accident or the algorithms that have a better rate of success in the overall activity they engage in?[54] This is perhaps the thorniest aspect that elicits a legislative intervention, although algorithmic defectiveness could also be developed and

---

[50]   For the discussion of this point see Wagner (n 47) 41–2; Koch (n 36) 104–6.

[51]   Jean-Sébastien Borghetti, 'How can Artificial Intelligence be Defective?' in Lohsse, Schulze and Staudenmayer (n 31) 64; Wagner (n 47) 42. Woodrow Barfield, 'Liability for Autonomous and Artificially Intelligent Robots' (2018) 9 Journal of Behavioural Robotics 196, 196–7 discusses the problem of qualifying software as product or as service in the context of the US legal environment.

[52]   Francesco Mezzanotte, 'Risk Allocation and Liability Regimes in the IoT' in De Franceschi and Schulze (n 46) 178–9.

[53]   Koch (n 36) 106; Ernst Karner, 'Liability for Robotics: Current Rules, Challenges, and the Need for Innovative Concepts' in Lohsse, Schulze and Staudenmayer (n 31) 119; also European Commission, 'Report from the Commission to the European Parliament, the Council and the European Economic and Social Committee on the safety and liability implications of Artificial Intelligence, the Internet of Things, and Robotics' (n 10) 14.

[54]   Borghetti (n 51) 65–72; Selbst (n 39) 1325 shows how the notion of design defect is conceptually alien to AI products; Patti, 'Autonomous Vehicles' Liability' (n 46) 205–8.

refined by the courts and the legal literature, in line with the process that so far has led to the defining of the general notion of defectiveness.

In the path towards the definition of defectiveness for AI products, the regulatory efforts undertaken by the European Commission in order to develop guidelines for a trustworthy AI should not be underestimated. While trying to set up standards for building intelligent systems that are reliable, fair, safe and secure, this framework may help also to shape a benchmark against which to assess the inherent quality of said systems and the lack of essential safeguards for individual rights and freedoms. The same holds true for the measures that the AIA envisions, which shall integrate the existing requirements in the products' safety legislation.

The distribution of the burden of the proof between the parties adds to the problem discussed above. Although the liability is not fault-based, a claim will be successful by proving the defectiveness of the product and the nexus of causality between the defect and the harm suffered. In the case of complex products, the burden of the proof is heavier for the victims who are unable to identify the reasons why an accident occurred and trace back the damage to a defect. In turn, having recourse to technical expertise to formulate and substantiate a claim may be too costly, especially when compared to the damage suffered. It is often pointed out that a solution for this problem would be reversing the burden of proof with regard to the defectiveness – the producer would be considered liable unless they are able to demonstrate that the product was not defective.[55]

A more radical intervention would be to eliminate the concept of defectiveness and adopt a criterion of pure strict liability that holds the producer liable whenever one of their products is involved in an accident.[56] This outcome is not considered excessively disruptive of the current criteria for allocating liability. On the contrary, it is aligned with the goal of deterrence, since it places the incentives to enhance the safety of products and prevent accidents on the manufacturers, who, unlike the users, have a greater influence on the behaviour of autonomous systems.[57]

A partial relief to the difficulty of determining defectiveness and causality could also derive from the traceability of the system's behaviour ensured by digitalisation – all data on the activities performed could be registered within the system and made accessible to the parties in case a damage materialises.[58]

---

[55]   Wagner (n 47) 47; Gerald Spindler, 'User Liability and Strict Liability in the Internet of Things and for Robots' in Lohsse, Schulze and Staudenmayer (n 31) 139.

[56]   Wagner (n 47) 47; Borghetti (n 51) 72; Spindler (n 55) 136–8.

[57]   Wagner (n 47) 47.

[58]   Bertolini and Episcopo (n 8) 11, are sceptical about the real advantage for the victims of having access to data that are complex and require technical expertise to be interpreted.

In the sector of autonomous vehicles, the equipping of the car with an event data recorder (EDR) is a suggestion already included in several policy documents.[59] Obligations to install a 'black box' device and to provide the data to the parties who need it in relation to a legal claim have already been adopted by the newly reformed German Road Traffic Act, which has allowed highly automated cars to circulate in the road traffic.[60] As intelligent systems develop, it may become necessary to record and store data not just on the technical behaviour of the system, but also on the upstream decisions taken by the robot in front of difficult real-world scenarios. In other words, it should always be possible to find out why an autonomous system made a particular decision, as well as what the inputs of the 'ethical governor' (in the case that there is one) had been.[61]

The requirement within Article 7(b) that the defect is present when the product is put into circulation is another point that deserves consideration. It could be very difficult to show that a 'defect' in a self-learning, autonomous system had been present when it was first put in the stream of commerce, unless installing the capacity for independent decision-making for unforeseen actions is itself considered a defect.[62] More specifically, the requirement is at odds with goods that have a changing nature, continuously adapt their behaviour to the external stimuli and evolve in line with their learning abilities.

The development risk defence is also problematic, and there are indications of removing it through a legislative intervention at the European level or in single Member States.[63] Other points that may need clarification or reform are the concept of liable person, in order to include developers, providers of services and other subjects in the value chain, and the range of recoverable losses.

---

[59]   Communication from the Commission to the European Parliament, the Council, the European Economic and Social Committee and the Committee of the Regions, On the road to automated mobility: An EU strategy for mobility of the future COM(2018) 283 final, 10; European Parliament Resolution of 15 January 2019 on autonomous driving in European transport (2018/2089(INI)) § 13.

[60]   S VIa inserted in the Road Traffic Act by the Eight Law amending the Road Traffic Act of 16 June 2017. The French Decree n. 2018-211 of 28 March 2018 relatif à l'expérimentation des véhicules à délégation de conduite sur le voies publiques, contains a similar provision, obliging vehicles to be equipped with a device that registers and stores all data on automated driving (art 11).

[61]   Alan FT Winfield and Marina Jirotka, 'The Case for an Ethical Black Box' in Yang Gao and others (eds.), *Towards Autonomous Robot Systems* (Springer 2017) 262.

[62]   Herbert Zech, 'Liability for Autonomous Systems: Tackling Specific Risks of Modern IT' in Lohsse, Schulze and Staudenmayer (n 31) 196; Mezzanotte (n 52) 180.

[63]   Patti, 'Autonomous Vehicles' Liability' (n 46) 204–5; Francesco Paolo Patti, 'Machine Learning and European Product Liability' in André Janssen and Hans Schulte-Nölke (eds.), *Researches in European Private Law and Beyond: Contribution in Honour of Reiner Schulze's Seventieth Birthday* (Nomos, 2020) 115–16.

V.   EASIER CASES

As was anticipated, looking at innovative technologies in isolation may lead to hasty conclusions – the inherent features and the potential impact on fundamental rights and values that their use entails seem to suggest that only newly conceived frameworks can be up to the challenge of handling the situation. Upon a more careful examination, one can realise that among the current regimes there are some already operating according to strict liability criteria which suit the requirements of AI-powered systems.

A.   Self-Driving Cars

Self-driving vehicles are the innovative technology that has most elicited the attention of legal scholars when thinking in liability terms. Although the promise of autonomous cars is to dramatically increase the safety of traffic circulation, the substantial speed of operation and the extreme variety of difficult-to-interpret scenarios or unexpected events that can occur in unstructured environments, such as in common traffic, point to the risk of serious damage in the event of an accident. In addition, the shift in control from the driver to the car software challenges the usual modes of ascertaining liability. On these grounds, one is led to think almost intuitively that the advent of this technology will trigger a radical reconsideration of the current frameworks.[64]

However, once again, looking at the inherent features of the new technology, radically diverging from the ones exhibited by its analogue counterparts, appears misguided. The authentic novelty of the product compared to the existing ones does not mean that the available regimes are not suitable to deal with it, especially considering that they have been established out of the need for accommodating a hazardous technology, which motor vehicles generally are. As is well-known, the general reaction of the Western legal systems to technological developments was to replace negligence-based regimes with strict liability regimes. Although a comparative analysis of the EU liability systems for traffic accidents would show many differences in the details of the

---

[64]   Andrea Bertolini and Massimo Riccaboni, 'Grounding the Case for a European Approach to the Regulation of Automated Driving: The Technology-selection Effect of Liability Rules' (2020) 51 European Journal of Law and Economics 243, assume a specular view, arguing that the trajectory towards the diffusion of autonomous vehicles can be undertaken only by adopting a new type of liability rules, based on a risk management approach. In the same vein, Jonathan Sinclair and Burkhard Schafer, 'Autonomous Vehicles: The Path to Liability is Still Unclear' (*Jusletter IT*, 23 November 2017), stress the special risks deriving from external manipulation and hacker attacks to the technology.

rules adopted, it is accepted that a large majority are based on the joint liability of the driver and the owner of the car (or the custodian in the French *Loi Badinter*), which they can escape only in limited circumstances.[65] This solution is complemented in the European Union by mandatory insurance, due to the harmonisation ensuing from the Motor Insurance Directive.[66] Autonomous vehicles would fall within the field of application of the directive given the general definition of vehicle that is subjected to the third-party insurance obligation.[67] The combination of strict liability rules and compulsory insurance seems to enable the plain integration of self-driving cars into the common traffic without disruption of the current regimes dealing with road accidents.[68]

This line of reasoning does not apply perfectly in countries, like the UK, where the system of liability for road traffic accidents is still based on fault or negligence criteria. Accidents caused by fully autonomous vehicles could not be assessed according to these principles, and the owner or user of the vehicle would almost never be responsible (unless they were negligent in the maintenance or the updating of the software).[69] For such situations, the adoption of special rules at the European level is deemed necessary.[70]

It is no coincidence perhaps that the UK, which is at the forefront in testing experiments with autonomous vehicles, introduced the Automated and Electric Vehicles Act 2018 that places on the insurance company the liability for accidents caused by the vehicle driving itself in a public road or other public space

---

[65]   For such an analysis with regard to France and the Netherlands see Roeland de Bruin, 'Autonomous Intelligent Cars on the European Intersection of Liability and Privacy. Regulatory Challenges and the Road Ahead' (2016) 7 European Journal of Risk Regulation 485, 492–3.

[66]   Directive 2009/103/EC of the European Parliament and of the Council of 16 September 2009 relating to insurance against civil liability in respect of the use of motor vehicles, and the enforcement of the obligation to insure against such liability [2009] OJ L263/11.

[67]   The Motor Insurance Directive applies to 'any motor vehicle intended for travel on land and propelled by mechanical power, but not running on rails, and any trailer, whether or not coupled' (art 1.1). See also European Commission, 'Report from the Commission to the European Parliament, the Council and the European Economic and Social Committee on the safety and liability implications of Artificial Intelligence, the Internet of Things, and Robotics' (n 10) 13.

[68]   Patti, 'Autonomous Vehicles' Liability' (n 46) 190, highlights the different situation in the United States: since the adoption of compulsory insurance rule is rare in the various jurisdictions, the analyses prefer to concentrate on the liability of the manufacturers.

[69]   Although even in the UK system, where fault of the driver is still required in theory, in practice courts have set a strict standard of diligence.

[70]   Borghetti (n 51) 74; Karner, 'Liability for Robotics: Current Rules, Challenges, and the Need for Innovative Concepts' (n 53) 121–2.

(with some limited exceptions).[71] With the adoption of these special rules for automated vehicles, the UK has commanded a solution that in other countries was already law in action. The reform of the traffic code that was undertaken in Germany in order to enable the circulation of highly automated vehicles seems to confirm this hypothesis:[72] the basic principle that imposes liability on the owner in case the driver is not at fault was left untouched, probably because it was considered adequate to cover the new risks brought about by automated driving and not excessively burdening the victims. Likewise, in Italy the ministerial decree of 28 February 2018, which authorises the experimental testing of autonomous cars on public roads, has implicitly maintained the mechanism that combines liability of the driver/owner with compulsory insurance, setting a coverage cap four times higher than that applicable for the same vehicle not equipped with the technology for autonomous driving (Article 19).

A significant point of divergence exhibited by the UK reform is instead the requirement to have compulsory first-party insurance that meets the need of compensating the users in case they suffer damage while driving in automated mode; otherwise, they would be left only with an action against the manufacturer.[73]

Applying the sectoral regime for road accidents has the additional advantage of avoiding confusion and overlaps at a stage when highly automated vehicles will circulate together with conventional cars. The introduction of a special regime for self-driving cars would impose on the victim an obligation to investigate the mode of operation before deciding against whom to take legal action and, depending on the choice, identify the diverse requirements for the action and gather the relevant information. This undesirable scenario confirms that new rules are at least premature since a transition phase of mixed circulation is to be expected for several years.

In any event, liability for defective products is not pre-empted by the sectoral regime of traffic accidents. In theory, a victim could claim damages from the producer of the automated car when there is evidence that the accident was caused by flaws in the embedded software or by defective sensors integrated in the car. However, it is highly unlikely that someone would choose such an option, since it entails a much heavier burden to discharge in terms of the elements to prove and the evidence to collect.[74] Moreover, the claimant would have to renounce the simplified (and, in substance, administrative) procedure

---

[71] S 2(1). For a commentary on the new rules see Katie Atkinson, 'Autonomous Cars: A Driving Force for Change in Motor Liability and Insurance' (2020) 17(1) SCRIPT*ed* 125, 148–51.

[72] Eight Law amending the Road Traffic Act, n 59.

[73] Bertolini and Riccaboni (n 64).

[74] Patti, 'Machine Learning and European Product Liability' (n 63) 111.

that the involvement of an insurance company guarantees thanks to the mechanism of direct action. Much more plausible is that the insurance company seeks redress from the manufacturer – insurers are professional operators who have the technical expertise and the financial resources to decide if a claim for a defective product is sound and to make an assessment of the cost-benefit ratio.[75]

In a more distant future, when the transition towards autonomous vehicles has been completed, it is possible to imagine that liability will concentrate exclusively on the producer, who will also bear the cost of insurance and factor it into the price of the cars. This option places liability on the party who is in the best position to prevent accidents from happening, and aims to spread the cost of insurance; conversely, the different prices of diverse car models, driven by the same algorithm, will reflect indirectly the level of safety of the car itself.[76]

B.   Robotics and AI in Healthcare

AI and robotics systems deployed in medicine and healthcare represent another special case,[77] which is better addressed with traditional rules, especially where updates have recently taken place.[78] The technologies used in this field are of a great variety, ranging from surgical robots to rehabilitation systems, from appliances for robot-enhanced psychotherapy and motor sensory applications in active prostheses to robotic nanocapsules for exploring the inner body. Robots are also used in hospitals for the delivery of pharmacy medications or laboratory specimens and for transporting heavier loads such as meals or linen.[79] In terms of purely digital systems, the most important example is expert systems that process and analyse medical data for diagnosis.

---

[75] Wagner (n 47) 51; Patti, 'Autonomous Vehicles' Liability' (n 46) 196–7.

[76] Patti, 'Autonomous Vehicles' Liability' (n 46) 201–2.

[77] Many studies analyse the legal implications of the deployment of AI devices and systems in healthcare: Ernst Karner, 'Liability for Medical Robots and Autonomous Medical Devices' in Ernst Karner and others (eds.), *Essays in Honour of Helmut Koziol* (Vienna 2020); George Maliha and others, 'Artificial Intelligence and Liability in Medicine: Balancing Safety and Innovation' (2021) 99(3) The Milbank Quarterly 629; Fruzsina Molnar-Gabor, 'Artificial Intelligence in Healthcare: Doctors, Patients and Liability' in Thomas Wischmeyer and Timo Rademacher (eds.), *Regulating Artificial Intelligence* (Springer, 2020).

[78] As is the case of the Italian Law n 24 of 8 March 2017, which introduces incentives to sue for compensation from healthcare institutions, while shielding individual physicians.

[79] For real-life examples see aethon.com/ accessed 5 November 2021.

First, this area is characterised by an extremely detailed regulatory scheme for medical devices, enabling a complex architecture of governance of the safety of all appliances used for medical purposes. This scheme has been recently reformed and Regulation 2017/745 has replaced the two previous directives that had become obsolete. In the process of reforming this field, several problematic issues have been dealt with and some criticalities have been solved.[80] Specific provisions addressing software have been introduced to the effect that AI systems used in medicine and healthcare and not embedded in tangible goods can be classified as medical devices when intended by the manufacturer to be used for one or more medical purposes.[81] Further, Regulation 2017/745 is now applicable to high-risk devices, regardless of the labelling that the producer has adopted. In order to fill a gap in the previous scheme, which did not extend to devices without an intended medical purpose, a special category of devices that present a severe risk of harm was created. All products falling within this class, and listed in Annex XVI to the Regulation, need to comply with the safety requirements and procedures set out therein.[82] This particular reform has overcome the problem of devices marketed for enhancement purposes, which could escape the relevant regime even if comparable, in terms of potential for harm, to genuine medical devices. The clinical evaluation and clinical investigation phases, previously poorly regulated with a simple recall to very general principles on human experimentation, have been strengthened and aligned with the current paradigms for clinical trials, including measures for protecting the members of vulnerable communities.[83]

This enhanced regulatory framework, now applicable to software medical devices based on AI,[84] has a bearing on the overall level of safety of the technologies introduced into the healthcare environment. In turn, we can expect that the issue of liability will also be positively affected by the enactment of measures that take into account the specific features and risks of said devices and steer the advancements in the sector. In sum, the issue of liability steps in

---

[80] See Erica Palmerini, 'A Legal Perspective on Body Implants for Therapy and Enhancement' (2015) 29(2–3) International Review of Law, Computers and Technology 226, 228–36, for an overview of the main drawbacks of the old framework as regards advanced bodily implants such as active prostheses or devices for deep-brain stimulation.

[81] Art 2.1.

[82] Art 1(2).

[83] Arts 61–82.

[84] For an analysis of the interplay between the MDR and the proposed AIA see Sofia Palmieri, Paulien Walraet and Tom Goffin, 'Inevitable Influences: AI-Based Medical Devices at the Intersection of Medical Devices Regulation and the Proposal for AI Regulation' (2021) 28 European Journal of Health Law 241.

as part of a wider ecosystem that has already been adapted to the challenges brought about by AI-empowered and robotic devices.

Having in mind the possible scenarios of use of AI and robotics in medical practices, a preliminary observation relates to the high variety of assignments that they can perform. Although medical robotics, unlike autonomous vehicles, have a wide range of tasks to which they can be applied, in many instances robots and AI used in healthcare will be tools in the hands of physicians,[85] who will maintain control to a large extent over the practice they are executing.[86] These factual circumstances will likely position most legal actions undertaken by patients harmed in a diagnostic, therapeutic or surgical intervention under the umbrella of medical malpractice. This area of tort law falls within the national Member States' competences and only a comprehensive comparative analysis could articulate a possible answer to the inquiry about the fate of a claim of algorithmic or robotic liability in this sector.[87] Common patterns detectable in several jurisdictions, however, suggest that such a claim would be administered according to criteria favourable to the patients harmed in the course of medical treatment involving the use of AI devices. Different factors lead to this conclusion: a general expansion of liability for medical malpractice, the improvement of standards of good care, mechanisms such as the *res ipsa loquitur* argument and the tendency to impose the burden of submitting evidence upon the party who is in the best position to acquire and track the relevant pieces of knowledge. The propensity to attribute the responsibility for organisational failures to healthcare institutions, together with the penetration

---

[85]   Jessica Morley and others, 'The Ethics of AI in Health Care: A Mapping Review' (2020) 260 Social Science & Medicine 113172, describe this situation in terms of AI-clinicians' cooperation to suggest that AI will be mainly used for supporting medical decision-making. Eric J Topol, 'High-performance Medicine: The Convergence of Human and Artificial Intelligence' (2019) 25 Nature Medicine 44, 52, also suggests that AI in medicine will never reach full autonomy level, humans being required instead to oversee algorithmic interpretation of images and data: 'Human health is too precious – relegating it to machines, except for routine matters with minimal risks, seems especially far-fetched'.

[86]   Guang-Zhong Yang and others, 'Medical Robotics – Regulatory, Ethical, and Legal Considerations for Increasing Levels of Autonomy' (2017) 2 Science Robotics.

[87]   More generally, for comparative studies on medical liability in Europe see Ewoud Hondius (ed.), 'The Development of Medical Liability' in John Bell and David Ibbetson (eds.), *Comparative Studies in the Development of the Law of Torts in Europe* (CUP, 2010). See also the research undertaken under the auspices of the European Centre on Tort and Insurance Law (ECTIL): Bernhard A Koch (ed.), *Medical Liability in Europe. A Comparison of Selected Jurisdictions* (De Gruyter, 2011); Ken Oliphant and Richard W Wright (eds.), *Medical Malpractice and Compensation in Global Perspective* (De Gruyter, 2013); Michael Faure and Helmut Koziol (eds), *Cases on Medical Malpractice in a Comparative Perspective* (Springer, 2001).

of the 'ideology of enterprise liability' in the practice of medicine,[88] is another factor that points in the direction of the ability of the existing regimes to deal with the occurrence of damage deriving from algorithmic flaws.

In sum, healthcare systems that rely heavily on AI-powered systems can be expected to improve the quality of care provided, thanks to the enhanced safety of said systems and the top performance in medical services, such as diagnosis and therapy recommendation, which some scientific evidence already shows. At the same time, on the inevitable occasions where patients will suffer harms, healthcare providers will probably be called to bear the related costs under the logic that sees them as better positioned both to prevent the eventuating of accidents and to afford the costs of liability. Jurisdictions, such as the Nordic countries, that have adopted insurance schemes to cover the injuries sustained by patients in the provision of medical care could be less inclined, in an initial phase, to include the risk of technological failures in the coverage. However, we can expect that following the introduction of AI systems in routine health-care, they will align with the general tendency.

A remaining problem deserves to be mentioned: the damages caused by AI-powered medical devices used in the provision of medical services will likely pertain to the medical malpractice domain and be administered according to the rules of that sector. Robotic devices destined to be integrated permanently in the body of the recipient, such as advance bionic prostheses or neural implants for brain stimulation, may fall outside this domain. Even when they have been inserted through a surgical procedure, the damage may derive exclusively from a defect of the product, and perhaps manifest later in time, thus excluding the liability of the professional who performed the intervention. In such situations, the regime of defective product liability will be available, but with all the uncertainties and difficulties that such a claim for redress presents. In fact, the regulatory scheme for medical devices has already shown gaps in the protection of victims of faulty devices, which the European Court of Justice has tried to remedy by way of inventive interpretation.[89]

VI. VICARIOUS LIABILITY AND THE CONCEPT OF AUXILIARY

The question to be asked at this stage of development is whether there are areas, outside the domains already regulated according to strict liability crite-

---

[88] Robert L Rabin, 'Tort Law in Transition: Tracing the Patterns of Sociolegal Change' (1988) 23 Valparaiso University Law Review 1, 6.

[89] Case C-503/13 and C-504/13 *Boston Scientific Medizintechnik GmbH v AOK Sachsen-Anhalt- Die Gesundheitskasse e Betriebskrankenkasse RWE* [2015].

ria, where AI-powered systems can be used and present comparable risks in terms of seriousness and likelihood that they will materialise.

Another element to be factored into this assessment is whether contractual remedies will apply. In the case where the victim is in a contractual relationship with the operator, the availability of contractual liability eases the position of the damaged person. Algorithmic applications of huge economic and social relevance can be found in the market for financial services, as tools such as robo-advisors and automated portfolio management become more widely available. In these instances, the investor that has incurred considerable losses due to the flaws of the system providing expert advice cannot resort to product liability, which is not applicable to services, but the contractual relation that underpins the use of automated decision-making seems to afford a sufficient level of protection against the professional.

On the contrary, when the damaged person is not in a contractual relation with the wrongdoer, they will have to rely on general tort law rules that are not strict liability based. The problem arises especially for autonomous robots that are used by commercial operators. Current examples refer to carrier robots used for the delivery of goods,[90] which can move on pavements and navigate crowds;[91] or to autonomous robots used for cleaning in large commercial spaces. Harms caused by AI systems that pose significant risks due to their mobility, weight, speed and/or shape would be dealt with under a fault-based regime. Therefore, the operators and users of these products would profit from a more favourable treatment; correspondingly, the victims of accidents would face a heavier burden to articulate their claims. Since this conclusion seems unacceptable, alternative hypothetical regimes have been explored. One consists of establishing an equivalence between a human auxiliary and a machine deployed in functions that would normally be executed by humans.[92] Since professionals who use workers or employees to perform part of the economic activities are liable for their conduct according to a rigorous criterion, the same should apply in the case where the work is carried out by machines. The rationale behind the attribution of liability to the employer expressed by the phrase *cuius commoda eius et incommoda* (who receives the benefits should also bear

---

[90]   An example of personal delivery robots is Starship: www.starship.xyz/ accessed 9 November 2021.

[91]   See the H2020 EU project Crowdbots investigating technical, ethical, and legal problems of robots designed to navigate in crowded environments: crowdbot.eu/ accessed 9 November 2021.

[92]   Karner, 'Liability for Robotics: Current Rules, Challenges, and the Need for Innovative Concepts' (n 53) 120; Christiane Wendehorst, 'Strict Liability for AI and Other Emerging Technologies' (2020) 11(2) Journal of European Tort Law 150, 159; Expert Group on Liability and New Technologies (n 8) 45–6.

the costs) applies also when essential functions are delegated to machines. This solution may even be achieved by analogy without requiring a legislative intervention.[93]

Another model that could be used as a paradigm or directly applied by analogy is the liability of animal keepers that exists in many jurisdictions, which appears especially convincing, according to some opinions, for systems embedding artificial neural networks whose cognitive capacities resemble those of small animals.[94]

VII.   TOWARDS AN EXPANSION OF STRICT LIABILITY?

Solutions based on the extensive interpretation of provisions on vicarious liability or implemented by analogy with previous cases can provisionally reduce the gaps in protection. However, quite understandably, proposals for introducing special liability rules for autonomous systems of more practical importance and presenting high risks are also advanced, in order to complement the sectoral regimes.[95]

For instance, the European Parliament Resolution on liability for AI focuses on the concept of the operator being held responsible according to strict liability criteria,[96] irrespective of the fact that the AI system operates virtually or in the physical world; joint responsibility should be introduced in the case of more than one operator;[97] and strict liability should be complemented by mandatory insurance[98] and compensation caps.[99] Activities that do not create high risk would remain regulated under a regime of fault liability, but fault should be presumed.[100]

The Report of the Expert Group on Liability and New Technologies considers the operator's strict liability an appropriate legal response for emerging digital technologies that are operated in non-private environments and may typically cause significant harm.[101]

---

[93]   Karner, 'Liability for Medical Robots and Autonomous Medical Devices' (n 77) 67.

[94]   Zech (n 62) 197–8; Richard Kelley et al., 'Liability in Robotics: An International Perspective on Robots as Animals' (2010) 24:13 Advanced Robotics 1861.

[95]   Karner, 'Liability for Robotics: Current Rules, Challenges, and the Need for Innovative Concepts' (n 53) 122–3.

[96]   Art 4.

[97]   Art 11.

[98]   Art 4(4).

[99]   Art 5.

[100]   Art 8.

[101]   Expert Group on Liability and New Technologies (n 8) 39–42.

Hypothetical rules of this kind need to be attentively discussed having in mind the potential scenarios in which they will operate: a general rule of strict liability imposed on the owner/operator of an autonomous system would apply to the professional that uses a fleet of robots to deliver packages and to the elderly people who are assisted by a care robot.[102] Confining the rule of strict liability to operators that use the AI system within their organisation and commercial or professional activity might avoid imposing too heavy a burden on individual owners deploying the machine for private purposes. However, a rule of this kind would connect strict liability to the status of the operator of the AI system and not to the type of activity performed or the context of use. This is quite an uncommon basis; in turn, it may result in the victim needing to make a more complex assessment in order to identify whom to sue and under which regime.

In addition, a strict liability rule could be very burdensome even for small business activities that deploy AI-powered systems. In such cases, the introduction of strict liability is considered by some premature, the mere reversal of the burden of the proof looking more appropriate at the current state of development.[103]

In any event, strict liability does not appear as a stand-alone solution, requiring instead to be complemented by insurance mechanisms that provide incentives for claim redress against the producers. Where the deployment of AI systems creates high risks, a regime of strict liability even for non-commercial users, provided mandatory insurance and caps for recoverable losses are in place, is deemed acceptable.[104]

VIII.   OLD AND NEW TYPES OF HARM

The hypothesis of adapting the current liability regimes to the harms caused by new technologies seems to be appropriate especially in the area of tangible harms: to life, bodily integrity and property. In other words, it deals quite well with 'new ways to inflict old harms',[105] such as in the case of cyber-physical systems that happen to injure someone or damage their property. Robotic technologies, despite frequent outcries to the contrary, are not disruptive of

---

[102]   Wendehorst (n 92) 157, 178, expresses strong criticism towards a rule of strict liability that would equally apply to professional operators and to consumers.

[103]   For this criticism, Hacker (n 30) 16–17.

[104]   Spindler (n 55) 140 f.

[105]   Jonathan Morgan, 'Torts and Technology' in Roger Brownsword, Eloise Scotford and Karen Yeung (eds.), *The Oxford Handbook of Law, Regulation, and Technology* (Oxford University Press, 2017) 524.

the legal order and remain compatible with the foundational assumptions of tort law.

On the contrary, in the area of AI systems used for decision-making in the private and public sector, we are faced with both new ways to inflict harm and 'new kinds of harm'.[106] These new kinds of harm can be economic losses of tremendous proportions, such as in the flash crisis of 2010 generated by automated computer programs;[107] or can be material or immaterial harms incurred as a consequence of biased decisions in the fields of employment, housing or the credit market, or derived from manipulative information such as in personalised newsfeeds. Privacy infringements and violations of dignity can occur with massive surveillance enabled by AI tools or predictive policing. In the area of electronic commerce, practices such as price discrimination or targeted advertising can have an impact on the commercial behaviour of individuals, leading to compulsive consumption and pecuniary losses. Psychological harm (not amounting to damage to health) may derive from the use of mental health apps, and algorithmic practices embedded in social networks such as fake news or hate speech may cause mental distress.

The distinction between embodied AI systems, on the one hand, that are more likely to create physical damage and software-based AI applications, on the other hand, causing damage to fundamental rights different from health and bodily integrity or other kinds of harm[108] is disregarded in the general definition of AI system provided in Article 3(1) of the AIA. However, it finds a rough correspondence with the binary classification of high-risk systems adopted therein. High-risk systems can be AI products or components of a product already subjected to European safety legislation requiring third-party conformity assessment (for instance, machinery, toys and medical devices).[109] Alternatively, they can be stand-alone AI applications in certain contexts of use such as management of critical infrastructure, employment, education or access to private and public services for essential needs.[110]

---

[106] ibid. 527.

[107] Tom CW Lin, 'The New Investor' (2012–13) 60 UCLA Law Review 678; Yesha Yadav, 'The Failure of Liability in Modern Markets' (2016) 102 Virginia Law Review 1031.

[108] Even purely digital AI may cause physical damage: for instance, an expert system provides a wrong diagnosis or recommends an inappropriate dosage of a drug or radiotherapy, and as a consequence the patient is harmed. However, in such cases the mistake is normally mediated by human action and the responsibility rests on the professional who relied on the machine's output.

[109] Art 6(1).

[110] Art 6(2). Annex III contains a list of eight areas in which the use of AI systems is considered high-risk. Other devices can be added to the list pursuant to the criteria and procedure regulated in Article 7.

Roughly speaking, the first type of high-risk systems seems to pose primarily tangible risks that, as such, are covered by European safety legislation. The safety measures in place focus especially on risks to health, while they do not address risks to other fundamental rights (nor even include mental health risks);[111] these measures would continue to apply but would be complemented by the new requirements set out by the AIA.

Stand-alone AI systems to be used in the areas included in Annex III are (with some exceptions) more likely to cause social types of harms[112] that for several reasons are refractory to the liability perspective. The criticalities we can point to are the difficulty of identifying the tortfeasor, which exists especially for offences taking place in the digital realm (such as in e-commerce practices or in the context of social networks), the difficulties in accessing the evidence needed to substantiate a case, and the often modest amount of the damage that would be recovered. All these factors would discourage legal action, and therefore deprive the instrument of tort law from achieving its main goals, that is, prevention of accidents and compensation of the individuals who are wronged.

The placing on the market of safe and trustworthy AI products requires the creation of a system of legality by design that directly invests the architecture of the said systems,[113] and ensures that they comply from the outset of the development process with fundamental rights and with the basic tenets of the legal order.

Therefore, it is to be appreciated that the proposal for a regulation on AI introduces strict requirements in terms of transparency, documentation management and traceability, human oversight, robustness, security and data quality that have to be respected in the design of the algorithm and in the subsequent development and testing phases.[114] These measures will improve

---

[111] European Commission, 'Report from the Commission to the European Parliament, the Council and the European Economic and Social Committee on the safety and liability implications of Artificial Intelligence, the Internet of Things, and Robotics' (n 10) 8, called for the inclusion of mental health risks among the potential damage to be prevented with dedicated product safety rules. Said damage may derive, for instance, from the collaboration with humanoid robots, especially in the case of vulnerable persons.

[112] The dichotomy between physical and social risks, and the different treatment they should receive, is clearly depicted in the Response (n 35), 6–8. On the category of 'social risks' see also Wendehorst (n 92) 163–4.

[113] Nemitz (n 37), 10–13; Hacker (n 30).

[114] Roger Brownsword, *Law, Technology and Society. Re-imagining the Regulatory Environment* (Routledge, 2019) 264, stressing how design and technological measures embedded in the products will supplement traditional rules and more and more serve regulatory purposes.

the safety and reliability of any AI device, thus diminishing the risk of harm to the users.

However, safety and liability legislation are complementary:[115] the AIA is an ex ante instrument, including oversight mechanisms, aimed at the minimisation of the risks of harm, while liability initiatives deal with the ex post compensation once such harm has occurred. Therefore, next to the regulatory oversight that is accomplished through the pre-emptive conformity assessment of a product by specialised agencies, tort law will continue to play a regulatory role – more precisely, it will serve to assess the risks in the context of the actual injury, and it will provide insights into the type of harms inconceivable ex ante. In turn, the knowledge gained in this process may lead to expansion of the scope of preventative measures and make them more effective.

Moreover, until the Regulation is enacted, tort law is, as often happens with new technologies, the only available regulation of these phenomena,[116] to be tested in its adequacy to tackle the challenge of wrongs involving the use of AI systems. A wide-reaching framework for addressing these harms is the General Data Protection Regulation (GDPR): Article 82 applies in the case of damage deriving from any treatment of personal data that infringes the GDPR. A broad definition of personal data makes almost inevitable the processing of personal data when using AI tools for decision assistance or mere profiling. In addition, the GDPR adopts a strict liability model[117] that is aimed at easing the position of the victim, given the complexity of automated processing and the intense protection afforded to identity, privacy and data protection rights. By allowing the processor or controller to escape liability only by demonstrating that he is 'not in any way' responsible for the event causing the damage, the GDPR has increased the objective nature of liability. Both tangible and intangible losses are recoverable under this scheme, and this feature suits the peculiar instances of the damage that can occur in this area.

The application of Article 82 of the GDPR to AI-enabled torts has some drawbacks: the burden of proof for the claimant can be heavy to discharge[118] since it demands identification of the controller of the processing among potential multiple operators involved; the claimant has to prove that the pro-

---

[115] Wendehorst (n 92) 153–5. In light of the expected EU legislation aimed at addressing liability issues related to AI systems, the Commission Staff Working document accompanying the text of the proposal (SWD(2021) 84 final, 21.4.2021, 9) details that 'compliance with the requirements of the AI horizontal framework will be taken into account for assessing liability of actors under future liability rules'.

[116] Morgan (n 105) 523.

[117] Brendan Van Alsenoy, 'Liability under EU Data Protection Law. From Directive 95/46 to the General Data Protection Regulation' (2016) 7 JIPITEC 271, 273.

[118] ibid. 275.

cessing violated a provision of the GDPR; and also has to show the causality between the unlawful processing and the actual damage.

Notwithstanding these limitations, Article 82 appears a suitable remedy to deal with many of the accidents involving the use of automated decision-making: it covers material and immaterial losses, thus allowing for the recovery of damage to fundamental rights; it can be complemented with the form of collective redress regulated in Article 80, in order to overcome the problem of the lack of incentives to sue for small claims. The explicit acknowledgement that internet intermediaries remain subject to the E-commerce Directive and the liability exemptions established therein (Article 2(4)) does not seem to constitute a problem: on the one hand, the E-commerce Directive is under revision and the Digital Services Act will also introduce new obligations for internet service providers; on the other hand, the intermediary that performs operations going beyond mere storage or distribution of content activities could be considered a *de facto* controller.

IX.   ROBOTS AS E-PERSONS

An attentive evaluation needs to be devoted to the proposal of endowing robots and autonomous systems with legal personality. This option was first formulated in the context of the European Parliament Resolution of 2017, which recommends exploring the possibility of 'creating a specific legal status for robots in the long run, so that at least the most sophisticated autonomous robots could be established as having the status of electronic persons responsible for making good any damage they may cause, and possibly applying electronic personality to cases where robots make autonomous decisions or otherwise interact with third parties independently'.[119] Other documents, for instance a POSTnote of the UK Parliamentary Office of Science and Technology dealing with robotics in social care, echoed this proposition, including 'legal personality' among the regulatory challenges in this field.[120]

More generally, the idea sparked a rich debate both in science and technology journals[121] and in the legal doctrine. The immediacy of the reaction was sometimes to the detriment of the depth of the analysis, and thus to the

---

[119] Para 59(f).

[120] Houses of Parliament, Parliamentary Office of Science & Technology, POSTnote n 591 December 2018 'Robotics in social care' 4.

[121] More than 150 experts from several European countries wrote an Open Letter to the European Commission, 'Artificial Intelligence and Robotics' www.robotics -openletter.eu/ accessed 9 November 2021, expressing strong disapproval. With a following letter to Nature, this initiative was backed by Luciano Floridi and Mariarosa Taddeo, 'Don't grant robots legal personhood' (2018) 557 Nature 309.

strength and relevance of the criticism. In the 2017 Resolution, attributing legal status to robots appears a practical solution for alleviating the position of victims of accidents involving an autonomous machine. Such a scheme would ensure a one-stop shop for the damaged person and a faster procedure to gain relief, were the legal personality accompanied by an absolute criterion for liability and, possibly, the adoption of insurance. Regardless of the clarity of this rationale (highlighted also by the order of appearance of the proposal in the document – a sort of last resort, in case the models previously listed were considered insufficient or inappropriate), misunderstandings have occurred, leading to it being labelled as 'ideological and non-sensical and non-pragmatic'[122], or 'counterintuitive' since robots do not possess the 'qualities typically associated with human persons'.[123]

A technical and functional outlook is more appropriate instead, that contextualises the proposal and evaluates it on its own merit. On these premises, we can rebut other types of criticism: for instance, observing that it would be unreasonable to hold a robot liable since it has no assets to compensate for the damage[124] neglects the fact that equipping the robot with an asset is an obvious implication of the proposal, which does not even need to be expressly stated. The same applies to the claim that 'standards of "conduct" for these e-persons' are necessary in order to assess their liability,[125] when it is clear that legal personhood would go hand in hand with strict, if not absolute, liability.

The appeal of the creation of legal persons in the area of tort liability deserves a deeper reflection that dives into the conceptual and practical reasons put forward by the legal doctrine in support of such an extension of the traditional category. These can be articulated along two lines of reasoning: on the one hand, legal personhood for robots would guarantee that there is always a remedy available for harms caused by intelligent systems; on the other hand, qualifying the latter as legal agents would mirror the factual delegation of tasks to robots that is happening in many sectors. On a practical level, attributing legal personhood to the machines would be an effective tool for handling the consequences of wrongful interactions; in the symbolic sphere, it would reflect more accurately the reality of activities performed autonomously and without human input.

The first argument is especially concerned with potential gaps in the protection that traditional regimes could leave open: for instance, when a defect in the product is not detectable or the activity carried out cannot be considered

---

[122] Open Letter (n 121).
[123] UNESCO World Commission on the Ethics of Scientific Knowledge and Technology (COMEST), 'Report on Robotics Ethics' (14 September 2017) para 201.
[124] Koch (n 36) 115.
[125] ibid.

extra-hazardous. Holding the robot liable under a strict liability principle would offer a practical solution also for accidents whose dynamics are unexplainable, at the same time reducing the transactional cost of ascertaining the different responsibilities in very complex ecosystems.[126]

A possible answer to these concerns lies in the analysis developed above that has tried to prove the aptness of tort law systems at the European and national level to govern the emergence of new technologies. Admittedly, some features of robotic and AI systems put a strain on the current regimes, and situations could arise in which none of them is fitting and applicable due to the specificities of the facts. However, contingencies of this kind seem quite rare, therefore for the time being they do not seem to be a very sound basis to support the adoption of such a breakthrough innovation. Once introduced, e-personhood would not have a punctiform quality, operating only in the interstices where a gap in protection manifests itself. On the contrary, its adoption would entail an overall recourse to the category and, more generally, a radical change in the architecture of (at a minimum) the tort law department, to the point of appearing exorbitant compared to the aims that drive this idea. Having in mind a pragmatic approach to the inquiry about legal personhood for artificial agents,[127] one is led to wonder whether such an approach is not doomed to open up more problems than it solves. Focusing on the technicalities, some have argued that holding (only) the AI system liable is not desirable for it negatively affects the goal of deterrence: no one would be exposed to the incentives inherent in the rules allocating liability, since the accountable 'person' is intrinsically immune from their influence.[128] In the case where the producers were obliged to contribute to a large extent to the robot funding – as a way of apportioning the costs of liability according to a prediction of the potential impact of the various players in the causation of damages – they would pass these costs on to the purchasers by raising the price of the products,[129] and would continue not to perceive the deterrent effect of liability. Schemes that are even more complex could be envisioned, in which different subjects are called on to contribute to building the robot's assets. This model

---

[126] Samir Chopra and Laurence F White, *A Legal Theory for Autonomous Artificial Agents* (University of Michigan Press, 2011) 119–51; David C Vladeck, 'Machines Without Principals: Liability Rules and Artificial Intelligence' (2014) 89 Washington Law Rev 141–50.

[127] Mireille Hildebrandt, *Law for Computer Scientists and Other Folk* (Oxford University Press, 2020) 246, condenses the inquiry into three sub-questions: what problems such attribution solves; what problems it does not solve; and what problems it creates.

[128] Wagner (n 47) 57.

[129] Wagner (n 47) 58–9.

would distribute the costs associated with liability among the various players active in the value chain: in order to reflect different shares of responsibility, each player could contribute in proportion to the level of involvement in the creation of risks. However, the lack of immediate accountability may lead to a lessening of the incentives to invest in safety and security.

Other drawbacks derive precisely from the surrounding requirements of legal personhood: since its functioning requires nonetheless identifying the person who is obliged to fund the robot or to purchase insurance for it, this person could be held directly liable, thus avoiding an 'unnecessary complication'.[130] Establishing the robot as the liable entity would in fact have the practical advantage of limiting the resources destined to compensate damages to the separate asset of the e-person. However, limited liability is seen as problematic since it can leave the victims without appropriate redress. Further, if that effect were precisely the aim of the reform, it would be better to tackle the problem of setting caps for liability directly,[131] instead of arriving at the same result through such a convoluted route.

The argument that appeals to the representational and classificatory function of the law points instead to the necessity of reconciling the substance of robots and AI systems acting as true agents and the formal category that can more accurately express this reality.[132] When the delegation of human tasks, such as driving or making a medical diagnosis, to robots becomes common, describing them as mere tools and their failures as manufacturing or design defects does not render justice to the expressive role of legal qualifications.[133] The notion of legal agents would be more accurate at a conceptual level and more useful as to the governance of the effects of their actions.

This position has an apparent sound logic, but to some extent it assumes a reality that has not taken place yet, and it will probably never materialise as such. One flaw of this reasoning is precisely that it overestimates the autonomy of intelligent systems: what can be appreciated from a technological viewpoint does not exist in a social and economic meaning. The activities that the robot autonomously carries out have to be understood as tasks that the machine performs in order for a human or a company to benefit personally, professionally or commercially from it. An intelligent system can never be represented in

---

[130] Borghetti (n 51) 73; Wendehorst (n 92) 156.

[131] Wagner (n 47) 59; and for a thorough analysis, Gerhard Wagner, 'Robot, Inc.: Personhood for Autonomous Systems?' (2019) 88 Fordham Law Review 591; Karner, 'Liability for Robotics: Current Rules, Challenges, and the Need for Innovative Concepts' (n 53) 123.

[132] Chopra and White (n 126) 150.

[133] Jason Millar and Ian Kerr, 'Delegation, Relinquishment, and Responsibility: The Prospect of Expert Robots' in Ryan Calo, A Michael Fromkin and Ian Kerr (eds.), *Robot Law* (Edward Elgar Publishing, 2016) 114–15.

isolation because it will always be part of a human-machine unit that gives meaning and direction to its activities. Therefore, we perhaps need novel ways to seize and express this condition in legal terms, but we can reasonably exclude the idea that robot personhood is the most appropriate of these.

4.   AI-Generated Torts

Ryan Abbott[1]

AI already diagnoses disease, drafts legal contracts and provides translation services. But what happens when these AI systems cause harm? What happens when a machine fails to diagnose a cancer, writes a faulty agreement or starts a war? How should the law respond to accidents caused by AI? With an already existing body of law developed to deal with accidents, tort law will play a central role in answering these and other questions. A tort is a harmful civil act, as opposed to a criminal one, other than under contract, where one person is damaged by another, and it gives way to a right to sue. The goals of tort law are many: to reduce accidents, provide a peaceful means of dispute resolution, promote positive social values and so forth.[2]

Whether tort law is the best means for achieving all these goals is debatable, but jurists are united in considering accident reduction one of the central aims, if not the primary one, of tort law.[3] By creating a framework for shifting the costs of accidents from injured victims to those who caused harm (tortfeasors), tort law deters unsafe conduct. A purely financially motivated rational actor will reduce potentially harmful activity to the extent that the cost of accidents exceeds the benefits of the activity.[4] This liability framework has far-reaching

---

[1]   Professor of Law and Health Sciences, University of Surrey School of Law and Adjunct Assistant Professor of Medicine, David Geffen School of Medicine at University of California, Los Angeles. This chapter was adapted from Ryan Abbott, 'The Reasonable Computer: Disrupting the Paradigm of Tort Liability' (2018) 86 Geo Wash L Rev 1.
[2]   See George L Priest, 'Satisfying the Multiple Goals of Tort Law' (1988) 22 Val U L Rev 643, 648.
[3]   See for example, George L Priest, 'The Invention of Enterprise Liability: A Critical History of the Intellectual Foundations of Modern Tort Law' (1985) 14 J Legal Stud 461; see also Robert F Blomquist, 'Goals, Means, and Problems for Modern Tort Law: A Reply to Professor Priest' (1988) 22 Val U L Rev 621 (arguing that economic theory and moral philosophy both require accident reduction to be the primary aim of tort law).
[4]   See *United States v Carroll Towing Co.* 159 F.2d 169, 173 (2d Cir. 1947) (applying a rule that balances the burden of additional protections on the actor with the probability and gravity of an injury).

and sometimes complex impacts on behaviour.[5] It can either accelerate or impede the introduction of new technologies.

This chapter primarily considers US law, although there is substantial overlap between tort liability systems in common law jurisdictions, and even civil law jurisdictions. In the US, most injuries caused by people are evaluated under a negligence standard in which liability depends on whether there was unreasonable conduct. This generally requires proof that a defendant acted unreasonably considering foreseeable risks. The standard is premised on what an objective and hypothetical 'reasonable' person would have done under the same circumstances. When an AI causes those same injuries, however, a strict liability standard applies. Strict liability is a theory of liability without fault; it applies without regard to whether a defendant's conduct is socially blameworthy. This distinction has financial consequences and a corresponding impact on the rate of technology adoption. It discourages automation because there is a greater risk of liability when an AI performs the same activity as a person. It also means that in cases where automation would improve safety, the current framework to prevent accidents may have the opposite effect.

I have argued elsewhere in favour of a regulatory principle of 'AI legal neutrality' by which the law should tend not to discriminate between human and AI behaviour in order to help the law better achieve its underlying goals.[6] In the context of tort law, the principle of AI legal neutrality suggests that differential treatment of AI and human behaviour is problematic, and that the acts of AI tortfeasors should be evaluated under a negligence standard, rather than a strict liability standard, in cases where an AI behaves like a human tortfeasor in the traditional negligence paradigm. Liability would be based on an AI's behaviour rather than its design. Such a system would help to encourage the adoption of AI in cases where it outperforms people from a safety perspective. It would also provide an added benefit in cases where AI activity would currently be evaluated under a strict 'product liability' framework which may require injured parties to demonstrate the existence of a design defect in an AI in order to establish liability. When an AI causes harm, it may be difficult to prove a design defect due to system complexity or limited explainability.

---

[5]   See *Helling v Carey* 519 P.2d 981, 983 (Wash. 1974) (holding that the standard of care in the profession of ophthalmology should not insulate providers from failure to test for glaucoma); Gideon Parchomovsky and Alex Stein, 'Torts and Innovation' (2008) 107 Mich L Rev 285, 286 (discussing how the role of custom in tort law impedes innovation). Nor is the idea that tort liability is a barrier to developments in AI new. See Steven J Frank, 'Tort Adjudication and the Emergence of Artificial Intelligence Software' (1987) 21 Suffolk U L Rev 623, 639.

[6]   Ryan Abbott, *The Reasonable Robot: Artificial Intelligence and the Law* (Cambridge University Press, 2020).

A negligence-based framework based on an AI's behaviour rather than its design would help to avoid this problem. For the purposes of ultimate financial liability, the AI's supplier (e.g. manufacturers and retailers) should still be responsible for satisfying judgments, which is largely the case under standard principles of product liability law.

The most important implication of this line of reasoning is that just as AI tortfeasors should be compared to human tortfeasors, so too should humans be compared to AI. Once AI becomes safer than people and practical to substitute for people, AI should set the baseline for the new standard of care. This means that human defendants would no longer have their liability based on what a hypothetical reasonable person would have done in the situation, but what an AI would have done. In time, as AI comes to increasingly outperform people, this rule will mean that someone's best efforts would no longer be sufficient to avoid liability. It would not mandate automation in the interests of freedom and autonomy, but people would engage in certain activities at their own peril. Such a rule is consistent with the rationale for the objective standard of the reasonable person, and it would benefit the general welfare. Eventually, the continually improving 'reasonable AI' standard should apply to AI tortfeasors, at which point AI should cause so little harm that the primary effect of the standard would make human tortfeasors essentially strictly liable for their harms.

The chapter, divided into three sections, reconstructs tort law for the time when AI becomes a safer and more practical alternative to humans. Section 1 provides background on injuries caused by machines and how the law has evolved to address these harms. It also discusses the role of tort law in injury prevention and the development of negligence and strict product liability. Section 2 argues that while some forms of automation should prevent accidents, the current tort framework may act as a deterrent to adopting safer technologies. This section proposes a new categorisation of AI-generated torts, contends that the acts of AI tortfeasors should be evaluated under a negligence rather than a strict liability standard and goes on to propose rules for implementing the system. Finally, Section 3 contends that once AI becomes safer than people and automation is practical, the reasonable AI, or the 'reasonable robot' in the case of a physically embodied AI, should become the new standard of care. It explains how this standard would function, considers when the standard should apply to AI tortfeasors and argues that the reasonable AI standard works better than the standard of a reasonable person using an AI. At some point, AI will be so safe that the standard's most significant effect would be to internalise the cost of accidents on human tortfeasors.

I.   LIABILITY FOR MACHINE INJURIES

A.   A Brief History

For as long as people have used machines, injuries have resulted – and machines have been with us for quite some time. The earliest evidence of simple machines, tools that redirect force to make work easier like pulleys and levers, dates back millions of years to the beginning of the Stone Age. In fact, the Stone Age is so named because it is characterised by the use of stone to make simple machines such as axes. The primary function of these tools was to hunt and cut meat, but they were also used to facilitate violence against people – and no doubt used negligently as well. As the use and complexity of simple machines grew, so too did the resultant injuries – Mesopotamian surgeons botched procedures and Greek construction zones were so dangerous they required that physicians be on-site. Such injuries continued unabated from the time complex machines were invented by the ancient Chinese and Greeks to the time of the first modern industrial machines.

The Industrial Revolution marked a turning point in the role of machines in society. Major technological advances in textiles, transportation and iron-making occurred during this period, and these resulted in the development of machines for shaping materials and the rise of the factory system as well as a dramatic increase in the number and severity of machine injuries. Working in industrial settings was dangerous business, in part because employers often had minimal liability for employee harms. These dangerous working conditions persisted well into the twentieth century before the US government began collecting data on work-related injuries in a systematic way. In 1913, the Bureau of Labor estimated that 23,000 workers died from work-related injuries (albeit an imperfect proxy for machine injuries) out of a workforce of 38 million, a rate of 61 deaths per 100,000 workers.[7]

In the modern era, the rate of work-related injuries has declined significantly. In 2017, for example, the Bureau of Labor reported 5,147 fatal work injuries, a rate of 3.5 per 100,000 workers.[8] There are several reasons for this decline: changes to tort liability, evolved societal and ethics norms that place a greater priority on human welfare, a modern system of regulations and criminal liability that protects worker well-being and improvements in safety

---

[7]   'Improvements in Workplace Safety – United States, 1900–1999' (1999) 48 CDC Morbidity & Mortality Wkly. Rep. 461, 461. The National Safety Council estimates that 18,000–21,000 workers died from work-related injuries in 1912.

[8]   Bureau of Labor Statistics, US Department of Labor, 'National Census of Fatal Occupational Injuries in 2017' (Bureau of Labor Statistics 2018) 1 www.bls.gov/news .release/pdf/cfoi.pdf.

technology. Yet, despite significant progress in workplace safety, accidents are still a serious societal concern. Every year, just in the United States, workplace accidents cost around $190 billion and are responsible for about 4,000 deaths. More broadly, unintentional injuries cost around $850 billion and kill more than 150,000 people annually, around 6 per cent of all deaths.[9] According to the Centers for Disease Control and Prevention (CDC), unintentional injuries are the fourth leading cause of death.[10]

B.   Tort Law as a Mechanism for Accident Prevention

Part of the reason for the decline in workplace injuries is that tort law provides a stronger financial incentive for safer conduct. The law has evolved from a system designed to insulate employers and manufacturers from liability to one with greater regard for worker and consumer health. In its quest to reduce accidents, tort law has far-reaching and sometimes complex impacts on behaviour; it can either accelerate the introduction of new technologies, as is the case with the use of glaucoma testing (the obligatory puff of air one has come to expect in an optometrist's office), or discourage the use of new technologies, as is generally the case in medical care, a field in which the standard of care is usually based on customary practice.[11] Torts are typically categorised based on the level of fault they require (or based on the interests they protect). At one end of the spectrum are intentional torts involving intent to harm or malice; on the other are strict liability torts, which do not require fault. Covering the 'great mass of cases' in the middle are harms involving negligence.[12]

C.   Negligence

The concept of negligence is the primary theory through which courts deal with accidents and unintended harms. In practice, to prevail in most personal injury cases, a plaintiff (or claimant) must prove by a preponderance of evidence (more likely than not) that the defendant (or respondent) owed the plaintiff a duty of reasonable care, the defendant breached that duty, the breach caused the plaintiff's damages, and the plaintiff suffered compensable damages. This generally requires proof that the defendant acted negligently, which is to

---

[9]   National Safety Council, 'Injury Facts: 2016' (3rd ed., 2016) 8.
[10]   CDC, 'Accidents or Unintentional Injuries' www.cdc.gov/nchs/fastats/accidental-injury.htm accessed 25/03/2022.
[11]   See note 5 supra.
[12]   Oliver Wendell Holmes Jr, 'The Theory of Torts' (1873) 7 Am L Rev 652, 653 in Sheldon M Novick (ed.), *1 The Collected Works of Justice Holmes* (University of Chicago Press, 1995) 327.

say, they acted unreasonably considering foreseeable risks. This standard is premised on what an objective and hypothetical reasonable person would do under the same circumstances. Thus, if the courts determine that a reasonable person would not have headed out to sea without a radio (the means by which to receive warnings of inclement weather),[13] manufactured a ginger beer with a snail inside[14] or dropped heavy objects off the side of a building[15] (all real and famous cases involving careless behaviour), then these activities could expose a defendant to liability.

Society has interests in sometimes competing values: reducing injuries and compensating victims as well as encouraging economic growth and progress. One way that tort law attempts to achieve a balance is by permitting recovery in negligence, only where there has been socially blameworthy conduct. Thus, where a defendant has acted reasonably, even if the defendant has caused serious injury to a plaintiff, there will generally be no liability. Juries play a key role in determining the reasonable person standard as applied to the facts of a case.

D.   Strict and Product Liability

While negligence governs virtually all accidents, there are exceptions. For instance, defendants may be strictly liable – liable without fault – for harms they cause as a result of certain types of activities like disposing of hazardous waste or using explosives. Thus, a defendant corporation that takes every reasonable care to prevent injury before dusting crops might nevertheless find itself liable for injuries it causes to a bystander. One of the most important modern applications of strict liability is to product liability, which refers to responsibility for the commercial transfer of a product that causes harm because it is defective, or its properties are falsely represented. Product injuries cause upward of 200 million injuries a year in the United States.[16] In most instances, members of the supply chain (e.g. manufacturers and retailers) are strictly liable for defective products.[17] The bulk of product liability cases involve claims for damages against a manufacturer or retailer by a person injured while using a product.[18] Typically, a plaintiff will try to prove that an injury was the result of some inherent defect of a product or its marketing, and that the product was flawed or falsely advertised. Defendants, in turn, attempt

---

[13]   See *The TJ Hooper* 53 F.2d 107 (SDNY 1931).
[14]   See *Donoghue v Stevenson* [1932] AC 562 (HL) (appeal taken from Scot.).
[15]   See *Byrne v Boadle* (1863) 159 Eng. Rep. 299.
[16]   David G Owen, *Products Liability Law* (3rd ed., Thomson West, 2014) 1.
[17]   ibid. 3.
[18]   ibid.

to prove that their products were reasonably designed, properly made, and accurately marketed. Defendants may argue that plaintiff injuries were the result of improper and unforeseeable use of the product, or that something other than the product caused the harm.

Product liability was not always governed by strict liability. Originally, US courts followed the historic English doctrine of *caveat emptor* (let the buyer beware) for product liability claims, reflecting a national philosophy embracing individualism and free enterprise. Toward the end of the nineteenth century, however, states began increasingly employing the doctrine of *caveat venditor* (let the seller beware) and an implied warranty of merchantable quality. Under this doctrine, '[s]elling for a sound price raises an implied warranty that the thing sold is free from defects, known and unknown [to the seller]'.[19] Yet even so, manufacturers were in large part able to avoid liability for defective products by essentially arguing that they lacked a contract with consumers (privity of contract). This was possible because in most cases consumers purchased products from third-party retailers rather than directly from manufacturers.

This changed in 1916 with the New York Court of Appeals decision in *MacPherson v Buick Motor Co*,[20] a case involving a motorist who was injured when one of the wooden wheels of his Buick collapsed. He subsequently attempted to sue the manufacturer (Buick) rather than the dealership where he purchased the vehicle. The court, in rejecting a defence based on privity of contact, held that if 'the manufacturer of such a foreseeably dangerous product knows that it will be used by persons other than the purchaser, and used without new tests, then, irrespective of contract, the manufacturer of this thing of danger is under a duty to make it carefully'.[21] *MacPherson* spurred negligence claims against manufacturers across the country as one by one state courts adopted the case's holding. This shift was accompanied by growing public support for consumer protection, together with the understanding that liability would not unduly burden economic activity. Businesses are often in the best position to prevent product injuries and can distribute liability through insurance. In 1963, the Supreme Court of California decided *Greenman v Yuba Power Products Inc*,[22] which held that manufacturers of defective products are strictly liable for injuries they cause. This case represents the birth of modern product liability law in the United States. After this decision, the doctrine of strict product liability spread rapidly across the nation.

---

[19] *Gardiner v Gray* (1815) 171 Eng Rep 46, 47 (KB).
[20] 111 N.E. 1050 (N.Y. 1916).
[21] ibid. 1053.
[22] 377 P.2d 897 (Cal. 1963) (in bank).

Of course, today's product liability law is not as simple as this brief narrative suggests. It combines tort law (e.g. negligence, strict liability and deceit), contract law (e.g. warranty), both common and statutory law (e.g. statutory sales law under Article 2 of the Uniform Commercial Code) and a hodge-podge of state 'reform' acts. State statutes have attempted to reform product liability law, often to limit the rights of consumers in order to protect manufacturers. For our purposes, however, it suffices to say this: as a general matter, manufacturers and retailers are strictly liable for injuries caused by defective products.

II.   AI-GENERATED TORTS

A.   Automation Will Prevent Accidents

On 18 March 2018, an autonomous vehicle (AV) operated by Uber killed a pedestrian in Arizona.[23] The AV, a Volvo XC90 SUV, was in autonomous mode when it struck Elaine Herzberg, who was crossing the street with her bicycle, at around 10 p.m. The AV was equipped with a light detection and ranging system (lidar), which illuminates targets with pulsed laser light and measures the reflected pulses with a sensor. Lidar should reveal objects hundreds of feet away at night as well as during the day. Indeed, Uber's self-driving software detected Herzberg but failed to stop in time. Because the AV was still in testing, Uber had a 'backup' driver in the vehicle to take control in the event that the software failed. However, the driver was watching *The Voice*, a TV show, on her mobile phone and failed to notice Herzberg in time. For that matter, Herzberg was crossing an unmarked, unlit segment of road at night. There seems to have been plenty of blame to go around, but nothing absolves the AV of failing to stop. This event is the first pedestrian fatality involving an AV, and it is generally considered the first death caused by an AV. Earlier fatalities had occurred with Tesla drivers operating in autopilot mode, but regulators did not consider the AV at fault in those cases.

Surveys of attitudes toward self-driving cars have produced mixed results but have often uncovered negative opinions. A 2016 survey by the American Automobile Association reported that three out of four US drivers surveyed said they would feel 'afraid' to ride in a self-driving car.[24] Only one in five said they would trust a driverless car to drive itself while they were inside. Another survey found that most UK citizens would feel uncomfortable with

---

[23]   Kate Conger, 'Driver Charged in Uber's Fatal 2018 Autonomous Car Crash' *New York Times* (New York, 15 September 2020).

[24]   Erin Stepp, 'Three-Quarters of Americans "Afraid" to Ride in Self-Driving Vehicle' (*AAA NewsRoom*, 1 March 2016) newsroom.aaa.com/2016/03/three-quarters-of-americans-afraid-to-ride-in-a-self-driving-vehicle/ accessed 24 March 2022.

self-driving vehicles on the road, and more than three-quarters would want to retain a steering wheel.[25] Regulators are more optimistic, but they are still being cautious. Until 2016, California required human drivers be present in all self-driving cars being tested on public roads. Unmanned vehicles can now operate on public roads under certain circumstances.[26]

Yet much of the public discourse on self-driving cars is misguided. The critical issue is not whether AI is perfect (it is not), but whether it is safer than people (it will be). Nearly all crashes, 94 per cent, involve human error.[27] A human driver causes a fatality about every 100 million miles, resulting in tremendous human and financial costs.[28] The US Department of Transportation estimates the economic costs of those accidents at more than $240 billion.[29] More than 35,000 people die from motor vehicle accidents each year in the United States, and more than a million die each year worldwide.[30] Someone is killed in a motor vehicle accident on average about once every twenty-five seconds.

By contrast, the Uber fatality was the first known death in hundreds of millions of miles driven by AVs. It is also important to note that driverless technologies are in their infancy, but they will be dramatically improved in a decade. At the point where automated cars are ten times safer than human drivers, that could reduce the annual number of US motor vehicle fatalities to about 3,500. This is the conclusion of a report from the consulting firm McKinsey & Company, which predicts AVs will reduce the number of auto-mobile deaths by about 30,000 a year.[31] However, the report estimates that

---

[25]   David Neal, 'Over Half of Brits Won't Feel Safe Using the Streets with Driverless Cars' (*The Inquirer*, 17 October 2016) www.theinquirer.net/inquirer/news/2474351/over-half-of-brits-wont-feel-safe-using-the-streets-with-driverless-cars accessed 24 March 2022.

[26]   Susmita Baral, 'Driverless Car Laws in California Get Major Changes in September' (*International Business Times*, 3 October 2016) www.ibtimes.com/driverless-car-laws-californiaget-major-changes-september-2425689 accessed 24 March 2022.

[27]   National Highway Traffic Safety Admin, US Department of Transport, 'Federal Automated Vehicles Policy: Accelerating The Next Revolution In Roadway Safety' (2016) 5–7.

[28]   Alexander Hars, 'Top Misconceptions of Autonomous Cars and Self-Driving Vehicles' (*Inventivio*, 2016) www.Inventivio.Com/Innovationbriefs/2016-09/Top-Misconceptionsof-Self-Driving-Cars.Pdf.

[29]   Insurance Institute for Highway Safety, 'General Statistics' (December 2017) www.iihs.org/iihs/topics/t/general-statistics/fatalityfacts/overview-of-fatality-facts.

[30]   ibid.

[31]   Michele Bertoncello and Dominik Wee, 'Ten Ways Autonomous Driving Could Redefine the Automotive World' (*McKinsey & Co.*, 1 June 2015) www.mckinsey.com/

self-driving technologies will not be adopted widely enough to permit this outcome until the middle of the century.

AVs may be the most prominent and disruptive upcoming example of AI's automating activities with a significant risk of harm, but automation has the potential to improve safety in a variety of settings. For instance, IBM's AI Watson works with clinicians to analyse patient medical records and provide evidence-based cancer treatment options. Like self-driving cars, Watson does not need to be perfect to improve safety – it just needs to be better than people. Medical error is one of the leading causes of death. Estimates vary, but a 2016 study in the *British Medical Journal* reports that it is the third leading cause of death in the United States, behind cardiovascular disease and cancer (the CDC currently ranks unintentional injuries as the fourth leading cause of death but does not include medical error in cause of death rankings).[32] Some companies already claim their AI outperforms doctors at certain tasks, and those claims are believable. Why should AI not be able to outperform a person when the AI can access the entire wealth of medical literature with perfect recall, benefit from the experience of directly having treated millions of patients and be immune to fatigue?

B.   Strict Liability Discourages Automation

To see why the current tort framework discourages automation, let us turn to the question of when it makes economic sense for a business to replace a person with an AI. In practice, it may be complex to calculate the cost of a human driver versus a self-driving vehicle. Human employees have costs in excess of their salaries and wages, such as tax liability for employer portions of social security tax, Medicare tax, state and federal unemployment tax, and workers' compensation; employer portions of health insurance; paid holidays, vacations and sick days; and contributions toward retirement, pension, savings and profit-sharing plans. AI costs may be simpler to estimate, but they are also uncertain. There are likely to be costs associated with repair, maintenance and operation in addition to purchase or licence costs and taxes.

Added to the direct financial costs associated with employing an operator, there may be indirect financial and non-financial costs, known and unknown, that guide a decision. For example, a person may require vocational training

---

industries/automotive-and-assembly/our-insights/ten-ways-autonomous-driving-could -redefine-the-automotive-world accessed 24 March 2022.

[32]   Martin A Makary and Michael Daniel, 'Medical Error – The Third Leading Cause of Death in the US' (2016) 353 BMJ 2139, 2139; see also Linda T Kohn, Janet M Corrigan and Molla S Donaldson (eds.), *To Err Is Human: Building a Safer Health System* (Institute of Medicine, 2000).

or be unable to work due to sickness; AI may require software updates or malfunction. Employing human operators may result in greater expenses for legal fees, administrative and overhead costs, and compliance with regulatory and employment requirements. AI may infringe patents or result in negative publicity. Businesses deciding whether to automate may also consider broader social policies. For instance, they may choose not to automate because of a perception that it promotes income inequality and unemployment. But businesses are required to act in the best interests of shareholders, and most interpret this duty as a mandate to maximise profit rather than primarily promote social responsibility. The decision whether to employ a person or an AI, even where the two are capable of functioning interchangeably, will therefore be a complex one. Nevertheless, these are precisely the sorts of decisions that businesses are skilled at making – estimating uncertain future costs and making decisions as rational economic actors. Tort liability will only be one factor to consider when businesses are deciding whether to automate. But, in the aggregate, tort liability will influence AI adoption.

As with some of these other factors, the costs of tort liability may not be straightforward. For instance, a business end user might not be directly liable for harms caused by AI. The AI's manufacturer and other members of the supply chain will generally be liable if the harm was caused by a defect in the AI. By contrast, businesses will generally be liable for negligent harms caused by their employees, although they can attempt to limit this liability by, say, relying on independent contractors whose negligent harms businesses will not usually be liable for. Yet, even in cases where liability rests with a business supplier or an independent contractor, such liability should indirectly impact a business. A manufacturer or retailer might pass along its costs in the form of higher prices, or a business might need to pay an independent contractor more than an employee to have the contractor assume risk. The percentage of cost passed on to the business or consumer will depend on the market and price elasticity for that product. Although tort liability can be indirect and complex, and businesses can purchase insurance to manage risk, this does not change the fact that tort liability has a financial cost that influences behaviour.

If both human and AI operators cost a business the same amount to employ, the decision about which to utilise should be neutral. However, if a business introduces the variable of tort liability into the decision, assuming that an AI and person are competitive in terms of safety, a human operator would be the preferred hire. Harms caused by a person will be evaluated in negligence while those same harms caused by an AI will be evaluated in strict liability. It is generally easier to establish strict liability than negligence. Strict liability does not require careless manufacturer behaviour, only that a defect be present in a product or its marketing. The law favours people over AI, at least with regard to tort liability. This will hold true as long as AI is treated as an 'ordinary product' in which strict liability is – and will be – the default rule.

C.   AI-Generated Torts Should Be Negligence-Based

Holding AI-generated torts to a negligence standard would result in an improved outcome – it would accelerate automation where doing so would improve safety. Of course, moving from a strict liability to negligence standard will have some drawbacks. As mentioned earlier, strict liability creates a stronger incentive for manufacturers to make safer products, and manufacturers are likely better positioned than consumers to insure against loss. Indeed, this is why courts initially adopted strict product liability. AI-generated torts, however, differ from other product harms in that automation will result in net safety gains once AI becomes safer than people.

To illustrate this, imagine that an AV with current technology is ten times safer than a human driver. In this case, it would be better that one human driver be replaced by an AV than the same AV becoming a hundred times safer than a human driver. To see why this is so, assume a closed system with only two vehicles, where the risk of injury for a human driver is one fatality per 100 million miles driven and the risk of injury for an AV (model C-A) is one fatality per one billion miles driven. C-A is ten times safer than a person. Over the course of ten billion miles driven by the person and C-A, there will be an average of 110 fatalities. Now, imagine that C-A is improved an additional tenfold, such that its risk of causing injury is reduced to one fatality per ten billion miles (C-A+). Then, over the course of ten billion miles driven by the person and C-A+, there will be a total of 101 fatalities. If, however, instead of focusing efforts on improving C-A, the human driver is simply replaced with another C-A, then over the course of 10 billion miles driven by C-A and C-A, there will be a total of 20 fatalities. Once AI becomes safer than people, and particularly once AI becomes substantially safer than people, automating would result in very significant reductions in accident rates. At some point, it will be preferable to increase the adoption of safer technologies at the cost of weakening the incentive to incrementally improve product safety.

A negligence standard would, nevertheless, still influence manufacturers to improve AI safety in order to reduce their liability. If an AI causes an accident a person would have avoided, the AI's behaviour would fall below the standard of reasonable care and result in liability. Of course, automating with AI that is less safe than a person is not desired, and this is a reason why jurisdictions prohibit unrestricted use of fully autonomous vehicles. Because AVs cannot currently outperform human drivers in any condition, their use is limited to controlled settings, a pre-emptive alternative to waiting for them to cause accidents and then fighting over compensation.

However, to the extent that tort liability is relied on to limit the introduction and use of comparatively less safe technologies rather than regulatory prohibitions, holding AI-generated torts to a negligence standard would have the desired effect – AI manufacturers would be financially liable when their AI causes accidents a person would have avoided. This could occur if AI is mistakenly predicted to be safer than it really is at the time of its rollout, or if there are other compelling reasons to automate. For example, it might be that Tesla has reason to believe its self-driving cars are significantly safer than human drivers, but once its cars enter the marketplace they fail to meet expectations because, say, Tesla's research fails to consider the reactions of drivers to self-driving vehicles in states other than California.

Even an AI that is generally safer than a person will still cause accidents. If it causes an accident a person would have avoided, this will result in liability. An AV might cause an accident on average once every billion miles compared to a person who might cause an accident every hundred million miles, but any particular accident caused by the AV might still fall below the standard of reasonable care. Manufacturers will likely have the best information available to determine whether it would be better to pay to further reduce accident risks (e.g. whether an additional \$10,000 per AV is worth a 1 per cent reduction in accident risk, or whether to pay claims for additional accidents). Higher safety levels will not always be preferable as inefficiently high safety levels might result in prohibitively high prices for consumers. To the extent that society is not satisfied with a manufacturer's risk-benefit analysis on optimum safety levels, non-tort mechanisms could be brought to bear, such as regulatory mandates for minimum safety standards. Finally, if risk spreading is a concern, even though businesses are better positioned to acquire insurance, consumers also have options to purchase insurance, particularly in the automobile context.

There is further justification for separating out harms caused by ordinary products like *MacPherson*'s Buick and AI tortfeasors like Uber's AV. Society's relationship with technology has changed. Machines are no longer just inert tools directed by individuals. Rather, in at least some instances, AI is taking over activities once performed by people and causing the same sorts of harm these activities generate. What distinguishes an ordinary product from an AI tortfeasor in this system are the concepts of independence and control. Autonomous AI is given tasks to complete, and functionally determines for itself the means of completing those tasks. In some instances, machine learning can generate unpredictable behaviour, such that the means are not predictable either by those giving tasks to the AI or even by the AI's original programmers. Nonetheless, the difference between ordinary products and AI tortfeasors should not be based on predictability, only on social and practical outcomes. It makes no difference to a person run over by a self-driving car what type of AI was operating the vehicle. The physical outcome is the same whether an AI acts according to fixed or expert rules created by programmers or more complex machine learning algorithms such as neural networks that generate new and sometimes unforeseen behaviours. Ultimately, tort law should be functional and aspire to lower accident rates.

D.   Identifying AI-Generated Torts

Not all injuries in which a machine or AI is involved would be AI-generated torts. To illustrate, consider two hypothetical accidents:

(1) A crane operator drops a steel frame on a passer-by after incorrectly identifying the location for drop-off.
(2) A crane operator is appropriately manipulating a crane under normal conditions when it tips over and lands on a passer-by.

In the first example, as between the machine and the operator, it seems obvious (and it can be assumed) that the operator is at fault (although a creative plaintiff's attorney may argue that the crane was negligently designed to allow such an outcome). The machine did not interrupt a direct and foreseeable chain of events set in motion by the operator's action, even though the accident could not have occurred without the machine's involvement, making it a factual cause of the injury in tort's vernacular. It was essentially functioning as an extension of the operator. In the second hypothetical example, allocating fault is once again intuitively obvious. The machine was at fault rather than the operator. The operator acted with reasonable care, and the injury was due to (again it can be assumed) a flawed crane.

These two scenarios would result in different liability outcomes. In the first, the operator, and possibly the operator's employer, would be liable to the passer-by in negligence because the operator failed to exercise reasonable care. In the second, the manufacturer and retailer of the crane would be strictly liable to the passer-by, even if the manufacturer had exercised the utmost care in the design and construction of the crane. In both scenarios, an operator was using a crane in much the same way cranes have been used in construction for thousands of years. Granted, today's cranes utilise more sophisticated designs, are built from sturdier materials and have electric power; nevertheless, the basic dynamic between man and machine has changed little. The cranes used to build skyscrapers, the pulleys used to build the Giza pyramids and the cranes used to build the Parthenon all involved human operators controlling the movements of a simple or complex machine to redirect and amplify force.

Now imagine a third scenario:

(3) An AI-operated, unmanned crane drops a steel frame on a passer-by after incorrectly identifying the location for drop-off.

The law now treats Examples 2 and 3 the same way because they both involve defective products. Yet, in important respects, Examples 1 and 3 are more closely related. They involve the same sort of action and physical result. In Example 2, the machine is being used as a tool. In Example 3, an AI replaces a person, and it performs in essentially the same manner as a person. If the AI were a person, it would be liable in negligence and held to the standard of a reasonable person. Changing how these accidents are treated and holding suppliers of AI tortfeasors to a negligence standard require rules for distinguishing between AI-generated torts and other harms. The goal is to distinguish between cases in which a machine is used as a mere instrument and a person is at fault (Example 1), cases in which an ordinary product is at fault (Example 2) and cases in which there is an 'AI tortfeasor' (Example 3).

AI-generated torts could be those cases in which an AI engages in an activity that a person could engage in and acts in a manner that would be negligent for a human tortfeasor. If this rule is applied to the crane examples, Example 1 would result in human liability because the human operator acted carelessly and because the crane did not interrupt a foreseeable chain of events. There would be strict manufacturer liability in Example 2 because a person could not reasonably be substituted for a crane. Example 3 would require negligent manufacturer liability since the AI was automating a task that a person could have performed.

Sometimes this rule will have a clear application. For example, an AI that mistakenly 'reads' a chest X-ray in place of a radiologist would be occupying the position of a human tortfeasor, whereas a malfunctioning X-ray machine would be an ordinary product. In other instances, this distinction would not be clear-cut. Electrocardiogram (ECG) machines, a vital feature of emergency rooms where they are used to evaluate patients for heart conditions, often provide interpretation of raw data but generally state that any analysis is preliminary and that health care providers are ultimately responsible for diagnosis.

In the context of the self-driving car, under the most widely adopted framework, vehicles are categorised on a zero to five scale based on 'who does what, when'.[33] At level zero, the human driver does everything; at level five, the vehicle can perform all driving tasks under all conditions in which a human driver can perform. In between, there are various degrees of assistance, control and interaction between man and machine. So, autonomy exists on a continuum, and while it might be clear in some cases that an AI is acting like a person

---

[33] See SAE International, 'Taxonomy and Definitions for Terms Related to Driving Automation Systems for On-Road Motor Vehicles, J3016_202104' (*SAE International*, 30 April 2021) www.sae.org/standards/content/j3016_202104/ accessed 24 March 2022 (describing the SAE taxonomy).

or an ordinary product, in other cases there might be an overlap of responsibility and decision-making between people and AI.

When an individual and an AI contribute to a harm, they might both be liable, either jointly or individually, in proportion to their wrongdoing. When a human driver and an AI driver are both at fault, as may have been the case when Uber's system failed to stop in time for a pedestrian and the backup driver was watching a TV show, they could be found equally negligent. The sort of analysis that commonly used ECGs perform has value, but it is widely understood not to be at the level of a human physician and is legitimately not intended to replace a human diagnosis. ECGs are better considered an ordinary product, and holding them to the standard of a physician would result in their routinely being found liable for medical negligence. This would likely result in manufacturers no longer providing analysis that now has value to doctors.

However, a supplier should not be able to avoid liability simply by disclaiming liability for a product that is obviously automating human activity. Also, it should not be necessary for an AI to actually replace a human operator for negligence to apply, but it should be sufficient that an AI is performing a task that a person could reasonably do. Thus, if a new taxi company goes into business using only a fleet of AVs, the company would not have replaced human operators with AI; AI would be doing work that human drivers could have done. By contrast, the portions of the taxis other than the self-driving software (e.g. the engine) could not be reasonably substituted for a person. So, while the software operating the self-driving taxi could qualify as an AI tortfeasor, the other parts of the vehicle could not.

The negligence test should focus on whether the AI's act was negligent rather than whether the AI was negligently designed or marketed. Again, the AI is taking the place of a person in the traditional negligence paradigm, and this would treat the AI more like a person than a product. It makes no difference to an accident victim what an AI was 'thinking', only how it acted. Accident victims have a right to demand careful conduct, regardless of how well an AI tortfeasor might have been designed.

There is another important reason why focusing on an AI's act is more appropriate than focusing on its design: many AI systems, such as those utilising machine learning, are becoming increasingly complex and have limited explainability, making it difficult or impractical for anyone, including an AV supplier, to determine why a self-driving car, say, ran a red light. But if the harmful act stems from defective software, then such a determination might be necessary to prove that a product has a defect and thus to establish liability. Even worse, it will almost certainly be substantially more challenging for a plaintiff to establish a product defect than it would be for a defendant. The plaintiff might need to hire (quite expensive) experts to investigate a self-driving car's AI, which presupposes a court would permit external access to a supplier's (likely) proprietary AI system. The cost of such an inquiry probably puts it beyond the feasibility of accidents without at least hundreds of thousands or millions of dollars in damages.

In the US system (although not the UK system), plaintiffs usually cannot recover their legal costs even when they prevail in court. For some injured victims then, lawyer and expert fees would exceed any likely recovery, which means that some meritorious claims would not be pursued. By contrast, a negligence test focused on an AI's act and whether it falls below the standard of a reasonable person would simply ask if the AV ran a red light and whether a reasonable person would have done the same. This is a far simpler and less expensive case to prove.

Of course, it is sometimes possible when alleging negligence, or even a defective product, for a plaintiff to prove their case with inference on the basis of reason, logic, bad behaviour by a party or common sense. As one example, a legal doctrine known as *res ipsa loquitur* – 'the thing speaks for itself' – allows circumstantial evidence to permit an inference that a defendant is at fault. For example, if a barrel falls off a building striking a pedestrian and causing harm, the pedestrian may have a difficult or impossible time proving what caused the accident. But, because barrels tend not to fall off buildings absent careless behaviour, the mere fact of the barrel's falling may be sufficient to establish negligence absent compelling contradictory evidence from a defendant.

Similarly, when a medical instrument is left in a patient after surgery, it tends to be adequate to establish negligence, even though a patient may have no way of proving what occurred.[34] However, inference, including through application of *res ipsa loquitur*, is not a panacea to the challenges posed by AI tortfeasors – at least as currently applied by courts. For example, *res ipsa loquitur* is not recognised by every state in the United States. Some states require that a defendant has exclusive control over a product (which can be problematic with the involvement of multiple parties), and not all states allow for the presumption of a product defect. There are similar restrictions on the use of inference more generally in many jurisdictions to avoid speculation and unfairness to defendants. Just because an accident occurs with a product does not necessarily mean there was a defect.[35]

---

[34] See for example, *Scott v Rayhrer* (2010) 185 Cal.App.4th 1535.
[35] Restatement (Third) of Torts: Product Liability (1998).

E.   Financial Liability

AI cannot be directly financially liable for its harms whether in strict liability or negligence since it does not have property rights. In fact, AI is owned as property and would not be influenced by the spectre of liability in the way a person can be influenced. For the purposes of financial liability, the AI's manufacturer and other members of the supply chain should still be responsible for satisfying judgments under standard principles of product liability law, which already has rules for allocating liability in complex cases where several parties contribute to the design and production of an ordinary product, or where several parties are involved in the distribution chain. Those rules could apply in a case where Apple and Delphi jointly design self-driving car software, which General Motors licenses and incorporates into its vehicles, and an independent retailer leases the vehicles to Lyft. Default liability rules could be altered by businesses in the supply chain through contracts. This would be particularly likely to occur in cases where manufacturers and retailers are large, sophisticated entities, such that General Motors could indemnify Apple, Delphi and Lyft in return for more favourable licensing and leasing terms.

Alternately, the AI's owner could be liable for its harms, which would be somewhat akin to treating AI tortfeasors as employees and making owners liable under theories of vicarious liability – that is, when someone is held responsible for the actions of another person. It is particularly easy to imagine owners purchasing insurance for harms caused by AI in the context of a self-driving car. Insurance policies may soon come with a rider (or discount) for AV software. Owner liability may further incentivise the production of autonomous AI given that manufacturers would have less liability, but this could also reduce adoption since owners would be taking on that liability. These two effects may offset each other if reduced manufacturer liability were to result in lower purchase prices. Ultimately, owner liability is not an ideal solution because owners may be the most likely victims of AI tortfeasors, and because manufacturers are still in the best position to improve product safety and weigh the risks and benefits of new technologies.

In practice, the economic impact of different liability standards for accidents by self-driving cars will be seen in insurance costs. Insurers base their premiums on risk, and insurance rates will decrease for self-driving cars, perhaps even increase for human drivers, once self-driving cars become significantly safer than human drivers. This should have a nudging effect on the adoption of self-driving cars, as financially sensitive individuals consider automobile premiums in deciding whether to drive. Even lower premiums for self-driving cars would be expected to the extent that they are judged under a more lenient negligence standard, thus further incentivising their adoption. If manufacturers and retailers rather than car owners are held responsible for accidents, the burden of insurance would shift from owners to manufacturers, although this cost may then be reflected in higher car purchase prices.

F. Alternatives to Negligence

The shift from a strict liability to negligence standard is not the only means of encouraging automation. The government could provide financial incentives to manufacturers and retailers to promote the creation and sale of safer technologies, since in other contexts such efforts have been effective at promoting innovation. For example, incentives could take the form of grants for research and development, loans to build production facilities, enhanced intellectual property rights, prizes, preferential tax treatments or government guarantees. The government could even provide credits to consumers for purchasing self-driving cars, similar to what it did under the Car Allowance Rebate System (CARS), better known as 'cash for clunkers', which provided consumers trading in old vehicles with vouchers worth between $3,500 and $4,500 to purchase new cars.[36] It was a $3 billion US federal programme designed as a short-term economic stimulus to benefit US automobile manufacturers and to promote safer, cleaner, more fuel-efficient vehicles. Ultimately, while critics dispute the effectiveness of the programme at stimulating the economy and promoting domestically produced automobiles, CARS did succeed at improving fuel-efficiency and safety, and it was popular with consumers. In a similar manner, the government could provide consumers who trade in their conventional vehicles with vouchers to purchase self-driving cars.

Even if incentives are limited to tort liability, there are still alternatives to shifting to negligence. Manufacturers could have their liability limited through state or federal tort reform acts that would place caps on damages, limit contingency fees (the ability of lawyers to obtain a percentage of a client's recovery as a fee for services), mandate periodic payments or reduce the statute of limitations (the time limit for suing). Mandatory regulations are another mechanism by which the government can promote safety. This could involve requirements that industries achieve minimum safety targets or direct requirements before adopting certain technologies. For example, human driving could be prohibited when self-driving cars become ten or a hundred times safer than human drivers. Regulatory solutions may be most appropriate when the benefits of automation are overwhelming, and when it is undisputed that automation would result in massive safety gains.

---

[36] Ted Gayer and Emily Parker, 'Cash for Clunkers: An Evaluation of the Car Allowance Rebate System' (2013) www.brookings.edu/wp-content/uploads/2016/06/cash_for_clunkers_evaluation_paper_gayer.pdf.

Yet, there is reason to think that shifting from strict liability to negligence without mandating automation is a preferred mechanism. It is both a consumer- and business-friendly solution. While consumers may have more difficulty seeking to recover for accidents, they should also benefit from a reduced risk of accidents. Most consumers would probably prefer to avoid harm rather than improve their odds of receiving compensation. Businesses would have lower costs associated with liability (which could also result in lower consumer prices). A market shift to negligence would not require government funding, additional regulatory burdens on industry or new administrative responsibilities. It would provide an incremental solution that relies on existing mechanisms for distributing liability and builds upon the established common law. There may be less risk that shifting from strict liability to negligence would produce unexpected outcomes than with more radical regulatory solutions. Therefore, a negligence standard for AI should be a politically feasible solution. Ultimately, to the extent that policymakers agree that automation should be promoted when it improves safety, there is no need to rely on a single mechanism. Such a shift could operate alongside government grants for research and development and consumer credits and be combined with direct regulations in certain instances.

III.   THE REASONABLE AI

A.   When Negligence Is Strict

Negligence may function almost like strict liability for people with below-average abilities. Individuals with special challenges and disabilities may not be capable of always exercising ordinary prudence and may be unable to maintain 'a certain average of conduct'. This issue was at the heart of a case in 1837, *Vaughan v Menlove*,[37] that concerned a defendant who lacked average intelligence. The defence argued that it would be unfair to hold him to the standard of an ordinary person, and that he should instead be held to the standard of a person with low intelligence. The court disagreed, holding that ordinary prudence should apply in every case of negligence. As famed judge Oliver Wendell Holmes Jr later articulated, '[t]he law considers ... what would be blameworthy in the average man, the man of ordinary intelligence and prudence, and determines liability by that. If we fall below the level in those gifts, it is our misfortune.'[38] This remains the case today – a modern defendant

---

[37]   (1837) 132 Eng. Rep. 490, 492; 3 Bing. (N.C.) 468, 471.
[38]   Oliver Wendell Holmes Jr, *The Common Law* (Boston, Little, Brown, & Co., 1881) 108.

cannot generally escape liability for causing a motor vehicle accident because they have slow reflexes, poor vision or anxiety while driving.

There are benefits to such a rule. Logistically, as the court noted in *Vaughan*, it is difficult to take individual peculiarities into account when determining a defendant's actual mental state. Better for administrative purposes to work with an external, objective standard than to prove individual capacities and state of mind. Substantively, the rule reinforces social norms, creates greater deterrent pressure and strengthens each person's right to demand normal conduct of others. As Holmes expressed, damage caused by individuals with reduced capabilities is no less burdensome than that caused by ordinary people. This rule thus benefits the general welfare but at the cost of telling some individuals that their best is not good enough. Those with diminished capabilities drive at their own peril, or they 'should perhaps refrain from driving at all'.[39]

B.   The New Hasty and Awkward

Collectively, people are not the best drivers, even when they do not drink behind the wheel, fall asleep on the highway or collide into police cars while playing Pokémon Go. But compared to AI? It will not be long before AI is safer than the average human driver, and then safer than any human driver. Principles of harm avoidance suggest that once it becomes practical to automate, and that doing so is safer, an AI should become the new 'reasonable person' or standard of care. In practice, this would mean that the defendant would be judged against what an AI would have done instead of judging their action against what a reasonable person would have done. For instance, today a defendant may not be liable for striking a child running in front of their car if a reasonable driver would not have been able to stop. But that person would soon be liable under the exact same circumstances if an AV would have, more likely than not, prevented the injury. In fact, it may be that the AV is only able to prevent such an accident because it has superhuman abilities, such as software capable of ultra-fast decision-making and access to external cameras that expand peripheral view beyond that of a person.

With the reasonable person test, jurors are asked to put themselves in the place of a reasonable person and decide what that person would have done. It may be a challenge for a juror to follow that reasoning in the case of a reasonable AI, but it is a far less nebulous and fictional concept than the reasonable person. The term 'reasonable' in the context of an AI is an anthropomorphism to assist people conceptually. To take a simple case, imagine an individual driving on a dry road surface at 40 miles per hour and then colliding with

---

[39]   *Roberts v Ring* 143 Minn 151, 153 (1919).

a child who runs into the road 150 feet ahead of the driver's vehicle. To determine whether the driver is liable under the reasonable AI standard, a plaintiff could present a jury with evidence that the same make and model of car that is being operated by automated software under the same conditions stops in about 100 feet. This means that the reasonable AI would not have collided with the child, and the human driver would be liable. Juries would not need to take distraction into account, the reaction time of AI would be known, and the braking distance could be standardised if the driver's vehicle could not be compared directly because it was not a vehicle type operated by self-driving software.

A defendant may argue that it is unfair for their best efforts to result in liability. A reasonable AI standard essentially makes people strictly liable for their accidental harms. This is the case now for below-average drivers, and the underlying rationale for the rule will not change when an above-average human driver becomes a below-average driver due to AI. It may appear unfair to impose liability on human drivers for doing their best, but it would be more unfair to prevent accident victims from recovering for harms that would have been avoided had an AI been driving. It does not matter to an accident victim whether they were run over by a person or an AI.

Tort liability would not prohibit people from driving even when AVs become substantially safer than people. If that were a desired outcome, it could be accomplished through a legislative ban on human driving. Instead, an AI standard of care would mean that people drive at their own risk, and this would have a significant impact on behaviour. If a driver causes an accident, they will be liable for the resultant damages. A tort-based incentive may be preferable to an inflexible statutory mandate because there are benefits to human driving unrelated to accidents, such as for promoting freedom and autonomy. Individuals who particularly value their freedom may still choose to drive and accept the consequences of their accidents. Making individuals and businesses effectively strictly liable for their harms will discourage rather than outright prevent certain undertakings. In the context of the self-driving car, it would likely result in far fewer human drivers as insurance rates for traditional vehicles would become more expensive relative to self-driving cars. Though, this would also depend on the cost of self-driving cars versus traditional vehicles.

A rule requiring automation at the time it first becomes available would be too harsh. AI may be prohibitively expensive or only available in limited quantities, which is likely early in a technology's life cycle. It would be unfair to penalise people for not automating when doing so would be impossible or impractical. Therefore, to introduce a reasonable AI standard, a plaintiff should have to show that a person was performing a task that could be performed by an AI and that it would have been practicable for the defendant to automate. This means that a defendant would not be judged against the standard of an AI where (1) no such AI existed at the time of the accident, (2) no AI was available to the defendant, (3) an AI was prohibitively expensive or (4) there were other overriding interests for not automating (e.g. regulatory requirements for a human driver). If Tesla could manufacture a completely safe AV at a cost of $1 million, it would not be reasonable to require that all consumers automate.

C.   Reasonable People Use AI

An alternative to the reasonable AI standard could be the reasonable person using an AI. For example, once self-driving cars become safer than people, a jury may find that it is unreasonable to drive yourself rather than to use an AV. When the reasonable person using an AI standard is applied to the earlier hypothetical involving a child who runs into the street, the human driver's negligence would not be based on failing to stop in 100 feet as a self-driving car would have; rather, liability would be based on them driving in the first place. A reasonable person would not have driven; a reasonable person would have chosen to automate.

Under either the reasonable person or reasonable AI standard, a human driver would be compared with a self-driving car but in different ways. With the reasonable AI standard, courts would evaluate the human driver's proximally harmful act, whereas they would evaluate the human driver's initial decision to automate based on the reasonable person standard (a bad decision would then be considered the harmful act). Maintaining the reasonable person standard would be more in line with the existing negligence regime. And, while it would be conceptually easier to keep the reasonable person standard, in practice it would be less desirable. The goal is to compare the harmful act of the person and AI, not target the initial decision to automate. It is problematic to base liability on the decision to automate because it must focus on the question of whether automation is either generally or situationally beneficial. A general focus fails to consider instances where a person will outperform an AI, and a situational focus must still compare the harmful act of a person versus an AI.

AI is and will be safer at automating not all but certain activities. For instance, an AI that is working to diagnose disease may be superior to physicians at detecting some conditions but not others. Self-driving cars may be safer than human drivers on average but not safer than professional or above-average drivers. AVs may also be safer under most conditions but may be relatively poor at, for example, driving off-road. So, while automation may generally improve safety, optimal accident reduction may require a mix of AI and human activity. Suppose, for example, an AV is ten times safer than a human driver generally but only half as safe as a human driver in icy conditions. Now, imagine a human driver encounters a patch of black ice and causes an accident under circumstances when they would not be negligent by comparison to a reasonable human driver. If courts were to hold them to the standard of a reasonable AI, they would escape liability if the AI would have been unable to avoid the accident (which is likely if the AI is half as safe in icy conditions). If the reasonable person using an AI test focuses on whether an AI is generally safer, however, they would be liable. This test would conclude that it would have been unreasonable not to use a self-driving car since it is generally safer. This would penalise human action even when it would be preferred.

Alternately, the reasonable person using an AI evaluation could be situational. For instance, it could be reasonable not to use an AI but only in icy conditions. However, this is just a more convoluted version of the reasonable AI test because it requires evaluating whether an AI would be safer than a person in a particular instance. This essentially asks how the AI would have acted in a situation – which would be the application of the reasonable AI standard. It would then require asking, based on that knowledge (which may be impractical for a person to have), whether an earlier decision to automate was reasonable. In the black ice hypothetical, it could require that the driver knows in advance of activating or deactivating self-driving software whether there are icy conditions and how the AI would perform in icy conditions to determine if the risk of using the AI in icy conditions outweighs the benefits of using it for other parts of the trip.

D.   The Reasonable AI Standard for AI Tortfeasors

AI tortfeasors should be held to a negligence standard, and their acts ought to be compared to those of a reasonable person. Further, the reasonable person standard should be replaced with the reasonable AI standard once automation is practicable, and AI is safer than the average person. Eventually, this means that AI tortfeasors will be held to the reasonable AI standard. For instance, if a self-driving Audi collides with a child who ran in front of the vehicle, the negligence test could take into account the stopping times of self-driving Google cars.

There is more than one way of determining the reasonable AI standard (e.g. considering the industry customary, average or safest technology). Under any test, this is different to the current strict liability standard where the inquiry focuses on whether a product is defectively designed or its properties are falsely represented. As AI improves, the reasonable AI standard will grow stricter, which is acceptable, because once AI is exponentially safer than a person, it is likely that AI tortfeasors will rarely cause accidents. While the economic impact of tort liability on automation adoption may be slight, the primary effect of the reasonable AI standard would be to internalise the cost of accidents on human tortfeasors.

Nonetheless, there may be instances in which it will still make sense to apply the reasonable person standard to AI tortfeasors. As described earlier, there will be cases in which a human defendant would not be judged against the standard of an AI, such as where automation is prohibitively expensive or AI is not widely available. In these cases, it would not be appropriate to hold an AI tortfeasor to a higher standard than a human defendant. In some industries and for certain types of automation, it may take decades – a lifetime, even – after the introduction of autonomous technologies for the use of such tools to become routine.

E.   Further Thoughts

In the future, there are likely to be few activities where AI cannot outperform people. Self-driving cars will eventually be a thousand times safer than the best human driver, at which point AI will cause so little harm that the economics of negligence versus strict liability will be irrelevant to AI manufacturers. AI will have become so ubiquitous that the constantly improving reasonable AI should set the benchmark for most or all areas of accident law, thereby preventing countless losses and injuries. It has become acceptable for more than a million people a year to die in traffic accidents worldwide, but only because a reasonable alternative has not yet been within reach. But there could soon be a world where practically no one dies from unintended injury, the fourth leading cause of death. We would then just be left to deal with the leading two causes of death: cardiovascular disease and cancer. Artificial inventors, a different type of AI, may eliminate those as well.[40]

---

[40]   Ryan Abbott, 'I Think, Therefore I Invent: Creative Computers and the Future of Patent Law' (2016) 57 BC L Rev 1079.

5. Civil Liability Applicable to Artificial Intelligence: A Preliminary Critique of the European Parliament Resolution of 2020

Henrique Sousa Antunes[1]

I. BACKGROUND

On 20 October 2020, the European Parliament approved a Resolution with recommendations to the Commission on a civil liability regime for artificial intelligence[2] (the 'Resolution'). The Resolution highlighted the importance of defining a clear and harmonised civil liability regime in Europe for the development of artificial intelligence ('AI') technologies and the products and services that benefit from them, so as to provide due legal certainty for producers, operators, affected persons and other third parties.

The same motivation had previously led the European Parliament to put forward a series of proposals on the subject of liability in its 2017 Resolution.[3] There are some important differences between the two documents. These differences reflect the deeper analysis that the European Commission, in particular, has been engaged in with regard to civil liability for harm attributable to AI systems. On this subject, we may note, lastly, the Report on the safety and liability implications of Artificial Intelligence, the Internet of Things and

---

[1] Associate Professor, Universidade Católica Portuguesa, Faculty of Law (Lisbon School). Co-ordinator of the working group 'Law and Artificial Intelligence' of the Católica Research Centre for the Future of Law. The text was completed on November 22, 2020, and revised on 16 July 2022 (a reference to the AI Act Proposal was made for this publication).
[2] Resolution with recommendations to the Commission on a civil liability regime for artificial intelligence (2020/2014(INL)).
[3] Resolution of 16 February 2017 with recommendations to the Commission on Civil Law Rules on Robotics (2015/2103(INL)).

Robotics,[4] which accompanies the European Commission 2020 White Paper on AI[5] ('White Paper').

One important element underpinning the 2020 Resolution is the distinction made between two different regimes for establishing civil liability for harm attributed to AI systems: strict liability for high-risk situations, and subjective liability with a presumption of fault, in other situations.[6] The aim of this chapter is, on the one hand, to provide a critical assessment of how far this option corresponds to the assumptions on which the Resolution is based, also taking a brief look at the concept of wrongdoing proposed and the scope of compensable harm, and, on the other hand, to assess the adequacy of the distinction indicated in light of the choices made in the 2017 Resolution and, above all, in light of the challenges that the development of AI raises for the traditional foundations on which compensation regimes have been based up to the present.

II.   THE 2020 RESOLUTION

A.   The Assumptions

The Resolution now approved by the European Parliament contains recommendations for a civil liability regime for operators of AI systems and also calls on the European Commission to review the Product Liability Directive ('PLD').[7] In the annex, the Resolution presents '[d]etailed recommendations

---

4   (report) COM(2020) 64 final.

5   (communication) COM(2020) 65 final, of 19 February 2020.

6   The model was suggested, in greater detail, in the important report published at the end of 2019 on the transformation of civil liability in the era of digitalisation (Expert Group on Liability and New Technologies, New Technologies Formation, 'Liability for Artificial Intelligence and Other Emerging Digital Technologies' (Report for the European Commission 2019)). For a detailed dialogue about this text, see, Mafalda Miranda Barbosa, 'O futuro da responsabilidade civil desafiada pela inteligência artificial: as dificuldades dos modelos tradicionais e caminhos de solução' (2020) 2 Revista de Direito da Responsabilidade 280–326. The model has also been welcomed in other legal writings. See, for example, Ernst Karner, 'Liability for Robotics: Current Rules, Challenges, and the Need for Innovative Concepts' in Sebastian Lohsse, Reiner Schulze and Dirk Staudenmayer (eds.), *Liability for Artificial Intelligence and the Internet of Things – Münster Colloquia on EU Law and the Digital Economy IV* (Nomos, 2019) 122–3; and Gerald Spindler, 'User Liability and Strict Liability in the Internet of Things and for Robots' in Sebastian Lohsse, Reiner Schulze and Dirk Staudenmayer (eds.), *Liability for Artificial Intelligence and the Internet of Things – Münster Colloquia on EU Law and the Digital Economy IV* (Nomos, 2019) 136–41.

7   Council Directive 85/374/EEC of 25 July 1985 on the approximation of the laws, regulations and administrative provisions of the Member States concerning liability for defective products.

for drawing up a European Parliament and Council Regulation on liability for the operation of artificial intelligence-systems' (the 'Proposal'). The Proposal does not include rules for the producer, its scope being limited to front-end and back-end operators (and, in the case of the latter, as long as their liability is not already covered by the product liability rules). In short, the Proposal is aimed at operators who exercise control over a risk connected with the operation and functioning of an AI system.

In our view, the structure of the Proposal appears to be based on five essential themes contained in the Resolution: the characteristics of AI systems; the equivalence between the operators' control of such systems and the control over risk that a car owner exercises in relation to their vehicle; convergence between the liability of the operator and the liability of the producer of AI systems; the requirement of proportionality, reflecting a balance between liability models and the development of AI, for the benefit of the community; and the creation of conditions that promote the appearance of markets offering civil liability insurance for operators of AI systems, thereby protecting research and innovation.

One aspect of our reflection centres around a possible difference between the assumptions contained in the Resolution and the regulatory choices made by the European Parliament. It will be recalled that the document is founded on the fundamental distinction between high-risk AI systems and other AI systems, with liability being, respectively, risk-based and fault-based, although with a presumption of fault in the latter case.

B.   The Dualistic Nature of Liability, Objective and Subjective: A Legitimate Choice?

The emergence of different liability regimes according to different degrees of risk is, it would seem to us, in contrast with the lessons drawn in some of the Resolution's assumptions. The common systems of liability of a car owner for the risk of a vehicle and the grounds for liability of the producer provide clear evidence for this conclusion.

The European Parliament pursued a route already opened up by the European Commission in the White Paper. In that document, a risk-based approach is followed, and the Commission suggests that clear criteria must be defined to distinguish between different AI systems.[8] Strict liability is regarded

---

[8]   The subsequent Proposal for a Regulation of the European Parliament and of the Council laying down harmonised rules on Artificial Intelligence (Artificial Intelligence Act) and amending certain Union legislative acts (COM(2021) 206 final), 21.4.2021, has reinforced the said approach: 'In order to introduce a proportionate and effective set of binding rules for AI systems, a clearly defined risk-based approach should be fol-

as appropriate for activities with a high level of risk, which is determined both by the sector in which the system is employed (healthcare, transport, energy and parts of the public sector) and by the risk of significant and unavoidable harm to the affected persons (uses with a significant impact on the affected persons). According to the Commission, these high-risk sectors should be identified exhaustively by regulatory means, although it also recognised the legitimacy of extending this concept of high risk, in order to prevent certain forms of harm, in particular in the employment context or in the use of intrusive surveillance technologies.

This approach clearly influenced the option in the 2020 Resolution to limit strict liability to high-risk AI systems. And, yet, the higher probability of harm occurring or of such harm being severe when compared to common activities falls within the concept of risk which, without any divisions in this context, forms the basis of objective liability regimes. This is accepted in the Resolution: referring to national laws, Recital C mentions this in relation to risks for the public (cars or hazardous activities) or risks that the actor cannot control (animals).

Now, AI systems involve risk. The European Parliament acknowledged this, when expressing the dangers associated with the development of new products and services in general ('[e]specially at the beginning of the life cycle…, after being pre-tested, there is a certain degree of risk for the user as well as for third persons that something will not function properly')[9] and, also, in view of the specific nature of AI:

> [t]he rise of AI, however, presents a significant challenge for the existing liability frameworks. Using AI-systems in our daily life will lead to situations in which their opacity ('black box' element) and the multitude of actors who intervene in their lifecycle make it extremely expensive or even impossible to identify who was in control of the risk of using the AI-system in question or which code or input caused the harmful operation. That difficulty is compounded by the connectivity between an AI-system and other AI-systems and non-AI-systems, by its dependency on external data, by its vulnerability to cybersecurity breaches, as well as by the increasing autonomy of AI-systems triggered by machine-learning and deep-learning capabilities.[10]

---

lowed. That approach should tailor the type and content of such rules to the intensity and scope of the risks that AI systems can generate. It is therefore necessary to prohibit certain AI practices, to lay down requirements for high-risk AI systems and obligations for the relevant operators, and to lay down transparency obligations for certain AI systems' (Principle 14).

[9] Proposal, recital 2.
[10] ibid. recital 3.

Hence, the characteristics of these systems fit within a concept of potential for harm that is legally relevant for formulating a duty to compensate without fault. The common characteristics of the various AI systems would justify a unified approach.

It is true that different degrees of autonomy will imply different levels of control of an AI system, with control serving as a justification for liability of the operator.[11] It is also true that the application of strict liability requires an assessment of any potential harmful implications of the AI system.[12] And, lastly, it is true that the definition of high risk can only be found by combining these two elements:

> an AI-system that entails an inherent high risk and acts autonomously potentially endangers the general public to a much higher degree; ... based on the legal challenges that AI-systems pose to the existing civil liability regimes, it seems reasonable to set up a common strict liability regime for those high-risk autonomous AI-systems.[13]

This approach indicates, however, that the European Parliament recommended as a condition for liability without fault that the operation of the system had to be dependent on factors beyond the operator's control.[14] Disruption of the control exercised by the operator is the true risk. Knowing, however, that that risk is evident due to certain features that are common in AI systems, in particular connectivity, dependency on external data or vulnerability to cyber-security breaches, what, strictly speaking, the European Parliament proposes is softening the risk-based liability, and removing from that regime situations in which there is no autonomy or in which, where there is, the potential for harm is less important.

Our conclusion on the alleviation of liability is also influenced by the acknowledgement that autonomy, as described, is a characteristic of future times. For the moment, therefore, subjective liability will prevail. This is the conclusion that can be drawn from the European Parliament's analysis

---

[11]   ibid. recital 10.
[12]   ibid. recital 13, Art 3(c).
[13]   Resolution, recital 14.
[14]   This is the concept of the autonomous system, influenced by technologies such as neural networks and deep-learning processes: 'an AI-system that operates by inter-preting certain input and by using a set of pre-determined instructions, without being limited to such instructions, despite the system's behaviour being constrained by, and targeted at, fulfilling the goal it was given and other relevant design choices made by its developer' (Proposal, Art 3(b)).

regarding the introduction of mandatory insurance for operators of high-risk AI systems:

> a mandatory (civil liability) insurance regime for high-risk AI-systems should cover the amounts and the extent of compensation laid down by the proposed Regulation; the (European Parliament) is mindful of the fact that such technology is currently still very rare, since it presupposes a high degree of autonomous decision making and that, as a result, the current discussions are mostly future-oriented.[15]

Proportionality serves as a justification for the relaxation of liability described. In the words of the Resolution:

> whereas the diversity of AI-systems and the diverse range of risks the technology poses complicates efforts to find a single solution, suitable for the entire spectrum of risks; whereas, in this respect, an approach should be adopted in which experiments, pilots and regulatory sandboxes are used to come up with proportional and evidence-based solutions that address specific situations and sectors, where needed.[16]

The European Parliament is clearly determined to put the principle of proportionality to work in the protection of emerging AI industries:

> [a] careful examination of the consequences of any new regulatory framework on small and medium-sized enterprises (SMEs) and start-ups is a prerequisite for further legislative action. The crucial role that such enterprises play in the European economy justifies a strictly proportionate approach in order to enable them to develop and innovate.[17]

The principle of proportionality cannot, however, lose sight of parallel areas of liability. And it cannot silence the European Union's commitment to increasing citizens' confidence in the development of emerging digital technologies (AI, the Internet of Things or robotics).[18] As we shall see later on in this text, openness to solutions other than classic civil liability frameworks would bring the comfort of providing the affected party with a guarantee of effective compensation for harm caused by high-risk systems, without compromising the protection required in other situations involving the creation or use of AI.

---

[15] Resolution, recital 24.
[16] ibid. recital L.
[17] Proposal, recital 5.
[18] See, in particular, European Commission, 'Ethics Guidelines for Trustworthy AI, High-Level Expert Group on Artificial Intelligence' (2019), which was produced by the independent High-Level Expert Group on AI set up by the European Commission in June 2018; 'White Paper'; and Proposal, recital 1.

In particular, the requirements of parallel regimes appear to rock the foundations of the Resolution. And, let it be noted, convergence with those liability regimes is affirmed by the European Parliament as a condition that the European legislator must be subject to when defining the new rules which it is now proposing.

The European Parliament does this, firstly, by equalising the treatment of identical harm, whether or not AI is involved: 'fair compensation procedures mean that each person who suffers harm caused by AI-systems or whose property damage is caused by AI-systems should have the same level of protection compared to cases without involvement of an AI-system'.[19] Accordingly, the identical nature of the regimes is a principle of the Proposal: '[c]itizens should be entitled to the same level of protection and rights, irrespective of whether the harm is caused by an AI-system or not, or if it takes place physically or virtually, so that their confidence in the new technology is strengthened'.[20]

Secondly, it highlights the liability regime for owners of a land vehicle: '[t]he liability of the operator under this Regulation is based on the fact that he or she exercises a degree of control over a risk connected with the operation and functioning of an AI-system, which is comparable to that of an owner of a car'.[21]

Lastly, it stresses the need for articulation with the product liability rules:

> [t]he introduction of a new liability regime for the operator of AI-systems requires that the provisions of this Regulation and the review of the Product Liability Directive be closely coordinated in terms of substance as well as approach so that they together constitute a consistent liability framework for AI-systems, balancing the interests of producer, operator, consumer and the affected person, as regards the liability risk and the relevant compensation arrangements.[22]

It seems to us that a prohibition of retrogression in relation to acquired rights would mean it would not be feasible to remove the strict liability of the producer of digital content and services which a review of the Directive might extend to. In other words, producers' liability does not seem able to accommodate two systems of liability with differentiation between high-risk systems and other ordinary-risk systems. Moreover, in abstract terms, it does not seem justifiable to place a greater burden on the operator than on the producer.

Taking a closer look, we may, first of all, consider the liability regime for car owners. In accidents caused by land vehicles, factors relating to the context

---

[19]   Resolution, recital J.
[20]   Proposal, para A(7), 'Principles and Aims of the Proposal'.
[21]   ibid. recital 10.
[22]   ibid. recital 23.

also lead to higher degrees of potential for harm, but here the legislator does not make provision for different types of liability. Whether a vehicle is being driven for commercial purposes or for personal activities, whether it is a new or used vehicle, whether it is large or small or is being driven in an urban or rural environment, and regardless of other variable personal conditions (e.g. age, experience, skill), it is treated in the same way by the legislator.

Evidence of this aggregation of various degrees of potential for harm under the same objective liability rules is provided, even more clearly, by product liability. Indeed, the history of the regime demonstrates the error of restricting liability without fault to high-risk activities.

It will be recalled that the Resolution accepts that there is an inevitable risk associated with the creation of new products and services: '[t]his process of trial-and-error is… a key enabler of technical progress without which most of our technologies would not exist'.[23] Accordingly, it also accepts that it is important to have liability legislation which tends to mitigate those inevitable risks: '[s]o far, the risks accompanying new products and services have been properly mitigated by strong product safety legislation and liability rules'.[24] We remember that apportionment of liability without fault is an appropriate instrument for preventing the occurrence of risks connected with the exercise of certain activities, due to the greater diligence adopted by actors in the course of their activities.[25]

Against this backdrop, the solution that European law found for the challenges posed by the combination of the risk involved in designing new products and services and the industrial scale of production was to pass the PLD. Indeed, the legislator said as much in its recitals: 'liability without fault on the part of the producer is the sole means of adequately solving the problem, peculiar to our age of increasing technicality, of a fair apportionment of the risks inherent in modern technological production'.[26]

Mass supply had increased the common risk of production, and this justified the fact that, irrespective of the specific degree of potential for harm of the goods in question, the producer was to be held liable without fault. In fact, according to Article 2 of the PLD, the rules relate to:

> all movables, with the exception of primary agricultural products and game, even though incorporated into another movable or into an immovable. 'Primary agricultural products' means the products of the soil, of stock-farming and of fisheries,

---

[23] ibid. recital 2.
[24] ibid. recital 2.
[25] See, in particular, João Calvão da Silva, *Responsabilidade civil do produtor* (Almedina, 1990) 499–500.
[26] Paragraph 6 of the recital to the Product Liability Directive.

excluding products which have undergone initial processing. 'Product' includes electricity.

The European legislator did not establish any distinction in the regime applicable to products on the basis of their greater or lesser proximity to the public or the greater or lesser probability of serious harm arising from them. The impact of the technological revolution on production is the *ratio legis* behind the strict liability of the producer. In Calvão da Silva's more detailed description on this matter, we can find, without doubt, some important features of the digital revolution:

> the increasing automation of the production process, the complex industrial organisation structured around specialisation and division (both vertical and horizontal) of work and the inseparable combination of man and machine involve the production and launch onto the market of products with defects that 'have to happen', with inevitable and anonymous defects that cause numerous harmful accidents which, even if they are not attributable to the fault of the producer, are considered in the field of distributive justice as having to be borne by him – *ubi commoda ibi incommoda*.[27]

If this situation led to the adoption of a single regime for apportioning harm, it does not seem possible to accept that an increase in the risk factors indicated weakens the liability of the actor.

In the Resolution, the lack of alternatives to the notion of civil liability, or to a certain idea of it, seems to require that liability for an activity with known risks will be subject to the reprehensible behaviour of the actor. The operator of a dangerous activity is protected from a duty to compensate without fault, which, in view of the benefit associated with the danger created for third parties, would generally be justified in the use of AI systems. And we are dealing with a danger of serious harm:

> [i]n addition to [the] complex features and potential vulnerabilities, AI-systems could also be used to cause severe harm, such as compromising human dignity and European values and freedoms, by tracking individuals against their will, by introducing social credit systems, by taking biased decisions in matters of health insurance, credit provision, court orders, recruitment or employment or by constructing lethal autonomous weapon systems.[28]

Accordingly, only the paradox of subjective liability serving as a basis for the duty to compensate for the exercise of activities which, in the abstract,

---

[27]   Calvão da Silva (n 25) 496–7.
[28]   Proposal, recital 3.

are likely to cause serious injury allows us to understand the *raison d'être* of another paradox, referring to the causes for excluding fault-based liability.

The severity of the harm associated with the risk of an AI system is not a singular criterion of strict liability. The application of this is determined by a combined assessment of the seriousness of the potential harm and the probability of the risk occurring, the degree of autonomy of the system and the manner and context in which the system is used. This combined approach enables confirmation of a high risk, which is defined as 'a significant potential in an autonomously operating AI-system to cause harm or damage to one or more persons in a manner that is random and goes beyond what can reasonably be expected'.[29]

To this extent, the possibility of exempting an actor from strict liability for serious harm caused by the use of an AI system is a real scenario. It was perhaps that *risk* that led the European Parliament to recommend a heterodox subjective civil liability, with clear elements of objective apportionment.

Generally speaking, liability is dependent on fault – Article 8(2) of the Proposal states:

> [t]he operator shall not be liable if he or she can prove that the harm or damage was caused without his or her fault, relying on either of the following grounds: a) the AI-system was activated without his or her knowledge while all reasonable and necessary measures to avoid such activation outside of the operator's control were taken, or b) due diligence was observed by performing all the following actions: selecting a suitable AI-system for the right task and skills, putting the AI-system duly into operation, monitoring the activities and maintaining the operational relia-bility by regularly installing all available updates.

The European Parliament finds in subjective liability a basis for the duty to compensate for harm attributed to third parties, establishing a legal presump-tion of fault: 'the existing fault-based tort law of the Member States offers in most cases a sufficient level of protection for persons that suffer harm caused by an interfering third party like a hacker or for persons whose property is damaged by such a third party, as the interference regularly constitutes a fault-based action'.[30] It should be noted that this assumption of fact is ques-tionable, given that the diligence expected varies according to whether or not the operator is acting in a professional capacity[31] and given that AI systems are characterised by connectivity, dependency on external data and vulnerability.

Accepting, however, the implication of potential for harm of some features of AI systems, the operator is objectively liable for an action of a third party, if

---

[29] ibid. Art 3(c).
[30] Resolution, recital 9.
[31] Proposal, recital 18.

it is impossible to locate that third party or for the affected party to obtain compensation from him: '[w]here the harm or damage was caused by a third party that interfered with the AI-system by modifying its functioning or its effects, the operator shall nonetheless be liable for the payment of compensation if such third party is untraceable or impecunious'.[32] Likewise, if the AI system has given rise to an autonomous activity, device or process that caused the harm, it will not suffice to allege such autonomy.[33] Only proof of due diligence or of a situation of force majeure will exonerate the operator in such cases.[34]

The regime established in Article 8(3) of the Proposal unequivocally exempts subjective liability: 'for specific cases, including those where the third party is untraceable or impecunious, ... the addition of liability rules to complement existing national [fault-based] tort law seem[s] necessary'.[35]

And what can be said regarding harm attributed to the autonomy of the AI system?[36] For fault-based liability, although a demonstration of diligent conduct will exonerate liability,[37] the law excludes, in those cases, the alternative possibility of reversing a presumption of causation which is, generally, associated with the presumption of fault.[38] What the Proposal does is render the presumption of causation irreversible if the presumption of fault is not reversed. The injuring party may not be exempted from liability by proving that, even with due diligence, the harm would have been caused. This is the choice of the European Parliament, when it presumes that the risk of autonomy

---

[32]   ibid. Art 8(3).

[33]   ibid. Art 8(2)(2). The Portuguese version refers to a fact 'based' on the AI-system; the English version states: '[t]he operator shall not be able to escape liability by arguing that the harm or damage was caused by an autonomous activity, device or process driven by his or her AI-system'.

[34]   ibid. Art 8(2)(2).

[35]   Resolution, recital 9.

[36]   It will be recalled that autonomy enabled by particularly sophisticated technologies, such as neural networks and deep-learning processes, appears as an essential condition for strict liability in high-risk systems. It is understood, in fact, that opacity and autonomy make it very difficult to trace back to the human decisions in the design or operation of the system, and, therefore, to demonstrate the fault of the producer, a third party or the operator (Proposal, recital 7).

[37]   ibid. Art 8(2).

[38]   The assessment of subjective reprehensibility in relation to the conduct of the actor only has meaning if the latter has an adequate chain of causation in relation to the effect of the wrongdoing. See Henrique Sousa Antunes, *Responsabilidade civil dos obrigados à vigilância de pessoa naturalmente incapaz* (Universidade Católica Editora, 2000) 270–86.

of the AI system is allocated to the operator, even in a system that is not high risk:

> it should always be clear that whoever creates, maintains, controls or interferes with the AI-system, should be accountable for the harm or damage that the activity, device or process causes. This follows from general and widely accepted liability concepts of justice, according to which the person that creates or maintains a risk for the public is liable if that risk causes harm or damage, and thus should ex-ante minimise or ex-post compensate that risk.[39]

A subjective liability regime is applicable, and yet beyond the scope of fault-based liability.

This is the only explanation for the exception of force majeure, which is also available in relation to strict liability for high-risk systems. The formula appears to include a broad understanding of force majeure situations which, in legal instruments of reference, appear as separate causes of exclusion of strict liability (natural and human facts). We may take Article 7:102 of the Principles of European Tort Law ('PETL'), on the exclusion or limitation of strict liability, as an example: '(1) Strict liability can be excluded or reduced if the injury was caused by an unforeseeable and irresistible a) force of nature (force majeure), or b) conduct of a third party'. The rule demonstrates the use of different terminology on this matter. The following is written in the PETL commentary on the article:

> [w]hile war or terrorism also often fall under that notion [force majeure], which is rather conduct of third parties, we reduced the meaning to natural events of massive impact. It is frequently addressed in international conventions as an 'exceptional natural phenomenon that is not avoidable, unpredictable and irresistible'.[40]

In short, the criticisms set out above suggest some fragilities of a regime that is not in tune with the classic lessons of civil liability. It is important, as we shall see, to rethink the paradigms of compensation.

C.   Wrongdoing and the Scope of Compensable Harm

An assessment of the procedural requirements that are met by the choice between strict liability and subjective liability, and an analysis of the conse-quences of the drawing of boundaries that has been mentioned, are, naturally, influenced by the conclusions reached as a result of our previous reflection.

---

[39]   Proposal, recital 8.

[40]   European Group on Tort Law, *Principles of European Tort Law – Text and Commentary* (Springer, 2005) 128.

Irrespective, however, of the basic choice indicated, several solutions are questionable, also from the perspective of the assumptions on which the Resolution rests. Where this is justified, Portuguese Law will serve as a reference, it being an emblematic regime of common liability options. In particular, the rules on accidents caused by vehicles will be highlighted.

Establishing the boundaries of the concept of wrongdoing, determining which harm is compensable and ascertaining the terms for limiting compensation are some of the questions that will be covered.

The European Parliament preferred the German model of a limited general clause of wrongdoing.[41] Liability is determined, firstly, by damage to life, health, physical integrity and property. The provision also adds '*significant* immaterial harm resulting in a verifiable economic loss'.[42] The formula appears to include various dimensions of personality rights or offences against intangible property, such as the breach or destruction of data: '[s]ignificant immaterial harm should be understood as meaning harm as a result of which the affected person suffers considerable detriment, an objective and demonstrable impairment of his or her personal interests'.[43] However, 'a verifiable economic loss' is included as a condition for liability.

Given that violation of personality rights is often accompanied by severe emotional distress, it is difficult to understand why the European Parliament made compensation for it dependent on an economic repercussion of the offence, 'having regard, for example, to annual average figures of past revenues and other relevant circumstances'.[44] First of all, drawing the boundaries of wrongdoing according to the dignity of the harmed rights seems incompatible with subjecting this assessment to the practical consequences of the harm. Secondly, in the context of defining compensable harm, this limitation appears to be illegitimate, in light of tradition in European laws. Once again, we may regard the PETL Article 10:301(1) as a paradigm:

> [c]onsidering the scope of its protection (Article 2:102), the violation of an interest may justify compensation of non-pecuniary damage. This is the case in particular where the victim has suffered personal injury; or injury to human dignity, liberty, or other personality rights.

---

[41] Proposal, Art 2(1). See, for all, Luís Manuel Teles de Menezes Leitão, *Direito das Obrigações*, vol 1 (15th ed., Almedina, 2018) 286–8.

[42] Proposal, Art 2(1).

[43] ibid. recital 16.

[44] ibid.

There is, admittedly, a restriction to access to justice, which cannot, therefore, be accepted. In the words of the 2020 Resolution:

> the proposed Regulation should also incorporate significant immaterial harm that results in a verifiable economic loss above a threshold harmonised in Union liability law, that balances the access to justice of affected persons and the interests of other involved persons.[45]

Another matter that warrants a critical eye are the maximum amounts of compensation established for harm caused by high-risk systems. The limits are set out in Article 5(1) of the Proposal: two million euros in the event of the death of or harm caused to the health or physical integrity of an affected person, and one million euros if the damage relates to harm to property or in the other relevant situations of wrongdoing (in the terms previously indicated). In the latter case, the same limit applies to situations where several items of property of the affected person have been damaged by a single operation of the same high-risk system. Equally with regard to Article 5(1)(b), where the affected person also brings a contractual liability claim against the operator, payment of compensation is denied if the total amount of damages is below 500 euros.[46]

Article 5(2) of the Proposal also lays down that the limits apply to several affected persons, stating:

> [w]here the combined compensation to be paid to several persons who suffer harm or damage caused by the same operation of the same high-risk AI-system exceeds the maximum total amounts provided for in paragraph 1, the amounts to be paid to each person shall be reduced pro-rata so that the combined compensation does not exceed the maximum amounts set out in paragraph 1.

The Proposal now being put forward follows the European legislator's solution in Article 16 of the PLD, but differs from the latter regarding the criteria used to determine the amounts in question and the respective maximum amount:

> [t]his Regulation should set out a significantly lower ceiling for compensation than that provided for in the Product Liability Directive, as this Regulation only refers to the harm or damage of a single person resulting from a single operation of an

---

[45] Resolution, recital 19.

[46] It should be stressed, however, that there are voices in favour of eliminating the same threshold set out in Article 9 of the PLD. The 2020 Resolution also appears here to be rowing against the tide. See, for example, Bernhard A Koch, 'Product Liability 2.0 – Mere Update or New Version?' in Sebastian Lohsse, Reiner Schulze and Dirk Staudenmayer (eds.), *Liability for Artificial Intelligence and the Internet of Things – Münster Colloquia on EU Law and the Digital Economy IV* (Nomos, 2019) 103.

AI-system, while the former refers to a number of products or even a product line with the same defect.[47]

In other words, the system's potential for causing harm to the community is not reflected in the corresponding provision on a compensation regime, and redress for damage suffered is limited to individual harm.

The establishment of maximum limits for compensation is accepted as a natural condition of the operation of mandatory insurance regimes. However, the European Parliament seems to forget that in the definition of high risk the level of collective impact of the harm is one of the fundamental grounds for assessing the severity of the damage:

> [t]he degree of severity should be determined based on relevant factors such as the extent of the potential harm resulting from the operation on affected persons, including in particular effects on fundamental rights, the number of affected persons, the total value for the potential damage, as well as the harm to society as a whole.[48]

It will suffice to imagine the risk of cyber-attacks on systems that control land or air mobility or on systems for the supply of essential goods or services to the community (health, water, electricity, gas, communications and so on).

It would, perhaps, make more sense to set incremental limits according to the foreseeable impact of the harm calculated by the number of people harmed. In Portuguese law, for example, the maximum limits of compensation in the çase of traffic accidents differ depending on whether the transport is individual or collective (Article 508 of the Civil Code).

By basing high-risk systems on civil liability and mandatory insurance regimes, the European Parliament finds that it needs to present maximum limits that are sufficiently attractive for the purpose of creating an insurance market for liability for harm attributable to high-risk systems. It does this on the basis of individual harm. It sacrifices compensation for collective harm, which is only protected by a fund created by the Member States, which is exceptional and temporary in nature, and if 'the compensation significantly exceeds the maximum amounts set out in this Regulation'.[49]

The 2020 Resolution fails, basically, to fulfil the paradigm of social responsibility: '[t]he very society that creates the risks develops within it increasingly improved processes to dilute or absorb the costs of repairing harm, to operate

---

[47] Proposal, recital 16.
[48] ibid. recital 13.
[49] ibid. recital 22.

a "distribution of losses", making the cost of these fall directly on the whole of the collective'.[50] The scope of the collective can, of course, be moulded.

III. IN DEFENCE OF ANOTHER PARADIGM

The guidelines of the European Parliament set out in the 2020 Resolution to some extent follow the positions it took in the 2017 Resolution. In particular, we may note similar reflections on the proportionality of the compensation solution, on the similarity with traffic accident liability and, for that reason, on the establishment of a mandatory insurance regime.

In terms of liability, the aim of establishing stricter levels of liability according to the additional level of autonomy is clearly expressed in the 2017 Resolution:

> ...once the parties bearing the ultimate responsibility have been identified, their liability should be proportional to the actual level of instructions given to the robot and of its degree of autonomy, so that the greater a robot's learning capability or autonomy, and the longer a robot's training, the greater the responsibility of its trainer should be.[51]

Regarding insurance contracts, the parallel with traffic accidents allowed the European Parliament, in 2017, to advocate making these mandatory for the use of AI systems, in particular when, due to the autonomy that the robots would gain, the harm could not be attributed to human failure:

> ...a possible solution to the complexity of allocating responsibility for damage caused by increasingly autonomous robots could be an obligatory insurance scheme, as is already the case, for instance, with cars; ... nevertheless, ... unlike the insurance system for road traffic, where the insurance covers human acts and failures, an insurance system for robotics should take into account all potential responsibilities in the chain.[52]

This similarity with the 2020 Resolution does not, however, extend to two fundamental ideas that the European Parliament supported in the 2017 text. These were the establishment of compensation funds of broad scope and the creation of a status of responsible electronic persons.

---

[50] Jorge F Sinde Monteiro, *Estudos sobre a responsabilidade civil* (Almedina, 1983) 76.

[51] Resolution of 16 February 2017 with recommendations to the Commission on Civil Law Rules on Robotics (2015/2103(INL)) recital 56.

[52] ibid. recital 57.

Given that there may be many participants in the operation of an AI system, a fund financed by all the entities involved would reduce the problems associated with determining which actor was responsible. The European Parliament called on the European Commission to consider the impact of a solution that allowed the manufacturer, the programmer, the owner or the user to benefit from limited liability if they contributed to a compensation fund or if they jointly took out insurance to guarantee compensation where damage is caused by a robot.[53]

In the 2017 Resolution, the European Commission is called on to assess the implications of solutions intended to ensure 'that a compensation fund would not only serve the purpose of guaranteeing compensation if the damage caused by a robot was not covered by insurance'.[54] Compensation funds are therefore expected to overcome the lack of insurance. Encouraging the making of a financial contribution by limiting liability demonstrates this. The European Parliament suggested that the European Commission should examine whether to allocate to compensation funds the management of compensation claims for harm caused by more sophisticated AI systems:

> deciding whether to create a general fund for all smart autonomous robots or to create an individual fund for each and every robot category, and whether a contribution should be paid as a one-off fee when placing the robot on the market or whether periodic contributions should be paid during the lifetime of the robot.[55]

This contrasts greatly with the 2020 Resolution. In the latter, these funds are merely supplementary:

> [i]n exceptional cases, such as an event incurring collective damages, in which the compensation significantly exceeds the maximum amounts set out in this Regulation, Member States should be encouraged to set up a special compensation fund, for a limited period of time, that addresses the specific needs of those cases. Special compensation funds could also be set up to cover those exceptional cases in which an AI-system, which is not yet classified as high-risk AI-system and thus, is not yet insured, causes harm or damage.[56]

However, a European approach involving public funding is rejected: 'a compensation mechanism at Union level, funded with public money, is not the right way to fill potential insurance gaps'.[57] Moreover, in the 2020 Resolution,

---

[53]   ibid. recital 59(c).
[54]   ibid. recital 59(b).
[55]   ibid. recital 59(d).
[56]   Proposal, recital 22.
[57]   Resolution, recital 25.

more sophisticated AI systems are subject to a strict liability regime, which places limits on the affected party resulting from the need that requirements for liability are met.[58] In fact, an insurance scheme is also dependent on those requirements being fulfilled. The compensation funds approach is different.[59]

The contrast is also evident with regard to the issue of the electronic person. In the 2017 Resolution, it was accepted that the creation of this category might simplify assessment of the harmful act. The European Parliament suggested that the European Commission should assess the impact of creating 'a specific legal status for robots in the long run, so that at least the most sophisticated autonomous robots could be established as having the status of electronic persons responsible for making good any damage they may cause'.[60] Conversely, the 2020 Resolution rejects electronic personality.[61]

The author is of the opinion that the 2020 text lacks the ambition required for a paradigm shift in liability associated with the features of AI systems. Moving past an anthropocentric and monocausal model of civil liability is seen as a unifying event in the important report published at the end of 2019 on the transformation of this area in the era of digitalisation.[62] The immediate condition of the harm is removed from the action of the individual, in intersubjective relationships, to an automated decision, where, also seeking to recognise the human will, the multitude of actors and the interoperability of digital technologies has meant that the standard of a single cause of the harm has been replaced by a framework of multiple causes.

As the author has written elsewhere, considering the need to protect the injured party, a bold move is required to surpass the anthropocentric and monocausal model of liability.[63] It is time to acknowledge that resorting to traditional liability solutions will amount to tinkering which is insufficient to guarantee redress for the harm suffered by the affected party. Hence, estab-

---

[58]   It is acknowledged, however, that it is difficult to implement a mandatory insurance regime for harm attributable to AI systems: '[a] lack of access to, or an insufficient quantity of, high quality data could be a reason why creating insurance products for new and emerging technologies is difficult at the beginning.' (Proposal, recital 21).

[59]   On this topic, see, recently, Thierry Vansweevelt and others, 'Comparative Analysis of Compensation Funds. Differences, Common Characteristics and Suggestions for the Future' in Thierry Vansweelvelt and Britt Weyts (eds.), *Compensation Funds in Comparative Perspective* (Intersentia, 2020) 189–213.

[60]   Resolution of 16 February 2017 with recommendations to the Commission on Civil Law Rules on Robotics (2015/2103(INL)) recital 59(f).

[61]   Resolution, recital 7; Proposal, recital 6.

[62]   Expert Group on Liability and New Technologies, New Technologies Formation (n 6) 19.

[63]   *Direito e Inteligência Artificial* (Universidade Católica Editora, 2020) 50–51.

lishing the liability of an electronic person is justified, which will, of course, require the construction of a financial system for that entity.[64]

In the absence of such liability, the impossibility of determining the perpetrator of the harm or the cause of the damage are circumstances which, in situations of high risk, should place a burden on the operator of the AI systems, justifying leaving the orthodoxy of liability rules to relations between injuring parties themselves, in search of a fair and efficient means of allocating costs. The injured party should benefit from provision of a social kind, which is not bound by assumptions of liability.[65]

In this scenario, compensation should fall to the social security authorities or to an autonomous compensation fund, funded in both cases by the operators of AI systems. This approach gives effect to liability in the case of compensation owed by an electronic person, harm caused by activities that are not high risk and exercise of the right of recourse between the perpetrators of the harm.[66]

IV.   CONCLUSIONS

The 2020 Resolution made a fundamental distinction between two different regimes for establishing civil liability for harm attributed to AI systems: strict liability for high-risk situations, and subjective liability with a presumption of fault, in other situations. The structure of the Proposal appears to be based on five essential subject matters contained in the Resolution: the characteristics

---

[64]   The benefit that this solution presents in terms of disputes regarding identification of the responsible party is obvious. On this topic, see, for example, Gerhard Wagner, 'Robot Liability' in Sebastian Lohsse, Reiner Schulze and Dirk Staudenmayer (eds.), *Liability for Artificial Intelligence and the Internet of Things – Münster Colloquia on EU Law and the Digital Economy IV* (Nomos, 2019) 60–61. Rejecting this route, see Mafalda Miranda Barbosa, 'O futuro da responsabilidade civil desafiada pela inteligência artificial: as dificuldades dos modelos tradicionais e caminhos de solução' [2020] Revista de Direito da Responsabilidade 296–315.

[65]   Compensation funds have this clear advantage as an alternative to civil liability. See, in particular, Monteiro (n 50) 74–83, Georg Borges, 'New Liability Concepts: the Potential of Insurance and Compensation Funds' in Sebastian Lohsse, Reiner Schulze and Dirk Staudenmayer (eds.), *Liability for Artificial Intelligence and the Internet of Things – Münster Colloquia on EU Law and the Digital Economy IV* (Nomos, 2019) 159–60, and Vansweevelt and others (n 59) 207–13. Redirecting compensation funds to a complementary intervention, see, recently, Barbosa (n 64) 295–6, 317.

[66]   These limitations of liability still enable the preventive aim referred to in Resolution 2020 to be met: '[t]he concept of "liability" plays an important double role in our daily life: on the one hand, it ensures that a person who has suffered harm or damage is entitled to claim compensation from the party held liable for that harm or damage, and on the other hand, it provides the economic incentives for persons to avoid causing harm or damage in the first place' (Proposal, recital 1).

of AI systems; the equivalence between the operators' control of such systems and the control exercised by a car owner; convergence between the liability of the operator and the liability of the producer of AI systems; the requirement of proportionality; and the promotion of a market offering civil liability insurance for operators of AI systems. In the author's opinion, the emergence of different liability regimes according to different degrees of risk seems to be in contrast with the lessons drawn in some of the Resolution's assumptions.

Disruption of the control exercised by the operator is the true risk. Considering, however, that that risk is indisputable due to certain features that are common in AI systems, especially connectivity, dependency on external data or vulnerability to cybersecurity breaches, what, strictly speaking, the European Parliament proposes is softening the risk-based liability, removing from that regime, which may be called on by the nature of things, situations in which there is no autonomy or in which, where there is, the potential for harm is less important. This relaxation of liability finds a justification in the principle of proportionality. The principle cannot, however, lose sight of parallel regimes of liability. And it cannot silence the European Union's commitment to increasing citizens' confidence in the development of emerging digital technologies.

The scope of parallel regimes includes the liability of car owners and that of the producer. In accidents caused by land vehicles, factors relating to the context also lead to higher degrees of potential for harm, but here the legislator does not establish different types of liability. Whether a vehicle is being driven for commercial purposes or for personal activities, whether it is a new or used vehicle, whether it is large or small or is being driven in an urban or rural environment, and subject to other variable personal conditions (e.g. age, experience, skill), it is subject to the same regime. The European legislator also did not make any distinction between the rules applicable to products on the basis of their greater or lesser proximity to the public or the greater or lesser probability of serious harm arising from them. The impact of the technological revolution on production is grounds for strict liability of the producer.

In the 2020 Resolution, only the paradox of subjective liability serving as a basis for compensating damages caused by the exercise of activities which, in the abstract, are likely to cause serious injury allows us to comprehend the *raison d'être* of another paradox, referring to the conditions for excluding fault-based liability – the European Parliament recommended a heterodox subjective civil liability, with clear elements of objective apportionment.

Several other solutions are questionable, also from the perspective of the assumptions on which the Resolution rests. Establishing the boundaries of the concept of wrongdoing, determining which harm is compensable and ascertaining the terms for limiting compensation illustrate some of the doubts raised.

On the topic of wrongdoing, it seems difficult to understand why the European Parliament made compensation for violation of personality rights dependent on an economic repercussion of the offence. Drawing the boundaries of wrongdoing according to the dignity of the harmed rights appears to be incompatible with subjecting this assessment to the practical consequences of the harm. Then, when defining compensable harm, knowing that violation of personality rights often causes severe emotional distress, this limitation appears to be illegitimate, bearing in mind the tradition in European laws. This restricts access to justice, which cannot be accepted. Another matter that deserves criticism is the maximum amounts of compensation established for harm caused by high-risk systems, since the European Parliament seems to forget the use of collective impact of the harm as one of the fundamental grounds for assessing the severity of the damage.

The author is of the opinion that the 2020 text lacks the ambition required for a paradigm shift in liability associated with the features of AI systems. It should be acknowledged that, moving past an anthropocentric and monocausal model of civil liability,[67] resorting to traditional solutions is insufficient to guarantee redress for the harm suffered by the affected party.

Hence, establishing the liability of an electronic person is justified, which will, of course, require the construction of a financial system for that entity. In the absence of such response, situations of high risk justify benefiting the injured party with the provision of a social kind, which is not bound by assumptions of liability. The orthodoxy of liability rules should be left to relations between injuring parties themselves, in search of a fair and efficient means of allocating costs. Compensation should, then, fall to the social security authorities or to an autonomous compensation fund, funded in both cases by the operators of AI systems.

The referred approach restricts liability to the case of compensation owed by an electronic person, to harm caused by activities that are not high risk and to exercise of the right of recourse between injurers, without compromising the preventive aim that the 2020 Resolution refers to, within Recital 1 of the Proposal.

---

[67] Expert Group on Liability and New Technologies, New Technologies Formation (n 6) 19.

6. Liability for Complex Systems: The Challenge of Robotic Technology in Private Law

Attila Menyhárd[1]

I. INTRODUCTION

The aim of this chapter is to assess whether the implementation of robotic technology requires the revision of the existing framework of liability in tort and, if yes, to what extent such a revision is needed. Although e-personality is not in the focus of this chapter, it is addressed as a preliminary question for liability issues. The role and function of liability, the conceptual framework of tort law and relevant specific forms of liability are considered. It is argued that although the existing framework of tort law is able to manage liability issues that emerge with robotic technology, policy issues are certainly to be revisited and a more complex approach is needed. Thus, the higher the importance of the protected interest interfered with is, the higher the required standard of conduct should be, and a more risk-averse attitude is required in decision-making. Interests protected at a lower level tolerate more risks. Issues like programmed unlawfulness, the victim's contributory negligence and the context of liability for breach of contract are also addressed. It is argued that, contrasted with tort law, regulation shall play a decisive role. This may make it necessary to reconsider the relationship between tort and regulatory law. It is also argued that the benefits of insurance as a risk-spreading mechanism would justify using insurance as a primary risk allocation regime contrasted with tort law.

---

[1]   Professor of Civil Law and the Head of the Department of Civil Law, Eötvös Loránd University, Budapest.

II.   PROPERTY AND PERSONALITY

A.   The Fundamental Structure of Law

According to an 'urban legend' in Hungary, a professor calls a student to the window of the faculty building during an exam when the student is not able to give the proper answers to the professor's questions. The professor requests the student to look at the street and to tell them what they see. The student, staring at the street, desperately tries to answer: 'I see people, trees, cars, dogs, buildings, bicycles ...' The reaction of the professor is negative. As the student, who does not have any further ideas, gives up, the professor provides the answer that they expected: 'Everything that you see is either the subject or object of rights.' What is taught by the professor to the student is the fundamental inherent structure of the law.

Law is a purely abstract phenomenon. It exists as a social reality, transforming social relationships into rights and obligations enforced by the state. Insofar as social relationships aim at reallocating economic resources in the widest sense, they create rights and obligations over material objects. This way the reality of the physical world becomes part of social and legal relationships. Social relationships may occur between the members of society, while the object of such relationships (the economic resources) are the parts of the physical world (things in a legal sense) that are the objects of rights and obligations. Assuming that the elements of the physical reality are either members of the society (persons) or the object of their relationships (property), they are either the subject or the object of legal relationships. That is a binary choice: physical reality is divided into two categories in the eyes of the law. It is either the subject or object of rights and obligations (that is, the law).

The division of the material reality in the world into subjects of rights and obligations (persons), on the one hand, and objects of rights and obligations (property), on the other hand, is a closed and intact system. Everything that exists in the real world can and shall be categorised in the law either as the subject of legal relationships (persons) or the object of the legal relationships (property). There is *nothing* that could not be categorised either as the subject or as the object of legal relationships and there is *nothing* in the physical reality that would fall under *both* of these categories. Although the boundaries between property and personhood are, at some points, not as clear as we would like them to be,[2] the abstract structure of law requires a choice between these categories reflecting the real world in the realm of law. Rights and obligations

---

[2]   Margaret Jane Radin, 'Property and Personhood' (1982) 34 Stanford Law Review 957.

are allocated to persons and persons cannot be the object of rights and obligations – something or someone cannot be both person and property at the same time. This is so, not on the basis of moral considerations, but on the basis of the internal logic of law.

B.   Robots as Persons (Much Ado About Nothing?)

If one considers the liability for damages caused by the operation of automated systems, the primary question is whether duties and liabilities could or should be allocated to the automated system as such. It follows from the internal logic of law that the victim bears the loss unless it can be shifted to other persons. The tool for such risk allocation is liability. This is the case if automated systems are qualified as persons. If the automated system shall not qualify as a person, a person has to be vested with liability provided that the law attempts to shift risks to persons other than the victim. That is why the preliminary question of liability for automated systems is legal personality. If the automated system, that is, the robot, does have a legal personality, then it is vested with rights, duties and obligations including liability for damages. If the robot is not vested with legal personality, it cannot be held liable, and risks of damage caused by it are to be allocated either to the victim or to other persons (e.g. to the producer, owner, operator or user of the automated system).

Legal personality has never been a category to be derived from the internal logic of law or which could be seen as given by nature. Neither could a theoretical definition of personality be provided. It is the law that determines and defines the potential holder of rights and the potential subjects of obligations, that is, persons. Law is an *artificial product* of society and so is the *concept* of person. Legal personality is an artificial product of the society as well. The person is the entity to whom personality was given by the law. Not even human beings are necessarily persons; in ancient Roman law, legal personality was denied for slaves who were qualified as things.[3] Rather, legal personality could be provided to anything. Due to the artificial construction of law, there are *no natural legal* phenomena; law as such is an artificial product and all that exists as part of the law is established on social values. Law is to protect legally protected interests. The beneficiary of the legally protected interests (the person) can be anything held by the community as worthy of protection.[4]

---

[3]   '*Servi res sunt*'; see William Buckland, *Roman Law of Slavery: The Condition of the Slave in Private Law from Augustus to Justinian* (Cambridge University Press, 1908) Ch 2; J. Inst. 1.3.2.

[4]   Alexander Nékám, *The Personality Conception of the Legal Entity* (Harvard University Press, 1938) 33.

Personality of legal entities is not derived from the legal entity of natural persons. Granting them personality is possible because they have legal representatives. Natural persons are able to represent anything. That is, from the point of view of the structure of law, anything can be a legal person because anything can have legal representation. Personality of the legal entity does have a clear function, that is, providing a simple solution for structuring social and legal relationships.[5] There is no abstract content behind the concept of legal personality. Thus, AI can also be provided with personality in the eyes of the law. While considering the opportunity of providing AI with legal personality, it cannot be limited to liability but has to be considered as the capability of having rights and obligations in general, that is, the capability of acquiring property, contracting, establishing companies or having certain inherent rights if such rights are provided to legal entities in the legal system (e.g. right to data, privacy, good reputation, etc.).

The concept of person and personality involves two types of persons: human beings and organisations as legal entities. Human beings are provided with legal personality because they are the members of society. Organisations are provided with legal personality because legal personality converts property rights and contractual relationships into shareholders' (membership) rights in order to ensure stability for the assets belonging to the legal entity. As legal personality is always the result of a decision based on social values and policy, the question is *why* should AI be provided with legal personality? Are there any kinds of social benefits for providing AI with legal personality? If this question is to be answered in the affirmative, then AI should be provided with legal personality. If the answer is negative, then it should not be done. That is, the question is not if AI *has* a legal personality but if AI *should have* a legal personality. The answer depends on the moral (social) evaluation of AI. As the law converts social values into norms,[6] the fundamental question is the moral one. Technically, the law can provide legal personality to anything in the physical or social reality including non-existing phenomena. The only prerequisite of legal personality is that the person has to be identifiable. If the person does not have the capacity or ability to act (e.g. because it does not exist in the physical world), a legal representative can act in its name. Representation is the key point for legal personality of organisations or environmental personhood. Thus, the ability of creating or expressing will or the ability to act are not preconditions of legal personality.

---

[5]   Ronald H Coase, 'The Nature of the Firm' in Oliver E Williamson and Sidney G Winter (eds.), *The Nature of the Firm: Origins, Evolution and Development* (Oxford University Press, 1993) 18–34, 22.

[6]   Jürgen Habermas, *Between Facts and Norms* (W Rehg tr, Polity Press, 1997) 255.

C.   Robots: Property or Personhood?

The real and only question is whether the social functions of legal personality justify providing it to something or someone. Legal personality is a tool of protecting interests: providing private autonomy to human beings, reducing transaction costs of economic organisations or protecting the environment. The fact that a robot may be similar to human beings is certainly not enough justification for providing it with legal personality – animals are able to feel, they communicate, their behaviour is driven by certain autonomous decision-making processes, and some species in many aspects can be similar to humans. In spite of this, they are not provided with personality, except in extremely rare anomalous cases in a limited number of jurisdictions which deviate from this mainstream approach.[7] I think that we are on the wrong track if we focus on similarities between robots (AI) and humans, because such similarity does not typically justify legal personality. The question is whether the legal personality of robots (and AI), that is, assessing them as persons in contrast to property, is justified by moral values, protected social interests and policy considerations. It also has to be taken into account that if robots are persons, this necessarily implies that they are *not* property. It is also unlikely that companies producing robots would accept that they produce persons that cannot be owned.

It seems to be obvious that if robots are provided with legal personality, then they have an autonomous liability, but that is not necessarily a final answer in tort law. There are structures of vicarious liability where persons are liable for the wrongdoing of others. From this point of view, the issue whether robots are things or persons is important but not necessarily decisive because persons can be held liable for things as well as for other persons.

III.   THE ROLE AND FUNCTION OF LIABILITY

Liability has been developed on a double track in legal history. The first track is the idea of liability as a tool for promoting corrective justice in social rela-tionships.[8] Early forms of liability addressed the consequence of wrongdoing

---

[7]   There are extremely rare instances where animals have been provided with legal personality, see for example: 'Orangutan Sandra granted personhood settles into new Florida home' (*Guardian*, 7 Nov 2019) www.theguardian.com/world/2019/nov/07/sandra-orangutan-florida-argentina-buenos-aires accessed 23 August 2022, where the orangutan was granted limited legal personhood by an Argentinian judge.

[8]   Aristotle, W D Ross and Lesley Brown, *The Nicomachean Ethics* (Oxford University Press, 2009); Ernest J Weinrib, *The Idea of Private Law* (Oxford University Press, 2012); Ernest J Weinrib, *Corrective Justice* (Oxford University Press, 2012).

while sanctioning wrongful behaviour with a payment of compensation. In ancient law, in the absence of a division of the legal system into private law and public law, it was not at all clear (and not important), whether such payment was to be seen as *damages* providing a restoration of the original state to the victim or as a *punishment*. The Roman law *lex Aquilia*, which provided compensation to the injured owner and is often held as the root of fault-based liability for damages in civil legal systems, was not private law. It also has been argued that deriving fault-based liability from *lex Aquilia* is simply a misunderstanding.[9]

This, however, does not change the fact that liability for damages is about distinguishing between right and wrong. In a way, the whole development of private law can be seen as replacing the *talio* with a monetary obligation, because liability defines protected interests and protected interests are the building blocks of property law as well as contract law. Property law and contract law can be understood as a product of tort law. Looking at tort law from this angle, tort law defines wrongful behaviour[10] and the consequence of wrongful behaviour is paying damages. This first track is underlined with the policy of preventing wrongdoing.

The other track is the idea of liability as a tool for risk allocation. If liability is seen purely as a method of risk allocation, it is not the wrongful conduct that is the focus but the idea that the costs shall be allocated where the benefit is realised. If costs are not allocated within the profit-making enterprise, externalities occur, which undermines efficiency in social relationships. That is the primary basis of environmental liability ('polluter pays' principle), product liability,[11] liability for extra-hazardous activity or the strict liability of employers.[12]

Law is about creating incentives; this comes from its role in society. Prevention is an incentive for the tortfeasor to avoid committing wrong or an incentive for the victim to defend themself against wrongdoing. Thus, prevention, as a function of law, is not the result of implementing policy but it comes with the nature of law. One can establish that compensation and prevention are the main functions of tort law.

---

[9]   Géza Marton, *A polgári jogi felelősség* (*Civil Law Liability*) (TRIORG, 1993) 53.

[10]   John C P Goldberg and Benjamin R Zipursky, *Recognizing Wrongs* (Harvard University Press, 2020) 9.

[11]   Helmut Koziol, 'Introductory Lecture' in H Koziol and others (eds.), *Product Liability – Fundamental Questions in a Comparative Perspective* (De Gruyter, 2017) 13–25, 20.

[12]   Note Douglas Brodie, *Enterprise Liability and the Common Law* (Cambridge University Press, 2010).

A.   Liability and Prevention

The main goal of *conduct-based* and *risk-based* forms of liability is to reach an optimal level of risk allocation in society. That is, in terms of economic efficiency, liability establishes the obligation of taking precautionary measures between the tortfeasor and the victim. The function of tort law has never been simply about establishing liability but also about drawing its limits – the risk of the victim starts where the liability of the tortfeasor ends. Losses that are not covered by the tortfeasor's liability shall fall to the victim. The primary tools for limiting a tortfeasor's liability are the limits of the required standard of conduct (by fault-based liability), doctrines of limiting causation and the victim's contributory negligence. When it comes to efficient risk allocation, the liability of the victim depends on the costs of precautionary measures, as was established by Judge Learned Hand in a judgment handed down in the case *United States v Carroll Towing Co.* in 1947.[13] According to the 'Hand formula' (or 'Hand rule'), the owner's duty to provide against resulting injuries is a function of three variables: (1) the probability of occurrence of loss; (2) the gravity of the resulting injury; and (3) the burden of adequate precautions. In algebraic terms: 'if the probability be called P; the injury, L; and the burden, B; liability depends upon whether B is less than L multiplied by P: i.e., whether $B < PL$'.

However, establishing liability may have a preventive effect only insofar as it is capable of influencing the tortfeasor's behaviour. If the probability of occurrence of loss cannot be reduced via creating incentives for preventing it, there is no sense in establishing liability, at least not from the point of view of prevention. That is, there are basically two prerequisites for reaching a preventive effect of liability in an efficient way: the first is the potential influence upon the behaviour, the second is the lower social costs of prevention compared to imposing liability on the other party.

B.   Liability and Compensation

Compensation puts the function of liability as a risk allocation mechanism into the foreground. The idea behind compensation is Aristotelian corrective justice. While distributive justice addresses the distribution of goods among the members of society, corrective justice addresses voluntary and involuntary transactions, that is, torts and contracts. The key element of justice is equality or fairness.[14] In the context of distributive justice, injustice occurs if

---

[13]   159 F.2d 169 (2d. Cir. 1947).

[14]   John Rawls, *A Theory of Justice* (Oxford University Press, 2000) 3–46.

one of the members of the society has too much in contrast to the other. Both distributive and corrective justice construe equality but they do it in different ways. Distributive justice allocates social resources according to the merits of the members of the society, while corrective justice maintains and restores equality between the parties of the transaction. In the context of corrective justice, injustice emerges when one party has a gain and the other party has a corresponding loss.[15] The paradigmatic justice of private law, however, is that equal situations are to be decided the same way, while different situations are to be decided in different ways. This requirement holds equally vis-à-vis the legislator as well as the courts.

Compensation as a policy goal can be achieved not only with liability but also via insurance. The main benefit of insurance on a social level is that insurance does not simply allocate risks but spreads them too, because the members of the risk community contribute to the insurance fund, spreading the risks amongst them. The possibility of replacing tort law as a risk allocation system with insurance is considered below.

IV.   TORT AND REGULATORY LAW

Producing and operating robots and AI does not come into a legal vacuum. There is a growing demand for detailed regulation. Presumably, due to the obvious need for state regulation over producing and operating robots and AI, statutory law and a system of individual or statutory permissions would cover this activity. In the context of liability, this raises the issue of the consequences of the public-private divide. In legal systems, where a wall is raised between administrative law and civil law, this wall is built on the autonomous concepts of unlawfulness and fault (or wrongfulness) in tort law. These concepts are independent from administrative regulation. Public law is the law governing the structure and activity of the state and state organisations,[16] while administrative law is the law governing the organising, decision-making, executive and arranging activity of state organs.[17] There is not a generally accepted (and distinguished from public and administrative law) concept for regulatory law. From the autonomous concept of unlawfulness, it follows that the compliance of the tortfeasor's conduct with a statutory provision or administrative per-

---

[15]   Ernest J Weinrib, 'Corrective Justice in a Nutshell' (2002) 52(4) The University of Toronto Law Journal 349.

[16]   Tamás Lábady, *A Magyar magánjog (polgári jog) általános része* (*The General Part of Hungarian Private (Civil) Law*) (2002) 22.

[17]   Miklós Világhy and Gyula Eörsi, *Magyar Polgári Jog I* (*Hungarian Civil Law*) (1962) 15.

missio does not in itself prevent the tortfeasor from being held liable.[18] The violation of a statutory provision may play, however, an important role in the qualification of the damage. If the qualification of the damage is important from the point of view of establishing the applicable regime (e.g. whether the liability is strict or a fault-based one), the violation of a specific regulation would orient the courts. Administrative law regulation may play an important role in considering fault as well. The tortfeasor may exempt themself from liability by proving that they acted according to the required standards of conduct. Compliance with the provisions of administrative law regulation in itself does not mean that the tortfeasor cannot be at fault, but regulation may provide important reference points on what the required standards of conduct in that certain case could and should be.[19]

The fundamental difference between tort law and regulation in addressing social behaviour is that while regulation provides ex ante measures with clear rules, liability is an ex post reaction of the law based on open standards. Liability – like private law in general – is designed for judicial enforcement in horizontal relationships of individuals. Liability reaches its limits when it comes to a potentially great number of cases or potentially big losses, because the risk of being found liable is not predictable for the potential tortfeasors ex ante. Statutory law and administrative control may prevent losses with ex ante measures.[20] This means that *optimal* risk allocation should be provided by the legislator instead of the courts. This kind of predictability would increase efficiency. The consequences of the public-private divide in tort law shall, however, be revisited, because the efficiency of such a system requires the provision of immunity against liability claims in the case of compliance with the statutory regulation or individual permissions. State intervention also may mean maintaining statutory compensation schemes for victims of development risks insofar as they can comply with the exclusionary nature of a product liability regime. The experiences with reducing the risks in medicines via the administrative control of putting medicines into the market, disclosure and compensating the losses that may occur *could* be a good pattern for certain parts of the industry. Such systems which protect the producers of medicines should be introduced for reducing the development risks for producers of robotics technology and AI.

---

[18] Barnabás Lenkovics, 'A környezetszennyezés polgári jogi szankciói' (The civil law sanctions of environmental damage) in L Asztalos and K Gönczöl (eds.), *Felelősség és szankció a jogban (Liability and sanction in the law)* (1980) 317 ff, 324.

[19] Willem H van Boom, 'On the Intersections Between Tort Law and Regulatory Law – A Comparative Analysis' in Willem H van Boom and others (eds.), *Tort and Regulatory Law* (Springer, 2007) 419–43.

[20] ibid.

V.   THE NATURE AND CONCEPT OF AUTOMATED SYSTEMS

Without going into the different aspects of robotics, for the purposes of this chapter, robots are defined as artificially manufactured automated systems which are capable of acting in the world without being controlled by human or non-human intervention, on the basis of algorithms and analysing data. I would not go as far as defining robots as human-like things, such as describing robots as a constructed system that displays physical as well as mental agency while not being a living organism in the biological sense.[21] Basically, I would address sophisticated automated systems (machines) as robots, assuming that they are able to receive and transmit information independently (connectivity), respond to outside input by engaging in physical motion independently (autonomy) and learn from experience by receiving, evaluating, using and transmitting information, with their learning ability determining their future responses (intelligence).[22]

Complexity and data dependence are inherent qualities of such systems. They are operated via algorithms that also interact and have to cooperate. They are programmed to react; their learning ability is also programmed. That is, the human factor mostly plays a role in the course of producing and operating robots as well as when robots interact with humans. The fundamental structure of risk allocation in private law comes from the internal logic of the law. That is, the victim has to bear the risk if it cannot be shifted to another person (*casum sentit dominus*). Liability shifts the risk to the tortfeasor, while insurance shifts the risk to the insurer then spreads it among the members of the risk community.

VI.   CORE PROBLEMS WITH THE LIABILITY REGIME

From the point of view of liability, the primary question is whether liability for damages caused by the operation of robots can be managed within the existing conceptual and structural framework of tort law. Assuming that robots are not persons, the question is whether conduct-based forms of liability (normally the basic norm of fault-based liability) and the application of specific forms

---

[21]   Neil Richards and William D Smart, 'How Should the Law Think about Robots?' in Ryan Calo, A. Michael Froomkin and Ian Kerr (eds.), *Robot Law* (Edward Elgar, 2016) 6.

[22]   F Patrick Hubbard, 'Allocating the Risk of Physical Injury from "Sophisticated Robots": Efficiency, Fairness, and Innovation' in Calo and others (n 21) 25.

of conduct-independent, no-fault forms of liability can provide the toolkit for shifting the risk to persons other than the victim. Shifting the risk to persons other than the victim is reasonable only if the chance of establishing liability may create incentives for preventing the loss via influencing the tortfeasor's conduct or if the tortfeasor is the one acquiring the benefit (profit) of the activity that caused the loss and establishing liability avoids externalities.

From this angle liability for robots seems to be much more an old issue in new clothes rather than a brand-new one. Animals, just like robots, are able to receive and transmit information, are able to respond to outside input by engaging in physical motion independently, and they can learn by experience. As to liability for damage caused by animals, Roman law has already provided answers, and there are answers for this form of liability in all modern-day jurisdictions.[23] Forms of liability for things, liability for extra-hazardous activity, product liability and other forms of strict liability are not conduct-based and they are applicable when considering liability for robots. I don't think that there is a *need* to rethink this framework in order to allocate liability for damage caused by robots. The flexible system of tort law[24] provides a conceptual framework built on rather open concepts which allows a wide playing field for the courts to decide cases according to the social evaluation of the case.

Liability for robotics, however, requires an innovative approach in liability and insurance systems. This innovative approach is needed, however, not on the level of structural framework but on the level of *policy*. The problem with robotic technology lies – at least from the point of view of liability issues – with its *complexity* and with the *time-dimension* of its application, that is, that it normally is assumed to perform over a long run. Complexity means that robotic technology based on AI is driven by algorithms designed on analyses of data. Algorithms produced by different developers interact and communicate in an environment of hardware and peripheries produced also by different entities, while the outcome of operating such complex systems in rather sensitive sectors like transport or biotechnology is determined by processed data. This complexity makes it rather difficult to identify conduct or causal links as well as the costs and benefits that could establish liability. This makes presenting evidence rather difficult in civil procedures. This phenomenon, called *Beweisnotstand* in German terminology,[25] resulting in reverse of burden of proof is not new in private law and litigation. The complexity of applying

---

[23] Cosima Möller, 'Haftungskonzepte im Römischen Deliktsrecht' in Sabine Gless and Kurt Seelmann (eds.), *Intelligente Agenten und das Recht* (Nomos, 2016) 119–40.

[24] Helmut Koziol, 'Das bewegliche System: Die goldene Mitte für Gesetzgebung und Dogmatik' [2017] Austrian Law Journal 160.

[25] Wannes Vandenbussche, 'Dealing with Evidentiary Deficiency in Tort Law' (2019) 9 IJPL 50.

robotic technology makes, however, its use rather limited. As such technology is assumed to operate on a longer run, the approaches that assess liability at the moment of performing the contract (liability for breach of contract), putting the product into circulation in the market (product liability) or wrongdoing (tort), normally followed in tort law or in liability for breach of contract, are not tenable anymore. An approach that implies the time-dimension of operating such systems and the reliance upon them shall be followed in relevant cases.

On the level of policy, the legal systems are required to comply with two contradictory aspects. The first is that persons and property are to be protected and this protection is provided – in private law – mostly via lability rules. The second is the public interest and the public demand for supporting innovation.

The underlying features of robotic technology are data dependency, autonomy, communication and interactions. Important elements of this complex system are protected with monopolies, that is, disposal over data and intellectual property rights. Creating incentives for innovation, that is, public interest, underlies these monopolies. Due to the consequences of the complexity, the limits of such monopolies are to be revisited and it shall be considered how far a duty of disclosure could limit such monopolies either vis-à-vis consumers or vis-à-vis other parties contributing to the operation of such systems. The failure of robotic technology may result in interference with interests protected on the highest level in society – life, health and bodily integrity – which would push the legal systems for a rather strict liability. If the risk of liability is too high, it creates strong incentives for the potential tortfeasor to avoid such risks which is often a barrier to innovation.

Innovation is a key factor for development of societies and a key factor in increasing the competitiveness of the economy. Thus, the law must support innovation. Innovation, however, necessarily implies risks. If such risks are shifted to the developers and appliers of innovative technology, this creates incentives for risk avoidance which will reduce incentives for developing innovative technology. An important part of the underlying legal environment for technological development is the allocation of the risks of research and development. The cornerstones for such risk allocation are liability and insurance. It already seems to be obvious that risk allocation, with the liability of research institutes, producers and service providers for the development and implementation of AI and biotechnology, will soon reach its limits. The healthcare sector, the food industry and transportation (including motor vehicle production) are the most vulnerable branches of industry. Life, health and bodily integrity are the values protected at the highest level of society, and the products and services made and distributed by those sectors create specific risks of personal injury. For this reason, the allocation of such risks is of utmost importance, and it is a rather sensitive issue in tort law. The problem is, however, that the proper assessment of fault (compliance with the required standard of conduct) and causal link will be almost impossible, due to the complexity of the technology and the network of cooperation behind producing such products and providing such services.

The contradictory requirements shall lead to heterogeneity in the policy. It means that the higher the level of the protected interest interfered with is (e.g. in cases of personal injury), the higher the required standard of conduct is and the more risk averse the required decision-making attitude is. Interests protected on a lower level (e.g. monetary interests) tolerate more risk; a good example could be the 'business judgment rule' in the context of the liability of directors of companies. That is, tort law, to a certain extent can tolerate the taking of risk if it is justified by protected interests. Tort law also may tolerate violation of statutory rules if it is necessary to prevent personal injury or other serious loss (e.g. exceeding the speed limit in road traffic in order to prevent an accident). I believe that one of the most challenging ethical and legal paradoxes in this field is to what extent illegality can be programmed and whether such programmed unlawfulness can be required if it may prevent accidents or other damaging events.

VII. FORMS OF LIABILITY AND RISK ALLOCATION CONCERNING AUTOMATED SYSTEMS

The system of liability in private law is built upon liability in tort and liability for breach of contract. It is common in both regimes that liability is a consequence of breaching a duty but while in tort law it is the violation of a duty imposed by the law that triggers liability, liability for breach of contract is the consequence of a failure to comply with a duty undertaken voluntarily by the party. The voluntary nature of contractual obligations justifies a strict approach of liability for breach of contract. A further peculiarity of contractual relationships is that – within the limits of freedom of contract – the parties are free in designing their duties and allocating the risks between them. The contract as such can be seen as a risk allocation mechanism.

In a statutory system of liability, unified or harmonised law in particular shall have to take into account this dichotomy of the liability system. As to liability in tort, due to the different regimes of specific forms of liability in jurisdictions, I will focus on the potential tortfeasors instead of trying to consider the different specific forms of liability that can play a role in allocating the risks of robotics technology. Primarily, there are three persons that potentially can be held liable for compensating the harm caused by robotic technology: the producer of the machine and equipment, the operator of the technology and the user who simply uses it.[26] There are also other market players involved in liability issues concerning robotic technology (and AI), like distributors, importers, service providers, professional or non-professional consumers. For the purpose of considering the framework of different forms of liability in tort, however, it seems to be apt to address the liability of the producer, the operator and the user.

It is assumed, as it seems to be realistic today, that the human factor should not be eliminated from liability issues. This holds not only for the potential victims but also for potential tortfeasors as well. It means that we shall consider technologies that are developed and controlled by humans. From this it follows that liability issues can be compatible with the structure of private law addressing social conduct and with the conceptual framework of liability law. The planning, producing and marketing of robotics technology is assisted by human behaviour and is the result of human decision-making. The same is true for the operation and control of robotics technology. That is, the liability for robotics technology is embedded in the system of social relationships.

A.   Liability of Producers

The liability of the producer of robotics technology is covered by harmonised law on the European playing field. The framework of product liability is provided by the EU Product Liability Directive.[27] Article 7(e) of the Product Liability Directive provides for exclusion of liability for the producer if he proves 'that the state of scientific and technical knowledge at the time when he put the product into circulation was not such as to enable the existence of the defect to be discovered'. This development risk defence is a highly controversial opportunity for the producer to escape liability. On the one hand, considering the importance of supporting research and development, such a policy seems to be reasonable. It is also reasonable because such risks of research and development cannot be easily calculated and insured. On the other hand, it does not seem to be fair that society as a whole enjoys the advantages of product development while a limited number of victims should bear the damage. This tension between the contradictory policies will only be stronger in the future, if specific regulation is provided with the aim of providing a better environment for innovation. The problem is that in order to increase the competitiveness of the economy and of the legal environment not simply innovation, the rapid implementation of the innovation in practice

---

[26]   Gerhard Wagner, 'Robot Liability' in Sebastian Lohsse and others (eds.), *Liability for Artificial Intelligence and the Internet of Things* (Nomos, 2019) 27–62.

[27]   Council Directive 85/374/EEC of 25 July 1985 on Product Liability.

(application in production and providing services) shall also be supported. This certainly increases the development risks. This results in a growing gap between the interests and the position of the victims and the beneficiaries. I believe that the colliding interests cannot be successfully balanced within the system of liability law. The only way of counterbalancing this disadvantage is through a developed social security system. The success of this counterbalancing primarily depends on the level of social welfare.

The issue of applicability of a 'learned intermediary' doctrine has not been seriously raised in European legislation and it seems that the European Court of Justice (ECJ) does not find it compatible with the Product Liability Directive to extend its scope to intermediate distributors.[28] From the point of view of the impacts of further developments on the structure of tort law, it has to be taken into account that the ECJ established very clearly that the European Product Liability Directive provides for an exclusionary regime.[29] That means that cases falling under the scope of the Directive shall not be decided according to any alternative liability regime offered by national law, even if the alternative regime would be more beneficial for the victim; for example, in most of the legal systems liability for breach of contract is a strict liability not allowing exoneration on the basis of development risk defence. Thus, if the producer is the seller of the thing it produced, it may occur that it can escape liability with the development risk defence via application of the product liability rules, although it could be held liable on the basis of liability for breach of contract. In such situations, the beneficiary of the European product liability legislation is the producer and not the victim.

The existing framework of product liability shall certainly be revised in the very near future. The European Union's White Paper on AI,[30] based on the Commision Report on the safety and liability implications of AI, the Internet of Things, and Robotics,[31] expresses a strong resolution for and commitment to improving the business and legal environment for technological development in the European Union. This is inevitable if the European Union wants to increase its competitiveness against the United States and Asia. According to

---

[28] ECJ C-327/05, *Commission v Denmark*.

[29] ECJ 25 April 2002 – C-183/00, *Maria Victoria González Sánchez v Medicina Asturiana* [2002]; ECJ 25 April 2002 – C-52/00 *EC Commission v French Republic* [2002]; ECJ 25 April 2002 – C-154/00 *EC Commission v Hellenic Republic* [2002]; ECJ C-327/05, *Commission v Denmark*.

[30] White Paper on Artificial Intelligence: a European approach to excellence and trust – Brussels, 19.2.2020 COM(2020) 65.

[31] Report from the Commission to the European Parliament, the Council and the European Economic and Social Committee/Report on the safety and liability implications of Artificial Intelligence, the Internet of Things, and Robotics – Brussels, 19.2.2020 COM(2020) 64.

the AI White Paper, there is an urgent need for revising the European frame-work of liability. The scope of the EU legislation as of today covers the pro-ducing and purchasing of goods only; the scope shall be extended to providing services, in particular in financial, transportation and healthcare sectors. There is also the need for the revision of product liability for AI-driven goods and services, because the growing complexity of the products and services makes it impossible to assess liability under the existing regime (uncertain causation, the application of integrated software that may change the function of the product, etc.). The liability of intermediaries has to be reconsidered and the liability shall be allocated in a more sophisticated manner, because it does not seem to be reasonable to shift the risks of defects in software to the producer. The AI White Paper tries to identify the risks involved in the applications of AI like opaque decision-making, the impossibility of revealing the causal link that resulted in the injury and the identification of the person responsible for it, the potential danger of discrimination and so on, but it does not provide even the main contours or the main directions of the possible solutions. It is not clear how the time-dimension of liability can be assessed, that is, the reference point for the liability of the manufacturer when the product was put into circulation in the market.

B.   Liability of Operators

Although the basic norm of fault-based liability, prevailing in most legal systems, assesses the conduct of the wrongdoer, there are specific forms of liability elaborated by the legislator or established by doctrines developed by the courts which shift the blame on to the person operating the thing or the activity that caused the damage, even if the operator did not perform any wrongful conduct; for example; if a hospital buys surgical robot equipment and permits use of it by doctors of another hospital as well, the owner of the equipment shall qualify as the operator while the doctors actually using it qualify as users. This specific form of liability is also addressed by soft law in Europe. The Draft Common Frame of Reference provides for such liability for the keeper of a motor vehicle (DCFR VI-3:205) and for the keeper of a sub-stance or an operator of an installation if the substance or the emission from the installation caused damage (DCFR VI-3:206). The Principles of European Tort Law provide that a person carrying on an abnormally dangerous activity is strictly liable for damage characteristic of the risk presented by the activity and resulting from it (PETL Art 5:101). The explanatory notes to the Principles establish that carrying on an abnormally dangerous activity does not require that the person ultimately liable had been directly and actively involved in the activity in the sense of hands-on action.[32]

C.   Liability of Users

The user is the person who actually uses the robotics technology and causes harm with it. The liability of the user, provided that they shall not be qualified as an operator of the robotics technology, is normally a fault-based liability. Fault is failure to comply with the required standard of conduct (required duty of care). That is, fault shall not be assessed as the status of mind, actual knowledge or personal abilities of the person acting. The conduct of the person shall be contrasted with the expectations that come from the social evaluation under the given circumstances of the case including the position of this person. The liability of the user is independent from the liability of the operator. From this it follows that the user and the operator can be qualified as multiple tortfeasors if their liability (according to the different tests applicable to each of them) is to be established.

As far as the required duty of care for users of robotics technology is concerned, it is rather difficult to conclude any general statements because it is true that with the development of robotics technology and its expanding use, members of society would get used to the application of it, including the risks it involves. Yet, the operating mechanisms of robotics technology are normally not clear or transparent for the user. Robotics technology, however, would most often be used by professionals against whom the level of the required standard of conduct can be set higher than that against non-professionals.

A key factor in using robotics technology is education and professional training, which may certainly help in reducing the risk of potential harms. This is not only a social responsibility but the responsibility of the producers as well as operators and employers. Robotics technology may put employment law liability in a new context too. This may be rather critical in legal systems which make the employee jointly and severally liable with the employer for damage caused by the employee in the course of the employment relationship. If vicarious liability provides immunity for the employee against the direct claims of the victim, this issue primarily remains an employment law issue.

D.   The Victim's Contributory Negligence

One of the shortcomings of the discussions on liability for robots is that they normally focus on the tortfeasor but fail to take into account the responsibility

---

[32]   *Principles of European Tort Law: Text and Commentary* (Springer, 2005) 108.

of the victim. As it has already been stressed, humans can become accustomed to the existence of robots, their operation and the risks involved with using them.[33] The victim is normally also charged with the duty to prevent the occurrence of loss according to the required standard of conduct. That is, if the victim was or ought to have been aware of the risks that are inherent within the actual automated system, they may be obliged to avoid such risks. If they failed to comply with this obligation, it leads to a proportional liability as between the tortfeasor and the victim. That is, if the victim was or ought to have been aware of the possibility of the failure of the automated system, they may be obliged to take reasonable precautionary measures in order to prevent damage.

VIII.   CONTRACTUAL RELATIONSHIPS

Producing and marketing goods and providing services is realised via chains of contractual relationships which can be rather complex. This makes liability issues rather complex as well because the contracts between the parties at different levels of the production and marketing chain are not grounded in the same bargaining position and may fall under different rules, including mandatory rules of contract law. Although the paradigm is freedom of contract, enforcement of clauses that limit the liability for breach of contract may fall under different tests in standard contract terms or in consumer contracts.

Clauses excluding or limiting liability for breach of contract are the most important tools of risk allocation in the hands of the contracting parties. There are, however, statutory or doctrinal limits of enforcing such clauses.[34] As a kind of standard approach, it can be established that excluding or limiting liability for intentional or grossly negligent breach of contract or liability for damage in human life, physical integrity and health shall not be enforceable. Regulatory and judicial restriction of contractual limitation and exclusion of liability for breach of contract has been a general answer in modern legal systems to the abuse of bargaining power. Limitation clauses reaching beyond the acceptable degree in most of the cases appeared in standard contract terms. This might be the reason for the reaction of the legal systems generally being twofold. One of the answers of the courts and later legislation was to disclaim exclusion clauses, the other was the control of standard contract terms.[35] One of the main arguments in favour of regulatory or judicial restriction on the

---

[33]   Curtis E A Karnow, 'The Application of Traditional Tort Theory to Embodied Machine Intelligence' in Calo and others (n 21) 76.

[34]   See for instance Council Directive 93/13/EEC of 5 April 1993 on Unfair Terms in Consumer Contracts.

[35]   See Hein Kötz, *European Contract Law* (2nd ed., Oxford University Press, 2017) Ch 8.

enforceability of exclusion clauses is that if the party to a contract was allowed to exclude their liability for all kinds of breach, it would deprive the contract as a legal instrument of its substance because the contract would not actually create any rights and obligations.

An adverse consequence of the statutory restriction of exclusion clauses is that the restriction may prevent contracting parties from defining the scope of their liability and adjusting it to the agreed price of their performance.

If, for instance, the seller of a car equipped with developed driver assistance systems stipulates in its standard contract terms that the drive assisting system may produce failures and the user is assumed to be aware of such risks, the seller shall not be liable for the failure of the driver assistance systems; the enforceability of this provision shall be tested according to the law (statutory law and court practice) addressing standard contract terms, consumer contracts and the general rules and doctrines upon enforceability of exclusion clauses. The primary aim of producers and sellers of robotics technology is certainly to describe the risks of using robotics technology in as much detail as possible and also to exclude or limit their liability for failure of such technology in order to escape liability. In light of the policy of promoting innovation and providing a legal environment that supports research and development as well as having regard to self-reliance, the courts should not be too restrictive by enforcing these clauses. These contractual provisions make the position of the buyer and third parties as victims different – as the buyer's claims may be limited by such clauses, the liability of the producer or the operator is not affected by them.

IX.   INSURANCE

The problems of assessing liability will push the role of insurance to the foreground. Over the last couple of decades, one of the most important structural issues in tort law has been the relationship between liability and insurance, especially the debate on whether no-fault compensation systems based on a compulsory insurance could replace tort law and liability.

It is a challenging, useful and important idea to consider how and to what extent insurance can replace or complement the system of liability in tort and this is also worthy of thorough discussion, in particular in the context of liability for automated systems. Such a system, normally, can be in compliance with systems of tort law in different jurisdictions.

A no-fault compensation scheme was introduced in New Zealand and replaced tort law with an overall insurance-based compensation scheme.[36]

---

[36]   László Sólyom, *A polgári jogi felelősség hanyatlása* (*The fall of liability in tort*) (Akadémiai Kiadó, 1977) 36 ff.

The compulsory third-party insurance system for operating motor vehicles in Europe[37] also supports the idea that insurance can become the primary regime for risk allocation, pushing damages into the background at least in some specific areas of tort law. It might, however, be a mistake to assume that an overall system of insurance can successfully be introduced as a replacement for a tort regime. One should rather consider the possibility of introducing such a system – at least as a first stage – for properly circumscribed and defined cases like cases of personal injury. As in most cases claims for non-pecuniary damages (or *solatium doloris*, that is, *Schmerzensgeld*) are combined with claims for recovery of pecuniary damages (typically compensation of lost income and maintenance costs), such a system should cover both in order to provide considerable social benefits. It is, however, far from being proven that insurance – either as a first-party or as a liability insurance – could replace the tort regime. Insurance is a system of risk-spreading among members of a community of homogeneous risk on the basis of probabilities of the occurrence of loss. The insurance pool finances itself.[38] Thus, the individuals belonging to the risk community contribute to the fund according to the potential risk they run. The tort system covers risks that are *too heterogeneous to be capable of creating a pool*. Maintaining an overall system of insurance may also involve considerable administration costs.

One of the main problems with the idea of replacing tort with insurance is the *contract-tort divide*. Liability for the breach of a contract or the compensation of losses suffered as a result of a breach of contract cannot be brought under any general insurance regime due to the *heterogeneous and specific nature of contractual rights and obligations*. A liability regime covering torts recognises the need to make distinctions between liability in tort and liability for breach of contract although it would be extremely difficult to manage; it can be possible only in legal systems which draw a clear dividing line between contract and tort.[39] The same holds true for liability for damages and restitution. Unjust enrichment claims and claims for damages often overlap[40] which can make it practically impossible to distinguish them. Such cases do not necessarily cause problems in court practice which may be flexible enough

---

[37]   Directive 2009/103/EC of the European Parliament and of the Council of 16 September 2009 relating to insurance against civil liability in respect of the use of motor vehicles, and the enforcement of the obligation to insure against such liability; Robert Merkin and Maggie Hemsworth, *The Law of Motor Insurance* (2nd ed., Sweet & Maxwell, 2020).

[38]   Jane Stapleton, 'Tort, Insurance and Ideology' (1995) 58 MLR 820, 821.

[39]   K Bárd, 'Kártérítési felelősség és biztosítás. Vázlat' (1998) 4 Collega Szakmai folyóirat joghallgatók számára 7, 9.

[40]   James Edelman, *Gain-Based Damages* (Hart, 2002) 65ff.

to address these situations, but an insurance regime covering only torts would make such distinctions necessary in the course of managing the claims against the insurance fund. Regarding the law of obligations, such distinctions would comply with the structure of Hungarian private law, which makes a sharp distinction between liability for torts and liability for breach of contract.

Even in the case of having an overall insurance-based compensation scheme, what relationship such an overall compulsory third-party insurance system could have with the social security system remains open. There are two possible ways of defining this relationship. One is that the compulsory liability insurance regime covers claims and losses that are *not covered* by social security (thus, this system would supplement the social security system); the other is that such claims will be covered by this system entirely and will be *picked out* from social security. This latter way is, in my view, unnegotiable, since as a matter of administering the system such claims cannot be separated from compensating injuries which were not – or were only partially – caused by other persons, but are, for example, the result of an act of the victim or of natural events.

Preserving the preventive effect of the system and the question of providing recourse rights is a sensitive problem that should not be underestimated. I think that, here, the devil lurks in the details. Whether or not a recourse right is provided, a specific system for calculating the cost of the insurance should be created, with higher fees to be paid by those who cause damage. The preventive effect of the recourse right can certainly be questioned, but I do not think that we should propose a system which does not manage the problem of moral hazard in insurance. Furthermore, a solution to the other challenge of insurance, adverse selection, should also be given in this system. Thus, the fee to be paid as a premium should be individualised. A further issue concerns who would establish the fee to be paid as a premium and, if a premium is individualised, could such a decision on the fee be challenged in court? Providing a recourse right necessarily involves the general problem of recourse rights as well. Insurance is a regime that should finance itself. If we assume that the insurance premium is the contribution to the fund that is created for covering damage caused (or suffered) by the persons belonging to the risk community, and we also assume that this fund is sufficient to cover the risks, the money recovered by the insurer via exercising its recourse right is merely an additional profit for the insurer. However, if the insurer is deprived of this advantage, there will be no incentive to exercise this right, which makes recourse pointless. In sum, I would be in favour of a system without recourse rights but containing a scheme to avoid moral hazard, providing an answer to adverse selection, and maintaining a preventive effect.

In any consideration of an overall insurance system, the relationship between this regime and the social security and national healthcare systems also has to be clarified. Insurance and socialisation of risks are two different risk allocation regimes.[41] The national healthcare system is part of the social welfare regime which can be seen as a tool for providing a minimum compensation for personal injury.

Assuming that the principle of full compensation should be maintained, a central issue of such a system is: *who pays* (i.e. who bears the risk) at the end of the day? One has to assume that all members of society, including legal entities, are potential wrongdoers or, considering a first-party insurance system, every natural person (and if the regime were to be extended to personal injuries, legal entities as well) is a potential victim. Thus, their contribution to this insurance fund (the fee they have to pay) is a kind of tax. If this fund is not adequate to cover all losses, a state subsidy should be provided in order to provide compensation to victims. If there is a surplus, it is very difficult to decide what to do with this and how to share it. Also, a problem is how potential wrongdoers (or victims) could pay the fee if they do not have any income or their income is very low. Especially in societies where a great majority of people are poor, they are unable to pay any kind of contribution to a fund such as this. If their contribution is financed by other members of the risk community, for example from the state budget, the result can be socially unjust and unacceptable. If this were the case, the system is actually not an insurance regime but a regime of socialisation of risks. Considering these factors, one has to conclude that introducing an overall system of insurance is basically a question of policy and social welfare.

X. CONCLUSIONS

Since the concept of person is an artificial product of society, technically robots could be qualified as persons; however, such a qualification would exclude treating them as property. Nevertheless, robotic legal personality is not justified by moral values, protected social interests or policy considerations, and any kind of similarity to humans is irrelevant in this respect. Liability is justified either by sanctioning wrongful conduct or by allocating the costs in order to prevent externalities. Both conduct-based and risk-based liability create incentives to optimise risk allocation. There are in essence two prerequisites for liability to have an efficient preventive effect: the first is the potential influence upon behaviour, the second is the lower social costs of prevention compared to imposing liability on the other party. Risk allocation of robotics technology could efficiently be provided by ex ante measures of regulation with clear rules instead of ex post liability based on open standards. This may

---

[41] Stapleton (n 38) 821ff.

require revisiting the intersection between tort law and regulatory law, because such a system requires the exclusion of liability in the case of compliance with statutory regulation or individual permissions. Shifting the risk to persons other than the victim is reasonable only if the chance of establishing liability may create incentives for preventing the loss via influencing the tortfeasor's conduct or if the tortfeasor is the one acquiring the benefit (profit) of the loss-causing activity and establishing liability avoids externalities. Liability for robotics requires an innovative approach in liability and insurance systems, balancing the protection of persons and property – mostly via lability rules, with the public interest and the public demand for supporting innovation.

Tort law tolerates the taking of a risk if it is justified by protected interests. It also may tolerate the breach of statutory rules if such breach was necessary to prevent personal injury or other serious loss.

Human factors should not be eliminated from liability issues. Within liability the main players are the producers, the operators and the users, and each should have their liability assessed differently. While the need for the revision of the European product liability legislation has been stressed in the AI White Paper, it is not clear at all how the time-dimension of liability can be assessed.

One of the shortcomings of the discussions on liability for robots is that they normally focus on the tortfeasor but fail to take into account the victim's contributory negligence. If the victim was or ought to have been aware of the possibility of the failure of the automated system, they may be obliged to take reasonable precautionary measures in order to prevent damage.

Producing and marketing goods and providing services is realised via chains of contractual relationships which can be complex. This may complicate liability issues, and in some circumstances the contracts may fall under different mandatory rules of contract law. Although the paradigm is freedom of contract, enforcement of clauses that limit the liability for breach of contract may fall under different tests in standard contract terms or in consumer contracts.

Insurance seems to be a better solution for allocating and spreading the risk of operating robotics technology but replacing tort with insurance is problematic as well. The contract-tort divide in the liability system is an obstacle to such a change. Moreover, maintaining preventive effect, managing moral hazard and adverse selection are big challenges as well.

Notwithstanding the problems it may raise, a system of compulsory insurance based on a no-fault liability regime seems to be the best tool for allocating and spreading the risks of innovation. Such a system could be implemented either as a statutory scheme or as a result of product liability. Product liability internalises the costs of compensating the victims, then spreads them among the product's buyers as the costs are incorporated into the price of the product. Due to the complex nature of AI-driven products and services or those derived from biotechnology, it is rather difficult to allocate the costs of compensation via product liability among the producers as primary risk bearers. The administration of a statutory scheme, however, may generate higher social costs. The social costs of maintaining such a system can be reduced by constant monitoring and analysing individual risks using smart tools. Exploiting the potential of the internet of things may help to reduce the costs of moral hazard and adverse selection in the context of insurance, which should result in an overall social insurance regime at lower costs.

7. Artificial Intelligence and Medical Decision-Making: Wind of Change for Medical Malpractice Liability and Insurance?

Özgün Çelebi[1] and Ayşegül Buğra Şar[2]

I. INTRODUCTION

Under the pressure of the ever-expanding quantity of medical information, the requirements of evidence-based medicine and the raising of expectations from the patient's side as to what medicine can achieve, the task of the physicians has become increasingly difficult. Based on their ability to parse through large amounts of data, the development of clinical decision support systems ('CDSSs') has therefore become a major preoccupation in various areas of healthcare. The systems which may be qualified as CDSSs have the common function of aiding clinical decision-making by matching the characteristics of an individual patient to a computerised clinical knowledge base and presenting patient-specific assessments.[3] The introduction of deep learning paved the way for new perspectives in this field. Research on artificially intelligent CDSSs, designed to assist physicians in their daily task of diagnosis, has constantly

[1]   Assistant Professor of Civil Law, Koç University Law School.
[2]   Assistant Professor of Maritime and Insurance Law, Koç University Law School.
[3]   Ida Sim and others, 'Clinical Decision Support Systems for the Practice of Evidence-based Medicine' (2001) 8(6) J Am Med Inform Assoc 527, 528. For a broad definition, see also E H Shortliffe, 'Computer Programs to Support Clinical Decision Making' (1987) 258(1) JAMA 61.

gained momentum[4] to such an extent that it is predicted that almost every type of clinician will be using artificial intelligence ('AI') technology in the future.[5]

Since the CDSSs operate merely by making a recommendation to the user and require their outputs to be applied by a human physician,[6] they can only cause harm through the intervention of humans.[7] Since the device is not supposed to replace, but to augment the physician's capabilities, the physician will carry the responsibility for deciding to rely on the outputs of such a system. Inversely, a physician also risks being held liable for not having recourse to such technology, if it can be shown that the harm suffered by the patient could have been avoided with the assistance of a CDSS. The physician's decisions regarding the use of an available CDSS fall within the sphere of application of negligence-based tort liability. In the case of an available technology, the negligent action is normally evaluated with respect to the diligent and responsible use of such technology.[8] However, some of the AI-based, complex CDSSs have characteristics which distinguish them from the previous technologies. As will be detailed below, the CDSSs which function as black boxes risk significantly altering medical decision-making processes[9] and thereby pose new

---

[4]   For examples of the use of AI in different fields of health care, see Eric J Topol, 'High-performance Medicine: The Convergence of Human and Artificial Intelligence' (2019) 25 Nature Medicine 44ff; Aliza Becker, 'Artificial Intelligence in Medicine: What is it Doing for Us Today?' (2019) 2(8) Health Policy and Technology 198, 199; Vivek Kaul, Sarah Enslin and Seth A Gross, 'History of artificial intelligence in medicine' (2020) 92(4) Gastrointestinal Endoscopy 807, 809–810. See also Rong Liu, Yan Rong and Zhehao Peng, 'A Review of Medical Artificial Intelligence' (2020) 4(2) Global Health Journal 42, 43.

[5]   Topol (n 4) 44.

[6]   Similarly, Andrew D Selbst, 'Negligence and AI's Human Users' (2020) 100 Boston University Law Review 1315, 1319. See also Andrea Bertolini, 'Artificial Intelligence and Civil Liability' (July 2020) www.europarl.europa.eu/RegData/etudes/STUD/2020/621926/IPOL_STU(2020)621926_EN.pdf accessed 25 September 2021, 113.

[7]   Arguing that to be the difference between IBM's Watson and other AI-driven tools such as self-driving cars, Jason Chung and Amanda Zink, 'Hey Watson – Can I Sue You for Malpractice? Examining the Liability of Artificial Intelligence in Medicine' (2018) 11 Asia Pacific J Health L & Ethics 51, 77–8.

[8]   Michael D Greenberg, 'Medical Malpractice and New devices: Defining an Elusive Standard of Care' (2009) 19(2) Health Matrix 423, 442–3. For the trend focusing on the reasonableness of the physician's judgment, regardless of the tool used, see Iria Giuffrida and Taylor Treece, 'Keeping AI under Observation: Anticipated Impacts on Physicians' Standard of Care' (2020) 22 Tul J Tech & Intell Prop 111, 114–16.

[9]   The view that black box systems bring radical changes to the medical decision-making process is not unanimously adopted. See, for instance, Alex John London, 'Artificial Intelligence and Black-Box Medical Decisions: *Accuracy versus Explainability*' (2019) 49(1) Hastings Center Report 15, 18, claiming that 'opacity, independence from an explicit domain model, and lack of causal insight' seen in

challenges to the traditional liability structure. The high degree of imprecision as to what a diligent action would mean in the context of the use of a black box system and the subsequent difficulty of assessing the risk of liability creates a strong need for formal guidelines for the user.[10] Some efforts have already been made in this direction.[11] Nevertheless, unless more precise legal guidelines are adopted, the integration of these systems into medical practice is likely to take place under the influence of interpretation of medical liability rules by the courts and the realities of the insurance market.

This chapter aims to provide an overview of the potential evolution of the well-established liability and insurance mechanisms in reaction to the use or failure to use black box CDSSs by physicians. The chapter will first explain in which ways the black box CDSSs challenge the negligence-based medical liability rules. It will then cover how the standard of care expected from the diligent physician may evolve with regard to the physician's decision regarding the use of the black box CDSS. Finally, the chapter will analyse how the insurance market may respond to the imprecisions created by the risk of liability based on the availability of black box CDSSs.

---

machine learning approaches 'are not radically different from routine aspects of medical decision-making'. Nevertheless, according to the view also adopted in this paper, whereas in traditional decision-making, reliance on opaque procedures may occasionally be the case, in the case of black box algorithms, lack of explainability is of a principled nature; on this issue, see Jens Christian Bjerring and Jacob Busch, 'Artificial Intelligence and Patient-Centered Decision-Making' (2021) 34 Philosophy & Technology 349, 363ff doi.org/10.1007/s13347-019-00391-6 accessed 25 September 2021. See also Julia Amann and others, 'Explainability for Artificial Intelligence in Healthcare: A Multidisciplinary Perspective' (2020) 20:310 BMC Medical Informatics and Decision Making 7.

[10]   Stressing the need for guidelines, see Becker (n 4) 202; W Nicholson Price II, Sara Gerke and I Glenn Cohen, 'Potential Liability for Physicians Using Artificial Intelligence' (2019) 322(18) JAMA 1765, 1766. See also Jessica S Allain, 'From Jeopardy to Jaundice: The Medical Liability Implications of Dr Watson and Other Artificial Intelligence Systems' (2013) 73 La L Rev 1049, 1051, underlining the necessity of a streamlined approach for assessing liability against AI systems.

[11]   Expert Group on Liability and New Technologies – New Technologies Formation set up by the European Commission, 'Liability for Artificial Intelligence and Other Emerging Digital Technologies' (2019) 6–7; The Royal Australian and New Zealand College of Radiologists, 'Ethical Principles for Artificial Intelligence in Medicine' (August 2019) <www.ranzcr.com/college/document-library/ethical-principles-for-ai -in-medicine> accessed 25 September 2021.

II.   CHALLENGES POSED BY BLACK BOX CDSSS TO THE TRADITIONAL MEDICAL LIABILITY RULES

Except for the areas which are subject to a no-fault approach in a limited number of jurisdictions,[12] liability for medical malpractice is based on negligence and requires proof that the provider of the service fell below the required standard of care.[13] This requirement stems from the idea that it is only when the harm could have been avoided through more careful conduct, as imposed by the applicable standard of care, that the physician can be held liable[14] and is therefore connected to the goal of deterrence of tort law.

AI-based CDSSs are capable of wrongs of their own, even when they would perform better than the average physician.[15] Where these systems depend on incorrect, insufficient[16] or potentially unrepresentative data,[17] this may lead to errors of judgment and even to systematic discrimination. When the AI-based

---

[12]   For France, see Florence G'Sell-Macrez, 'Medical Malpractice and Compensation in France: Part I: the French Rules of Medical Liability since the Patients' Rights Law of March 4, 2002' (2011) 86 Chi-Kent L Rev 1093, 1108–9; Genevieve Helleringer, 'Medical Malpractice and Compensation in France: Part II: Compensation Based on National Solidarity' (2011) 86 Chi-Kent L Rev 1125, 1126ff; for the US, see David A Hyman and Charles Silver, 'Medical Malpractice and Compensation in Global Perspective: How Does the U.S. Do It?' (2012) 87 Chi-Kent L Rev 163, 172; for the examples of Sweden, France, Belgium, see Kenneth Watson and Rob Kottenhagen, 'Patients' Rights, Medical Error and Harmonisation of Compensation Mechanisms in Europe' (2018) 25 European Journal of Health Law 1, 14–22.

[13]   For the US, see Hyman and Silver (n 12) 168; for the UK, see Richard Goldberg, 'Medical Malpractice and Compensation in the UK' (2012) 87 Chi-Kent L Rev 131, 143; for German law, see Marc S Stauch, 'Medical Malpractice and Compensation in Germany' (2011) 86 Chi-Kent L Rev 1139, 1144–5; for France see G'Sell-Macrez (n 12) 1098. See also, for German law, para 630a/II of the BGB (*Bürgerliches Gesetzbuch*) and in France, art. L1142-1 of the CSP (*Code de la santé publique*).

[14]   'No theory of negligence will assign liability where a tortfeasor could not have prevented the harm through greater care': Selbst (n 6) 1321.

[15]   A Michael Froomkin, Ian Kerr and Joelle Pineau, 'When AIs Outperform Doctors: Confronting the Challenges of a Tort-Induced Over-Reliance on Machine Learning' (2019) 61 Arizona Law Review 33, 59.

[16]   David D Luxton, 'Should Watson Be Consulted for a Second Opinion?' (2019) 21(2) AMA Journal of Ethics 131, 134. See also, Sim and others (n 3) 529ff: The authors underline the importance of the creation of machine-interpretable knowledge bases to enable the decision support systems to have direct access to the newest research for automated updating of their knowledge basis.

[17]   Selbst (n 6) 1357; on the potential systematic bias, see also Maximilian Kiener, 'Artificial Intelligence in Medicine and the Disclosure of Risks' (2021) 36 AI & Society 705, 709ff; Thomas Ploug and Soren Holm, 'The Right to Refuse Diagnostics and Treatment Planning by Artificial Intelligence' (2020) 23 Med Health Care and Philos 107, 109–10; Amann and others (n 9) 5; Thomas Grote and Philipp Berens, 'On

CDSS is constructed in such a way that it cannot explain the logic used to arrive at a particular decision, these flaws become more difficult to detect. The opacity of the decision-making process[18] and the lack of information as to why the system came up with a particular prediction is known as the 'black box' problem.[19] The danger of recourse to such systems lies in the fact that the user is not able to detect the errors of judgment made by the system and to make an informed decision as to whether or not to rely on its recommendations. As a result, the 'explainability' of the system, understood as the characteristic of an AI-driven system enabling the users to understand why or how a conclusion was reached,[20] has become a major preoccupation for the AI model choice both from a technical and a legal point of view.[21]

The difficulty of tracing back potentially problematic decisions made with the involvement of AI systems makes it challenging for the victims to obtain compensation under the current liability schemes.[22] One of the problems in this regard relates to the identification of the source of the harm, that is, whether it was caused by faulty data, by the system's self-learning or by the user's fault.[23]

---

the Ethics of Algorithmic Decision-Making in Healthcare' (2020) 46 J Med Ethics 205, 209.

[18] Commission, 'White Paper on Artificial Intelligence – A European approach to excellence and trust' COM (2020) 65 final, 12; Expert Group on Liability and New Technologies (n 11) 33; House of Lords Select Committee on Artificial Intelligence, *AI in the UK: Ready, Willing and Able?* (HL 2017–19, 100) para 89ff; Yavar Bathaee, 'Artificial Intelligence Opinion Liability' (2020) 35 Berkeley Tech LJ 113, 117.

[19] Zach Harned, Matthew P Lungren and Pranav Rajpurkar, 'Machine Vision, Medical AI, and Malpractice' (2019) Harv JL & Tech Dig jolt.law.harvard.edu/digest/machine-vision-medical-ai-and-malpractice accessed 25 September 2021, 4; Luxton (n 16) 134; W Nicholson Price II, 'Regulating Black-Box Medicine' (2017) 116(3) Michigan Law Review 421, 429–31; Yavar Bathaee, 'The Artificial Intelligence Black Box and the Failure of Intent and Causation' (2018) 31 Harv J L & Tech 889, 905.

[20] The Royal Society, *Explainable AI: The Basics – Policy Briefing* (November 2019) royalsociety.org/-/media/policy/projects/explainable-ai/AI-and-interpretability-policy-briefing.pdf accessed 25 September 2021, 8. For a similar use of the concept of explainability, see Amann and others (n 9) 2; Philipp Hacker and others, 'Explainable AI under Contract and Tort Law: Legal Incentives and Technical Challenges' (2020) 28 Artificial Intelligence and Law 415, 421; House of Lords Select Committee on Artificial Intelligence (n 18) para 100; Froomkin, Kerr and Pineau (n 15) 48. The use of the terms 'transparency', 'explainability' and 'interpretability' is not consistent (The Royal Society, 9) and they are sometimes used interchangeably (House of Lords Select Committee on Artificial Intelligence (n 18) para 91). In this chapter the term explainability refers to the characteristic of the system which enables the user to understand the reasoning behind the conclusion reached by the system in individual cases.

[21] Hacker and others (n 20) 417.

[22] COM (2020) 65 final (n 18) 12.

[23] Phillip Morgan and others, 'Review of Legal Frameworks, Standards and Best Practices in Verification and Assurance for Infrastructure Inspection Robotics' (8 July

The victims of harm incurred through the involvement of AI-based technology may therefore be in a weaker position to establish causation than in other tort cases.[24] Proof of causation becomes more complicated when, as is the case for decision support tools, the system recommends a course of action rather than taking an action itself.[25] Identification of the physician's negligence is also tainted with the same level of difficulty. Negligence liability requires proof that the harm could have been avoided if a higher degree of care had been deployed and such analysis is to be made by comparing the action taken by the physician with the action expected under the applicable standard of care. In the case of recourse to black box CDSSs, the problem lies precisely in determining what to expect from the reasonable physician. The unexplainable character of the logic behind the system's recommendations may make it impossible for the physician to understand whether the system's judgment, differing from their personal views, is the result of a better performance or simply an error of judgment.[26] If whether the system has committed an error or not would become impossible to detect and thus the potential errors qualify as unforeseeable, the physician who would be allowed or encouraged to use such systems could not be held liable for failing to take precautions against an unforeseeable risk.[27] Unable to understand and filter the outputs of the machine, the physician can no longer play a significant role in the decision-making process and may become a mere instrument for conveying the premonitions of an 'oracle' to the patient,[28] exempt of all liability for the harm caused. The problem of compatibility with the European data protection law is also one of the legal concerns raised with regard to unexplainable AI systems.[29]

2020) papers.ssrn.com/sol3/papers.cfm?abstract_id=3645997 accessed 25 September 2021, 29–30; similarly, Expert Group on Liability and New Technologies (n 11) 33; highlighting the potentially large number of 'alternative causation' cases, see Bertolini (n 6) 100.

[24]   Expert Group on Liability and New Technologies (n 11) 50; similarly, Bertolini (n 4) 11; Morgan and others (n 23) 30.

[25]   Miriam C Buiten, 'Towards Intelligent Regulation of Artificial Intelligence' (2019) 10 European Journal of Risk Regulation 41, 56.

[26]   Hacker and others (n 20) 422.

[27]   See Selbst (n 6) 1362, claiming that 'without interpretable or explainable AI, it is essentially impossible to claim that an AI error should have been foreseen ahead of time.'; on the issue of AI's unforeseeable actions and liability, see also Bathaee, 'Artificial Intelligence Opinion Liability' (n 18) 148 and Buiten (n 25) 56.

[28]   For the use of the term 'oracle' for accurate black box machines, see Harned, Lungren and Rajpurkar (n 19) 6.

[29]   See House of Lords Select Committee on Artificial Intelligence (n 18) para 101; Hacker and others (n 20) 417–18; Kristina Astromskė, Eimantas Peičius and Paulius Astromskis, 'Ethical and Legal Challenges of Informed Consent Applying Artificial Intelligence in Medical Diagnostic Consultations' (2021) 36 AI & Society 509, 514ff.

In reaction to the legal and ethical problems created by black box systems, draft legal instruments and documents issued by regulatory authorities have begun to mention the need for the development of systems whose reasoning is accessible to humans.[30] Unless approval criteria requiring human users to understand how a conclusion was reached are imposed,[31] models which do not have this quality may get the green light from regulatory authorities provided they fulfil the relevant criteria for their respective risk class. Since these systems seem to perform better than their explainable counterparts,[32] in the absence of clear legal guidance, the development of unexplainable assistance systems will not come to an end despite their shortcomings in terms of meaningful human supervision and subsequent problems regarding the user's liability.

III. POTENTIAL LIABILITY RISK UNDER THE NEGLIGENCE-BASED MEDICAL LIABILITY RULES

A. Standard of Care Based on the System's Accuracy

One of the possible scenarios regarding the evolution of the standard of care for the use of black box CDSSs can be based on the reliance on the level of

---

[30] Commission, 'Proposal for a Regulation of the European Parliament and of the Council Laying Down Harmonised Rules on Artificial Intelligence (Artificial Intelligence Act) and Amending Certain Union Legislative Acts', COM (2021) 206 final, states that operation of high-risk AI systems must be 'sufficiently transparent to enable users to interpret the system's output and use it appropriately' (art 13/1) and enable human oversight (art 14). Within the FDA, the Patient Engagement Advisory Committee has also underlined that '[o]ne way to gain the trust of patients and providers in AI/ML today is to explain the "why" of the algorithm output as well as the "what"' (US Food & Drug Administration, 'Executive Summary for the Patient Engagement Advisory Committee Meeting – Artificial Intelligence (AI) and Machine Learning (ML) in Medical Devices' (22 October 2020) www.fda.gov/media/142998/download accessed 25 September 2021, 9.

[31] Regulation (EU) 2017/745 of the European Parliament and of the Council of 5 April 2017 on medical devices, amending Directive 2001/83/EC, Regulation (EC) No 178/2002 and Regulation (EC) No 1223/2009 and repealing Council Directives 90/385/EEC and 93/42/EEC [2017] OJ L 117/1 (Medical Device Regulation) does not contain a general requirement for AI-driven medical devices to be explainable or interpretable: Johan Ordish, Hannah Murfet and Alison Hall, 'Algorithms as Medical Devices' (PHG Foundation, University of Cambridge, 2019) www.phgfoundation.org/media/74/download/algorithms-as-medical-devices.pdf?v=1&inline=1 accessed 25 September 2021, 29.

[32] Buiten (n 25) 58.

accuracy of the CDSS. If the success rates of the CDSS become the principal criterion for determination of the standard of care, in the case that the level of accuracy of the CDSS supersedes that of human physicians, the failure to consult the device[33] and to rely on its recommendations[34] may become difficult to justify with regard to what would be done by a reasonable physician. Since the goal and benefit of such systems is precisely to surpass human knowledge,[35] the mere lack of concordance with human knowledge would not be an acceptable basis for refusing to rely on their recommendations. Thus, the more authoritative a CDSS is in terms of success rate, 'the greater the liability risk of the professional who disregards the system's advice'.[36] Conversely, if the physician follows the recommendations of a highly performant CDSS, they would not be deemed negligent for doing so, even though these recommendations are not intelligible.[37] Obviously, an accuracy-based scenario becomes attractive only if the accuracy level has been demonstrated in a satisfactory way. Small sizes of the cohorts studied, a lack of a sufficient number of independent studies and a lack of validation in real-world clinical settings[38] may cast doubts on whether the difference between the system's performance and human decision-making has been adequately shown.[39]

Nevertheless, even in the case where the accuracy level may be the starting point for the determination of diligent conduct, the high level of accuracy may

---

[33] For computer-based expert systems in general, see, DI Bainbridge, 'Computer-Aided Diagnosis and Negligence' (1991) 31 Med Sci & L 127, 135; for medical AI technology, see, Giuffrida and Treece (n 8) 116. See, Hacker and others (n 20) 423, arguing that use of a black box model can become obligatory if its performance becomes exceptionally high, and under the condition that it can be reasonably integrated into the medical workflow and if it is cost-justified.

[34] Arguing that there would be in this case an 'epistemic obligation' to rely on the system, similar to the requirement to rely on the advice of an expert, however, that if such reliance conflicts with other values, such as patient-centred medicine, this might be a reason to dispense with this epistemic obligation, see Bjerring and Busch (n 9) 351. For an analogy with a consultant physician, for determination of the negligence of the consulting physician, see Michael Lupton, 'Some Ethical and Legal Consequences of the Application of Artificial Intelligence in the Field of Medicine' (2018) 18(4) Trends Med 1, 4–5.

[35] Selbst (n 6) 1338.

[36] Joseph A Cannataci, 'Law, Liability and Expert Systems' (1989) 3 AI & Soc 169, 178; similarly, Froomkin, Kerr and Pineau (n 15) 36, 61–2.

[37] Similarly, Bathaee, 'Artificial Intelligence Opinion Liability' (n 18) 117–18.

[38] Hacker and others (n 20) 421; on this issue, see also Topol (n 4) 44ff.

[39] It has also been asserted that 'the superiority of the model cannot be measured only in terms of its accuracy (i.e., the ratio of correct over all predictions); rather, other performance metrics, such as sensitivity (a measure of false negatives) or specificity (a measure of false positives), also need to be considered': Hacker and others (n 20) 421.

not always be enough to turn the failure to use it into negligence. The diligent conduct expected from the physicians does not always require the physician to be in touch with the highest technology, even in the case where the high performance of such technology is accepted. Legal systems may indeed have different approaches as to how strongly they incentivise new technologies. Depending on the legal policy adopted in this regard, the physician may remain in a safer area if they cling to the customary practice. In Germany, 'unless agreed otherwise, the treatment must take place according to the medical standards that are generally recognised at the time of the treatment' (BGB para 630a/II). In France, the law states that the patient is 'entitled to receive the most appropriate care and to receive treatment whose effectiveness is recognised, and which guarantees the best level of safety and the best possible relief of pain in light of established medical knowledge' (art. L1110-5 CSP). Likewise, 'the acts of prevention, investigation, or treatment should not, in the state of medical knowledge, make the patient take risks that are dispro-portionate to the expected benefits' (art. L1110-5 CSP). Although they do not mean prohibition of new approaches, these principles seem to privilege patient safety and lead towards the implementation of what has already become part of general practice. Nevertheless, the standard of care may also be conceived in a way that incentivises innovation more aggressively. The reasonableness of using a new device may require avoiding a judgment based merely on the fact that it has not yet been widely adopted and instead require reflecting 'on the circumstances under which physicians generally adopt and use new devices, even where those adoptions entail a substantial change from customary care'.[40] Some decisions given in the US seem to require the use of new technology even in cases where such technology has not become part of customary prac-tice. In a well-known decision it was held that, because the benefits of radios were well-known, two tugs which were not equipped with radio receivers were unseaworthy and the tug company was not living up to the necessary standard of care, although having these receivers was not common practice at the time.[41] This reasoning was also applied to medical liability. In a case where the court had to determine whether an ophthalmologist should have ordered a glaucoma test for a certain age group of patients even though standard practice did not require the test for such age group, it was held that the ophthalmologist should have ordered the test notwithstanding the contrary general practice and was negligent for not doing so.[42] Scholars report that the medical liability law in

---

[40]   Greenberg (n 8) 431.
[41]   *T. J. Hooper* 60 F.2d 737 (2d Cir. 1932).
[42]   *Helling v Carey* 83 Wash. 2d 514, 519 P.2d 981 (1974).

the US has been evolving in this direction.[43] These cases show that law may evolve in a way that compels the use of new technologies and will not allow reliance on the customary practice to shield physicians from liability. The rise of evidence-based medicine, encouraging the physicians to apply current scientific evidence before it becomes customary practice, may speak in favour of such evolution.[44]

It must also be noted that even in the scenario where reliance on the system's recommendations due to its accuracy levels may become a reasonable justification for the use of black box systems, the physician may still be required to fulfil additional conditions to avoid falling below the standard of care. The physician would be required to be aware of the capabilities of the system, with sufficient knowledge on how it functions,[45] for which tasks it is appropriate and whether it is safe or superior to conventional treatment alternatives.[46] This involves knowledge and consideration of the 'risks posed by that device in connection with particular types of procedures or patients'.[47] In addition, they would still have to check whether the results reached by the CDSS are absurd or out of context.[48] In the case where poor data quality or its biased character is detectable, reliance on the outputs of the device may also give rise to liability.[49] Finally, determination of the physician's sphere of liability may require making a sharper distinction between the diagnosis and the choice of the treatment. Although a CDSS may assist the physician both in diagnosis and treatment options, when it comes to determining the most appropriate treatment option, morality may dictate 'a variety of optimal solutions based on a multitude of personal sets of values and circumstances'.[50] Advice about what to do for a patient cannot be formulated without the preferences of the patient[51] and balancing the costs and benefits of action.[52] Consequently, in a context

---

[43]   Froomkin, Kerr and Pineau (n 15) 55–6. For the example of the rapid introduction of the requirement to use X-rays to diagnose fractures, see Froomkin, Kerr and Pineau (n 15) 56.

[44]   Froomkin, Kerr and Pineau (n 15) 58.

[45]   Greenberg (n 8) 435; Giuffrida and Treece (n 8) 121.

[46]   Greenberg (n 8) 435; similarly, for computer-based expert systems, Bainbridge (n 33) 131.

[47]   Greenberg (n 8) 436. For potential liability arising from the failure to use warnings in these systems, Giuffrida and Treece (n 8) 119.

[48]   For an example of how the system's outcomes may contradict common sense, see Froomkin, Kerr and Pineau (n 15) 49, fn 84; Kiener (n 17) 710–11.

[49]   Bathaee, 'Artificial Intelligence Opinion Liability' (n 18) 161. For a proposal on the steps to be taken to minimise liability, see Giuffrida and Treece (n 8) 121–2.

[50]   Chung and Zink (n 7) 64.

[51]   Ploug and Holm (n 17) 109; Bjerring and Busch (n 9) 360ff.

[52]   Shortliffe (n 3) 62.

where the decisions are mainly based on the level of accuracy of the device, the physician's negligence would necessarily be shifted towards the competence to use the CDSS and the adoption of the treatment option which is best suited to the specific patient. However, under a scenario where the standard of care evolves on the basis of the system's level of accuracy, it would not be possible to find the physician negligent merely for relying on the diagnosis made by the device, even though the reasoning was not intelligible.

B.   Standard of Care Based on the System's Explainability

The creation of an area of immunity for harms caused by a judgment error committed by the CDSS as the result of a trade-off with its general level of accuracy may be problematic.[53] Hence the opinion that the use of black box CDSS is a major threat for the rights of patients and for the development of trust in new technologies. This observation leads to the possibility of law evolving towards a system where the standard of care would be based on meaningful human participation in the decision-making process, which requires the reasoning of the CDSS to be accessible to the human physician. The tendency of underlining the importance of developing tools in a way to enable human supervision, referring either to transparency or explainability, particularly in situations where confidence is critical,[54] suggests that the standard of care may also evolve in this direction. For instance, the European Commission's 'Report on the safety and liability implications of Artificial Intelligence, the Internet of Things and Robotics' stresses the necessity to 'consider requirements for transparency of algorithms, as well as for robustness, accountability and when relevant, human oversight and unbiased outcomes'.[55] It also encourages development of systems where 'humans can be able to understand how the algorithmic decisions of the system have been reached'.[56] The European Parliament Resolution of 16 February 2017 with recommendations to the Commission on Civil Law Rules on Robotics states that 'it should always be possible to supply the rationale behind any decision taken with the aid of AI that can have

---

[53]   Some scholars also point to the impacts of such evolution on medical practice: by providing a normative justification for their decision, the deployment of machine learning algorithms may impose mechanisms of defensive medicine among clinicians: Grote and Berens (n 17) 208.

[54]   Astromskė, Peičius and Astromskis (n 29) 512, arguing that, for some minor procedures, opacity may not be required or linked with the trustworthy dialogue between the patient and the physician, but in life and death situations where confidence is critical, the benefits of AI can be out of reach without interpretability.

[55]   Commission, 'Report on the Safety and Liability Implications of Artificial Intelligence, the Internet of Things and Robotics' COM (2020) 64 final, 9.

[56]   COM (2020) 64 final, 9.

a substantive impact on one or more persons' lives' and that 'it must always be possible to reduce the AI system's computations to a form comprehensible by humans'.[57] According to the White Paper on Artificial Intelligence, there should be requirements 'regarding the keeping of records in relation to the programming of the algorithm, the data used to train high-risk AI systems, and, in certain cases, the keeping of the data themselves', to 'allow potentially problematic actions or decisions by AI systems to be traced back and verified'.[58] The European Commission's High-Level Expert Group on Artificial Intelligence's Ethics Guidelines for Trustworthy AI (2019) states that 'an explanation as to why a model has generated a particular output or decision … is not always possible', but concludes that the 'degree to which explicability is needed is highly dependent on the context and the severity of the consequences if that output is erroneous or otherwise inaccurate'.[59] More recently, the European Commission's Proposal for a Regulation of the European Parliament and of the Council Laying Down Harmonised Rules on Artificial Intelligence (Artificial Intelligence Act) and Amending Certain Union Legislative Acts has also stated the necessity of systems which enable human oversight. The House of Lords Select Committee on Artificial Intelligence also stresses that the 'development of intelligible AI systems is a fundamental necessity if AI is to become an integral and trusted tool'.[60] Some professional bodies also have expressed discomfort in the face of unexplainable decisions reached by algorithms. The Royal Australian and New Zealand College of Radiologists' Ethical Principles for Artificial Intelligence in Medicine provides that when machine learning ('ML') or AI is used in medicine, 'the doctor must be capable of interpreting the basis on which a result was reached, weighing up the potential for bias and exercising clinical judgement regarding findings'.[61]

---

[57] Parliament, 'European Parliament Resolution of 16 February 2017 with Recommendations to the Commission on Civil Law Rules on Robotics' 2015/2103(INL) para 12.

[58] COM (2020) 65 final (n 18) 19.

[59] High-Level Expert Group on Artificial Intelligence set up by the European Commission, 'Ethics Guidelines for Trustworthy AI' (8 April 2019) digital-strategy.ec.europa.eu/en/library/ethics-guidelines-trustworthy-ai accessed 25 September 2021, 13.

[60] The House of Lords Select Committee on Artificial Intelligence (n 18) para 105. See, however, Secretary of State for Business, Energy and Industrial Strategy, *Government Response to House of Lords Artificial Intelligence Select Committee's Report on AI in the UK: Ready, Willing and Able?* (CM 9645, 2018) which recommends carefully weighing the benefits of deep learning techniques against the requirement for transparency and states that '[o]ver-emphasis on transparency could deter the use of AI, and in doing so, could deny patients access to an important component of their care' (para 26).

[61] Royal Australian and New Zealand College of Radiologists (n 11) 5.

To address the difficulties for claimants to establish fault and causation, the Expert Group on Liability and New Technologies mentions the possibility of alleviating or reversing the burden of proof.[62] As far as the proof of facts necessary for the establishment of fault is concerned, the reversal of the burden of proof may be justified by the opacity and limited predictability of the systems and the asymmetry between the potential claimant and the defendant.[63] Although such a solution may strengthen the position of victims of harm caused by complex systems, it does not answer the question of what negligence may mean in the face of highly performing black box algorithms and how one can establish or presume negligence if no control is possible. An alternative solution is the one mentioned by the House of Lords Select Committee on Artificial Intelligence, which states that 'it is not acceptable to deploy any artificial intelligence system which could have a substantial impact on an individual's life, unless it can generate a full and satisfactory explanation for the decisions it will take'. The Committee also suggests that '[i]n cases such as deep neural networks, where it is not yet possible to generate thorough explanations for the decisions that are made, this may mean delaying their deployment for particular uses until alternative solutions are found'.[64] In the absence of implementation of a regulatory approach in the direction of development of explainable devices, this approach may also be followed by the courts with the aim of preventing the creation of an immunity area for the use of unexplainable CDSSs in the field of health care. If the standard of care is shaped in a way to encourage 'meaningful human participation',[65] reliance on a system which does not create any areas for human supervision may be the indication of falling below what is expected from a reasonable physician[66]. Accordingly, instead of concluding that the impossibility of control leads to

---

[62] Expert Group on Liability and New Technologies (n 11) 49–55.

[63] Expert Group on Liability and New Technologies (n 11) 55.

[64] House of Lords Select Committee on Artificial Intelligence (n 18) para 105.

[65] Froomkin, Kerr and Pineau (n 15) 38.

[66] See Helen Smith and Kit Fotheringham, 'Artificial Intelligence in Clinical Decision-Making: Rethinking Liability' (2020) 20(2) Medical Law International 131, 135, arguing that 'the court might decide that for a clinician to abrogate their personal responsibility and instead delegate clinical decision-making to an AIS [AI system] is conduct so specious that the claim could proceed on this ground', and Hacker (n 20) 429, stating that 'explainability is often at least as important as predictive performance to determine whether the law allows or even requires the use of ML tools under professional standards of care'. See also Bathaee, 'Artificial Intelligence Opinion Liability' (n 18) 154–5, who mentions the possibility of considering reliance on AI without any human supervision to be the evidence that the creator or user of the AI fell below a given standard of care, in cases where 'there is a great amount of uncertainty as to how the AI is making its decisions or as to how it will perform in the real world'.

the absence of negligence, the courts may be tempted to conclude that reliance on the unexplainable AI in fields with risky consequences is per se constitutive of negligence and will thereby regulate the use and development of AI-based CDSSs through tort law. If such an approach is adopted, the intervention of unexplainable CDSSs in the decision-making process will be a factor which increases risk of liability for the physician unless they can support the CDSS's outcomes with their personal knowledge, and this may also limit the development of black box CDSSs.

IV.   POTENTIAL ROLE OF MALPRACTICE LIABILITY INSURANCE ON THE ADOPTION OF BLACK BOX CDSSS

Receiving marketability approval by regulatory authorities is a first step towards the use of black box CDSSs. However, for their widespread adoption, they would have to receive insurance reimbursement[67] under public and private health insurance schemes[68] and presumably be endorsed also by malpractice insurers that grant cover for physicians' civil liability arising from the physician's acts amounting to malpractice.[69] As taking out malpractice insurance is usually required for physicians,[70] not only the risk of liability, but also whether potential civil liability based on the use or failure to use a CDSS will be covered by an insurance policy may be of key importance to the decision of the physician to have recourse to such a tool, thereby affecting the adoption and development of CDSSs. Malpractice insurers are therefore likely to play a role in the deployment of black box CDSSs through their assessment of risks in connection with these systems and their decisions as to which types of system should be used in healthcare settings.

---

[67]   For a view that insurance reimbursement is a challenge for black box medicine, see W Nicholson Price II, 'Black-Box Medicine' (2015) 28(2) Harv J L & Tech 419, 462.

[68]   Price II, 'Black-Box Medicine' (n 67) 462.

[69]   The malpractice liability risk can be insured in private insurance markets via malpractice liability insurance. However, systems governing the management of medical malpractice liability may be diverse and the financing of malpractice liability may as well be carried out by states whereby the parties affected by malpractice can be compensated through state funds, OECD, *Policy Issues in Insurance no. 11 – Medical Malpractice: Prevention, Insurance and Coverage Options* (2006) 10 ('OECD Report').

[70]   It is either mandatorily required by law or imposed by medical professional bodies or medical establishments as a prerequisite for practising as a physician. See, OECD Report (n 69) 76–82 for the position in OECD countries.

For estimating to what extent black box CDSSs will become part of medical practice, similarities and divergences of the approval requirements of regulatory authorities, the reimbursement criteria of public and private health insurers and the endorsement conditions of malpractice liability insurers may be important. A multitude of criteria would connote that more efforts would be required for CDSSs to receive the support of all these parties to perform in real-world settings.[71] Regulatory authorities and health and malpractice insurers act independently, not only in determination of their criteria, but also in the management of their approval, reimbursement and endorsement decision processes.[72] Health insurers' and malpractice insurers' roles begin after the systems are already approved by regulatory authorities, which poses a risk for those who are faced with the decision to use or not to use them: even though the systems may be marketable, the costs related to the use of the system may not be reimbursed by health insurers, or malpractice insurers may decide not to approve the use of the systems by the physicians that they insure. The section below will present a tentative approach as to the likely position to be adopted by malpractice insurers regarding the use of black box CDSSs.

As malpractice insurers undertake to indemnify physicians' malpractice liability, they have to assess their own risk of having to compensate for it. Therefore, they would require information on any eventuality which may have an impact on the malpractice liability risk.[73] In order to minimise the potential compensation they may end up paying, they would be expected to endorse diagnostic systems that are not likely to increase the malpractice risk

---

[71] For instance, application of different legal standards by authorities for their determination of approval and reimbursement (FDA requiring the devices to be 'safe and effective' and Centers for Medicare & Medicaid Services ('CMS') requiring them to be 'reasonable and necessary' for diagnosis and treatment) have resulted in uncertainties for device manufacturers as to whether their FDA-approved devices would receive reimbursement from CMS, see Rachel E Sachs, 'Delinking Reimbursement' (2018) 102 Minnesota Law Review 2307, 2342.

[72] Price II, 'Regulating Black-Box Medicine' (n 19) 465 suggests that there could be a 'collaborative governance' in regulating complex algorithms where other health system actors, including 'insurers', could also play a role (the author does not specifically mention malpractice insurers in their work). It was also considered in Sara Gerke and others, 'The Need for a System View to Regulate Artificial Intelligence/Machine Learning-Based Software as Medical Device' (2020) 3(53) npj Digital Medicine doi .org/10.1038/s41746-020-0262-2 accessed 25 September 2021, that AI/ML-based software may be evaluated through a 'full system approach' whereby regulatory authorities would need to take into account, among other things, the reimbursement decisions of insurers.

[73] For instance, some insurers require the disclosure of whether electronic health records are being used by physicians to better assess and rate their malpractice risk, as this is accepted as a practice reducing the risk.

too greatly, or that would contribute to the reduction of it. Malpractice insurers will not have to make a robust selection among systems in the far future, in case reliance by physicians on highly accurate diagnostic systems – whether or not they are black box – becomes the standard of care because this will reduce the malpractice liability risk altogether. Their position will not be highly affected either if the applicable standard of care evolves in the direction of requiring the use of explainable systems: in this case, as the physician's liability will be assessed in reference to how they interpret the recommendations of an intelligible system, evaluating the liability risk will not be significantly different from how malpractice insurers assess the physician's liability risk arising from the use of the existing technologies. In either circumstance, the real question will lie in whether black box systems will be likely to be endorsed by malpractice insurers until a firm standard of care is established. For the time being, uncertainty remains as to the tools that courts might use to decide what may amount to malpractice in such conditions. This would create unpredictability for malpractice insurers as to both whether they would be ordered to pay compensation in like circumstances and costs they may have to incur in defending physicians against victims' claims. For this reason, until liability schemes surrounding the use of black box systems become perceptible, malpractice insurers would presumably rather endorse systems the reliance on which would present a higher degree of predictability as to whether it would constitute malpractice.

In the context of black box medicine, reimbursement decisions of both public and private health insurers will be vital.[74] One of the possible criteria for reimbursing black box medicine for these insurers has been suggested to be the reputation of the training data of the algorithm,[75] as a tool expected to increase its reliability. Indeed, it may be claimed that algorithms trained by highly skilled physicians being 'a proxy signal of quality' could deserve reimbursement more, compared to those that are not.[76] This may also be relevant for the liability insurers' reimbursement decisions. However, such a criterion is not without problems regarding the risk of liability. Due to the fact that medical AI is usually trained in high-resource institutions,[77] the use of algorithms in low-resource settings with different patient populations and human resources

---

[74]   Price II, 'Black-Box Medicine' (n 67) 462. The author also suggests at 462–3 that overall adoption may be facilitated where public insurers are encouraged to reimburse black box medicine.

[75]   W Nicholson Price II, 'Medical AI and Contextual Bias' (2019) 33(1) Harv J L & Tech 66, 87. Reputation of the training data is referred to as 'data from excellent doctors in high-resource settings', see 86.

[76]   Price II, 'Medical AI and Contextual Bias' (n 75) 87.

[77]   ibid. 66.

may in turn create less accurate algorithmic decision-making in those settings.[78] As a consequence, the requirement of the reputation of the training data as a condition of reimbursement by health insurers may become a factor which may allow the creation of bias and judgment of errors in the algorithmic decisions in some settings. Detectability of bias inherent in the CDSS by healthcare providers would presumably be contingent upon the system's reasoning being intelligible by the physician. If the standard of care evolves in a way to be based on the accuracy levels of the system, high-performance levels will create an area of immunity for the physician, which will also benefit the malpractice insurer. However, in the current state, whether or not the physician will be held liable for having used a system whose bias cannot be detected is tainted with uncertainty. Conversely, using an explainable system will enable the physician to assess the appropriateness of its recommendations for the individual patient and will therefore create predictability as to when they may be deemed negligent. Under these circumstances, as much as a physician's reliance on a system with a detectable bias would mean for the malpractice insurers that they could be required to compensate,[79] the system being explainable will at least assist them in predicting the potential extent of their liability to compensate. In this regard, given the need for predictability, the condition of a safe risk assessment by malpractice insurers[80] can best be satisfied through the use of explainable systems, and these insurers may be tempted to lead the medical practice in this direction. As a result, although reputation of the training data of the system may be a factor that malpractice insurers could take into consideration, explainability is also likely to play an important role in the assessment of what

---

[78]   ibid. 67. The use of algorithms becoming the standard of care may encourage reliance on algorithms that give rise to inaccurate decisions where the algorithm is supported as a result of its use in high-context settings, see Charlotte Tschider, 'Medical Device Artificial Intelligence: The New Tort Frontier' (2021) 46(6) Brigham Young University Law Review 1551, fn. 68.

[79]   As the physician would be considered as negligent which would give rise to its liability.

[80]   It was stated in Kenneth S Abraham, *Distributing Risk: Insurance, Legal Theory, and Public Policy* (Yale University Press, 1986) 46 that with the introduction of new medical procedures and products, predicting malpractice liability for injuries becomes even more daunting. Through the example of unpredictability of liability costs for toxic substances, the author discusses that the difficulty in prediction will cause problems in accurately pricing the risk (48) and elaborates on the possibility of managing this difficulty by prohibiting or limiting the amount of liability insurance coverage for toxic substances (47). Mark A Geistfeld, 'Legal Ambiguity, Liability Insurance, and Tort Reform' (2011) 60 DePaul Law Review 539, 540 also emphasises that liability insurers endorse measures of tort reform that diminish the unpredictability of the liability costs, as this facilitates the setting of premiums.

kind of systems will be encouraged to be used by (or imposed on) physicians to benefit from an adequate malpractice insurance cover.

In addition to having to compensate for losses arising from malpractice, insurers may also be required to cover the costs incurred in the defence of the physician against a malpractice claim by the victim,[81] whether or not the claim eventually succeeds.[82] For malpractice insurers to decide whether or how they will defend the physician, first the victim must have suffered a loss and claimed for their loss. Malpractice insurers would then have to make an internal assessment as to whether the victim's claim is persuasive, and this would necessitate them incurring expenses for investigating the claim. Where, upon such determination, the insurer decides that the victim's claim is not justified, it could defend the physician in order to prove that the claim should fail. Where the insurer is uncertain about whether the claim is justified, it could again fight the claim to avoid paying for compensation. Where the insurer believes that the victim's claim is justified on a legal basis yet not as to its quantum, it may either settle the claim or prefer to defend the physician with the hope that the court will decide in their favour. In all these circumstances, insurers will incur litigation costs as well as expenses for claim investigation which may both qualify as defence costs[83] to be paid by insurers. These costs are usually less than the compensation paid for medical liability, nevertheless they may be substantial[84] and malpractice insurers would have to factor them in when insuring healthcare providers against malpractice.[85]

---

[81]   Legal systems may have different rules regarding the compensation of defence costs by insurers. In some systems, defence costs may be paid by insurers only where the insurers contractually agree to pay for them. Under some instruments, however, insurers may be required to reimburse them (e.g. Principles of European Insurance Contract Law (PEICL) Art 14:101) whereby contracts excluding the reimbursement of defence costs may not be allowed, see Jürgen Basedow and others, *Principles of European Insurance Contract Law* (2nd expanded edition Ottoschmidt, 2016) 287.

[82]   Basedow and others (n 81) 287.

[83]   Basedow and others (n 81) 287.

[84]   For the ratio of loss/defence & cost containment expenses provided in a US-wide summaryofmedicalprofessionalliabilityinsuranceforthecalendaryearsof2005–2019,see content.naic.org/sites/default/files/inline-files/MED%20MAL%20RPT%202019_0. pdf accessed 25 September 2021. See also Charles Silver, 'Basic Economics of the Defense of Covered Claims' in Daniel Schwarcz and Peter Siegelman (eds.), *Research Handbook on the Economics of Insurance Law* (Edward Elgar, 2015), 447.

[85]   For the view that defence costs play a fundamental role for malpractice insurers in setting premiums as well as insurance payouts and number of claims filed, see Aaron E Carroll, Parul Divya Parikh and Jennifer L Buddenbaum, 'The Impact of Defense Expenses in Medical Malpractice Claims' (2012) 40 (1) Journal of Law, Medicine & Ethics 135, 141.

In this regard, the criterion of improved patient outcomes taken into consideration by health insurers in evaluating their reimbursement decisions[86] may also be of use to malpractice insurers. Indeed, with regard to the use of CDSSs, malpractice insurers would likely take into account whether the number of claims to be made by victims decreases where the system is used, compared to where it is not. Should the system succeed in decreasing the number of claims, insurers would have to investigate fewer claims and incur fewer investigation and litigation expenses. Where it is demonstrated that the use of the diagnostic system improves patients' health conditions compared to the situation where the patient is treated without the diagnostic system, there would be less cause for a claim and accordingly less costs for malpractice insurers. Clinical evidence of improved patient outcomes may therefore be an important condition for endorsing a system, especially for malpractice insurers, as such evidence would assist them in reducing their potential liability for defence costs. For this reason, they would have an interest in endorsing systems having clinical evidence as to improved medical outcomes. However, such evidence may not always be available for black box systems,[87] especially where they are approved by regulatory authorities through pathways not strictly requiring this type of data. In the absence of such explicit clinical evidence demonstrating improved patient outcomes, black box systems are not likely to improve the position of the malpractice insurers with regard to their defence costs[88] until post-market evaluation of such devices as to patient outcomes can be effectively made through real-world performance data. In comparison to what is needed for a claim involving an explainable CDSS, the unpredictable nature of how the negligence claims will be shaped around unexplainable systems may make the process more difficult to manage for the insurer and thereby increase the defence costs. As a result, malpractice insurers may be tempted to endorse explainable systems due to the safer area they provide in terms of defence costs.

---

[86] It was submitted in Price II, 'Black-Box Medicine' (n 67) 464 that absent an approval received under a stringent scheme requiring strong clinical data, public and private insurers usually require clinical evidence of improved patient outcomes.

[87] Price II, 'Black-Box Medicine' (n 67) 464.

[88] It is also anticipated that black box systems lacking such clinical evidence by design may significantly reduce their chance of being reimbursed unless the reimbursement criteria are reconsidered for these types of systems by health insurers; Price II, 'Black-Box Medicine' (n 67) 464.

V.   CONCLUSION

CDSSs which do not reveal the reasoning behind the recommendations they make create important challenges to the negligence-based liability structure, in terms of proof of causation and determination of the standard of care applicable to the user, who may either refuse to use them or embrace their unintelligible outcomes. At the same time, these systems promise to improve medical services since they present the advantage of performing better than their explainable counterparts. In the absence of legal guidance on whether or not the focus must be placed on their explainability in the process of their development, the presence of such systems in the market will leave the courts in the difficult position of determining how to apply traditional liability principles to the case of physicians. The standard of care may evolve in the direction of reliance on the general level of accuracy, in which case the physician would be under the pressure of relying on the black box CDSS's recommendations. However, in this scenario, the concept of accuracy and whether the standard of care relies on customary practice or incentivises the use of new technologies will also have a role to play in the determination of the standard of the reasonable physician. In addition, the physician will still have to take personal decisions as to the appropriateness of the CDSS for the case at hand and as to the best treatment option dictated by moral or economic considerations. The downside of this system would be the creation of an immunity area for the physician relying on an overall accurate but unintelligible CDSS and the subsequent incentivisation of defensive medicine practices to avoid liability. As a result, 'policy debates across the world increasingly feature calls for some form of AI explainability, as part of efforts to embed ethical principles into the design and deployment of AI-enabled systems'.[89] If such debates are not reflected in rules regulating the deployment of AI-based CDSSs, the courts may eventually fulfil this role by setting the standard of care in such a way as to deem unreasonable all patient-related decisions based on a device whose recommendations are unintelligible. As for the potential reaction of malpractice insurers towards the use of black box systems, the main area of preoccupation seems to lie in the unpredictability of the physician's liability risk. As a result, the malpractice insurance market is likely to shape the physician's actions so that they remain in a more predictable area, which is better provided by explainable systems, both in terms of their obligation to compensate and defence costs. In conclusion, in parallel to the debates which relate to whether or not the focus of the

---

[89]   The Royal Society (n 20) 8.

policy makers/approval authorities must lie in the accuracy or explainability of the CDSS, the creation of structures which embed the requirement of explainability into the use and deployment of AI-based CDSSs by the courts and insurers is also a possibility.

8. Autonomous AI Torts: A Comparative Law and Economics Approach

Mitja Kovac[1]

I. INTRODUCTION

Autonomous artificial intelligence ('AI') and recent breakthroughs in machine-human interactions and machine learning technology are increasingly affecting almost every sphere of our lives. Such intelligence is on an exponential curve, with particular materialisations of it representing ever greater threats to privacy, possibly being ethically questionable, and even potentially dangerous, risky and harmful.[2] The creation of autonomous, non-natural, artificial super-intelligence that makes its own choices following an evaluative process raises one of the most debate-provoking questions facing the modern world. AI is unleashing a new industrial revolution where it is vital that lawmakers address the systemic challenges it brings and regulate its economic and social effects without stifling innovation. Current trends in favour of developing autonomous machines able to interact, learn and make autonomous decisions (and hypothetically even develop personhood) also point to several different concerns regarding their direct and indirect potentially harmful effects, which call for a substantive legal and economic response.

Russell, for example, argues that no one can predict exactly how the new AI technology will develop, but if autonomous machines far exceed human capacity and if we leave the mentioned concerns unaddressed, then autonomous AI could prove to be the last phenomenon in human history.[3] Moreover, Turner argues that Europeans have not come to grips with what is ethical, let alone

---

[1]   Professor of Civil and Commercial Law, University of Ljubljana School of Economics and Business (Slovenia).
[2]   Michal Kosinski and Wang Yilun, 'Deep Neural Networks are More Accurate than Humans at Detecting Sexual Orientation from Facial Images' (2018) 114 Journal of Personality and Social Psychology 246.
[3]   Stuart Russell, *Human Compatible: Artificial Intelligence and the Problem of Control* (Allen Lane, 2019) 4. See also Stuart Russell and Peter Norvig, *Artificial Intelligence: A Modern Approach* (3rd ed., Pearson, 2016).

with what the law should be, thus creating a growing legal vacuum in almost every domain affected by this unprecedented technological development.[4] At the same time, Buyers suggests that lawyers are currently wondering what happens when a self-driving car has a software failure and hits a pedestrian, or a drone fitted with a camera happens to catch an individual naked beside a pool or taking a shower, or a robot kills a human in self-defence.[5]

Having regard to such developments, the European Parliament and the European Commission together with many other lawmakers around the globe launched an intensive activity[6] to consider the issue of liability and other broader challenges posed by emerging digital technologies. The European Commission also established a special expert group on liability made up of the 'Product Liability Directive' formation and the 'new technologies' formation.[7] Another task these two expert groups faced is the issue of whether a) it is appropriate and necessary to intervene regulatorily in AI technologies; b) such intervention should be developed in a horizontal or sectoral way; or c) new legislation should be introduced at the EU level.[8]

Both the European Commission and the European Parliament consider the civil liability for damage caused by any form of artificial intelligence to be a crucial issue that must also be analysed and addressed at the EU level in order to ensure efficiency, transparency and consistency while also ensuring optimal risk prevention by establishing legal certainty across the EU. From the law and economics perspective, the role of such a civil liability system is to deter people and firms from injuring others, discourage and prevent risks, internalise the costs of risky events and compensate those who are injured. In

---

[4]   Jacob Turner, *Robot Rules: Regulating Artificial Intelligence* (Palgrave Macmillan, 2019) 81–6.

[5]   See John Buyers, *Artificial Intelligence: The Practical Legal Issues* (Law Brief Publishing, 2018) 21–35; Matt Harvey and Matthew Lavy, *The Law of Artificial Intelligence* (Sweet & Maxwell, 2020); Woodrow Barfield and Ugo Pagallo, *Advanced Introduction to Law and Artificial Intelligence* (Edward Elgar Publishing, 2020); and Charles Kerrigan, *Artificial Intelligence: Law and Regulation* (Edward Elgar Publishing, 2022).

[6]   See for example, European Commission, 'Proposal for a Regulation of the European Parliament and of the Council Laying Down Harmonised Rules on Artificial Intelligence (Artificial Intelligence Act) and Amending Certain Union Legislative Acts' (Communication) COM (2021) 206 final; European Parliament, 'Resolution of 16 February 2017 with recommendations to the Commission on Civil Law Rules on Robotics' (Resolution) P8_TA(2017)0051; and European Commission, 'Report on the safety and liability implications of Artificial Intelligence, the Internet of Things and Robotics' (Communication) COM (2020) 64 final.

[7]   European Commission, 'Artificial Intelligence for Europe' (Communication) COM (2018) 237 final.

[8]   ibid.

addition, one may wonder whether society's aims would be better served by reformulating our relationship with autonomous AI in a more radical fashion and whether the current rules indeed cover all of the potential risks generated by autonomous AI.

Incorporating the main insights from tort law and economics literature,[9] this chapter seeks to address the role played by public policy in regulating autonomous AI, the associated risks and civil liability for damage caused by such AI.

By applying law and economics insights to autonomous AI, this chapter is able to offer a set of recommendations for economically informed regulatory intervention which should deter hazardous enterprises, induce optimal precaution and simultaneously preserve dynamic efficiency (not distort incentives to innovate). The chapter stresses the need to understand how legal incentives might be reformulated for autonomous AI, although it is ultimately suggested that no revolutionary legal solution is needed to tackle the problem of AI-caused hazards. Moreover, the chapter supports the European Parliament

---

[9]   See for example, Steven Shavell, 'On the Redesign of Accident Liability for the World of Autonomous Vehicles' (2020) 49 The Journal of Legal Studies 243; Bryan Casey and Mark A Lemley, 'You Might be a Robot' (2019) 105 Cornell Law Review 287; Eric Talley, 'Automators: How Should Accident Law Adapt to Autonomous Vehicles? Lessons from Law and Economics' (2019) Columbia Law School Working Papers Series No. 19002; Alberto Galasso and Hong Luo, 'Punishing Robots: Issues in the Economics of Tort Liability and Innovation in Artificial Intelligence' in Ajay Agrawal, Joshua Gans and Avi Goldfarb (eds.), *The Economics of Artificial Intelligence: An Agenda* (National Bureau of Economic Research, 2018) 493–504; Andrea Bertolini, 'Robots as Products: The Case for Realistic Analysis of Robotic Applications and Liability Rules' (2013) 5 Law, Innovation and Technology 214; Hans-Bernd Schäfer and Claus Ott, *The Economic Analysis of Civil Law* (Edward Elgar Publishing, 2004) 107–273; Michael Faure, 'Toward a Harmonized Tort Law in Europe? An Economic Perspective' (2001) 8 Maastricht Journal of European and Comparative Law 339–50; Hans-Bernd Schäfer, 'Tort Law: General' in Budewijn Bouckaert and Gerrit De Geest (eds.), *Encyclopaedia of Law and Economics* (Edward Elgar Publishing, 2000) 569–96; Emons Winand and Joel Sobel, 'On the Effectiveness of Liability Rules When Agents Are Not Identical' (1991) 58 Review of Economic Studies 375; Steven Shavell, *Economic Analysis of Accident Law* (Harvard University Press, 1987); Mitchell A Polinsky and William P Rogerson, 'Product Liability, Consumer Misperceptions and Market Power' (1983) 14 Bell Journal of Economics 581; Steven Shavell, 'Strict Liability Versus Negligence' (1980) 9 Journal of Legal Studies 1; Kenneth J Arrow, 'Optimal Insurance and Generalized Deductibles' [1974] Scandinavian Actuarial Journal 1; Richard A Posner, 'A Theory of Negligence' (1972) 1 Journal of Legal Studies 29; Richard A Posner, 'Strict Liability: A Comment' (1973) 2 Journal of Legal Studies 205; Guido Calabresi, 'Some Thoughts on Risk Distribution and the Law of Torts' (1961) 70 Yale Law Journal 499, 499–553; Guido Calabresi, 'The Decision for Accidents: An Approach to Non-fault Allocation of Costs' (1965) 78 Harvard Law Review 713, 713–45; and Guido Calabresi, *The Costs of Accidents: A Legal and Economic Analysis* (Yale University Press, 1970).

and the European Commission's law-making activity by advocating anticipatory, ex ante regulatory intervention. The chapter also addresses the European Parliament's concerns about whether strict liability or the risk management approach should be applied in situations where AI causes damage, and offers arguments in support of suggestions made by the European Commission's expert groups on 'Liability and New Technologies' working on an amendment to the Product Liability Directive as well as the general frameworks for liability and AI.

The analysis presented here is both positive and normative. The analytical approach engages in interdisciplinary analysis and enriches it with concepts used in the economic analysis of law.[10] To make the economic analysis accessible to readers not acquainted with sophisticated mathematical reasoning, the law and economics toolkit relied upon follows the traditional comparative law and economics approach.[11]

This chapter is structured as follows: the first part offers the general background, recapitulates definitions and provides a manual for development and deployment in the AI field. In the second part, a synthesis of law and economics scholarship on an improved AI-related liability law regime is provided. The third part briefly comments on recent EU legislative activity. Finally, some conclusions are presented.

II.   GENERAL BACKGROUND AND KEY CONCEPTS

It is indisputable that humankind is facing an era when more sophisticated autonomous AI is unleashing a new industrial revolution that will profoundly change and transform all of society or at least major parts of it. Although some marvel at the capacity of AI,[12] others seem to worry that our species will mortally struggle with super powerful AI and that it will be humankind's 'final invention'.[13] Barrat, for example, also argues that AI indeed helps choose

---

[10]   See Gerrit De Geest, *Contract Law and Economics – Encyclopaedia of Law and Economics*, vol 6 (2nd ed., Edward Elgar Publishing, 2011); and Richard A Posner, *Economic Analysis of Law* (8th ed., Wolters Kluwer, 2011).

[11]   Roger Van den Bergh, *The Roundabouts of European Law and Economics* (Eleven International Publishing, 2018) 21–8.

[12]   Cade Metz, 'In a Huge Breakthrough, Google's AI Beats a Top Player at the Game of Go' (*Wired*, 27 January 2016) www.wired.com/2016/01/in-a-huge -breakthrough-googles-ai-beats-a-top-player-at-the-game-of-go/#:~:text=In%20a %20major%20breakthrough%20for,bedeviled%20AI%20experts%20for%20decades accessed 27 July 2022.

[13]   James Barrat, *Our Final Invention: Artificial Intelligence and the End of the Human Era* (Thomas Dunes Books, 2013).

which books you buy and which movies you see, it puts the 'smart' in your smartphone, will soon be driving our cars, is making the most of the trading on Wall Street, and controls vital energy, water and transport infrastructure.[14] However, AI combined with robotic systems completes tasks in ways that cannot be anticipated in advance, while robots increasingly blur the line between person and instrument.[15]

Curiously, there is no precise, straightforward, universally accepted definition of AI, or even a consensus definition of it. Calo, for example, argues that AI is best understood as a set of techniques aimed at approximating some aspect of human or animal cognition using machines.[16] This paper employs the more useful definition of AI provided by Nilsson: '[a]rtificial intelligence is that activity devoted to making machines intelligent, and intelligence is that quality that enables an entity to function appropriately and with foresight in its environment'.[17] Moreover, throughout this chapter the term 'AI' refers to autonomous AI that is capable of self-learning, interacting, making autonomous decisions, developing emergent properties, adapting its behaviour and actions to the environment, and has no life in the biological sense.

However, in recent years the field of AI has been shifting from simply building systems that are intelligent to building intelligent systems that are human-aware and trustworthy.[18] In particular, a set of techniques known as 'machine learning', supported in part by cloud computing resources and widespread, web-based data gathering, have propelled the field and been a considerable source of excitement. Machine learning ('ML') refers to the capacity of a system to improve its performance of a task over time.[19] ML develops algorithms designed to be applied to datasets with the main areas of focus being prediction (regression), classification and clustering or grouping

---

[14]   ibid.

[15]   Ryan Calo, 'Robotics and the Lessons of Cyberlaw' (2015) 103 California Law Review 513, 513–63.

[16]   Ryan Calo, 'Robots as Legal Metaphors' (2016) 30 Harvard Journal of Law & Technology 209; and Ryan Calo, 'Artificial Intelligence Policy: A Primer and Roadmap' (2017) 51 UC Davis Law Review 399, 399–435. See also Russell and Norvig (n 3).

[17]   Nils J Nilsson, *The Quest for Artificial Intelligence: A History of Ideas and Achievements* (Cambridge University Press, 2010).

[18]   See Jerry Kaplan, *Artificial Intelligence: What Everyone Needs to Know* (Oxford University Press, 2016); Peter Stone and others, 'Artificial Intelligence and Life in 2030' (Report of the 2015 study panel 50, Stanford University, 2016); and Pamela McCorduck, *Machines Who Think: A Personal Inquiry into the History and Prospects of Artificial Intelligence* (A.K. Press, 2004) 133.

[19]   Harry Surden, 'Machine Learning and Law' (2014) 89 Washington Law Review 87.

tasks (e.g. recognising patterns in datasets). Nowadays, ML is divided into two main branches: a) unsupervised ML (involving finding clusters of observation similar in terms of their covariates – dimensionality reduction; also, matrix factorisation, regularisation and neuro-networks); and b) supervised ML (using a set of covariates (X) to predict an outcome (Y)).[20]

The output, as Athey notes, of a 'typical unsupervised ML model is a partition of the set of observations, where observations within each element of the partition are similar according to some metric or vector of probabilities that describe a mixture of groups that an observation might belong to'.[21] Athey also states that 'on the other hand supervised ML focuses on a setting where there are some labelled observations where both X and Y are observed and the goal is to predict outcome (Y) in an independent test set based on the realized values of X for each unit in the test set'.[22] The mentioned author emphasises that 'the actual goal is to construct $\mu(x)$, which is an estimator of $\mu(x) = E\ (Y/X=x)$, in order to do a reliable job predicting the true values of Y in an independent dataset'.[23]

As Calo points out, ML has been dramatically propelled forward by the 'deep learning' technique (operating within ML), namely, a form of 'adaptive artificial neural networks trained using a method called backpropagation'.[24] Analytically speaking, deep learning (hereinafter 'DL') 'leverages many-layered structures to extract features from enormous data sets in service of practical tasks requiring pattern recognition, or uses other techniques to similar effect'.[25] These trends in ML and DL are now driving the 'hot' areas of research that encompass large-scale ML, reinforcement learning, robotics, computer vision, natural language processing, collaborative systems, crowdsourcing and human computation, algorithmic game theory and computational social choice, the Internet of Things and neuromorphic computing.

---

[20] See Sendhill Mullainathan and Jann Spiess, 'Machine Learning: An Applied Econometric Approach' (2017) 31 Journal of Economic Perspectives 87; Hal R Varian, 'Big Data: New Tricks for Econometrics' (2014) 28 The Journal of Economic Perspectives 3, 3–27; and David M Blei, Andrew Y Ng and Michael I Jordan, 'Latent Dirichlet Allocation' (2003) 3 Journal of Machine Learning Research 993.

[21] Susan Athey, *The Impact of Machine Learning on Economics* (National Bureau of Economic Research, 2018). See also Prem Gopalan, Jake M Hofman and David M Blei, 'Scalable Recommendation with Hierarchical Poisson Factorization' (2015) Proceedings of the 31st Conference on Uncertainty in Artificial Intelligence 326–35.

[22] ibid.

[23] Namely, the main estimation problem is, according to Athey, 'how to estimate Pr (Y = k/X = x) for each of k = 1, ..., K possible realizations of Y'; Athey (n 21).

[24] Calo (n 15).

[25] Russell and Norvig (n 3) 9–10.

Over the next 15 years, scholars expect a stronger focus on developing systems that are human-aware, meaning that they specifically model, and are specifically designed for, the characteristics of the people with whom they are meant to interact.[26] Such human-like systems will be able to find creative ways to develop 'interactive and scalable ways to teach other robots and to develop human-like characteristics, including decision-making, feelings and potential self-awareness'.[27]

III.   SYNTHESIS OF LAW AND ECONOMICS SCHOLARSHIP ON AI LIABILITY

As the above section demonstrates, AI might be able to perform several actions rather than merely process information and will exert direct control over objects in the human environment. Somewhere out there is stock-trading AI, teacher-training AI and economic-balancing AI that might even be self-aware. Such autonomous AI could then cause serious indirect or direct harm.[28] Calo, for instance, also argues that high-speed trading algorithms which could destabilise the stock market or cognitive radio systems that can interfere with emergency communications may hold the potential, alone or in combination, to create serious damage.[29] In order to mitigate these potentially serious hazards and damage, the combination of ex ante regulatory intervention (regulatory standards) and the ex post imposition of liability via tortious liability is at the lawmaker's disposal. In other words, this system of ex ante regulation and ex post sanctioning is designed to deter future harmful behaviour. Yet, the fundamental question is how would a lawmaker effectively modify the behaviour of AI? Moreover, the prospect that AI might behave in ways its designers or manufacturers did not expect challenges the dominant assumption made in tort law that courts only compensate for injuries that are foreseeable. Hence, would courts then simply refuse to find liability because the defendant could not foresee the harm the AI caused and assign it to the blameless victim? Or would strict product liability assigning the liability to manufacturers be applied as an alternative remedy?

This section offers a set of law and economics recommendations for an economically informed regulatory intervention which should deter hazards,

---

[26]   Stone and others (n 18).

[27]   ibid. See also Jordan Pearson, 'Uber's AI Hub in Pittsburgh Gutted a University Lab – Now It's in Toronto' (*Vice Motherboard*, 2017) www.vice.com/en/article/3dxkej/ubers-ai-hub-in-pittsburgh-gutted-a-university-lab-now-its-in-toronto.

[28]   Ryan Calo, *The Case for a Federal Robotics Commission* (Brookings Centre for Technical Innovation, 2014).

[29]   ibid.

induce optimal precaution and simultaneously preserve dynamic efficiency and not distort incentives to innovate.

A.   The Law and Economics of Torts

Tort law states the conditions in which a person is entitled to damage compensation if their action does not arise from a contractual obligation and encompasses all legal norms that concern the claim made by the injured party against the wrongdoer (tortfeasor). From the traditional legal viewpoint, the tort system's main goal is to protect and ex post compensate victims for potential unjust injuries.[30] From the law and economics perspective, the tort law system assigns liability to deter future injurers from engaging in hazardous behaviour while inducing the ex ante implementation of the optimal precautions.[31] Calabresi suggests that the economic rationale behind tort law is minimising the total costs of accidents.[32] Economically speaking, every 'reduction of an individual's utility level caused by a tortious act can be regarded as a damage'.[33] Tort law rules aim to draw a just and fair line between those noxious events that should lead to damage compensation and others for which the burden of the damage should lie where it falls. A thorough overview of tort law and economics literature exceeds the limitations of this chapter and can be found elsewhere.[34] Still, it should be stressed that tort law and economics literature traditionally address three broad aspects of tortious liability. The first is the assessment of its effects on incentives (including incentives to participate in activities and incentives to mitigate and reduce the risk) – analytically speaking, tort law is thus an instrument that improves the flow of inducements;[35] the second concerns risk-bearing capacity and insurance; while the third is its

---

[30]   Louis Visscher, *Debated Damages* (Eleven International Publishing, 2014).

[31]   Michael Faure, 'Attribution of Liability: An Economic Analysis of Various Cases' (2016) 91 Chicago-Kent Law Review 603.

[32]   Guido Calabresi, *The Cost of Accidents: A Legal and Economic Analysis* (Yale University Press, 1970).

[33]   Schäfer (n 9) 569–96.

[34]   See Robert Cooter and Thomas Ulen, *Law and Economics* (6th ed., Addison-Wesley, 2016) 287–373; Posner (n 10); and Schäfer and Ott (n 9) 107–273.

[35]   By adjusting tortfeasors' incentives to take precautions, the tort system actually induces them to internalise the costs of their behaviour (i.e. negative externalities) and thereby ex ante discourages them from engaging in such activities that might generate such negative externalities; Gerrit De Geest, 'Who Should be Immune from Tort Liability' (2012) 41 The Journal of Legal Studies 291. Moreover, as Gilead points out, tortious liability also promotes positive externalities (i.e. safety innovations in products and services) for society at large; Israel Gilead, 'Tort Law and Internalization: The Gap between Private Loss and Social Cost' (1997) 17 International Review of Law and Economics 589.

administrative expense comprising the costs of legal services, the value of litigants' time and the operating costs of the courts.[36] These three categories are then subjected to a rigorous cost-benefit analysis that should yield the marginal conditions for an efficient outcome. Wittman, for example, argues that the key is to find a liability rule where the equilibrium levels of prevention undertaken by the injurer and the victim coincide with the optimal levels.[37]

Still, it should be emphasised that, even after a long debate on the economic effects of tort law, questions still remain about the optimal institutional structure and the position of tort law in a modern regulatory environment. For instance, should tort law be institutionalised as a comprehensive deterrence-incentive system designed to regulate all sorts of hazards (and simultaneously provide incentives for efficient, productive behaviour)? Or should its domain, as suggested by Schäfer, be more restricted to the 'classical cases and leave complicated risks and hazards to other social institutions – safety regulations'.[38] The literature shows that the answer to these two broad questions relies on two foundational factors: a) the availability of private insurance against all sorts of events that might generate damage, and b) the capacity of civil courts to obtain and process the information needed for the optimal enforcement and operation of such a tort law system.[39] Yet, Schäfer also notes that 'independent from potential informational constraints the tort law system cannot be an efficient institution as long as reducing the scope of liability results in distortive incentive effects which are less costly than the resulting savings of costs of the judicial system and easier insurance coverage'.[40] Namely, as the administrative and procedural costs of a tort law case can be very high (or even prohibitive), alternative institutions like no-fault insurance schemes, strict liability or ex ante safety regulation might be more effective for reducing the overall costs of accidents than tort law liability.[41]

---

[36]   Steven Shavell, 'Liability for Accidents' in Mitchell A Polinsky and Steven Shavell (eds.), *Handbook of Law and Economics*, vol 1 (Elsevier 2007) 139–83.

[37]   Donald Wittman, *Economic Foundations of Law and Organization* (Cambridge University Press, 2006) 131.

[38]   Schäfer (n 9) 572. See also Mark F Grady, 'Unavoidable Accident' (2009) 5 Review of Law and Economics 179.

[39]   Schäfer (n 9).

[40]   ibid. 590.

[41]   Donald N Dewees, David Duff and Michael J Trebilcock, *Exploring the Domain of Accident Law: Taking the Facts Seriously* (Oxford University Press, 1996) 452.

B.   Liability for Harm versus Safety Regulation

In his seminal paper on liability for harm versus regulation of safety, Professor Shavell paved the way for analytical understanding of the optimal employment of tort liability and/or regulatory standards. Shavell instrumentally addressed the effects of liability rules and direct regulation upon the rational self-interested party's decision-making process.[42] Liability in tort and safety regulation are shown to be two different approaches for controlling activities that create risks of harm and that induce the optimal amount of precaution.[43] However, as Shavell emphasises, major mistakes have been made in the use of liability and safety regulation.[44] Regulation, when applied exclusively, had often proven inadequate for many problems, whereas tort liability might provide, due to causation problems, suboptimal deterrence incentives.[45] Shavell also argues that regulatory fines are identical to tortious liability in that they create incentives to reduce risks by making parties pay for the harm they cause.[46] Nevertheless, as Shavell stresses, regulatory fines have an advantage in situations where private suits (and related tortious liability) would not be brought due to difficulty in establishing causation or where harms are widely dispersed.[47]

In addition, Rose-Ackerman suggests that regulation (statutes) should generally dominate so long as agencies can make rules to shape policy.[48] The tort rules should thus be limited to areas of activity not covered by regulation and to situations in which courts can complement the regulatory (statutory) scheme with a supplementary enforcement and compensation mechanism. At the same time, Schmitz argues that the joint use of liability and safety regulation is optimal if wealth varies among injurers.[49]

---

[42]   Steven Shavell, 'Liability for Harm versus Regulation of Safety' (1984) 13 Journal of Legal Studies 357.

[43]   Tort liability is private in nature and works not by social command but indirectly, through the deterrent effect of damage actions that may be brought once harm occurs, whereas standards and ex ante regulations are public in character and modify behaviour in an immediate way through requirements that are imposed before the actual occurrence of harm; ibid.

[44]   ibid.

[45]   ibid. See also Richard A Epstein, 'The Principles of Environmental Protection: The Case of Superfund' (1982) 2 Cato Journal 9.

[46]   Yet fines also suffer from the inability to pay for harm and from the possibility that violators would escape public agency; Shavell (n 42).

[47]   ibid.

[48]   Susan Rose-Ackerman, 'Tort Law as a Regulatory System' (1991) 81 AEA Papers and Proceedings 2.

[49]   Patrick W Schmitz, 'On the Joint Use of Liability and Safety Regulation' (2000) 20 International Review of Law and Economics 371, 371–82.

C.   AI-Generated Hazards Should Be Clustered within the Realm of Fault-Based Liability Rather Than Product Liability

Law and economics scholarship has argued for the need to rethink legal remedies when applying them to AI torts.[50] For example, Shavell even argues that AI renders classic product liability law unable to create the optimal incentives for the use, production and adoption of safer AI technologies as it is currently designed.[51] AI-related hazards are essentially unknown risks and the law and economics literature has addressed the problem of imposing liability for such unknown and unexpected risks and argues that whether 'liability for unknown risks is desirable depends on what is more important: avoiding the marketing of products which are not safe enough, or not hindering the introduction of better new products'.[52] Landes and Posner suggest that such liability might actually induce producers to invest in safer technologies.[53]

More recently, in their novel approach Guerra, Parisi and Pi state that AI-generated accidents should be clustered within the realm of 'fault-based liability rather than product liability', where negligence-based rules should be blended with strict liability rules to create precaution incentives for AI operators and their potential victims, and R&D incentives for manufacturers' development of safer AI.[54] They offer a novel liability regime, which they refer to as the 'manufacturer residual liability' rule.[55] Under such a 'manufacturer residual liability' regime, the primary liability is held by either the AI human operator or the victim, and the residual liability – the assignment of the accident cost when neither party is negligent – then falls on the manufacturer.[56]

---

[50]   See for example, Mark A Lemley and Bryan Casey, 'Remedies for Robots' (2019) 86 The University of Chicago Law Review 1311; and Eric Talley, 'Automators: How Should Accident Law Adapt to Autonomous Vehicles? Lessons from Law and Economics' (2019) Columbia Law School Working Papers Series No. 19002.

[51]   Steven Shavell, 'On the Redesign of Accident Liability for the World of Autonomous Vehicles' (2020) 49 The Journal of Legal Studies 243–85.

[52]   Michael Faure, Louis Visscher and Franziska Weber, 'Liability for Unknown Risk – A Law and Economics Perspective' (2016) 7 Journal of European Tort Law 198.

[53]   William M Landes and Richard A Posner, 'A Positive Economic Analysis of Products Liability' (1985) 14 The Journal of Legal Studies 535.

[54]   Alice Guerra, Francesco Parisi and Daniel Pi, 'Liability for Robots II: An Economic Analysis' (2021) 18(4) Journal of Institutional Economics 553, 554.

[55]   ibid.

[56]   Such a liability regime makes operators and victims liable for accidents due to their negligence – hence, incentivising them to act diligently; and makes manufacturers residually liable for non-negligent accidents – thus, incentivising them to make optimal investments in R&D for robots' safety. In turn, as Guerra, Parisi and Pi argue, such a rule would bring down the price of safer robots, driving unsafe technology out of the market and, due to the percolation effect of residual liability, would induce opera-

Namely, human operators and victims should bear accident losses attributable to their own negligent behaviour and manufacturers should only be held liable for non-negligent accidents. The negligence of the AI human operator also marks the boundary between a human operator's fault-based liability and the manufacturer's strict residual liability. Further, manufacturer's liability would arise for two separate sources of accidents caused by AI: a) malfunctions;[57] and b) design limitations.[58] Finally, they show that such a liability regime might offer several advantages over simple negligence and strict liability, and might achieve four objectives of an AI tort law regime, one that induces: a) efficient human precautionary care; b) efficient activity levels; c) investments in the R&D of safer AI; and d) the adoption of safer technology.[59] Such a 'manufacturer residual liability' regime, however, assumes the existence of a human operator who is capable of directing the activity of the AI and eventually overriding its decisions (i.e. supervised AI). Hence, this proposed regime will not be sufficient for addressing the potential hazards in instances where AI is completely capable of self-determination (i.e. unsupervised AI). This scenario and potential legal remedies are addressed in the next section.

---

tors to adopt optimal activity levels in AI usage; ibid. See also Alice Guerra, Francesco Parisi and Daniel Pi, 'Liability for Robots I: Legal Challenges' (2021) 18(3) Journal of Institutional Economics 331.

[57] Malfunctions should be dealt with by ordinary product liability law already in place where victims may sue manufacturers directly, or by allowing operators to sue manufacturers in subrogating when operators face direct liability under conventional tort law; ibid. 333.

[58] Design limitations refer to accidents that occur when AI encounters a new unforeseen circumstance that causes it to behave in an undesired manner; ibid. 333.

[59] ibid. 333, 340. In addition, Cooter and Porat offer a 'total liability for excessive harm' rule for instances of multiple tortfeasors where officials can verify the total harm caused by all injurers but not the harm caused by an individual injurer. Under the 'total liability for excessive harm' rule, each individual injurer should be liable for the total harm that everyone causes in excess of the optimal harm. They suggest that a remarkable consequence of such a rule is that injurers respond to it by causing the optimal harm and their liability is nil; Robert D Cooter and Ariel Porat, *Getting Incentives Right: Improving Torts, Contracts and Restitution* (Princeton University Press, 2014) 74–89. For example, an AI agency could establish a safety target and announce that each producer of AI systems in a certain area is liable for the damage caused by all producers of AI systems in excess of the target. As Cooter and Porat suggest, the agency gains control over the damages (i.e. negative externalities) without having to monitor individual producers, while the producers do not have to pay damages or comply with bureaucratic regulations; ibid. 74.

D.   Liability Issues and Autonomous AI

The new generation of AI might completely autonomously learn from their own variable experience and hypothetically develop in an unpredictable, uncontemplated, unique manner its creator could never had reasonably foreseen. AI companies might also be judgment-proof due to their size and AI is by definition about design limitations. If one then employs the 'let the machine learn' concept, the argument that a designer should have anticipated the risk becomes harder to sustain. In other words, AI might become sentient enough to have legal standing and, while evolving in manners unplanned by the AI system's designers, may generate unforeseeable losses and the best thing we can argue in such instances is to not use the court system (classic tort or contract law) at all but to rely on the EU's regulatory intervention instead. The classic law and economics concept of the judgment-proof problem shows that if injurers lack sufficient assets to pay for the damage they cause, their incentives to reduce risk will then be inadequate.[60] Yet, the judgment-proof problem can also be defined much more broadly to include the problem of the dilution of incentives to lower the risk that emerges when an existing legal person engaged with AI is completely indifferent to both the ex ante possibility of being found legally liable for the harm done to others and the potential accident liability (given that the value of the expected sanction equals zero). Existing legal persons might thus be completely indifferent to the ex ante possibility of being found liable by the human-imposed legal system for harm caused, and hence their incentives to engage in risky activities might be weak. For example, since the actions of AI agents are likely to become increasingly unforeseeable, the designers or producers of AI might think that such unforeseeable development might excuse them from any tortious liability and, in such a scenario, the traditional tort law mechanism might (except at a very high level of abstraction and generality) become inadequate for dealing with the potential harm caused by AI agents.[61] It must be stressed that this problem of diluted incentives (a broad judgment-proof definition) is distinct from what scholars and practitioners often call a 'judgment-proof problem', generally described as when a tortfeasor is merely financially unable to pay for all of the losses, leaving the victim

---

[60]   Steven Shavell, 'The Judgment Proof Problem' (1986) 6 International Review of Law and Economics 45.

[61]   Moreover, such liability could result in the over-deterrence of such an AI data provider, operator or software engineer, and may be detrimental to innovation and hamper innovation activity. See Michael E Porter, *The Competitive Advantage of Nations* (Free Press, 1990).

without full compensation.[62] Accordingly, the judgment-proof characteristics of existing legal persons engaged with autonomous AI could undermine the deterrence and insurance goals of traditional tort law.

In my previous work, several mechanisms were proposed to address such 'judgment-proof' characteristics of existing legal persons (i.e. manufacturers) and what follows is a brief summary of potential remedies: a) lawmakers could require any principal to have a certain minimum amount of assets in order to be allowed to engage in a completely autonomous AI-related activity; b) lawmakers could introduce the compulsory purchase of liability insurance coverage in order for any principal to be allowed to engage in an autonomous AI-related activity; c) lawmakers could directly ex ante regulate the AI's risk-creating behaviour (i.e. regulatory agencies could ex ante set detailed standards for the behaviour, employment, operation and functioning of any autonomous AI); d) regulatory agencies could establish a detailed set of sector-specific safety standards (similar to those in the air travel or pharmaceutical industries); e) criminal liability for the human operator (i.e. the principal) could be introduced to provide additional pressure to optimise the principal's decision on whether to engage with the autonomous AI activity at all; f) lawmakers could extend liability from the actual injurer (the autonomous AI) to the company that engages or employs such an AI agent; g) lawmakers could introduce corrective ex ante taxes that would equal the expected harm; h) lawmakers could establish a regime of compulsory compensation or a broad insurance fund for instances of catastrophic losses that is publicly and privately financed; and i) lawmakers could introduce the AI manufacturer's strict liability supplemented by the requirement that an unexcused violation of a statutory safety standard is negligence per se.[63]

Finally, it is noted that regulation and the previously discussed tort law regime should be applied simultaneously to address different types of completely autonomous and supervised AI.[64]

---

[62]   See Gur Huberman, David Mayers and Clifford W Smith, 'Optimal Insurance Policy Indemnity Schedules' (1983) 14 Bell Journal of Economics 415, 415–26.

[63]   See Mitja Kovac, *Judgement-Proof Robots and Artificial Intelligence: A Comparative Law and Economics Approach* (Palgrave Macmillan, 2020); and Mitja Kovac, 'Autonomous Artificial Intelligence and Uncontemplated Hazards: Towards the Optimal Regulatory Framework' (2021) 13(1) European Journal of Risk Regulation 94.

[64]   Kovac also offers several law and economics arguments which suggest that for completely autonomous AI a new special electronic legal person should not be created; ibid.

E.   Empirical Evidence on Liability for Harm and Innovation

The traditional law and economics literature suggests that the allocation of liability to the producer might delay innovation and distort the producer's incentive to invest in groundbreaking, frontier-risky technologies.[65] Regarding the question of strict liability, law and economics scholarship has witnessed the transformation of the core of liability law around the world from simple negligence to the far more complex concept of strict product liability.[66] In the last few decades, law and economics scholarship has shifted its attention to the possible detrimental effects of different tort law regimes and product liability on innovative activity.[67] This change from simple negligence to strict product liability was declared by many to be a victory for consumers and safer products. In theory, enhanced quality, safety and innovation should have resulted from this revolution in liability. However, scholars found that the reverse occurred.[68] They showed that product liability costs in the USA had prompted some manufacturers to abandon valuable new technologies, life-saving drugs and innovative product designs.[69]

Another stream of literature investigated the related issues of the civil liability regime and its detrimental effects on innovations. Namely, liability should ideally promote efficient levels of safety, while misdirected liability efforts and various litigation mechanisms might actually depress beneficial innovations.[70] Viscusi and Moore examined these competing effects of liabil-

---

[65]   See for example, Alberto Galasso and Hong Luo, *Punishing Robots: Issues in the Economics of Tort Liability and Innovation in Artificial Intelligence* (University of Chicago Press, 2019); Gideon Parchomovsky and Alex Stein, 'Torts and Innovation' (2008) 107 Michigan Law Review 285; Peter Huber, 'Safety and the Second Best: The Hazards of Public Risk Management in the Courts' (1985) 85 Columbia Law Review 277; and Michael E Porter, 'The Competitive Advantage of Nations' (1990) 14 Competitive Intelligence Review 1.

[66]   Schäfer and Ott (n 9). See also Reimer H Kraakman, 'Vicarious and Corporate Civil Liability' in Gerrit De Geest and Boudewijn Bouckaert (eds.), *Encyclopaedia of Law and Economics*, vol 2 (Edward Elgar Publishing, 2000).

[67]   John F Manning, 'Textualism as a Nondelegation Doctrine' (1997) 97 Columbia Law Review 673, 685.

[68]   See for example, Paul A Herbig and James E Golden, 'Differences in Forecasting Behaviour between Industrial Product Firms and Consumer Product Firms' (1994) 9 Journal of Business & Industrial Marketing 60, 60–69; Richard W Mallot, 'Rule-governed Behaviour and Behavioural Anthropology' (1988) 11 Behavioural Analysis 181, 181–203; Manning (n 67); and Jean B McGuire, 'A Dialectical Analysis of Interorganizational Networks' (1988) 14 Journal of Management 109, 109–124.

[69]   Herbig and Golden (n 68).

[70]   For example, the literature suggests that existing liability regimes could disincentivise firms from investing in the development of AI technologies; Erica Palmerini

ity costs on product R&D intensity and the introduction of new products by manufacturing firms.[71] They suggest that at low to moderate levels of expected liability costs there is a positive effect of liability costs on product innovation,[72] whereas the effect is negative at very high levels of liability costs. Moreover, they show that at the sample mean, liability costs increase R&D intensity by 15 percent.[73]

However, in a study on the interrelationships between propensity to patent, innovative activity, and litigation and liability costs generated by different legal systems Kovac, Datta and Spruk show that product liability and the associated litigation costs across firms and countries do not account for the failure of pharmaceutical firms to acquire a valid patent.[74] The results in fact reveal that higher litigation and liability costs across firms, combined with damages caps, reversed causality and limited class actions, and broad statutory excuses between and within countries have a positive effect on the validation rate, application rate and the stock of EPO patents.[75] Empirical evidence may thus suggest that civil liability and related litigation might be perceived as a filter that screens hazardous innovation and provides the incentive for efficient, productive and safe innovations.

F.   Synthesis: Towards Economically Informed AI Torts

The previous points may be summarised in the following outline for an improved doctrine. There is a need to rethink legal remedies as we apply them to AI torts – AI makes traditional product liability law in its current design unable to create the optimal incentives for the use, production and adoption of safer AI technologies. For supervised AI, generated hazards should be clustered within the realm of fault-based liability rather than product liability.

---

and Andrea Bertolini, *Liability and Risk Management in Robotics* (Nomos, 2016); Andrea Bertolini, 'Robotic Prostheses as Products Enhancing the Rights of People with Disabilities. Reconsidering the Structure of Liability Rules' (2015) 29 International Review of Law, Computers & Technology 116; and Lilla M Montagnani and Mirta Cavallo, 'Liability and Emerging Digital Technologies: An EU Perspective' (2021) 11 Notre Dame Journal of International and Comparative Law 2.

[71]   Kip W Viscusi and Michael J Moore, 'Product Liability, Research and Development, and Innovation' (1993) 101 Journal of Political Economy 161, 161–84.

[72]   ibid.

[73]   The greater linkage of these effects to product R&D rather than process R&D is consistent with the increased prominence of the design defect doctrine; ibid.

[74]   Salvini Datta, Mitja Kovac and Rok Spruk, 'Pharmaceutical Product Liability, Related Litigation and the Propensity to Patent: An Empirical Firm-level Investigation' (2021) 11 SAGE Open 2.

[75]   ibid.

The 'manufacturer residual liability' rule should be introduced for supervised AI where the primary liability is held by either the AI human operator or the victim, and the residual liability – the assignment of the accident cost when neither party is negligent – then falls on the manufacturer. The judgment-proof characteristics of existing legal persons engaged with autonomous AI could undermine the deterrence and insurance goals of traditional tort law. In instances of unsupervised, completely autonomous AI, 'manufacturer residual liability' is not adequate and an additional regulatory ex ante intervention is required. In instances of completely autonomous AI, a new special electronic legal person should not be created. Finally, empirical evidence may suggest that civil liability might be regarded as a filter that screens hazardous innovation and provides the incentive for safe AI-related innovations.

IV.   COMMENT ON THE EU'S LEGISLATIVE INITIATIVES

In 2017, the European Parliament urged the European Commission to produce a legislative proposal containing a set of detailed civil law rules on robotics and artificial intelligence.[76] This proposal was also to include a set of precise recommendations and very broad proposals to the European Commission concerning civil law rules on robotics. These were to: a) address issues such as liability for damage caused by a robot; b) produce an ethical code of conduct; and c) establish a European agency for robotics and artificial intelligence.

The European Parliament emphasised that draft legislation is urgently needed to clarify liability issues, especially for self-driving cars, and called for a mandatory insurance scheme and a supplementary fund to ensure that victims of accidents involving driverless cars are fully compensated. In addition, the European Parliament wondered whether: a) strict liability; b) the risk management approach; c) obligatory insurance; or d) a special compensation fund should be applied in instances where AI causes damage.[77]

Regarding the specific legal status, in paragraph 59 of its Resolution on Civil Law Rules in Robotics the European Parliament suggests that the 'EU should create a specific legal status for robots, so that at least the most sophisticated autonomous robots could be established as having the status of *electronic persons* responsible for making good any damage they may cause,

---

[76]   European Parliament, 'Resolution of 16 February 2017 with recommendations to the Commission on Civil Law Rules on Robotics' (n 6).
[77]   ibid.

and possibly applying electronic personality to cases where robots (AI) make autonomous decisions or otherwise interact with third parties independently'.[78]

The European Parliament also proposed: a) a code of ethical conduct for robotics engineers; b) a code for research ethics committees; c) a system of registration; d) a licence for designers; and e) a licence for users.[79]

In its Communication from the Commission to the European Parliament on artificial intelligence for Europe,[80] the European Commission states that a thorough evaluation of the Product Liability Directive (85/374/EEC) was carried out which provides that 'although strict liability for producers of AI is uncontested, the precise effects of new technological developments will have to be more closely analysed'. The European Commission in this Communication also explicitly asks whether 'a regulatory intervention on these technologies appears appropriate and necessary and whether that intervention should be developed in a horizontal or sectoral way and whether new legislation should be enacted at the EU level'.[81] The European Commission also established the Expert Group on Liability and New Technologies that provides expertise on the applicability of the Product Liability Directive to traditional products, new technologies and new societal challenges (Product Liability Directive formation) and assists the European Commission in developing principles that can serve as guidelines for the possible adaptation of applicable laws on the EU and national levels relating to new technologies (New Technologies formation). Moreover, the European Commission has engaged in a series of activities looking at the issues of liability with a view to ensuring legal certainty during the uptake of AI technologies.

In October 2020, the European Parliament adopted a resolution on liability[82] which provides that 'there is no need for a complete revision of the well-functioning liability regimes, but that the complexity, connectivity, opacity, vulnerability, the capacity of being modified through updates, the capacity for self-learning and the potential autonomy of AI-systems, as well as the multitude of actors involved nevertheless represent a significant challenge to the effectiveness of Union and national liability framework provisions; [and it] considers that specific and coordinated adjustments to the liability regimes are necessary to avoid a situation in which persons who suffer harm or whose

---

[78]   ibid.

[79]   ibid.

[80]   European Commission, 'Artificial Intelligence for Europe' (n 7).

[81]   European Commission, 'Liability for Emerging Technologies' SWD (2018) 137 final.

[82]   European Parliament, 'Resolution of 20 October 2020 on a civil liability regime for artificial intelligence' (Resolution) 2020/2014(INL).

property is damaged end up without compensation'.[83] This finding is clearly in line with the previously discussed law and economics principles.

Further, in its resolution on liability the European Parliament abandons its earlier position on establishing a new legal personality and, consistent with law and economics principles, notes that 'it is not necessary to give legal personality to AI systems'.[84] In addition, in line with the outlined law and economics insights, the European Parliament states that 'the existing fault-based tort law of the Member States offers in most cases a sufficient level of protection for persons that suffer harm caused by an interfering third party like a hacker or for persons whose property is damaged by such a third party, as the interference regularly constitutes a fault-based action', and notes that 'only for specific cases, including those where the third party is untraceable or impecunious, does the addition of liability rules to complement existing national tort law seem necessary'.[85] The European Parliament also considers that it is

> appropriate ... to focus on civil liability claims against the operator of an AI-system [and] affirms that the operator's liability is justified by the fact that he or she is controlling a risk associated with the AI-system, comparable to an owner of a car ... [and that] the operator will be in many cases the first visible contact point for the affected person.[86]

However, such a shift of liability solely to the operator overlooks the role of a victim and might hence generate the opportunistic behaviour of potential victims. Recall that law and economics analysis suggests the introduction of the 'manufacturer residual liability' rule for supervised AI where the primary liability falls either on the AI human operator or the victim, and the residual liability – the assignment of the accident cost when neither party is negligent – then falls on the manufacturer.

The European Parliament also notes that an AI system that entails an

> inherent high risk and acts autonomously potentially endangers the general public to a much higher degree; [and] based on the legal challenges that AI-systems pose to the existing civil liability regimes, it seems reasonable to set up a common strict liability regime for those high-risk autonomous AI-systems.[87]

In other words, the potential judgment-proof problems discussed in previous sections related to autonomous AI call for a specific regulatory approach.

---

[83]   ibid. para 6.
[84]   ibid. para 7.
[85]   ibid. para 9.
[86]   ibid. para 10.
[87]   ibid. para 14.

The regulatory approach proposed by the European Parliament obviously corresponds generally with the discussed economic principles.[88] Yet, from the law and economics perspective, it could be developed and further refined by introducing the proposed 'manufacturer residual liability' rule coupled with a set of the offered ex ante regulatory interventions designed to address the judgment-proof problems linked to autonomous AI.

Finally, in April 2021 the European Commission reacted to the European Parliament's resolution on liability and published its proposal for a regulation that lays down harmonised rules on artificial intelligence[89] that establish a legal framework for trustworthy AI. This proposal prescribes harmonised rules for the development, placement on the market and use of AI systems in the EU following a proportionate risk-based approach.[90] The proposal also ex ante prohibits particularly harmful AI practices and defines high-risk AI systems that pose significant risks to the health and safety or fundamental rights of persons. Such AI systems will need to comply with a set of horizontal mandatory requirements for trustworthy AI and follow conformity assessment procedures before they can be placed on the EU market. For example, Article 9 of the proposed regulation introduces a risk management system that involves a continuous iterative process which runs throughout the entire life cycle of a high-risk AI system and from the economic perspective is designed as a regulatory tool to ex ante (i.e. before it actually occurs) decrease the possible AI-related hazards. The proposed regulation also introduces a set of obligations concerned with technical documentation, transparency and the provision of information to users, introduces the automatic recording of events (logs) and provides that 'high-risk AI systems should be designed and developed in such a way that they can be effectively overseen by natural persons during the period in which the AI system is in use'.[91]

The proposed regulation (Artificial Intelligence Act) additionally introduces a compulsory conformity assessment procedure, AI certification and the

---

[88]   For example, in the same resolution the European Parliament also considers compulsory liability coverage to be one of the key factors that defines the success of new technologies, products and services; it observes that 'proper liability coverage is also essential for assuring the public that it can trust the new technology despite the potential for suffering harm or for facing legal claims by affected persons; [and] notes at the same time that this regulatory system focuses on the need to exploit and enhance the advantages of AI-systems, while putting in place robust safeguards' ibid. para 23.

[89]   European Commission, 'Proposal for a Regulation of the European Parliament and of the Council Laying Down Harmonized Rules on Artificial Intelligence (Artificial Intelligence Act) and Amending Certain Union Legislative Acts' (n 6).

[90]   It also proposes a unified future-proof definition of AI; ibid. 3.

[91]   ibid. art 14. The regulation also introduces a detailed set of obligations for providers, importers, users, distributors or any other third-party of AI systems.

compulsory registration of high-risk AI systems in an EU database.[92] These requirements are obviously in line with the previously outlined law and economics findings and are designed to ex ante complement the ex post tort law regimes.

Generally speaking, the regulatory proposal is in harmony with the economic arguments presented above where the need for ex ante regulatory intervention was emphasised. From the law and economics perspective, such an ex ante regulatory approach is clearly welcomed, one where the providers and users of these AI systems will have to ensure safety and comply with existing legislation protecting fundamental rights throughout the whole AI system's cycle. The risk-based approach employed where regulation prohibits AI systems that pose an unacceptable risk[93] represents a precautionary approach and, economically speaking, is designed to address the judgment-proof problems and identified shortcomings of the national tort law systems and product liability rules currently in place. Regulation represents a first systematic regulatory approach to address the potential hazards of high-risk, autonomous AI systems and forms part of a wider comprehensive package of measures[94] that address the problems posed by the development and employment of AI systems.

Moreover, one may wonder whether this regulatory proposal (and also the forthcoming amended 'Product Liability Directive') should continue with a one-size-fits-all approach covering all products including AI systems or should they also include differentiated rules for certain sectors (sector-specific approach) for certain aspects of AI-related liability issues. From the law and economics perspective such a general one-size-fits-all approach might be justified from the transaction costs and information asymmetries perspective. Namely, implementation of a sector-specific approach would impose very high administrative transaction costs[95] and requires an informed regulator which might suffer from severe information asymmetries. Furthermore, one

---

[92]   The regulation also establishes a special European Artificial Intelligence Board and introduces the establishment of National Competent Authorities for governing the application and implementation of this regulation.

[93]   The prohibitions cover practices that hold significant potential to manipulate persons through subliminal techniques beyond their consciousness or exploit the vulnerabilities of specific vulnerable groups in order to materially distort their behaviour in a manner likely to cause them physical or psychological harm; ibid. 13.

[94]   See, for example, the European Parliament and Council Directive 2006/42/EC on machinery, and amending Directive 95/16/EC (recast) [2006] OJ L157/24 (Machinery Directive); European Parliament and Council Directive 2001/95/EC on general product safety [2002] OJ L11/4 (General Product Safety Directive), and initiatives that address liability issues related to AI technologies.

[95]   Transaction costs of administering, enforcing and implementing such sector-specific regulations.

could implement a rule of thumb where the question of a sector-specific or general approach would depend upon the size of the expected harm. Namely, if the size of the expected harm generated by the AI systems in a specific sector or industry exceeds the administrative and other regulatory transaction costs then a sector-specific approach might indeed be justified. In other words, one might set a version of the Learned Hand Formula,[96] where a sector-specific approach should be formulated as the one where the costs (C^d) of having such a sector-specific approach, discounted by probability (p) of actual occurrence of sector-specific events, are lesser than the expected damage ($D^p(p)$) caused by a certain sector-specific AI system.

The earlier discussion on the technical human-like, self-awareness, self-learning features of autonomous AI and the extrapolation of the main findings of the law and economics literature on autonomous AI suggests that EU lawmakers are facing the unprecedented challenge of how to simultaneously regulate potential harmful and hazardous activity while not simultaneously deterring innovation in the field of autonomous AI. Still, economically speaking, law is a much more resilient and robust mechanism than is often believed.[97] Insightfully, the old rules generally employ strict liability in cases of new technologies and, when there is no legitimate application[98] of current laws, the proposed EU regulatory initiatives and established legal mechanisms via such strict liability also provide a general, first-aid response to the potential responsibility of autonomous AI.

---

[96]   Judge Learned Hand's negligence formula, denoting P as probability of loss, L as magnitude of loss and B as the cost of precaution. Judge Hand wrote that a potential injurer is negligent if, but only if, B < PL (see *United States v Caroll Towing Co.* 159 F.2d 169, 173 (2d Cir. 1947)). Although the Hand Formula is relatively recent, the method it actualises has been used to determine negligence ever since negligence was first adopted as the standard to govern accident cases: see Richard A Posner, 'A Theory of Negligence' (1972) 1 Journal of Legal Studies 29; and Terry T Henry, 'Negligence' (1915) 29 Harvard Law Review 40. However, applying Posner's discussion on the Learned Hand Formula, one must compare those costs and discounted benefits in their correct marginal form; Posner (n 10) 168.

[97]   Namely, since every new technology in essence poses a certain conceptual problem to the existing jurisprudence, efficient legal institutions react and generally address such issues by, for example, requiring legal standards of reasonableness, a duty of care or good faith. See for example, *Guille v Swan*, Supreme Court of New York 1822; and *Rylands v Fletcher* (1868) LR 3 HL 330.

[98]   For example, ballooning over Manhattan (*Guille v Swan*, Supreme Court of New York 1822) or having a reservoir in England (*Rylands v Fletcher* (1868) LR 3 HL 330).

V.   CONCLUSIONS

The issue of autonomous AI has recently attracted increasing scholarly attention in economics, law, sociology and philosophy studies. A new industrial
revolution has been unleashed where it is vital that lawmakers address its
systemic challenges and regulate its economic and social effects. The current
trends in favour of developing autonomous machines able to interact, learn and
make autonomous decisions call for substantive regulatory treatment.

While applying law and economics insights, this chapter has sought to
address the role of public regulatory policy in regulating autonomous AI and
related AI torts. The main findings are: a) the EU's current law-making anticipatory activities and regulatory initiatives are in line with the theory of the
optimal timing of legislative action and correspond with law and economics
suggestions on efficient regulatory intervention; b) generally speaking, the
laws and legal mechanisms currently in place adequately address responsibility for AI; c) the 'manufacturer residual liability' rule should be introduced for
supervised AI where the primary liability is held by either the AI human operator or the victim, and the residual liability – the assignment of the accident cost
when neither party is negligent – by the manufacturer; d) the judgment-proof
characteristics of existing legal persons engaged with autonomous AI could
undermine the deterrence and insurance goals of traditional tort law; e) in
instances of unsupervised, completely autonomous AI, 'manufacturer residual
liability' is not adequate and additional regulatory ex ante intervention is
needed if the autonomous AI evolves in an unpredictable manner once it has
left the creator's lab – then the ex ante regulatory intervention is suggested;
f) the proposed shift of liability solely to the operator neglects the role of the
victim and might induce the opportunistic behaviour of potential victims; g)
implementation of sector-specific regulatory intervention depends upon the
size of the expected harm, administering transaction costs and information
asymmetries; and h) the classic debate on the two different means of controlling hazardous activities, namely ex post liability for harm done and ex ante
safety regulation, may boil down to the question of efficient ex ante regulation.

The analysis performed suggests that the EU's proposed regulatory interventions follow an economic logic and that, from a scientific viewpoint, it may
be possible to formulate the proposed regulatory interventions in an even more
accurate and robust way.

9. Civil Liability all at Sea: The Challenges of Unmanned Cargo Ships

Simon Baughen[1]

Unmanned ships are coming – and coming soon. Kongsberg's 'Yara Birkeland' was put into commercial operation in Porsgrunn in the spring of 2022. During the first two years of operation, the vessel will go through a gradual transition towards full autonomous sailing. 'Yara Birkeland' will be the world's first fully electric and autonomous container ship. It is equipped with various proximity sensors, radar, Lidar,[2] AIS,[3] camera and infra-red camera, and its connectivity and communication is through maritime broadband radio, satellite communications and GSM.[4] Loading and discharging will be done automatically using electric cranes and equipment. Berthing and unberthing will be done without human intervention, through an automatic mooring system. The ship will sail within 12 nautical miles of the coast, between three ports in southern Norway. There will be three centres to handle emergency and exception handling, condition monitoring, operational monitoring, decision support, surveillance of the autonomous ship and its surroundings and all other aspects of safety.

Where the 'Yara Birkeland' leads, other autonomous ships are sure to follow, initially with small coastal and inland waterway vessels. Autonomous ships offer the attraction of reducing accidents, with an estimated 80 per cent of maritime accidents being due to human error.[5] They also offer a reduction in wage costs, estimated to form 30 per cent of a shipowner's operating costs, by eliminating an on-board crew.[6] They may also offer fuel savings through the reduction in weight by eliminating the accommodation structure. However, autonomous vessels bring risks, notably that of a loss of control through mali-

---

[1]   Professor, The Institute of International Shipping and Trade Law, Swansea University.
[2]   Light, Detection and Ranging.
[3]   Automatic Identification System.
[4]   Global System for Mobile Communication.
[5]   marasco-marine.com/incl/23.php accessed 4 June 2022.
[6]   'Massive Cargo Ships Are Going Autonomous. Here Are the Companies & Trends Driving the Global Maritime Industry Forward' (*CB Insights*, 28 August 2018) www.cbinsights.com/research/autonomous-shipping-trends/ accessed 4 June 2022.

cious hacking, and loss of communication with shoreside control in periods of bad weather coupled with a reduction in datalink capacity. There will also be additional operational costs, such as the provision of shore-based controllers ('SBCs') who will monitor the ship and navigate it remotely during sections of its voyage, as well as taking over navigation through remote operation when the ship gets into difficulty if weather and traffic conditions change considerably. The lack of an on-board crew will mean that no maintenance work can be done during the voyage, resulting in increased time in ports for such work. The lack of an on-board crew will also rule out the use of heavy fuel oil which is maintenance intensive and will require the use of costlier marine diesel oil ('MDO') or marine gas oil ('MGO'). Additionally, owners may need to use port agents to perform functions relating to the loading and unloading of cargo, including the issuing of bills of lading, which are currently performed by the master and crew.

Unmanned vessels clearly pose challenges for compliance with the international regulatory framework established through the various conventions of the International Maritime Organization ('IMO').

The IMO's Maritime Safety Committee ('MSC') recently embarked on a regulatory scoping exercise on how safe, secure and environmentally sound Maritime Autonomous Surface Ships ('MASS') operations may be addressed in IMO instruments.[7] The MSC sets out the following four-point scale for MASS operations.

- MASS 1: Ship with automated processes and decision support, with seafarers on board to operate and control shipboard systems and functions. Some operations may be automated and at times be unsupervised but with seafarers on board ready to take control.
- MASS 2: Remotely controlled ship with seafarers on board but controlled and operated from another location. The seafarers on board are there to take control if necessary, and to operate the shipboard systems and functions.
- MASS 3: Remotely controlled ship without seafarers on board, the vessel being entirely controlled and operated from another location.
- MASS 4: Fully autonomous ship, whose operating system is able to make decisions and determine actions by itself.

---

[7]   The IMO's Maritime Safety Committee approved the framework and methodology for the regulatory scoping exercise on Maritime Autonomous Surface Ships (MASS) during its 100th session held on 3–7 December 2018, following the establishment of a correspondence group on MASS which was set up to test the framework of this regulatory scoping at the 99th Session of MSC on 16–25 May 2018.

The key factor differentiating levels MASS 3 and MASS 4 on this scheme would be the level of operational control that would have to be exercised by human shore-based controllers. It is worth noting that other more detailed scales of autonomous operation exist. There is Sheridan's ten-point scale from 1992[8], and alternatively, a six-point scale set out in 2017 by the Danish Maritime Law Association, itself adapted from Lloyd's Register.

The regulatory scoping exercise was completed on 26 May 2021 and considered by the IMO Legal Committee at the end of July 2021.[9] In general, the exercise concluded that MASS could be accommodated within the existing regulatory framework of the IMO conventions without the need for major adjustments or a new instrument. While some conventions can accommodate MASS as drafted, others may require additional interpretations or amendments to address potential gaps and themes that were revealed through the Regulatory Scoping Exercise, the most important being: the role and responsibility of the master; the role and responsibility of the remote operator; questions of liability; consistent definitions/terminology of MASS; and carriage of certificates.

So far, much of the attention has been on the regulatory challenges posed by these vessels of the future, which, along with increasing attention to climate change and international shipping, are likely to prove a feature of the new decade. However, so far, there has been little analysis of the impact of maritime robotics on civil liability for accidents arising out of the carriage of cargo by sea by vessels operating at MASS levels 3 and 4. It is this which this chapter seeks to rectify.

Currently, the civil liability map consists of national laws on contract and tort and international conventions that govern civil liability. There are three categories of international conventions, and it is on these that this chapter will focus its attention with respect to their operation in relation to cargo vessels with no on-board crew. First, there are three strict liability pollution conventions, and one strict liability convention on wreck removal. There is the International Convention on Civil Liability for Oil Pollution Damage ('CLC'), in its original 1969 iteration and in its updated 1992 Protocol, for oil pollution; the 2001 Bunker Oil Pollution Convention for pollution from escapes of bunkers; and the 1996 Hazardous and Noxious Substances Convention, as updated by the 2010 Protocol. The first two are in force, the third one is not, but is likely to be in force by the time we see the operation of unmanned cargo vessels. Secondly, there are the presumed fault liability conventions covering loss or damage to

---

[8]   T Sheridan, *Telerobotics, Automation, and Human Supervisory Control* (MIT Press, 1992).

[9]   Legal Committee, 108th session (LEG 108), 26–30 July 2021.

cargo. The principal convention is the 1924 Hague Rules,[10] and its amended version with the 1968 Visby Protocol.[11] Thirdly, there is a fault-based convention for collision liability, the Brussels Collision Convention 1910. In addition, there are two global tonnage-based limitation regimes for maritime claims, the 1957 and 1976 Limitation Conventions, as well as mandatory insurance requirements to be found in the strict liability conventions, and within the EU and the UK for maritime claims up to the limits of the 1996 Protocol to the 1976 Convention. The position of third parties involved in a maritime accident also needs to be considered from the perspective of recourse actions by the shipowner, and from their ability to rely on the provisions of the limitation conventions or on the channelling provisions in the strict liability conventions.

This leads to the question of whether the advent of uncrewed vessels should lead to a review of the third parties entitled to such protection. Two particular issues loom large. First is the status of independent contractors that might be used by shipowners to undertake remote navigation of their uncrewed vessels, an issue which affects the vicarious liability of the shipowner, as well as the protection of the contractor in the event of a maritime claim. Second, there is the difficulty of ascribing fault to defects in the navigational software. Particularly problematic is self-learning software that adapts over time – the so-called 'Skynet' problem where incorrect lessons are learned by the AI with disastrous consequences.[12]

I.   EXISTING STRICT LIABILITY REGIMES

There are two civil liability conventions currently in force that deal with compensation for pollution and clean-up costs from ships, as well as a convention on wreck removal.

The first civil liability pollution convention is the 1969 CLC for oil pollution and its 1992 Protocol, to which the UK has subscribed. These cover pollution damage resulting from spills of persistent oils suffered in the territory (including the territorial sea) of a State Party to the Convention, expanded in the 1992 Protocol to cover pollution damage caused in the exclusive economic

---

[10]   International Convention for the Unification of Certain Rules of Law relating to Bills of Lading ('Hague Rules'), and Protocol of Signature (Brussels, 25 August 1924).

[11]   Protocol to Amend the International Convention for the Unification of Certain Rules of Law Relating to Bills of Lading ('Visby Rules') (Brussels, 23 February 1968). Throughout this chapter the Hague Rules will be referred to save where there are references to new provisions in the Visby amendments.

[12]   Although not so disastrous as in 'Terminator 2' where the intelligent missile system 'Skynet' decided to launch a nuclear apocalypse to destroy its human creators.

zone ('EEZ') or equivalent area of a State Party. 'Pollution damage' is defined within Article I.6 of the 1992 Protocol as:

(a) loss or damage caused outside the ship by contamination resulting from the escape or discharge of oil from the ship, wherever such escape or discharge may occur, provided that compensation for impairment of the environment other than loss of profit from such impairment shall be limited to costs of reasonable measures of reinstatement actually undertaken or to be undertaken;
(b) the costs of preventive measures and further loss or damage caused by preventive measures.

Under both versions of the CLC the registered owner of the vessel is strictly liable, subject to very limited exceptions. Although liability is strict, under Article III.2 the shipowner may escape liability if it can prove that the discharge or escape or the threat of contamination:

(a) resulted from an act of war, hostilities, civil war, insurrection or an exceptional, inevitable and irresistible natural phenomenon; or
(b) was due *wholly* to anything done or left undone by another person, not being a servant or agent of the owner, with intent to do damage; or
(c) was due *wholly* to the negligence or wrongful act of a government or other authority in exercising its function of maintaining lights or other navigational aids for the maintenance of which it was responsible (emphasis added).

In respect of (b) and (c), the word 'wholly' is particularly important. If the shipowner can only prove that the damage fell partly within the events listed, it will be unable to claim the exemption. None of these exceptions involves any absence of fault on the part of the shipowner, so the liability regime will be unaffected by the problems of establishing or rebutting fault that will affect other civil maritime liability regimes.

There is, however, one aspect of the CLC which does involve fault, where there is the fault of the claimant, and the absence of fault of the shipowner. Article III.3 provides: 'If the owner proves that the pollution damage resulted wholly or partially either from an act or omission done with intent to cause damage by the person who suffered the damage or from the negligence of that person, the owner may be exonerated wholly or partially from his liability to such person'.

There are channelling provisions which ensure that oil pollution claims against the registered owner can be made only under the CLC. Claims for oil pollution against various associated parties are also excluded, save where the right to limit liability would be lost. Under the 1969 CLC these were simply the servants or agents of the owner. The 1992 Protocol is more extensive and encompasses, under Article III.4:

(a) the servants or agents of the owner or the members of the crew;
(b) the pilot or any other person who, without being a member of the crew, performs services for the ship;
(c) any charterer (howsoever described, including a bareboat charterer), manager or operator of the ship;
(d) any person performing salvage operations with the consent of the owner or on the instructions of a competent public authority;
(e) any person taking preventive measures;
(f) all servants or agents of persons mentioned in subparagraphs (c), (d) and (e).

Shore-based controllers should fall within either (a), (b) or (c) of the 1992 Protocol, and probably under the first heading in the 1969 CLC.

The CLC has its own provisions for limitation of liability which are virtually unbreakable. Liability insurance is mandatory for ships carrying more than 2,000 tons of oil and there is a direct right of action against the liability insurer. The insurer may rely on any defences available to the shipowner and may avoid liability on proof that the damage resulted from the wilful misconduct of the shipowner.

A separate tier of compensation is set up under the Fund Convention to compensate victims of oil pollution who were unable to receive adequate recompense from the shipowner under the CLC regime. This is financed by contributions from receivers of oil cargoes. The UK is a party to the 1992 Protocols, which set up a new fund convention with higher limits and provided for the eventual winding up of the 1971 Fund. From 16 May 1998, members of the 1992 Fund had ceased to retain membership of the 1971 Fund. On 24 May 2002, the 1971 Fund ceased to be in force. Some states that still apply the 1969 CLC are parties to the 1992 Fund. As from 1 November 2003, the limit is 203 million Special Drawing Rights ('SDRs'). An additional tier of compensation is provided by the 2003 Protocol, which came into force on 3 March 2005. This establishes a supplementary fund with an overall limit of 750 million SDRs for each incident for pollution damage in the territory of the State Parties to the Protocol. It will only cover claims for incidents that occur after the Protocol has entered into force for the state concerned.

The strict liability structure of the 1992 Protocol of the CLC is applied in the other two pollution conventions and in the 2007 Nairobi Wreck Removal Conventions.[13] The 2001 International Convention on Civil Liability for Bunker Oil Pollution Damage ('Bunker Oil Convention') entered into force on 21 November 2008. The Convention covers bunker oil spills outside the vessel, wherever they occur, which cause damage in the territory of State Parties. The Convention, however, defines 'shipowner' in Article 1(3) in terms wider

---

[13] Entry into force, 14 April 2015.

than those used by the CLC, as 'the owner, including the registered owner, bareboat charterer, manager and operator of the ship'. The 2010 International Convention on Liability and Compensation for Damage in Connection with the Carriage of Hazardous and Noxious Substances by Sea ('HNS'), which is not currently in force, imposes strict liability on shipowners who carry HNS cargoes, defined in Article 1(5) by reference to substances listed in various existing sources, such as the International Code for the Construction and Equipment of Ships Carrying Dangerous Chemicals in Bulk 1983. The HNS Convention, unlike the other two maritime pollution conventions currently in force also imposes liability for death or personal injury on board or outside the ship carrying the hazardous and noxious substances.[14]

Mandatory insurance requirements and a direct right of action against insurers appear in all the Conventions.[15] A specific limitation of liability regime, and the establishment of a second tier of compensation through a Fund, feature with the HNS Convention. The Bunker Oil Pollution Convention and the Wreck Removal Convention have neither of these features and provide for the owner's strict liability to be subject to the right to limit under any applicable national or international regime, such as the Convention on Limitation of Liability for Maritime Claims, 1976, as amended. There are no channelling provisions under these two Conventions, although as regards the Bunker Oil Pollution Convention the UK has introduced channelling provisions into the implementation of the Convention in the Merchant Shipping Act 1995.

There is also a strict liability public law clean-up regime in the EU under the 2004 Environmental Liability Directive ('ELD')[16] whose territorial maritime limits were expanded in 2013 by the Offshore Safety Directive ('OSD').[17] The ELD put in place an EU-wide framework for remediation of environmental

---

[14] Article 7 reiterates the familiar CLC defences and adds a new one where:
the failure of the shipper or any other person to furnish information concerning the hazardous and noxious nature of the substances shipped either (i) has caused the damage, wholly or partly; or (ii) has led the owner not to obtain insurance in accordance with Article 12; provided that neither the owner nor its servants or agents knew or ought reasonably to have known of the hazardous and noxious nature of the substances shipped.

[15] Under the Bunker Oil Pollution Convention liability insurance is mandatory for the registered owner of a ship having a gross tonnage greater than 1000 registered in a State Party, while under the Wreck Removal Convention the mandatory insurance requirement applies to ships of 300 gross tonnage and above and flying the flag of a State Party.

[16] Directive 2004/35/CE of the European Parliament and of the Council of 21 April 2004 on environmental liability with regard to the prevention and remedying of environmental damage.

[17] Directive 2013/30/EU of the European Parliament and of the Council of 12 June 2013 on safety of offshore oil and gas operations and amending Directive 2004/35/EC.

damage which is defined as damage to: '(a) protected species or natural habitats, or a site of special scientific interest, (b) surface water or groundwater, or (c) land'.

The ELD sets out two complementary public law regimes to require remediation of environmental damage, or any imminent threat of such damage, by operators, neither of which has retroactive effect. The first is a strict liability regime which applies to operators who professionally conduct risky, or potentially risky, activities listed in Annex III. Those relevant to shipping within Annex III are:

> Transport by road, rail, inland waterways, sea or air of dangerous goods or polluting goods as defined in: (c) Council Directive 93/75/EEC concerning minimum requirements for vessels bound for or leaving Community ports and carrying dangerous or polluting goods, as last amended by Directive 2002/84/EC.

This category would cover the carriage of hazardous substances, until the HNS Convention comes into force. A second, fault-based regime covers damage to protected species or natural habitats or a site of special scientific interest caused by all professional activities, including those outside Annex III, where the operator is at fault or negligent.

Article 4(2) of the Directive excludes an incident in respect of which liability or compensation falls within the scope of the 1992 CLC, or the 1992 Fund Convention, or the 2001 Bunker Oil Pollution Convention. Article 4(3) of the Directive also provides that it is without prejudice to the right of an operator to limit liability in accordance with the Convention on Limitation of Liability for Maritime Claims 1976. The Directive also excludes liability in relation to environmental damage caused by: (a) an act of armed conflict, hostilities, civil war or insurrection; (b) an exceptional natural phenomenon, provided the operator of the activity concerned took all reasonable precautions to protect against damage being caused by such an event; (c) activities the sole purpose of which is to provide protection from natural disasters.

There is no upper limit of liability for an operator under either of these regimes, but operators are not required to obtain liability insurance. Civil claims fall outside the Directive and remain subject to national laws.

The effect of the Directive in the maritime sphere was initially limited by the geographical ambit of damage to surface water. However, that changed with the implementation of the OSD Directive 2013/30 on safety of offshore oil and gas operations. Article 38 amends the Environmental Liability Directive so that the ambit of damage to surface water covers all EU waters including the EEZ (about 370 km from the coast) and the continental shelf where the coastal

Member States exercise jurisdiction. Member States had until 19 July 2015 to implement this provision, and the UK implemented the provisions on this day.[18]

II. PRESUMED FAULT REGIMES.
INTERNATIONAL CARRIAGE OF CARGO

Most cargo that is carried by sea is carried under contracts that are subject to one of the international conventions for carriage of goods by sea. Most common is the Hague Rules 1924, the subject of an amending protocol, the Visby Protocol in 1968 to which the UK and most European countries are party. There is also a newer convention, the Hamburg Rules,[19] to which a few countries, but no major maritime interests, subscribe. A further, more ambitious convention, which extends to multimodal carriage involving sea carriage, is the Rotterdam Rules 2008. This is not yet in force, so far receiving only 5 of the necessary 20 ratifications. The Hague Rule liability scheme involves a variant of a presumed liability scheme. Once the cargo claimant establishes that the loss or damage occurred during the carrier's period of responsibility, the carrier is presumptively liable for that loss or damage unless it can be shown that the loss or damage was caused by an excepted peril specified by the rule, or the carrier can positively prove that it took proper care of the cargo during its period of responsibility.

Under the Hague and Hague-Visby Rules,[20] their application is determined by the contract of carriage between the carrier and the shipper, the fact of carriage by sea and the existence, or contractual contemplation, of a bill of lading that determines the applicability of the Rules. The nature of the ship in which the goods are carried is of no import. The Rules do refer to 'the ship' as a party which is liable along with the carrier in Article IV(1) and (2) which establish the defences to liability for loss or damage, and in Article III(8) which renders void any clauses in the contract of carriage relieving the carrier or the ship

---

[18] In England through the Environmental Damage (Prevention and Remediation) (England) Regulations 2015, with similar, but not identical, Regulations in the other devolved nations. The Regulations remain in force as 'retained legislation' following Brexit.

[19] United Nations Convention on the Carriage of Goods by Sea (Hamburg, 1978) (the 'Hamburg Rules'). The Convention entered into force on 1 November 1992.

[20] With the Hague-Visby Rules the relevant provision is Article X, which provides: 'The provisions of these Rules shall apply to every bill of lading relating to the carriage of goods between ports in two different States if (a) the bill of lading is issued in a contracting State, or (b) the carriage is from a port in a contracting State, or (c) the contract contained in or evidenced by the bill of lading provides that these Rules or legislation of any State giving effect to them are to govern the contract; whatever may be the nationality of the ship, the carrier, the shipper, the consignee, or any other interested person.'

of liability, or of lessening liability, other than that as provided in the Rules. 'Ship' is widely defined as '[a]ny vessel used for the carriage of goods by sea' and does not presuppose that any particular type of ship is being used. There are some references to the 'master' and 'crew' which might be problematic for an unmanned vessel, but as this analysis will show, this is not the case.

The Hague and Hague-Visby Rules impose three duties on the 'carrier' which could be a charterer or a shipowner, which depends on the form of the bill of lading, in particular the way in which it is signed.

The carrier is under three obligations: to provide a seaworthy ship, before and at the start of the voyage (Article III(1)); to properly and carefully 'load, handle, stow, carry, keep, care for and discharge the goods carried' (Article III(2));[21] and to issue a bill of lading to the shipper containing three specified pieces of information (Article III(3)). This last obligation will be unaffected by the operation of unmanned ships and will not be discussed.

If cargo is lost or damaged during the carrier's period of responsibility under the Rules, which runs from the start of loading to the completion of discharge, there will be a presumed breach of Article III(2) which the carrier may rebut by showing that it took proper care of the cargo or by bringing itself within one of the exceptions afforded to it under Article IV(2). Article III(2) imposes a non-delegable obligation,[22] although some of these operations may be contractually allocated away from the shipowner to other parties such as charterers, shippers and receivers.[23] Crew intervention in cargo management is already diminishing and will disappear still further at levels 3 and 4. Operations such as opening and closing hatch covers during the voyage to ventilate grain cargoes may be done remotely by the SBC but there is no reason why these could not be done completely remotely through the programmed software with the SBC maintaining only a monitoring role.

If a presumptive breach of Article III(2) is established, the carrier can rebut it either by showing positively that it did properly and carefully perform the tasks set out in Article III(2) or by showing that the loss or damage was caused by one of the excepted perils set out in Article IV(2) which lists specific exceptions from (a) to (q). Of particular interest is the first of these, 'Act,

---

[21]   It should be noted that certain obligations, such as the carrier's delivery obligation, and also its obligation to proceed on the voyage with reasonable dispatch, fall outside the Rules, although it has been held that the one-year time bar applies to claims for misdelivery.

[22]   *Hourani v T & J Harrison* (1927) 27 Lloyd's Rep 415 (KB).

[23]   This is the position under English law, see *The Jordan II* [2004] UKHL 49, [2005] 1 WLR 1363, but in other jurisdictions applying the Hague Rules the shipowner is treated as having undertaken all seven of the functions listed in Article II and Article III(2).

neglect, or default of the master, mariner, pilot, or the servants of the carrier in the navigation or in the management of the ship'. The absence of an on-board crew might be thought to remove this exception when the goods are being carried by an unmanned vessel. However, it is possible to regard the SBC as the functional equivalent of the master and therefore the carrier would still be able to rely on the exception in respect of loss or damage caused by any errors of navigation on their part.

If the SBC is not regarded as the 'master' then they could constitute a 'servant of the carrier'. As the duties of the carrier under both Article III(1) and (2) are non-delegable, the servants of any independent contractor engaged to perform those duties will be treated as a servant of the carrier.[24] Accordingly, servants of the SBC will be 'servants of the carrier' for the purposes of the nautical fault defence.[25] It is doubtful whether negligence by the voyage programmer would fall within the exception, as such negligence would render the vessel unseaworthy. The duty is personal to the carrier and is non-delegable so there is no due diligence if the ship has been rendered unseaworthy by the negligence of the crew[26] or by that of an independent contractor.[27]

Human input at level 4 will probably be no more than an SBC inputting the start and finish of the voyage, and human SBCs assuming operation when the software dictates – everything else will be down to the algorithms, which will dictate when to involve human operators in remote navigation. This means that the nautical fault exception in Article IV(2)(a) effectively disappears in respect of goods carried on a level 4 vessel. Nor would defects in the software controlling the vessel's navigation be attributable to the fault of a legal person, as a software program has no personality, and the initial human creator of the software will have created it, along with its self-learning capacity, long before the commencement of the voyage in question. However, at level 4 it is conceivable that the SBC may be summoned into action by the vessel's navigational software, and the SBC's response to that call to arms in response

---

[24]   As regards Article III (2) see: *The Ferro* [1893] P 38; *Hourani v T&J Harrison: Brown & Co v Same* (1927) 28 Lloyd's Rep 120 (CA).

[25]   See, *Heyn and others v Ocean Steamship Co Ltd* (1927) 27 Lloyd's Rep 334 (KB); *Hourani v T&J Harrison: Brown & Co v Same* (1927) 28 Lloyd's Rep 120 (CA). More than one employer can be vicariously liable for the negligence of an employee under the direction of another. *Viasystems (Tyneside) Ltd v Thermal Transfer (Northern) Limited* [2005] EWCA Civ 1151, [2006] QB 510.

[26]   *Alize 1954 v Allianz Elementar Versicherungs AG (The CMA CGM Libra)* [2019] EWHC 481 (Admlty), [2019] 1 Lloyd's Rep. 595; aff'd [2020] EWCA Civ 293, [2020] 2 All ER (Comm) 1072, [2020] 2 Lloyd's Rep 565; aff'd [2021] UKSC 51.

[27]   *Riverstone Meat Co Pty Ltd v Lancashire Shipping Co Ltd (The Muncaster Castle)* [1961] AC 807 (HL).

to a compromised algorithm may be negligent. In this case, if that negligence is causative of the loss or damage, the defence will exonerate the carrier.

Another defence that is of interest would be (f) 'Act of public enemies'. This probably covers pirates but may also be extended to cover persons who hack into the vessel's computer system, on the grounds that they are the twenty-first century's '*hostes humani generis*', the old description used for pirates and slavers. The final defence is in heading (q) which provides:

> Any other cause arising without the actual fault or privity of the carrier, or without the fault or neglect of the agents or servants of the carrier, but the burden of proof shall be on the person claiming the benefit of this exception to show that neither the actual fault or privity of the carrier nor the fault or neglect of the agents or servants of the carrier contributed to the loss or damage.

This would cover a hack on the vessel's computer system but with the burden on the carrier of proving that there had been no fault on the part of its agents, servants or carrier. After the decision of the Supreme Court in *Volcafe Ltd and others v Compania Sud America de Vapores SA*[28] the carrier will also have to show it took reasonable care of the cargo, as regards the inherent vice exception in (m) and likely as regards all the other exceptions bar (a) which is based on the fault of the vessel's servants and agents in the navigation and management of the vessel or the fire exception in (b).[29]

Next, we must consider the issue of seaworthiness, an issue which pervades discussion of unmanned vessels. Article III(1) imposes an obligation on the carrier, before and at the beginning of the voyage, to exercise due diligence to: '(a) [m]ake the ship seaworthy; (b) [p]roperly man, equip and supply the ship; (c) [m]ake the holds, refrigerating and cool chambers, and all other parts of the ship in which goods are carried, fit and safe for their reception, carriage and preservation'.

If the carrier can rely on an exception under Article IV(2) it will lose its right if the claimant can show that the vessel was unseaworthy before and at the beginning of the voyage and that this unseaworthiness was a cause, not necessarily the exclusive cause, of the loss or damage in question. If the claimant succeeds in doing so, the burden will then shift to the carrier to establish under Article IV(1) that it took due diligence to make the vessel seaworthy.

Headings (a) and (c) would remain unchanged as they apply as regards the physical condition of the ship (a) and its cargo carrying spaces. With an unmanned cargo vessel, the relevant provision would be heading (b). This does

---

[28]   [2018] UKSC 61, [2019] AC 358.
[29]   *Glencore Energy UK Ltd v Freeport Holdings Ltd (The Lady M)* [2019] EWCA Civ 388, [2019] 2 All ER (Comm) 731, [2019] 2 Lloyd's Rep 109.

not prescribe what is necessary for proper manning, equipping and supplying of the ship. There is no requirement for any on-board manning, and this obligation would be satisfied through having sufficient, properly trained SBCs monitoring and, as necessary, navigating the vessel remotely, with proper software and communications systems to enable safe autonomous navigation, and the necessary, functioning cameras, sensors and Lidar to establish communication with the SBC. At level 4 there would be a query about whether the vessel could be said to be 'properly' manned in the absence of any human input into its navigation. However, there would likely be some form of continuing onshore monitoring and the shipowner's arrangements for this would fall under this heading.

In this context, seaworthiness will have to extend landward, extending to software and hardware onshore, as well as to the competence of the SBCs monitoring and, as necessary, operating the vessel. The obligation of the carrier under Article III(1) will involve the following aspects of the vessel's operation: the computer hardware on the vessel by which the software controlling the vessel will be operated; the software installed; the programming of the software for the voyage to be undertaken; and the competence of the human element, the SBCs who will monitor the vessel's progress and, if needs be, take remote control of its operation. The human element of the crew will no longer be tied in with the vessel and although this will have an impact on classification surveys which will need to assess those off-ship elements, it will not alter the basic legal analysis. The hardware and the software on the vessel are no different from existing navigational aids, such as satnav and radar on a vessel, while it is well-established that crew incompetence will render a vessel unseaworthy.[30] The preparation of a passage plan by the master is an incident of the vessel's initial seaworthiness before and at the start of the voyage,[31] and the same would apply as regards the inputting of voyage instructions by an onshore controller under levels 3 and 4. With increased web awareness in the vessel's software systems it is likely that in time the only input will be of the place of loading and discharge with all navigational details being determined by the software on the basis of up-to-date virtual charts.

If anything is wrong with any of these elements 'before and at the beginning of the voyage'[32] the ship will be unseaworthy and if that is a cause of the loss or damage to cargo then the shipowner will be in breach of Article III(1). This is something for the claimant to prove. The timing of the seaworthiness period

---

[30]   *The Star Sea* [1995] 1 Lloyd's Rep 651, (QB); *Hong Kong Fir Shipping Co Ltd v Kawasaki Kisen Kaisha Ltd* [1962] 2 QB 26 (CA).

[31]   *The CMA CGM Libra* (n 26).

[32]   A breakdown shortly after leaving port will give rise to an inference that the vessel was unseaworthy on sailing. *The Theodegmon* [1990] 1 Lloyd's Rep 52 (QB).

will fit slightly awkwardly into the brave new world of unmanned vessels and onshore remote operators. It is likely that several SBCs will be employed at different stages in the voyage, and each will also be simultaneously undertaking remote operation of other vessels. Will seaworthiness through the competence of the 'crew' attach at the time the voyage starts or will this be a moveable feast attaching each time the vessel passes into the orbit of a new set of SBCs?

Thereafter, the burden shifts and it will be for the shipowner to exonerate itself under Article IV(1) by showing that it took due diligence to make the ship seaworthy before and at the start of the voyage if it is to be able to rely on an exception in Article IV(2). As noted above, the duty is personal to the carrier and is non-delegable so there is no due diligence if the ship has been rendered unseaworthy by the negligence of the crew[33] or by that of an independent contractor.[34]

So, for example, problems caused by hacking of the vessel's computer systems would amount to a breach of Article III(1) if the necessary anti-virus programmes had not been kept up to date, no matter that this was a task undertaken by an independent contractor – nor would the shipowner be able to establish due diligence in this situation. A failure to update during the voyage would be different and would amount to a breach of Article III(2) in failing properly and carefully to carry and care for the cargo.

If the software installed on the vessel is itself defective, then the issue would be whether this failure occurred while the vessel was in the orbit of the shipowner. The shipowner's duty under Article III(1) does not start until the vessel comes into its 'orbit', which term is coextensive with ownership, service or control. In *The Happy Ranger*[35] the shipowner was not liable for the negligence of the shipbuilder prior to that date that had resulted in defects to the vessel's cranes. However, the shipowner had failed to exercise due diligence in relation to the period after the vessel came into its orbit by failing to proof test the hooks before loading began, having been aware that no such testing had been done by the shipbuilder. With the acquisition of an unmanned vessel, the owners would need to show that they had run the proper test on the software controlling its navigation.

Thereafter, the owners would need to show that proper tests had been run to ensure that the software was still functioning properly. With increasing likelihood of machine learning and adaptation of the program, a risk is that defects in the software may be generated over time which cannot be detected

---

33   *The CMA CGM Libra* (n 26).
34   *The Muncaster Castle* (n 27).
35   [2006] EWHC 122 (Comm), [2006] 1 Lloyd's Rep 649.

by such tests. A defect in the adapted navigational software would render the ship unseaworthy but if not detectable by proper testing prior to start of the voyage, the carrier would be able to invoke the defence of due diligence in Article IV(1) and then be able to rely on the defence in Article IV(2)(p) of latent defect.

New navigational software fitted after the acquisition of the vessel would be another matter. If defective before and at the start of the voyage, the vessel would be unseaworthy, and the carrier would not be able to show due diligence was taken to make the vessel seaworthy as the duty is non-delegable. The fault of the software programmer would be the fault of the carrier, as the fault of the ship repairer's servants was the fault of the shipowner in *The Muncaster Castle*.

The incompetence of the crew can sometimes go beyond negligence and amount to unseaworthiness.[36] In the context of an unmanned vessel, the crewing component of seaworthiness would extend to the competence of the SBCs monitoring the vessel's operation. For example, lack of familiarity with the vessel's navigational software, lack of training by the servants of the SBC, lack of sufficient operators to monitor multiple vessels or lack of proper shift durations would all render the ship unseaworthy through 'crew' incompetence.

The 'skynet' problem of self-learning navigational AI going out of control, beyond human detection and control, still remains and under the Hague Rules the carrier would have a due diligence defence under Article IV(1) in respect of loss or damage resulting therefrom. Is this enough to justify altering the cargo carriage regime? I would argue that this is not the case. This is also a problem with latent defects in physical seaworthiness for which the carrier is excepted, and the issue of loss or damage *to* cargo, as opposed to loss or damage caused *by* certain types of cargo, is not a public facing matter which may mandate a strict liability regime as with the CLC.

A.   The Hamburg Rules 1978

The Hamburg Rules attach to contracts of carriage as set out in Article 2 and impose liability on the carrier and the actual carrier. The basis of liability is established under Article 5 and is one of presumed fault. As with the Hague Rules it is the specified contract of carriage between the carrier and the shipper,

---

[36]   *Hong Kong Fir Shipping* (n 29). See, too, *Manifest Shipping Co Ltd v Uni-Polaris Insurance Co Ltd (The Star Sea)* [2001] UKHL 1, [2003] 1 AC 469, and *The Eurasian Dream* [2002] EWHC 118 (Comm), [2002] 1 Lloyd's Rep 719; *The CMA CGM Libra* (n 26).

the fact of carriage by sea, that determines the applicability of the Rules. The nature of the ship in which the goods are carried is of no import.

B.   Mandatory Insurance

Within the EU, insurance for maritime claims up to the limits of the 1996 Protocol to the 1976 Limitation Convention are mandatory under Directive 2009/20/EC on the insurance of shipowners for maritime claims. The implementing UK legislation, The Merchant Shipping (Compulsory Insurance of Shipowners for Maritime Claims) Regulations 2012, remains in force as 'retained legislation' after the end of the Brexit transition period on 31 December 2020. The Directive applies to ships of 300 gross tonnage or more and imposes an obligation on Member States to require that shipowners of ships flying its flag have insurance covering such ships and to require shipowners of ships flying a flag other than its own to have insurance in place when such ships enter a port under the Member State's jurisdiction. The insurance is to cover maritime claims subject to limitation under the 1996 Convention.[37] The amount of the insurance for each and every ship per incident shall be equal to the relevant maximum amount for the limitation of liability as laid down in the 1996 Convention.

III.   FAULT LIABILITY REGIMES. COLLISIONS

The 1910 Brussels Collision Convention, whose provisions were brought into effect in the UK in the Maritime Conventions Act 1911,[38] governs civil liability for maritime collisions and is explicitly fault-based. Article 2 provides: 'If the collision is accidental, if it is caused by force majeure, or if the cause of the collision is left in doubt, the damages are borne by those who have suffered them. This provision is applicable notwithstanding the fact that the vessels, or any one of them, may be at anchor (or otherwise made fast) at the time of the casualty.' Article 3 provides: 'If the collision is caused by the fault of one of the vessels, liability to make good the damages attaches to the one which has committed the fault' and Article 4 provides: 'If two or more vessels are in fault the liability of each vessel is in proportion to the degree of the faults respectively committed. Provided that if, having regard to the circumstances, it is not possible to establish the degree of the respective faults, or if it appears that the

---

[37]   The Protocol to the 1976 Convention on Limitation of Liability for Maritime Claims ('LLMC') which raised the limits of the LLMC. The limits were raised again in 2015 by amendment to the Protocol.

[38]   The relevant provisions now appear in The Merchant Shipping Act 1995.

faults are equal, the liability is apportioned equally.' Article 6 abolishes all legal presumptions of fault in relation to liability for collision. Under English law, the mere fact of a collision will be sufficient to attract the operation of the doctrine of *res ipsa loquitur*, so creating a rebuttable presumption of negligence. The presumption will be rebutted where the cause of the collision can be shown to be due to the fault of a third party for whom the defendant is not responsible.

It is unclear how the use of SBCs that are independent contractors servicing multiple shipowners will affect a shipowner's vicarious liability under a fault-based system for collisions. The law on independent contractors has developed rapidly in the last ten years. The essential distinction between independent contractors and employees or persons akin to employees has recently been restated by the Supreme Court in *Barclays Bank plc v Various Claimants*.[39] The case involved claims against a bank in respect of alleged abuse of its employees, committed by an independent contractor doctor who had been employed by the bank to carry out medical assessments as part of the bank's recruitment processes. Lady Hale stated: 'The question therefore is, as it has always been, whether the tortfeasor is carrying on business on his own account or whether he is in a relationship akin to employment with the defendant.' On this analysis, it is likely that an SBC would be regarded as a true independent contractor and not akin to an employee of the shipowner. It is, therefore, essential to a fault-based system that shipowners are vicariously liable for the acts and omissions of SBCs who are the human operatives of their vessels and to clarify matters it would be helpful to amend the Brussels Convention 1910 as follows:

(1) Where a ship in the course of navigation is under the control of a device not requiring human intervention, and a collision is caused by a defect in that device, the collision shall not be regarded as accidental or caused by force majeure within Article 2 of this Convention even if no one is proved to have been at fault in respect of the defect.
(2) Any liability imposed by Articles 1-4 shall attach notwithstanding that the collision is caused by the act, neglect or default of the servants and agents, not on board the vessel, of a third party, other than a charterer by demise, to whom control of the vessel has been entrusted.

---

[39] [2020] UKSC 13, [2020] AC 973.

IV.   THE EU PARLIAMENT'S PROPOSED REGULATION ON CIVIL LIABILITY FOR OPERATORS OF AI

On 22 October 2020 the European Parliament sent to the Commission a draft Regulation for a new strict liability regime for operators of AI systems.[40] The Regulation proposes a strict liability regime for operators of 'high risk' operations. The only defence is if the harm or damage was caused by force majeure. Due diligence will not be a defence. High risk is defined in Article 3 as 'a significant potential in an autonomously operating AI-system to cause harm or damage to one or more persons in a manner that is random and goes beyond what can reasonably be expected; the significance of the potential depends on the interplay between the severity of possible harm or damage, the degree of autonomy of decision-making, the likelihood that the risk materializes and the manner and the context in which the AI-system is being used'. This potentially would cover operations of autonomous ships at MASS levels 3 and 4. The Regulation is to apply 'where a physical or virtual activity, device or process driven by an AI-system has caused harm or damage to the life, health, physical integrity of a natural person, to the property of a natural or legal person or has caused significant immaterial harm resulting in a verifiable economic loss'. Article 5(1) provides comparatively low limitation limits of:

> (a) up to a maximum amount of EUR two million in the event of the death of, or in the event of harm caused to the health or physical integrity of, an affected person, resulting from an operation of a high-risk AI-system;
> (b) up to a maximum amount of EUR one million in the event of significant immaterial harm that results in a verifiable economic loss or of damage caused to property, including when several items of property of an affected person were damaged as a result of a single operation of a single high-risk AI-system; where the affected person also holds a contractual liability claim against the operator, no compensation shall be paid under this Regulation, if the total amount of the damage to property or the significant immaterial harm is of a value that falls below [EUR 500].

Article 7 sets out a 30-year limitation period from the date the harm occurred and 10 years for economic loss claims.

For AI operations which are not high risk Article 8 provides that the operator shall be '[s]ubject to fault-based liability for any harm or damage that was caused by a physical or virtual activity, device or process driven by the

---

[40]   The draft Regulation is on the lines of Expert Group on Liability and New Technologies, New Technologies Formation, 'Liability for Artificial Intelligence and Other Emerging Digital Technologies' (Report for the European Commission 2019).

AI-system'. The available defences to the operator are set out in Article 8(2) where the operator:

> [c]an prove that the harm or damage was caused without his or her fault, relying on either of the following grounds:
>
> (a) the AI-system was activated without his or her knowledge while all reasonable and necessary measures to avoid such activation outside of the operator's control were taken, or
>
> (b) due diligence was observed by performing all the following actions: selecting a suitable AI-system for the right task and skills, putting the AI-system duly into operation, monitoring the activities and maintaining the operational reliability by regularly installing all available updates.
>
> The operator shall not be able to escape liability by arguing that the harm or damage was caused by an autonomous activity, device or process driven by his or her AI-system. The operator shall not be liable if the harm or damage was caused by force majeure.
>
> 3. Where the harm or damage was caused by a third party that interfered with the AI-system by modifying its functioning or its effects, the operator shall nonetheless be liable for the payment of compensation if such third party is untraceable or impecunious.
>
> 4. At the request of the operator or the affected person, the producer of an AI-system shall have the duty of cooperating with, and providing information to, them to the extent warranted by the significance of the claim, in order to allow for the identification of the liabilities.

The territorial scope of the Regulation is 'the territory of the Union'. This would encompass the territorial sea of Member States, and would fall within the ambit of the proposed Regulation, in the light of the ECJ's decision in *Commune de Mesquer*,[41] loss or damage manifesting on land from an oil spill in the EEZ of a Member State, which gives rise to overlap with the IMO's civil liability conventions. The Parliament's proposed Regulation is stated to be 'without prejudice to any additional liability claims resulting from contractual relationships, as well as from regulations on product liability, consumer protection, anti-discrimination, labour and environmental protection between the operator and the natural or legal person who suffered harm or damage because of the AI-system and that may be brought against the operator under Union or national law'. This may remove the overlap. Would this exclude the CLC, say, as an environmental protection measure or does it not because it is not a 'regulation governing harm or damage because of the AI system', just an implemented convention on harm or damage due to pollution with no reference to AI; and what are 'regulations'? However, Article 4(2) of the Regulation requires the listing of AI systems and provides in Article 4(5):

---

[41] Case C-188/07 *Commune de Mesquer v Total France SA and Another* [2008] ECR I-4501.

'This Regulation shall prevail over national liability regimes in the event of conflicting strict liability classification of AI-systems.'

If autonomous ships are not included in the annex as high risk, civil liability from accidents deriving from them in the territory of the Union will fall under Article 8, which applies a fault regime, clearly inapplicable to the CLC, Bunker Oil Pollution Convention and HNS Convention. This is mitigated somewhat by Article 9 which provides: 'Civil liability claims brought in accordance with Article 8(1) shall be subject, in relation to limitation periods as well as the amounts and the extent of compensation, to the laws of the Member State in which the harm or damage occurred.'

However, there is still a clash between the basis of liability in Article 8 and that in the three IMO civil liability conventions. To avoid this, there should be a clear exclusion of claims arising under the Conventions of the sort utilised in the Environmental Liability Directive 2004, to which the Brussels Convention on Collisions 1910 should be added.

The Parliament's proposal was followed on 28 September 2022 by the European Commission's proposal for the AI Liability Directive.[42] Unlike the Parliament's proposal of October 2020, the Commission's proposal is framed as a Directive, and contains no substantive rules regarding liability arising out of use of an AI system. Instead, it applies to non-contractual fault-based civil law claims for damages, in cases where the damage caused by an AI system occurs after the end of the transposition period. Fault still has to be proved under the applicable Union or national laws, but the Directive lays down common rules on (a) the disclosure of evidence on high-risk artificial intelligence (AI) systems to enable a claimant to substantiate a non-contractual fault-based civil law claim for damages, contained in Art 3; and (b) the burden of proof in the case of non-contractual fault-based civil law claims brought before national courts for damages caused by an AI system contained in Art 4 The Directive does not affect rules of Union law regulating conditions of liability in the field of transport. With maritime transport the only such rules of Union law concerning fault-based civil law claims would be Directive 2009/20/EC on the insurance of shipowners for maritime claims.

The restriction to fault-based liability regimes means that the proposed Directive will have no application to the two current strict liability pollution regimes, the CLC and the Bunkers Convention, and will have no application to the HNS regime when it eventually comes into force. It will have application in the Member States to fault-based tort claims such as general pollution claims

---

[42] Directive of the European Parliament and of the Council on adapting non-contractual civil liability rules to artificial intelligence (AI Liability Directive) 28.9.2022 COM(2022) 496 final 2022/0303 (COD).]

and collision claims, as regards the rebuttable presumption of a causal link in the case of fault provided for in Art 4. Art 5 provides for the Commission to submit a report to the Parliament, the Council, and the Economic and Social Committee, assessing the Directive's achievement five years after its transposition. In particular, that review should examine whether there is a need to create no-fault liability rules for claims against the operator combined with a mandatory insurance for the operation of certain AI systems, as suggested by the European Parliament resolution of 20 October 2020 on a civil liability regime for artificial intelligence.

V.   CONCLUSION

Civil liability arising out of international shipping involves two types of policy issues. There is what might be called public facing liability where the maritime accident impacts on national publics, and private facing liability where the impact is on discrete private parties. Public facing liability is seen with pollution accidents and the resulting civil liability conventions have been premised on the need for adequate compensation for pollution damage and remedial measures. The shipowner should be on the line no matter what the position is as regards fault. This has led to strict liability regimes under the CLC, the Bunkers Convention, the nascent HNS Convention and the Nairobi Wreck Removal Convention. Compulsory insurance with a direct right of action against the liability insurer is a feature of these conventions. Some go further and provide an additional layer of compensation through a fund financed by receivers of the cargo subject to the convention. Not much needs to change with these conventions with the advent of crewless ships. The public will still be compensated if an autonomous tanker causes an oil spill, even if this happens without any fault on the part of the shipowner, as with a 'skynet' incident. These incidents will also involve issues of fault with regard to recourse actions but that involves private facing liability, and how the question of fault is addressed with robotic operation of vessels is not a pressing issue.

Private liability is involved with international carriage of goods where loss or damage will lead to claims by a subrogated insurer against a shipowner backed up by its liability insurer. There is less need to agonise about how fault manifests itself under the liability conventions when we enter the arena of robotic ships. The likeliest effect of this development is that Article IV.2(a) will start to wither away, certainly when dealing with vessels at MASS Level 4, although the 'skynet' issues will allow for the possibility of the carrier escaping liability through the operation of Article IV.1 and reliance on the defence under Article IV.2(p) of 'latent defects not discoverable with due diligence'. It is not a pressing public issue as to whether such cargo losses are picked up by the cargo insurer and not by the shipowner and its liability insurer. The balance of insurance may change somewhat but that is all. In practice, adequate liability insurance must be carried by vessels if they are to trade, and within EU and UK waters the 2009 Directive and the UK-implementing Regulation make it mandatory, up to the limits specified in the 1976 Limitation Convention (1996 Protocol), in respect of trading to and from EU and UK ports.

Collision liability could be regarded as either private or public facing. It is currently subject to a system of fault liability under the Brussels Convention 1910. This can be mitigated somewhat by the principle of *res ipsa loquitur*, and under English law it is also possible that the shipowner could be regarded as presumptively liable through the classification of autonomous vessels as 'extra hazardous' due to the problem of undiscoverable defects that develop in the self-learning navigational technology. This has led some to argue for the imposition of strict liability. This would mean that in a collision each vessel would be 100 per cent liable to the other and would have to pay the other's claims. Possibly the Brussels Convention could be amended to allow for strict liability but with a presumption of innocence for autonomous vessels that are stationary at the time of collision. Problems may arise, as with road vehicles, when collisions arise between an autonomous and a manned vehicle, where the former would be strictly liable, and the latter liable only on the basis of fault. If fault, the default position under tort and delict, remains the basis for liability, then the recording of data from the navigational software will become critical and should be addressed by the IMO in its current scoping exercise to impose similar obligations to maintain this and make it available, as is the case with manned vessels' paper logs. Vessels are already using a voyage data recorder ('VDR') and its regulation falls under the purview of the SOLAS Chapter V, Regulation 20 as well as Annex 10.

Even with strict liability, an element of fault will come in with respect to the situations in which the right to limit, whether it be the package limitation under the Hague and Hague-Visby Rules, the general right to global limitation of maritime claims under the 1957 and the 1976 Limitation Conventions or the exclusive limitation regime of the CLC and the HNS Conventions, can be lost where the claimant can show that the loss resulted from the person's personal act or omission, committed with the intent to cause such loss, or recklessly and with knowledge that such loss would probably result. This is already an almost insurmountable obstacle for claimants currently – the one successful instance is in *The Atlantik Confidence*,[43] involving loss of cargo following the scuttling of the vessel. Given that it requires some form of human agency, this issue will remain unchanged.

---

[43]   [2016] EWHC 2412 (Admlty), [2016] 2 Lloyd's Rep 525.

Discussion of limitation regimes also raises the question of who can rely on them other than the shipowner in the new situation of autonomous vessels. SBCs would almost certainly be entitled to limit under the 1976 LLMC and the 1996 Protocol[44] and would be protected under the channelling provisions of the CLC and HNS conventions. As matters stand, hardware manufacturers and designers of maritime software would fall outside these provisions. There is no good reason why they should be brought within their protective embrace.

A final concern is the potential overlap between EU legislation on civil liability of operators of AI systems and maritime civil liability conventions. This overlap, though present in the Parliament's proposed Regulation, does not appear in the Commission's proposed Directive. The proposed Directive will still affect all cases of non-contractual liability brought in Member States by any claimant for damage arising out of the operation of an AI system, such as from an autonomous vessel operating within the territory of the EU Member States. Under the proposed Directive the victim would still bear the burden of proof, but the presumption of causality would result in a targeted alleviation of the burden of proof regarding the question as to how or why an AI system reached a certain harmful output. The proposed Directive still has some way to go in the EU legislative process and its final form may contain amendments from the EU Commission's proposal. Strict liability remains a possibility for the future, with the five year review of the Directive by the Commission leaving open the prospect of the adoption of rules on strict liability and mandatory insurance.

---

[44] Either as an 'operator' within the definition of 'shipowner' in Art 1.2 or, if employed by the 'shipowner' 'as person for whose act, neglect or default the shipowner or salvor is responsible' under Art 1.4.

10. Robotics Regulation and Liability Issues Concerning Robotic Technologies in the Oil and Gas Sector

Kyriaki Noussia[1] and Maria Glynou[2]

I.   INTRODUCTION

A key characteristic of the new digital era in which we live is the convergence between industries, in general, but also more specifically the oil and gas industry, and the data generated by digitisation and connectivity as well as the transmission of that data which this entails. In the oil and gas sector, the increasing symbiosis between energy companies and technology companies – where data is increasingly used – has meant that the data exchanged and circulated in the digitised operations has also become a valuable commodity. Hydrocarbons are a product of the industry, as is data as well as artificial intelligence ('AI'), big data and the Internet of Things ('IoT'), all of which also constitute such commodities. The initial decline in oil prices in January 2016 and later on in March 2020 due to the Covid-19 pandemic, as well as the sharp rise in oil prices in early 2022 due to the war in Ukraine, have accelerated the push to digitisation which has become even more pronounced. The energy sector is more prone than any other sector to reflecting the shockwaves caused by external current affairs, extreme events and crises, be it wars or epidemics or pandemics or conflicts between states, and such an impact on the energy sector is then also reflected in all other areas of life, hence the demand for an accelerated pace of digitisation, in an effort to use its results and effects as a tool to empower companies to redesign processes across all aspects of the industry and the markets. However, this has brought about the need to protect the data generated, and oil

[1]   Associate Professor, School of Law, University of Reading.
[2]   LLM candidate and Research Assistant at the London School of Economics and Political Science (LSE), London.

and gas companies have begun expanding and applying innovation in areas such as clean tech, analytics, IoT and Big Data.[3]

Further, another distinctive feature of the oil and gas sector, namely the high-level risk for severe harm to be caused to individuals and/or the environment, gives rise to concerns regarding the liability arising from damages and accidents, such as ergonomic hazards, vehicle collisions, explosions and oil pollution.

This chapter examines the liability regime in robotics and more specifically in the oil and gas sector and the risks entailed. It discusses cyber security and robotics risks, the regulation of robots and the liability of robots from a general perspective as well as in relation to oil and gas operations. Issues addressed include questions such as to whom this liability is attributed, the ways in which the losses encountered could be mitigated as well as the liability incurred via insurance for cyber and robotics risks, the regulation of robotics and the attribution of liability issues that pertain to the accelerated use of robotics in oil and gas.

II. THE LIABILITY REGIME IN OIL AND GAS EXPROPRIATION AND TRANSPORTATION

The globalisation and digitisation of environmental risk which results from the 4th Industrial Revolution ('4IR') pose a mounting challenge for oil and gas operations as even to date the rules of responsibility for harm production remain under-developed, despite the negotiation and implementation of numerous international environmental agreements. In addition, those agreements lack detailed provisions stipulating the responsibility of state and non-state actors for environmental damage. Moreover, state practice often reflects a widespread reluctance to pursue environmental liability through interstate claims as well as a preference for increasing the importance of private liability attached to operators of risk-bearing activities as the main mechanism for progressing environmental liability.[4]

The civil liability regime for marine and oil pollution was the first of these regimes to broaden compensation obligations beyond personal injury and

---

[3] The National, 'Oil & Gas 4.0' (*Oilandgas4.thenational.ae*) oilandgas4.thenational .ae/#group-oil-and-gas-4.0-j2S3ckx2WV accessed 26 April 2022.

[4] Kyriaki Noussia, 'The BP Oil Spill – Environmental Pollution Liability and Other Legal Ramifications' (2011) 20 European Energy and Environmental Law Review 98, 98–101; Kyriaki Noussia, 'Cybersecurity and Environmental Impact: Insurance as a Better Protection Mechanism for Liability from Incidents in Oil and Gas Operations' in P Marano and K Noussia (eds.), *InsurTech: A Legal and Regulatory View. AIDA Europe Research Series on Insurance Law and Regulation*, vol 1 (Springer, 2020) 231.

property damage provisions to environmental impairment. Additionally, it has served as a model for liability rule development for all activities related to oil and gas expropriation and/or its transportation.[5]

The marine and oil pollution liability legal regime has been developed via the various conventions, resolutions and codes that the United Nations International Maritime Organization ('IMO') has enacted. The 1973/78 International Convention for the Prevention of Pollution from Ships ('MARPOL') is the main treaty in this area.[6] MARPOL was a treaty enacted after the Torrey Canyon oil disaster of 1967.[7] After the Exxon Valdez incident in 1989, the Oil Pollution Act 1990 ('OPA') was enacted in the US in 1990, which imposed stronger duties of care, included a right of action against operators and shifted the burden of liability to the side of the harm producer. Then, the International Convention on Civil Liability for Oil Pollution 1992 ('CLC 1992') and the International Convention on the Establishment of an International Fund for Compensation for Oil Pollution Damage (Fund) 1992, in force as of 1996, set the current terms of application of claims for compensation within contracting states.[8] Oil pollution liability under the international conventions has always deferred to the sovereign rights of contracting parties, for both the International Convention on Civil Liability for Oil Pollution 1969 ('CLC 1969') (Article II) and the Fund Convention 1971 (Article 3) apply only to pollution damage caused or impacting on the territory, including the territorial sea, of Member States. Article I(6) of the CLC 1969 defined pollution damage as 'loss or damage caused outside the ship carrying oil by contamination resulting from the escape or discharge of oil from the ship, wherever such escape or discharge may occur, and includes the cost of preventive measures and further loss or damage caused by preventive measures'. However, the

---

[5]   Michael Mason, *Transnational Compensation for Oil Pollution Damage: Examining Changing Spatialities of Environmental Liability* (no 69, Department of Geography and Environment, London School of Economics and Political Science 2002) 1–3; Björn Sandvik and Satu Suikkari, 'Harm and Reparation in International Treaty Regimes: An Overview' in Peter Wetterstein (ed.), *Harm to the Environment: The Right to Compensation and the Assessment of Damages* (Clarendon Press 1997) 57–71, 64–5.

[6]   Its Annex I, concerned with oil pollution, contains detailed technical provisions designed to eliminate intentional discharges. MARPOL is credited as instrumental in significantly reducing discharges from marine transportation; Mason (n 5) 4.

[7]   Mason (n 5) 4.

[8]   Mason (n 5) 6–7; Gavin Little and Jenny Hamilton, 'Compensation for Catastrophic Oil Spills: A Transatlantic Comparison' [1997] LMCLQ 554; Gotthard M Gauci, 'Protection of the Marine Environment through the International Ship-Source Oil Pollution Compensation Regimes' (1999) 8 Review of European Community and International Environmental Law 29; Noussia, 2011 (n 4), 98–101.

broadening of the geographical scope of the liability conventions was considered essential and was reinforced by an international agreement, which clarified that the liability Conventions cover measures – wherever taken – to prevent oil pollution damage within a territorial sea or exclusive economic zone ('EEZ').[9] The international regime for the compensation of pollution damage caused by oil spills from tankers is based on two treaties adopted under the auspices of the IMO, the CLC 1992 and the Fund 1992 Conventions, replacing two corresponding Conventions adopted in 1969 and 1971 respectively.[10] The strict marine oil pollution civil liability model, which was imposed by the CLC 1992 and the Fund 1992 Conventions, has been further extended to the International Convention on Liability and Compensation for Damage in Connection with the Carriage of Hazardous and Noxious Substances by Sea 1996 ('HN') and the International Convention on Liability for Bunker Oil Pollution Damage 2001 ('BOPD').[11]

All these Conventions broadly share the environmental reinstatement provisions and jurisdictional scope of CLC 1992. The BOPD, which covers fuel oil spills from vessels other than tankers, breaks with the liability channelling provisions of the CLC 1992, by exposing operators and charterers as well as registered owners to compensation claims, all with rights of limitation. This notable shift to multiple liabilities indicates pressure from the US and the European Commission on the IMO to accord more with the existing liability norms in this area of oil pollution, and it also reflects the need to make up for the absence of a second tier of supplementary compensation – as under the Fund Convention.[12]

In the US, on 11 May 2017 Executive Order 13800 on 'Strengthening the Cybersecurity of Federal Networks and Critical Infrastructure' ('EO 13800' or 'the cybersecurity EO') was issued and directed key departments and agencies to: (i) report on US government international engagement priorities in cyberspace; (ii) develop strategies to strengthen the deterrence posture of the US in cyberspace; and (iii) enable the US to engage proactively with all

---

[9] Mason (n 5) 11–12; 'International Convention on Civil Liability for Oil Pollution Damage (CLC)' (*Imo.org*, 1996) www.imo.org/en/About/Conventions/Pages/International-Convention-on-Civil-Liability-for-Oil-Pollution-Damage-(CLC).aspx accessed 26 April 2022.

[10] Måns Jacobsson, 'The International Oil Pollution Compensation Funds and the International Regime of Compensation for Oil Pollution Damage' in Jürgen Basedow and Ulrich Magnus (eds.), *Pollution of the Sea – Prevention and Compensation* (Hamburg Studies on Maritime Affairs vol 10, Springer, 2007) 138–50, 138–9.

[11] Mason (n 5) 20; Gavin Little, 'The Hazardous and Noxious Substances Convention: A New Horizon in the Regulation of Marine Pollution' [1998] LMCLQ 554.

[12] Mason (n 5) 20.

partners to address key issues in cyberspace. In May 2018, the US Department of State Report described the US Cyberspace Policy as one which enhances international cooperation and seeks to ensure that the internet and other connected networks and technologies remain valuable and viable tools for future generations, stating the aim to: a) increase international stability and reduce the risk of conflict stemming from the use of cyberspace; b) identify, detect, disrupt and deter malicious cyber actors, and protect, respond to and recover from threats posed by those actors, and enhance the resilience of the global cyber ecosystem, including critical infrastructure; c) advance an international regulatory environment that supports innovation and respects the global nature of cyberspace; d) uphold an open and interoperable internet where human rights are protected and freely exercised and where cross-border data flows are preserved; e) maintain the essential role of non-governmental stakeholders in how cyberspace is governed.[13]

Notwithstanding the above, what is also notable is the willingness of the global offshore energy insurance market to participate in efforts to establish and fix a new limit for environmental pollution liability.[14]

The energy insurance market and its insurance products as mitigating factors mirrored the increase in the limitation of liability required under the OPA, in that at least four of the OPA's elements and consequences were carried in the offshore energy insurance and reinsurance market: a) 'operators' extra expense' ('OEE') and 'excess liabilities' coverage had to be prioritised in terms of a single limit before the balance of the OEE insurance limits used for pollution clean-up and containment of oil spills; b) given the enormity of the BP oil spill, coverage has since been at a much higher premium; c) private commercial insurers were expected to not be as willing to commit financial capital to underwriting unknown new risks if no extra high premiums were to be agreed, since in effect the BP oil spill had triggered a 'hard' energy insurance market involving scarcity of coverage and high prices; d) many insurance market experts supported a more efficient pre-disaster risk financing approach to managing and financing large-scale oil spill disasters through 'reinsurance sidecars', catastrophe bonds ('CAT bonds') or energy insurance financial futures and options.

---

[13] 'Recommendations to the President on Protecting American Cyber Interests through International Engagement' (*State.gov*, 2018) www.state.gov/wp-content/uploads/2019/04/Recommendations-to-the-President-on-Protecting-American-Cyber-Interests-Through-International-Engagement.pdf accessed 26 April 2022.

[14] Rawle O King, 'Deepwater Horizon Oil Spill Disaster: Risk, Recovery, and Insurance Implications' (Congressional Research Service, 2010) 15–20 sgp.fas.org/crs/misc/R41320.pdf accessed 26 April 2022.

III. CYBERSECURITY RISKS IN THE OIL AND GAS SECTOR AND WAYS TO MITIGATE THE ARISING LIABILITY THROUGH INSURANCE

Cyber risks in oil and gas constitute a key, wide operational hazard and measures should be put in place to tackle the issue of liability exposure. Oil and gas companies should implement measures to prevent, detect and respond to cyber threats, such as taking cyber insurance coverage to help offset the potential financial impacts of a cyber-attack and the liability implications.[15] With the robotics penetration of the oil and gas industry it is expected that the market for cyber liability insurance will experience exponential growth, providing for one or more types of coverage such as: a) liability for security or privacy breaches, including loss of confidential information by allowing or failing to prevent unauthorised access to computer systems; b) the costs associated with a privacy breach (e.g. consumer notification and support post such a breach); c) the costs associated with restoring business assets stored electronically; d) business interruption and consequential losses related to a security or privacy breach; e) expenses related to cyber extortion and cyber terrorism; f) losses or corruption of data; g) liability as a result of breach of privacy due to theft of data, transmission of a computer virus or failure of network security on rendering of internet professional services; h) D&O (Directors & Officers) management liability costs; i) crisis management costs.[16]

The problems which have surfaced in the underwriting of such risks have included concerns about the way in which risks are assessed and priced, and the way in which exposures are managed, as what has been seen in practice is a material imbalance between premiums charged and exposures assumed due to the often noted discrepancy between the large amounts of capital needed to underwrite and the modest returns generated. In addition, a question that arises pertains to the way in which the risk of an oil-production-related accident (offshore or not) encompassing a cyber or robotics risk will be assessed to be better underwritten and addressed. As liability rules also have a role to play in the potential risks to be defined, the insurance coverage will subsequently also be influenced and affected. One approach to better respond to robotics, AI-related and cyber risks is to lift the severity of the liability involved in any such risk by making the insurance scheme mandatory. For such insurance to be effective

---

[15] 'The Road to Resilience: Managing Cyber Risks' (*World Energy Council*, 2016) www.worldenergy.org/publications/entry/the-road-to-resilience-managing-cyber-risks accessed 26 April 2022.

[16] Carrie E Cope and Ian Reynolds, *'Breaking Bad' in Cyberspace: A Challenge for the Insurance Industry* (LexisNexis, 2015) 85–102.

and pragmatically subscribed to by the insurance market, the difficulty of calculating the actual losses from robotics and cyber-related liability incidents in the oil and gas sector must be considered. Also, the intricacies of placing caps on such liabilities should be considered as well, in an effort to avoid the evolution and establishment of a 'hard' insurance market.

IV.   ROBOTICS IN THE OIL AND GAS SECTOR

Oil and gas companies have invested heavily in robot developments. The history of robotics in the oil and gas sector stretches back to the late 1950s when the Hughes Aircraft Company debuted the Manipulator Operated Robot ('MOBOT'). Resembling a cross between the Michelin Man and an octopus, the machine was intended for use in radioactive environments and was controlled from a safe vantage point with the aid of a 200ft cable. Although designed for the nuclear power industry, it was adopted and utilised in the oil and gas sector, where it proved most influential. Overall, a remote operation reduces risks to the human workforce as robots can also act as the first responder in explosive atmospheric conditions.[17]

Currently, the offshore industry is constantly looking for new technological innovations, and demand for robots in oil and gas is growing as the technology becomes more refined.[18] The oil and gas industry has geared up to deploy robotics across a wide range of applications in the upstream, midstream and downstream segments, primarily to drive productivity and efficiency amid volatility in crude prices. Robotics offers the potential to automate repetitive, yet critical, tasks in field operations, such as taking readings from instruments, cleaning and inspecting assets for signs of corrosion or wear. Recent technological advancements are enabling operators to deploy robots in terrestrial, aerial and underwater configurations to carry out tasks that may be too risky to be undertaken by field personnel. Moreover, ageing infrastructure is necessitating regular inspection of these assets and autonomous drones are being used due to their sheer number and issues related to accessibility.[19]

Some of the tasks for an offshore oilfield operation are dangerous, but recent advances in robotics technology could mean the removal of human beings from some of the riskiest situations encountered on the rig. This chapter identi-

---

[17]   Michael Shaw, 'How Robotics Technology is Improving Safety at Offshore Oilfield Operations' (*Nsenergybusiness.com*, 2020) www.nsenergybusiness.com/features/offshore-oilfield-technology-robotics/ accessed 26 April 2022.

[18]   Umar Ali, 'Robot Revolution: Five Robotics Developments in Offshore Oil and Gas' (*Offshore Technology*, 2019) www.offshore-technology.com/features/robotics-oil -gas/ accessed 26 April 2022.

[19]   ibid.

fies five distinctive applications of robotics in the offshore oil and gas industry. Firstly, ANYmal: autonomous mobile robots can offer comprehensive support through regular and automated inspection of machinery and infrastructure. Described as the world's first autonomous offshore robot, ANYbotics' ANYmal robotic platform is a quadrupedal robot designed to operate autonomously in challenging terrain. The robot can inspect offshore sites, and is equipped with visual and thermal cameras, microphones and gas detection sensors that allow it to generate a 3-D map of its surroundings to carry out inspections and operations more efficiently. ANYmal can use this map to learn more about and navigate the space it operates in autonomously, as well as be remotely operated from an onshore control site to provide its human operators with real-time data. A crucial task for energy providers is the reliable and safe operation of their plants, especially when producing energy offshore. ANYmal was first deployed on a North Sea platform in September 2018, performing 16 inspection points and carrying out several tasks, including reading sensory equipment and detecting leaks. Secondly, ARGONAUT: developed as part of the Total-funded ARGOS Challenge to develop the first autonomous surface robot for the oil and gas industry, the ARGONAUT is another robot designed with routine inspections and autonomous tasks in mind. The ARGONAUT was deployed in 2018, first working on Total's onshore Shetland gas plant before being relocated to the offshore Alwyn platform.[20] Thirdly, Eelume: the Eelume robot is designed to 'live' permanently underwater and perform subsea inspection, repair and maintenance tasks. Eelume connects to a docking station on the seabed, which makes it easier to deploy than a conventional remote-controlled robot that would need to be sent down from the surface.[21] Like the natural species of the Arctic lamprey, the robotic device resembling it spends almost all of its life submerged, moves through the water by flexing its entire body and has visual sensors, allowing it to move with greater efficiency while inspecting underwater infrastructure for oil and gas companies. Its unique snake-like body affords the robot greater manoeuvrability underwater, allowing it to enter restricted subsea areas that would otherwise be difficult to enter with existing technology. The robot also has a modular design, with several tools that can be attached to it to equip it for various jobs.[22] The unit is the latest example of a new generation of robots making life easier for energy companies by removing their human workforce from some of the riskiest tasks, thus reducing the occurrence of accidents and hence the liability to be

---

[20]   ibid.
[21]   ibid.
[22]   ibid.

borne by the oil and gas sector.[23] Fourthly, the Empowered Remotely Operated Vehicle ('E-ROV'): a self-contained, battery-operated system designed for subsea operations. The E-ROV operates remotely via an Ethernet connection, which allows the robot to be operated from a control room anywhere in the world. Equinor has also been developing a 4G network on the Norwegian Continental Shelf, with the E-ROV sending and receiving data via a buoy on the surface.[24] Fifthly, Oseberg H: operated by Equinor in the North Sea, the Oseberg H oil platform is the world's first fully automated oil and gas platform. With no living quarters and no facilities, the platform is entirely unmanned, only requiring one or two maintenance visits a year.[25]

The use of robotics in oil and gas indirectly increases the lifespan of infrastructure and prolongs the life of installations that would otherwise have been dismantled for being uneconomic. It also means less of an environmental footprint as people do not have to be deployed locally as such robotics can be controlled and operated remotely. [26] Remotely and autonomously operated robots have played a significant role in the provision of oil and gas from under-sea sources.[27] The potential of robotics in maintaining and decommissioning key energy infrastructure to provide security and minimise environmental impact is widely recognised. Nuclear plants, pipelines and distribution networks can also all benefit from advances in robotics technology.[28]

V. REGULATING ROBOTICS

Autonomous robots, as objects, fall under the broad definition of machinery within the EU Machinery Directive 2006/42,[29] and as products intended for the consumer markets they fall under the General Product Safety Directive

---

[23] Shaw (n 17).

[24] Ali (n 18).

[25] ibid.

[26] See S Tarantola, A Rossotti and E Flitris, 'Safety Aspects of Offshore Oil and Gas Operations in Arctic and Sub-Arctic Waters' (European Commission, Joint Research Centre (JRC), 2019); Shaw (n 17).

[27] A Shukla and H Karki, 'Application of Robotics in Offshore Oil and Gas Industry – A Review Part II' (2016) 75 Robotics and Autonomous Systems 508. www.sciencedirect.com/science/article/pii/S0921889015002018?casa_token= NKvO9ik9cN8AAAAA:f40X7UIumHxpxeyxyc6CGTKMiOIy0qbzx0Z5rbk6KuBZ MX7dwk9asLVbtcJ0nULx9xsSNyTHjQ accessed 16 April 2022.

[28] EuRobotics AISBL, 'Robotics 2020 Strategic Research Agenda for Robotics in Europe' (2014) www.eu-robotics.net/sparc/upload/topic_groups/SRA2020_SPARC .pdf accessed 26 April 2022.

[29] Directive 2006/42/EC of the European Parliament and of the Council of 17 May 2006 on machinery, and amending Directive 95/16/EC (recast) eur-lex.europa.eu/legal -content/EN/TXT/?uri=celex%3A32006L0042.

2001/95.[30] In the context of the Machinery Directive,[31] an evaluation was issued in 2018,[32] in the terms of which the Commission has identified the need for greater legal clarity for some of the Directive's provisions. Moreover, concerning the General Product Safety Directive,[33] in June 2021, the Commission issued a 'Proposal for a Regulation on general product safety, amending Regulation (EU) No 1025/2012 of the European Parliament and of the Council, and repealing Council Directive 87/357/EEC and Directive 2001/95/EC of the European Parliament and of the Council' which takes into consideration the legislative proposal on Artificial Intelligence, made in April 2021,[34] and thus constitutes a safety net for products and risks which fall outside the scope of the Artificial Intelligence Act. However, the liability issues in the robotics sector are still not clearly defined. The justification of liability asserts the capacity to have control over one's own behaviour or over produced, offered or sold products, or over actions for which one is responsible. Even though robots as machines are acting on their own sensory perceptions, based on computer coding embedded in them and self-learning abilities, they still do not classify as moral agents to which moral responsibility can be ascribed, as they perform tasks without any free will.[35]

In 2016, the European Parliament Committee of Legal Affairs published its first Report with Recommendations to the Commission on Civil Law Rules on Robotics (2015/2103(INL))[36]. The Report of 2016 was followed by two

---

[30]   Directive 2001/95/EC of the European Parliament and of the Council of 3 December 2001 on general product safety eur-lex.europa.eu/legal-content/EN/ALL/?uri=celex%3A32001L0095 accessed 26 April 2022.

[31]   ibid.

[32]   European Commission, 'Commission Staff Working Document, Executive Summary of the Evaluation of the Machinery Directive' (2018) 3 ec.europa.eu/transparency/documents-register/detail?ref=SWD(2018)161&lang=en accessed 26 April 2022.

[33]   Directive 2001/95/EC of the European Parliament and of the Council of 3 December 2001 on general product safety eur-lex.europa.eu/legal-content/EN/ALL/?uri=celex%3A32001L0095 accessed 26 April 2022.

[34]   European Commission, 'Proposal for a Regulation of The European Parliament and of The Council Laying Down Harmonised Rules on Artificial Intelligence (Artificial Intelligence Act) and Amending Certain Union Legislative Acts', COM(2021) 206 finaleur-lex.europa.eu/legal-content/EN/TXT/DOC/?uri=CELEX:52021PC0206&from=EN accessed 25 April 2022.

[35]   Thomas Kapitan, 'The Free Will Problem' in Robert Audi (ed.), *The Cambridge Dictionary of Philosophy* (2nd ed., Cambridge University Press, 1999) 326; Rolf H Weber and Dominic N Staiger, 'New Liability Patterns in the Digital Era' in TE Synodinou and others (eds.), *EU Internet Law* (Springer, 2017); Andrea Bertolini, 'Robots as Products: The Case for a Realistic Analysis of Robotic Applications and Liability Rules' (2013) 5 Law, Innovation and Technology 214.

[36]   European Parliament, 'Report with Recommendations to the Commission on Civil Law Rules on Robotics' 2015/2103(INL) www.europarl.europa.eu/doceo/docum

more Reports, with particular regard to AI and robotics (2018/2088(INI) and 2020/2012(INL)).[37] All of the reports addressed, *inter alia*, the impact of the rise of robotics, the flow of data and ethical principles, and made proposals regarding civil liability rules for robotics with increased autonomous and cognitive features.[38] The Reports also placed upon the Commission the role of proposing legislation on how to regulate robotics and AI, and whether strict liability should be adopted as a rule for all the parties involved in the liability chain, including the manufacturers, owners and users of robotics, which in oil and gas can be translated as the liability chain between designer, producer, commissioner or user responsible for robotics use in the oil and gas industry.[39] More specifically, in the latest Resolution (2020/2012(INL)), the European Parliament requests that the Commission propose a Regulation on ethical principles for the development, deployment and use of AI, robotics and related technologies, which establishes sufficient mechanisms for developers', deployers' and users' liability to be ensured.[40] In this context, in April 2021, the Commission made a proposal for a Regulation on Artificial Intelligence ('Artificial Intelligence Act') aiming at ensuring that AI systems are used appropriately, pursuant to safety requirements, and in accordance with fundamental rights. Moreover, it appears that, among others, one of the objectives of the proposed Regulation is to mitigate safety risks. Indicatively, by providing the increasingly autonomous robots as an example, the Commission underlines the prominence of their safe operation in complex environments.[41] The proposal lays down obligations that will apply to providers and users of

---

ent/A-8-2017-0005_EN.html accessed 26 April 2022.

[37]   European Parliament, 'European Parliament Resolution of 12 February 2019 on a Comprehensive European Industrial Policy on Artificial Intelligence and Robotics', P8_TA(2019)0081 www.europarl.europa.eu/doceo/document/TA-8-2019-0081_EN.html accessed 25 April 2022; European Parliament, 'European Parliament Resolution of 20 October 2020 with Recommendations to The Commission on a Framework of Ethical Aspects of Artificial Intelligence, Robotics and Related Technologies', P9_TA(2020)0275 www.europarl.europa.eu/doceo/document/TA-9-2020-0275_EN.html accessed 25 April 2022.

[38]   Aysegul Bugra, 'Room for Compulsory Product Liability Insurance in the European Union for Smart Robots? Reflections on the Compelling Challenges' in P Marano and K Noussia (eds.), *InsurTech: A Legal and Regulatory View. AIDA Europe Research Series on Insurance Law and Regulation*, vol 1 (Springer, 2020) 167–8.

[39]   ibid.

[40]   European Parliament, 'European Parliament Resolution of 20 October 2020 with Recommendations to The Commission on a Framework of Ethical Aspects of Artificial Intelligence, Robotics and Related Technologies' (n 37) 40.

[41]   European Commission, 'European Commission Proposal for a Regulation of The European Parliament and of The Council Laying Down Harmonised Rules on Artificial Intelligence (Artificial Intelligence Act) and Amending Certain Union Legislative Acts' (n 34).

high-risk AI systems. For providers,[42] it will create legal certainty and alleviate obstacles in relation to the cross-border provision of AI-related services and products. For companies using AI, it will promote trust among their customers. Moreover, the framework will envisage specific measures supporting innovation, including regulatory sandboxes and specific measures supporting small-scale users and providers of high-risk AI systems to comply with the new rules.[43]

Robotics as a term denotes a wide range of devices and uses and this further enhances the need for clarity as to whether the same civil liability and insurance regimes apply to all devices embodied in the term and their uses.[44] Appropriate legal and regulatory frameworks will have to be developed to support the more widespread deployment of robots, including those operated autonomously. Legal frameworks are needed to define where responsibilities lie, ensure the safe and effective functioning of robotics and autonomous robotics systems, and also offer guidance on how to handle disputes in areas where there are no existing legal precedents.[45] That said, a balance needs to be achieved and any governance regime should be cautiously implemented so as to not curtail innovation and hold back desirable progress by stifling technological advancement in the area. Nevertheless, liability needs to be defined and attributed in detail.[46]

A.   Robotics as 'Products' or 'Services': Liability and Insurance

At the EU level, the Product Liability Directive 85/374[47] is only applicable in the case of (physical) goods, but the non-coverage of services can be hardly justified in the digital era. In fact, according to the Commission's latest report on the application of the Product Liability Directive 85/374,[48] the relevance of

---

[42]   Who develop and place such systems on the Union market.

[43]   European Commission, 'Proposal for a Regulation of The European Parliament and of The Council Laying Down Harmonised Rules on Artificial Intelligence (Artificial Intelligence Act) and Amending Certain Union Legislative Acts' (n 34).

[44]   ibid.

[45]   Emma L Flett and Jennifer F Wilson, 'Artificial Intelligence: Is Johnny 5 Alive? Key Bits and Bytes from the UK's Robotics and Artificial Intelligence Inquiry' (2017) 23 Computer and Telecommunications Law Review 72, 73 www.kirkland.com/-/media/publications/article/2017/04/artificial-intelligence-is-johnny-5-alive-key-bits/computer-and-telecommunications-law-review-aiflett.pdf accessed 25 April 2022.

[46]   ibid 74.

[47]   Council Directive 85/374/EEC of 25 July 1985 on the approximation of the laws, regulations and administrative provisions of the Member States concerning liability for defective products eur-lex.europa.eu/legal-content/EN/TXT/?uri=celex%3A31985L0374 accessed 25 April 2022.

[48]   ibid.

the Directive's concepts, as these are currently expressed, has been put into question.[49] Moreover, in 2020, the Commission highlighted that an improvement to the existing legislative framework is of paramount importance, in order for new risks and situations to be sufficiently addressed.[50] Particularly, the Commission confirmed that the existing EU legislation's scope is limited to products. Therefore, services and, subsequently, services based on AI technology are excluded.[51] Hence, a new method on how to approach product liability related to 'goods' and 'services' features is needed – a position which was also upheld in the Inception Impact Assessment issued by the European Commission in June 2021;[52] the European Commission specifically highlighted that in the age of digital technologies and circular economy, not only liability cannot be properly established but also injured parties cannot claim for compensation efficiently under the current regime, namely the national civil liability rules and the Directive.[53] In this view, the European Commission issued an official proposal on the revision of the Product Liability Directive in September 2022, in order to adapt *inter alia* the definition of product to the digital world.[54] In the US, the legal framework for product liability encompasses a manufacturing defect, a design defect or a warning defect. In the case of robotics, for design defects to be established, it needs to be proven that the risk could have been reduced through a reasonable alternative design, and whether the risk was foreseeable by its programmer, as no matter the available

---

[49] European Commission, 'Report from the Commission to The European Parliament, The Council and The European Economic and Social Committee on The Application of the Council Directive on the Approximation of the Laws, Regulations, and Administrative Provisions of the Member States Concerning Liability for Defective Products (85/374/EEC)' COM (2018) 246 final 8-9. eur-lex.europa.eu/legal-content/EN/TXT/?uri=CELEX%3A52018DC0246 accessed 25 April 2022.

[50] European Commission, 'White Paper on Artificial Intelligence: A European Approach to Excellence and Trust' (2020) 15 ec.europa.eu/info/sites/default/files/commission-white-paper-artificial-intelligence-feb2020_en.pdf accessed 25 April 2022.

[51] ibid.

[52] European Commission, 'Inception Impact Assessment' (2021) 2–3 ec.europa.eu/info/law/betterregulation/have-your-say/initiatives/12979-Civil-liability-adapting-liabilityrules-to-the-digital-age-and-artificial-intelligence_en accessed 25 April 2022.

[53] ibid 3.

[54] European Commission, 'Commission Staff Working Document Impact Assessment Accompanying the Document Proposal for a Regulation of The European Parliament and of The Council on General Product Safety, Amending Regulation (EU) No 1025/2012 of The European Parliament and of the Council, and Repealing Council Directive 87/357/EEC and Directive 2001/95/EC of The European Parliament and of The Council' SWD (2021) 168 final 6 ec.europa.eu/info/sites/default/files/impact_assessment.pdf accessed 25 April 2022.

self-learning capabilities and ability to make autonomous decisions, robotics are still subject to the producer's instructions.[55] Because under EU law, 'product' in the Product Liability Directive[56] is confined to movables as tangible objects only and not to intangibles or services, manufacturers are liable where such provisions for liability exist in the domestic laws of the Member States. In addition, it is relatively more justified to provide compulsory insurance coverage if the certain use of robotics in oil and gas is defined as a 'product'. The rationale behind this is that compulsory insurance is required as producers need to take out liability insurance for robotic products, due to the latter being more likely to cause injury or property damage in comparison to robots classified as services.[57] Product liability as defined today does not meet the requirements for robotics product liability. Under the existing EU legal framework, robots cannot be made responsible for any actions because they are not capable themselves of acting individually, as there is always a person feeding commands to the machine.[58] Thus, only the manufacturer or owner of the robot should be held liable for robot actions as producer or owner, and for the causal link to be able to be established, the action must have caused the damage and it must have been reasonably foreseeable. In addition, as robotics collect data on individuals, the obligation to ensure compliance with the General Data Protection Regulation ('GDPR') exists and is the duty of the operator of robotics. As robotics devices involve multiple layers of commands, multiple liability levels arise, and multiple levels of data protection necessities emerge. Providing that data protection is already integrated into the respective technology when created (privacy by design), some of these data protection issues could be more easily resolved. By way of example, this could be achieved by including and developing data protection and data minimisation

---

[55]   David G Owen, John E Montgomery and Mary J Davis, *Products Liability and Safety: Cases and Materials* (Foundation Press, 2004) 40ff; see also Weber and Staiger (n 35) 203ff, whereby it is stated that '… if at the time of production of the robot, the risk fell beyond existing scientific knowledge this will shield the producer from liability. However, based on the risks robots create, an exception to the liability provisions or a reduction of liability does not seem warranted as otherwise the end-user would not be sufficiently protected'; *Feldman v Lederle Laboratories*, 479 A.2d 374 (NJ 1984).

[56]   Council Directive 85/374/EEC of 25 July 1985 on the approximation of the laws, regulations and administrative provisions of the Member States concerning liability for defective products eur-lex.europa.eu/legal-content/EN/TXT/?uri=celex %3A31985L0374 accessed 26 April 2022.

[57]   Bugra (n 38) 172.

[58]   See also Urs Freytag, 'Sicherheitsrechtliche Aspekte der Robotik' [2016] Sicherheit & Recht 111, for a discussion of the rules and laws that should apply to robotics; Weber and Staiger (n 35) 205.

procedures, such as encryption, access controls and automatic deletion tools, at the initial manufacturing stage of each robotic machine.[59]

The Product Liability Directive[60] applies in establishing smart robot producers' liability for third party damages and as such imposes a strict liability regime. Such strict liability ought to be backed by a compulsory insurance scheme, but the Product Liability Directive[61] contains no such duty to insure against potential third party claims. However, in the case of robotics, such insurance is necessary depending on the interpretation of the term 'robotics'.[62]

Because robots are products, product liability rules do apply. Product liability rules make the producer responsible for all damages caused by the user and third parties by the functioning of the device. In particular, when damage occurs as a consequence of the use of a robot, its design may be deemed defective and not sufficiently safe.[63] What kind of design may be deemed defective is, however, a matter of fact, decided ex post by a trial judge, influenced at the same time by the novelty of robotic technologies or the absence of sufficiently narrow-tailored technical standards, which augments the possibility for liability due to non-reliable safety standard mechanisms being in place. Liability is even more perplexing when human-machine interaction or machine learning ('ML') is involved, in particular the question of which party ought to be held liable for the harmful consequences arising from the use of the robot. Producers can be held liable for not having embedded the necessary safety measures to prevent the damage incurred, or users who 'taught' the robot may be considered liable as having contributed to changing the performance of the machine in a way deemed to be ex ante unpredictable by the producer.[64] This all can lead to refusal to insure some kinds of robotic devices, inadequate insurance being placed or the charging of higher premiums, hindering their

---

[59]   GDPR Article 23.

[60]   Council Directive 85/374/EEC of 25 July 1985 on the approximation of the laws, regulations and administrative provisions of the Member States concerning liability for defective products eur-lex.europa.eu/legal-content/EN/TXT/?uri=celex %3A31985L0374 accessed 26 April 2022.

[61]   ibid.

[62]   Andrea Bertolini, 'Robots and Liability – Justifying a Change in Perspective' in F Battaglia, J Nida-Rümelin and N Mukerji (eds.), *Rethinking Responsibility in Science and Technology* (Pisa University Press, 2014); Andrea Bertolini and others, 'On Robots and Insurance' (2016) 8 International Journal of Social Robotics 381, 387; Andrea Bertolini, *Liability for the Acts of Robots: Justifying a Change in Perspective* (Pisa University Press, 2014).

[63]   Bertolini and others (n 62); Bertolini, 'Robots and Liability – Justifying a Change in Perspective' (n 62).

[64]   Bertolini, 'Robots and Liability – Justifying a Change in Perspective' (n 62); Bertolini and others (n 62).

insurability, delaying their diffusion and embedding in our lives, and impairing their proliferation within the economy and the robotics-producing industry.

If robotics is perceived as 'services', then there is no requirement for compulsory commercial liability insurance.[65] That said, compulsory insurance is a way to mitigate and ensure the cover of losses and the compensation and protection owed towards third parties who are affected by the actions of the wrongdoer, serving the tort liability norm of compensatory justice.[66] In the case of robotics in oil and gas, different levels of risks will be present within the different functions of the oil and gas operation, and compulsory insurance may only be required and necessary for those robotics operations in the oil and gas chain that present a high level of risk of damage.[67] Under the Product Liability Directive,[68] manufacturers are not liable if they prove that the state of scientific and technical knowledge at the time, when the product was put into circulation, was not such as to enable the existence of the defect to be discovered. It has been argued in several instances whether unintended behaviour of smart robots resulting in damage to third parties may constitute a 'defect' within the meaning of the Directive and whether the development risk defence could relieve manufacturers of smart robots in a great number of cases on the ground that robotics technology is constantly evolving.[69] For the use of service robots, legal regulation can be achieved by resorting to private law either by gaining traditional indirect control through liability rules or via the implementation of imputation rules, and the implementation of liability for fault or strict liability via the establishment of a duty of care, via the enactment of compulsory insurance schemes, via the establishment of standards and through the control of general terms and conditions.[70] The use of robotics in oil and gas will also involve malfunctions and damages, which are to be expected[71] as it is anticipated that the use of service robots will lead to negative after-effects,

[65] Bertolini, 'Robots and Liability – Justifying a Change in Perspective' (n 62) 172–3.
[66] ibid 175.
[67] ibid 180.
[68] Council Directive 85/374/EEC of 25 July 1985 on the approximation of the laws, regulations and administrative provisions of the Member States concerning liability for defective products eur-lex.europa.eu/legal-content/EN/TXT/?uri=celex%3A31985L0374 accessed 26 April 2022.
[69] G Courtois, 'Robots Intelligents et Responsabilité: Quels Régimes, Quelles Perspectives?' (2016) 6 Dalloz IP/IT 287; Piotr Machnikowski, 'European Product Liability: An Analysis of the State of the Art in the Era of New Technologies' in Piotr Machnikowski (ed.), *European Product Liability* (Intersentia, 2016) 17–110.
[70] Thomas Dreier and Indra Spiecker genannt Döhmann, 'Legal Aspects of Service Robotics' (2012) 9 Poiesis & Praxis 201, 207-8.
[71] ibid 211–15.

unpredicted breakdowns and unintended side effects, and it is due to such malfunctions that third party liability issues will arise. Legal regulation should address the need to alter the damages owed and the liability threshold, which is currently low. The susceptibility to property damage caused by misguiding the robot can be potentially large and extensive. Hence, different levels of compensation should be available and the way to respond to damages sustained by third parties is via the introduction of mandatory liability insurance.

B.   Big Data and Data Protection

The emergence and widespread nature of the IoT and of robotics imply that the number of devices connected to the internet has already, for years, surpassed the number of people using the internet. What this has actually meant is that we have access to more data than ever before and have data about most things on the planet. This huge increase in the amount of data available means that we can use them to create a smarter world. Big data are different from other data because of four key elements: volume, velocity, variety and, perhaps most importantly, value. The best use of 'big data' can only occur if the data is presented and used in a way that works for a large group of people in society (public, organisation, etc.). Big data also needs to be carefully managed in order to be effective, especially where it is being used to analyse private information, so as to not breach privacy rights of the individuals concerned.[72] A key challenge is the users' concerns about their privacy. In addition, such robotics can cause damage; however, they also represent an important risk reduction tool.[73] A regulatory intervention that introduces strict liability of the user and/or the owner of automated machines, where strict liability means a responsibility that does not give relevance to the guilt or to the causal link between wrongdoing and losses, risks disincentivising the use of automation. Most of the literature and also the European institutions dealing with the issue of compensation for damage caused by autonomous systems have raised the question of the possible responsibility or co-responsibility of the producer and/ or programmer.[74] Hence, the most part of the efforts are on the reform of the

---

[72]   James Mullan, 'Re-Emerging Technologies: What's Hot and What's Not!' (2014) 14 Legal Information Management 168, 170.

[73]   R Eastwood, TP Kelly and E Landre, 'Towards a Safety Case for Runtime Risk and Uncertainty Management in Safety-Critical Systems' (8th IET International, 2013) 1–6.

[74]   See for example Patrick F Hubbard, '"Sophisticated Robots": Balancing Liability, Regulation, and Innovation' (2015) 66 Florida Law Review 1803; Samir Chopra and Laurence F White, *A Legal Theory for Autonomous Artificial Agents* (University of

Directive on manufacturer liability and on cybersecurity.[75] In seeking a solution, perhaps we need to focus attention on the importance of compensation and prevention, which usually find an answer in civil liability. In the event of damage that can be referred to an automated machine, prevention will be more easily guaranteed by the collection of additional data relating to cases in which defaults of the machine have been determined to improve the state of knowledge and reduce damage for the future.[76]

In these terms we can say that prediction is more important than liability and sanctions. It therefore appears that the objectives of compensation and prevention are better achieved by a system that allows for the compensation of those damaged, and at the same time the acquisition of data relating to the claims and its processing in order to provide new knowledge to better manage the risks of defaults in the future. The law has already made initial attempts through enabling the possibility of anonymisation and pseudo-anonymisation, and it is particularly important to take into account procedures in accordance with the current state of the art.

Big data, a phenomenon that consists of the fast and exponential data growth and data traffic, requires data analysis and data mining procedures. Ethics is an emerging issue related to big data, alongside data protection, privacy and awareness. Data collected and used implies also an ethical approach to robotics, AI, big data and the IoT ecosystem. In Europe, it is possible to address any matters related to ethics and robotics (including big data, AI, IoT, ML) through the GDPR. Outside Europe, instead, because of the lack of an international ethical standard, the matter should be addressed through policies or other contractual solutions.[77] Article 32 of the GDPR proposes some security solutions to protect personal data and manage the risks. Apart from the possible solutions (*inter alia*, pseudo-anonymisation and encryption of personal data), the

---

Michigan Press, 2011); Sabine Gless and Kurt Seelman, *Intelligente Agenten und das Recht*, vol 9 (Nomos, 2016).

In particular, these authors have rightly placed the attention on the concept of defect in view of what may be the 'defects' in the case of artificial intelligence and of a reasonable duty of safety and care.

[75]   David C Vladeck, 'Machines Without Principals: Liability Rules and Artificial Intelligence' (2014) 89 Washington Law Review 117, 130–7.

[76]   Nick Bostrom, 'When Machines Outsmart Humans' (2003) 35 Futures 759, 763; Yudkowsky Eliezer, 'Cognitive Biases Potentially Affecting Judgment of Global Risks' in Nick Bostrom and Milan Cirkovic (eds.), *Global Catastrophic Risks* (Oxford University Press, 2008).

[77]   Nicola Fabiano, 'Robotics, Big Data, Ethics and Data Protection: A Matter of Approach' in M Aldinhas Ferreira and others (eds.), *Robotics and Well-Being: Intelligent Systems, Control and Automation: Science and Engineering*, vol 95 (Springer, 2019).

ethical focal point is to protect personal data guaranteeing the dignity of each natural person. Article 25 of the GDPR provides for data protection by design and by default whereby the focus is on (a) data protection and (b) the user.[78] The principle of 'privacy by design' could serve as a superior approach to the specific legal approaches. According to this principle, data protection should already be considered in the initial drafts of the development of a new technology, in order to emphasise its importance. 'Privacy by design' is closely linked to the concept of 'privacy by default', where a high minimum level of privacy settings are implemented in the privacy settings of the new technological services. Subsequently, the user of the robotics system shall be able to decide for themself about additional data transfers. The inclusion of both approaches into the broad discussion would provide the potential for good problem-solving.

The IoT constitutes a significant piece of the autonomous systems landscape. Given that a vast portion of the data utilised by autonomous systems originates from IoT devices, the latter are often perceived as an additional hurdle to overcome in relation to liability for autonomous systems. Concerns about the interplay of IoT and liability regimes for autonomous systems relate to privacy, for example transparency, data 'ownership' and use or rights of data subject issues. In terms of liability, the difficulty in an IoT context relates to the fact that we are dealing with a complex chain of interconnected products which stem from different suppliers.[79] Hence, legislation specifically defining the boundaries of operational responsibility is needed to address uncertainty over liability.

C.   Applying the Law of Negligence to Robotics and AI

If harm is caused, the first question is whether anyone was under a duty not to cause, or to prevent, that harm. The second question is whether the duty was

---

[78]   It is stated that 'controllers must implement appropriate technical and organisational measures, such as pseudonymisation, which are designed to implement data-protection principles, such as data minimisation, in an effective manner and to integrate the necessary safeguards into the processing in order to meet the requirements of this Regulation and protect the rights of data subjects'. According to this rule, it is relevant to pay attention to set up appropriate technical and organisational measures. The pseudonymisation method is one of the possible actions to use for achieving the goal of integrating the necessary safeguards to protect the rights of data subjects into the processing. Moreover, according to the Article 25(2) 'the controller shall implement appropriate technical and organisational measures for ensuring that, by default, only personal data which are necessary for each specific purpose of the processing are processed'; see Nicola Fabiano (n 77).

[79]   Evelyn Studer and Jacques De Werra, 'Regulating Cybersecurity: What Civil Liability in Case of Cyber-Attacks?' [2017] Expert Focus 511, 512.

breached. The third question is whether the breach of duty caused the damage. The owner is not the only person who might be under a duty of care in the above situation. This might also apply to the designer of the AI or the person (if any) who taught or trained it. The level of duty can fluctuate upwards or downwards according to context. The precautions to be made depend on the statistical probability of harm occurring multiplied by the gravity of potential harm.[80] Strict liability refers to the situation where a party is held liable regardless of their fault. Product liability refers to a system of rules which establish who is liable when a given product causes harm. Often, the party held liable is the 'producer' of that product, though intermediate suppliers may be included as well. The focus is on the defective status of a product, rather than an individual's fault. Product liability regimes provide certainty as they specify in advance which party is to be held responsible. Product liability regimes are so-called because they relate to products, not services. Many commentators have assumed that product liability regimes will apply to AI without examining the important preliminary question of whether it is a good or a service. In the EU, products are defined as 'all movables' in Article 2 of the Product Liability Directive, which suggests that the regime applies only to physical goods. Consequently, a robot may be covered but some cloud-based AI may not. However, it is suggested that the best way of dealing with liability for AI is an insurance scheme and for at least some forms of AI insurance to be made mandatory so as to cover risks to third parties.[81]

This is especially so if the grave environmental and health hazards associated with the oil and gas industry are considered. To illustrate, a compulsory insurance scheme would be the most appropriate in cases of natural gas/oil leaks and spills, fall injuries in the workplace, heat illnesses caused to outdoor workers as well as respiratory diseases related to oil fields.[82]

D.   Tort and Delict: Different Approaches to Liability when Autonomous Systems are Involved

The different approaches in tort law and in the law of delict impose the need to investigate how liability in relation to autonomous systems is treated under each regime.

---

[80]   Jacob Turner, *Robot Rules: Regulating Artificial Intelligence* (Palgrave Macmillan, 2018).

[81]   ibid.

[82]   See United States Department of Labor, 'Oil and Gas Extraction' www.osha .gov/oil-and-gas-extraction/health-hazards#temperature accessed 23 April 2022.

With respect to tort in common law, a particular defendant is liable to repair a particular claimant's loss.[83] The three main elements of tortious liability, in negligence, are the following: the defendant's duty of care, the breach of the standard of care, namely the tortious conduct, and the proximate causation.[84] Furthermore, conduct is considered as tortious in cases where the defendant's action poses an unreasonable and foreseeable risk to the claimant.[85] The claimant, however, is not required to demonstrate that the specific chain of events was foreseeable by the defendant, rather that the resulting harm was foreseeable.[86] It is thus evident that autonomous systems pose challenges as to the fulfilment of tort liability's requirements. Particularly, the risk can hardly be foreseeable, given that the autonomous systems' algorithmic developments are unforeseeable.[87] Even more, initiating a process which leads to harm does not suffice for liability to be established, since liability requires a defendant's conduct to be unreasonably dangerous. Hence, the breach of duty on behalf of the manufacturer, owner or user is hard to establish. Moreover, the criterion of proximate causation is difficult to fulfil as well. Particularly, it is difficult to link autonomous systems' harmful effect to responsible human conduct, since the harmful effect is the result of an environmental – and not human – input[88] and the fact of the accident itself is not indicative of negligence.

Additionally, strict liability in common law also poses difficulties in establishing liability when autonomous systems are involved, since it requires objects that a) have tendencies to escape human control and b) are dangerous upon escape. While it could be reasonable to propose a strict liability regime specifically for autonomous systems deployed in extremely dangerous fields of the oil and gas industry, it would be too broad and general, hence also an inaccurate characterisation to classify altogether autonomous systems as ultra-hazardous activities. By way of example, such a regime could be established for particularly defined activities, such as the ones involving the workers' exposure to ergonomic hazards, electrical and other hazardous energy and confined spaces.

---

[83] In this paper, tort is examined following the work by Ernest Weinrib, *The Idea of Private Law* (Oxford University Press, 2012).

[84] ibid 169–70.

[85] Stephen Perry, 'Responsibility for Outcomes, Risk, and the Law of Torts' in Gerald J Postema (ed.), *Philosophy and the Law of Torts* (Cambridge University Press, 2001) 72.

[86] *Hughes v Lord Advocate* [1963] AC 837 (HL).

[87] Curtis Karnow, 'The Application of Traditional Tort Theory to Embodied Machine Intelligence' in Ryan Calo, A Michael Froomkin and Ian Kerr (eds.), *Robot Law* (Edward Elgar Publishing, 2016) 63–4, 72–4.

[88] Peter M Asaro, 'The Liability Problem for Autonomous Artificial Agents' [2016] AAAI Spring symposium series 191.

On the other side of the spectrum, the establishment of liability is challenging in the context of delict as well but from a different perspective. Delictual liability is established when a person, who is at fault, causes damage to another unlawfully. Its main elements are four: human act, damage to the rights of the injured person, fault of the injuring party and causal link between them. Unlawfulness can either arise out of the wrongfulness of the outcome or the breach of a duty on behalf of the injuring person. In cases where autonomous systems cause damage, for the user or owner to be held liable, it is questionable whether the unlawfulness derives from harming the injured person's legal rights. It rather derives from the user's or owner's breach of general duty to maintain safety,[89] especially when the system is not properly serviced. Concerning the requirement of fault, it can be classified as negligence, gross negligence or intent. Negligence is defined as failure to exercise necessary care, gross negligence is defined as failure to exercise necessary care up to a material extent and intent is defined as the will to cause an unlawful consequence.[90] In cases when an autonomous system causes damage, the injuring person's fault can hardly be identified and therefore the absence of its fault is highly likely to render the general delictual liability inapplicable. Hence, whereas tortious liability requires that the risk be foreseeable, and the harm be attributable to dangerous human conduct, delictual liability focuses mainly on the aspect of the injuring person's fault.

In the context of strict liability in civil law, according to which damage is caused by a greater source of danger regardless of fault, it is examined whether the harmful effect has been caused due to an activity which inherently imposes a higher risk.[91] In principle, the possessor or the person who is in actual control of the source of danger is held liable. However, when it comes to autonomous systems, the user or owner cannot be held liable, considering the autonomous systems' nature as machines acting on their own sensory perceptions. Therefore, the civil law approach sheds light on a matter different from the (mis)classification of autonomous systems as hazardous activities. It rather examines *inter alia* the extent to which the user or owner can control an autonomous system. This is one of the main reasons why strict liability under the civil law is harder to establish as compared to strict liability under the

---

[89]   Jänich M Volker, Paul T Schrader and Vivian Reck, 'Rechtsprobleme des Autonomen Fahrens' (2015) 28 Neue Zeitschrift für Verkehrsrecht 316.

[90]   Taivo Liivak and Janno Lahe, 'Delictual Liability for Damage Caused by Fully Autonomous Vehicles: The Estonian Perspective' (2018) 12 Masaryk University Journal of Law and Technology 49–74.

[91]   Helmut Koziol (ed.), *Basic Questions of Tort Law from a Comparative Perspective* (Jan Sramek Verlag, 2012) 234.

common law even when it comes to extremely hazardous activities such as the ones mentioned above.

Hence, in conclusion, while tort and delict may have essentially the same result, the difference lies primarily on the approach and the requirements in order for liability to be established under each of the regimes.

VI.   CONCLUSIONS

'Advances' in robotics will dramatically change the way we live and work, as autonomous robotics systems will change society and our life and bring groundbreaking changes in all sectors. Especially when it comes to the oil and gas sector, the exponential rise of self-learning machines is anticipated to extend the lifespan of subsea infrastructure, while simultaneously contributing to the protection of the marine environment from several sources of pollution. The paradox that needs to be bridged relates to the fact that technology is largely autonomous, that is, self-determinative, operating according to its own blind laws independently of human will, whereas the solutions suggested are not that technology-neutral but more inspired by the complexity of the technology.

To allow people to flourish in a society where AI is more prevalent, a robust liability regime and regulatory framework for robotics is needed, whether they are perceived as products or services through their actions. Insurance can play a role in disseminating its wide use and deployment in that it can act as a mitigating mechanism for liability entailed; however, a robust legal and regulatory regime will guarantee the availability of insurability and the non-creation of a hard insurance market, hence facilitating the robotics' wide use.

Robotics and AI technologies represent the 4IR impacting even more widely on human lives than computers and the internet. As robotics technology has been deep-rooted in every aspect of our daily lives, it demands a detailed plan and procedures for robotics based on ethical, legal and social norms. Thus, drafting a comprehensive guideline for robotics so that human/robot coexistence can be ensured with certainty, safety, security and trust is imperative and essential. As robotics applications and their deployment in various sectors vary, so do also the level and nature of liability arising, as such robotics vary from one another in terms of design, functions and behaviour with humans. This translates to an inefficacy to address all by a single tool. This diversity and widespread use of robotics also entails the realisation that traditional legal doctrines, for example tort, negligence or product liability, may not provide a conclusive answer to the question of attribution of liability. As this rising technology affects us in multifarious ways, it is imperative to design a robust regulatory framework so as to better address different liability considerations. Accordingly, in the context of the oil and gas sector, in particular, when forming a suitable liability regime, in order to achieve the optimal liability regime and the better attribution of compensation, the level of risk to cause damage by robotics operations may be assessed in conjunction with the different levels of compensation which should be available to injured parties.

Index